A TREASURY OF
SERMON ILLUSTRATIONS

A TREASURY OF SERMON ILLUSTRATIONS

Edited by
CHARLES L. WALLIS

Without a parable spake he not unto them.
—Matt. 13:34

ABINGDON PRESS
NASHVILLE ● NEW YORK

A TREASURY OF SERMON ILLUSTRATIONS

ISBN 0-687-42580-8
Library of Congress Catalog Card Number: 50-10619

SET UP, PRINTED, AND BOUND BY THE
PARTHENON PRESS, AT NASHVILLE,
TENNESSEE, UNITED STATES OF AMERICA

To my father

ROBERT SCOTT WALLIS

I venerate the man whose heart is warm,
Whose hands are pure, whose doctrine and whose life
Coincident, exhibit lucid proof
That he is honest in the sacred cause.
—WILLIAM COWPER, *The Task*

Preface

This treasury of illustrations is designed to be a ready and helpful companion for ministers and other religious leaders. The reader will find here stories and anecdotes, pungent and suggestive quotations, and brief quotable poems which will have a stimulating and warm appeal to both speakers and their hearers.

Included are old favorites which readers will wish to have in an easily accessible form and an abundance of stories which have been hitherto uncollected. The stories are told in a compact manner without elaboration or comment. The illustrations represent the universal experience of men, and all are timely or have a timeless interest.

For the best use of this book, the following suggestions are offered:

1. Browse through the book leisurely when opportunity permits. Although illustrations are listed under the most obvious headings in the indexes, the reader will find many stories which are adaptable to other themes.

2. Mark in the margin next to the story the date and place the illustration is used. This will become an informal record which will check overuse of particular illustrations.

3. Use the indexes. To make the volume more conveniently useful, five indexes are included. The first, "The Christian Year," draws attention to materials valuable for the observation of more than thirty special days and occasions in the church program. The second, "Children's Stories," lists 125 illustrations especially helpful in preparing children's sermons, church-school lessons, and other youth activities. The third, "Hymn Stories," identifies illustrations about hymn origins and hymn writers which may be adaptable to worship programs. The fourth, "Index of Names," includes the names of persons quoted or considered. Dates and biographical notes are listed. The fifth, "Index of Topics," is a definitive cross index of more than 900 significant subjects and makes possible a ready selection of illustrations on any of these topics.

It is impossible to give credit to many unknown individuals who first told most of the stories included. However, illustrations have been identified wherever possible.

CHARLES L. WALLIS

7

Contents

Contents

A

ACCOMPLISHMENT

1. Kagawa, the Japanese Christian evangelist, has said: "If you are willing to die for it, there is nothing you cannot accomplish."

2. After completing his oratorio *The Dream of Gerontius*, Sir Edward Elgar declared: "This is the best of me; for the rest, I ate, and drank, and slept, and loved, and hated, like another; my life was as the vapour, and is not; *but this I saw and knew*; this, if anything of mine, is worth your memory."

3. Leonardo da Vinci's great career as an artist began when he was asked by his sick teacher to finish a painting which the teacher had begun. The student protested that he was unable. "Do your best," the teacher said. Before the easel da Vinci prayed: "It is for the sake of my beloved master that I implore the skill and power for this undertaking." When the painting was completed, the teacher looked it over carefully and then said: "My son, I paint no more."

4. When Ralph Waldo Emerson failed one day to get a calf into a barn, a young girl thrust her finger into the animal's mouth and led it in. Emerson wrote in his *Journal* that day: "I like people who can *do things*."

5. The grave which marks the final resting place of Sir Christopher Wren is inscribed with these words: *Si monu-mentum quaeris, circumspice*—"If you seek his monument, look about you."

6.
Great things are done when men and
    mountains meet;
This is not done by jostling in the street.
    —BLAKE, "Gnomic Verses"

7. An old saying runs: "I am but one, but I am one; I cannot do everything, but I can do something. What I can do, by the grace of God, I will do."

AGE
Old Age

8. "No one," somebody has said, "grows old. You are old when you stop growing."

9. A young man committed suicide and left a note saying: "Died of old age at twenty-one."

10. Let me grow lovely, growing old—
    So many fine things do:
Laces, and ivory, and gold,
    And silks need not be new.
And there is healing in old trees,
    Old streets a glamour hold;
Why may not I, as well as these,
    Grow lovely, growing old? [1]
        —KARLE WILSON BAKER,
            "Growing Old"

11. The glory of that part of life which follows the halfway mark is expressed in

[1] From *Dreamers on Horseback*. Used by permission of the author.

these enthusiastic lines from "Rabbi Ben Ezra" by Robert Browning:

Grow old along with me!
The best is yet to be,
The last of life, for which the first
    was made.

12. When Adams was eighty years old, he met a friend who inquired, "How is John Quincy Adams today?" "Quite well, I thank you," replied the former president, "but the house in which he lives is becoming dilapidated, in fact, almost uninhabitable. I think John Quincy Adams will have to move out before long. But he himself is well, quite well."

13. Samuel Johnson, considering his broken health and failing memory, wrote in his *Prayers and Meditations*: "But I am now in my seventieth year; what can be done ought not to be delayed."

Present Age

14. A speaker who was attempting to show young people that our age is a great one, an age which has inherited the legacy of many generations and one which must offer a great future to persons yet unborn, told this striking story: While thinking on the subject he had selected, he looked from the window of a train named "The Century." Another train from the opposite direction sped past. That train was named "The Century Limited." Just then a passing porter smiled and said, "We're standing where the 'Centuries' meet."

15. "It is one of the illusions, that the present hour is not the critical, decisive hour," wrote Ralph Waldo Emerson. "Write it on your heart that every day is the best day in the year. No man has learned anything rightly until he knows that every day is Doomsday."

16. "Everyone is criticizing and belittling the times," said Emerson. "Yet I think that our times, like all times, are very good times, if only we know what to do with them."

17. During one of the darkest moments of World War II, Winston Churchill said: "Let us . . . so bear ourselves that if the British Commonwealth and Empire last for a thousand years, men will still say, 'This was their finest hour.'"

18. One of the characters in *Hans Frost* by Hugh Walpole speaks of certain people who "slap the face of the present with the dead hand of the past."

AGNOSTICISM

19. Robert Ingersoll, the famous agnostic, once visited Henry Ward Beecher, an equally famous minister. During his visit he noticed a beautiful globe which pictured the stars and constellations in the heavens. "This is an exquisite thing," Colonel Ingersoll said admiringly. "Who made it?" "Who made it?" Beecher replied with pretended surprise. "Why, Colonel, nobody made it. It just happened."

20. An early French academician, Butrau, surprised his friends one day by lifting his hat to a crucifix as he passed it on the street. "Ah, then," they remarked, "you are on better terms with God than we supposed?" "On bowing terms," came the reply; "we don't speak."—EDMUND GOSSE, *Aspects and Impressions*

ALIBI

21. An Arab went to his neighbor to borrow a piece of rope. "Sorry," said the neighbor, "but I need that rope to tie up my milk." "Tie up your milk! What do you mean?" "Oh," said the other, "when you don't want to do a thing, one excuse is just as good as another."—William S. Abernethy, *Left-handed Folks*

22. George Adam Smith, traveling in the Orient, asked a native to direct him to a certain destination. "Suffer me first to go and bury my father," the native said. Smith, surprised by the remark, was later told that such an answer represented a polite refusal.

23. "John, hast thee a purse?" asked an old Quaker. "No, sir," answered the lad with respect. "That is too bad," said the Quaker, "for I was going to give thee fifty cents to put in it." Two weeks later he met the boy again and inquired: "John, hast thee a purse now?" "Yes, sir," replied John in great glee. "That is too bad," said the Quaker, "for I was going to give thee fifty cents to buy one."

24. I sent a message to the fish:
I told them, "This is what I wish."
The little fishes of the sea,
They sent an answer back to me.
The little fishes' answer was
"We cannot do it, Sir, because—"
—Lewis Carroll, *Through
the Looking-Glass*

AMERICA

25. The following words by William Tyler Page were formally adopted as the American Creed by the House of Representatives on April 3, 1918: "I believe in the United States of America as a government of the people, by the people, for the people; whose just powers are derived from the consent of the governed; a democracy in a republic; a sovereign nation of many sovereign states; a perfect union, one and inseparable; established upon those principles of freedom, equality, justice, and humanity for which American patriots

sacrificed their lives and fortunes. I therefore believe it is my duty to my country to love it, to support its constitution, to obey its laws, to respect its flag, and to defend it against all enemies."

26.
God built Him a continent of glory and
    filled it with treasures untold;
He carpeted it with soft-rolling prairies
    and columned it with thundering
    mountains;
He studded it with sweet-flowing foun-
    tains and traced it with long winding
    streams;
He planted it with deep-shadowed for-
    ests, and filled them with song.
Then he called unto a thousand peoples
    and summoned the bravest among
    them.
They came from the ends of the earth,
    each bearing a gift and a hope.
The glow of adventure was in their eyes,
    and in their hearts the glory of hope.
And out of the bounty of earth and
    the labor of men,
Out of the longing of hearts and the
    prayer of souls,
Out of the memory of ages and hopes
    of the world,
God fashioned a nation in love, blessed
    it with
Purpose sublime—and called it Amer-
    ica! [2]
            —Rabbi Abba Hillel Silver

27. In 1876 Thomas Huxley visited America especially to speak at the new Johns Hopkins University, and this was his message: "I cannot say that I am in the slightest degree impressed by your bigness or your material resources, as such. Size is not grandeur; territory does not make a nation. The great issue, about which hangs a true sublimity and the terror of overhanging fate, is, What

[2] Used by permission of the author.

are you going to do with all these things?"

28.
America first, not only in things material,
But in things of the spirit.
Not merely in science, inventions, motors, skyscrapers,
But also in ideals, principles, character.
Not merely in the glad assertion of rights,
But in the glad assumption of duties.

Not flouting her strength as a giant,
But bending in helpfulness over a sick and wounded world like a Good Samaritan.
Not in splendid isolation,
But in courageous co-operation.

Not in pride, arrogance, and disdain of other races and peoples,
But in sympathy, love, and understanding.
Not in treading again the old, worn, bloody pathway which ends inevitably in chaos and disaster,
But blazing a new trail along which, please God, other nations will follow into the new Jerusalem where wars shall be no more.

Some day, some nation must take that path—unless we are to lapse into utter barbarism—and that honor I covet for my beloved America.
And so in that spirit and with these hopes, I say with all my heart and soul, "America First." [3]
—G. ASHTON OLDHAM,
"America First"

29.
Our country hath a gospel of her own
To preach and practice before all the world—

[3] Used by permission of the author.

The freedom and divinity of man,
The glorious claims of human brotherhood,
And the soul's fealty to none but God.
—JAMES RUSSELL LOWELL,
"America's Gospel"

30. Inscribed on the Statue of Liberty, Bedloe Island, New York harbor, are these words from "The New Colossus" by Emma Lazarus:

Not like the brazen giant of Greek fame,
With conquering limbs astride from land to land;
Here at our sea-washed, sunset gates shall stand
A mighty woman with a torch, whose flame
Is the imprisoned lightning, and her name
Mother of Exiles. From her beacon hand
Glows world-wide welcome; her mild eyes command
The air-bridged harbor that twin cities frame.
"Keep, ancient lands, your storied pomp!" cries she
With silent lips. "Give me your tired, your poor,
Your huddled masses yearning to breathe free,
The wretched refuse of your teeming shore.
Send these, the homeless, tempest-tost to me,
I lift my lamp beside the golden door."

31. Woodrow Wilson has been quoted as saying: "I am sorry that you do not wear a little flag of the union every day instead of some days. I can only ask you, if you do not wear the physical emblem, be sure that you wear it in your heart, and the heart of America shall interpret the heart of the world."

32. Before they left Europe for the new world, the Pilgrims heard these words read by the Rev. John Robinson: "And I will make of thee a great nation, and I will bless thee, and make thy name great; and thou shalt be a blessing" (Gen. 12:2).

33. John Adams in a letter wrote: "Posterity! You will never know how much it cost the present generation to preserve your freedom! I hope you will make a good use of it. If you do not, I shall repent it in heaven that I ever took half the pains to preserve it."

34. During the Constitutional Convention, George Washington said to the delegates: "It is too probable that no plan we propose will be adopted. Perhaps another dreadful conflict is to be sustained. If to please the people we offer what we ourselves disapprove, how can we afterwards defend our work? Let us raise a standard to which the wise and honest can repair. The event is in the hand of God."

35. Even though they realized that their signatures on the Declaration of Independence might mean the loss of property or even life itself, the signers did not hesitate to inscribe their names. Their spirit is indicated in the story of one of the number who signed himself Charles Carroll. "How will anyone know which Charles Carroll is meant, among all those called by that name in Maryland and elsewhere?" asked a friend who looked on. "Well, let there be no mistake," said the doughty fighter, and he signed in bold letters, "Charles Carroll of Carrollton."

36. Construction of the Capitol building in Washington was completed during the Civil War. Lincoln answered those who felt that materials and labor should be used for the war effort by saying: "Well, I reckon that as long as they see the Capitol going up, they will understand we intend the nation to go on."

37. When E. Stanley Jones was shown a beheading block in Canton, China, he said to his Chinese guide: "But you don't do this now, do you?" "Oh, no," the guide answered, "we a republic now; we hang 'em, the same as you."

38. Sinclair Lewis, Nobel prize-winning novelist, spoke words which many share when he said: "Intellectually I know that America is no better than any other country; emotionally I know she is better than every other country."

39. Fritz, a German immigrant boy, presented himself for military service. When advised that, being an alien, he did not need to enlist to fight against his fatherland, he replied: "When I come to America, I come *all*."—ERNEST RHODES

ANCESTORS

40. When an old rabbi was asked why God made only two people, Adam and Eve, the rabbi replied: "So that nobody can say, 'I came from better stock than you do.'"

41. "The man who has not anything to boast of but his illustrious ancestors is like a potato," wrote Sir Thomas Overbury in *Characters*, adding, "—the only good belonging to him is underground."

42. When a member of a prominent New England family was boasting to Will Rogers that her ancestors came over in the "Mayflower," the humorist, who was proud of his Indian blood, commented: "My ancestors were here to meet them."

ANGER

43. When a craftsman of limited training was seen often at the discussions in the Academy, a friend asked if he understood Latin, the language of the intellectuals. "No," said the craftsman, "but I can tell who is wrong in the argument." When asked how he determined this, the craftsman said: "Why, by seeing who is angry first."

44. "Anybody can become angry—that is easy," said Aristotle; "but to be angry with the right person, and to the right degree, and at the right time, and for the right purpose, and in the right way—that is not within everybody's power and is not easy."

45. "I learned," said Plutarch, "that anger is not incurable if one wants to cure it."

APPRECIATION

46. John Ruskin said: "The question is not what a man can scorn, or disparage, or find fault with, but what he can love and value and appreciate."

47. "Nothing upset him more than depreciatory talk of other people," someone said of Tennyson. "His own judgments were lenient; his appreciation of the work of others was unfailingly generous. He always respected human nature, even in the poorest and the least esteemed."

48. Once after an appreciative paper on Shelley's poetry had been read, one member of the group arose in the discussion, saying rather truculently that he could not see anything in Shelley, to which the reader of the paper, replying later, simply remarked: "Mr. So-and-So says that he does not see anything in Shelley. Poor devil."—HARRY EMERSON FOSDICK

49. Said Elbert Hubbard: "I would rather be able to appreciate things I cannot have than to have things I am not able to appreciate."

50. After Abbe Winkeman, the classical writer, had shown the famous statue "Apollo Belvidere" to his students, he said: "Go and study it, and if you see no great beauty in it to captivate you, go again. And if you still discover none, go again and again and again. Go until you *feel* it, for be assured it is there."

51. Once a man, dressed in evening clothes, was walking down a street in New York on a rainy, slushy night in winter. His heart was touched by two small boys dragging a huge box of kindling wood to their tenement home. He surprised them by taking hold of the rope to help. But as he pulled, one boy deserted for a glimpse in a shop window, and the other was lured off by a food vendor, until the gentleman in evening clothes found himself pulling kindling wood, alone, through the smiling crowd of a busy street. He quickly retired and let the boys know that he was a supplement but not a substitute for their activity.—ROBERT RUSSELL WICKS, *The Reason for Living*

Appreciation of Music

52. After a concert by Paderewski one man commented: "Yes, I came, but it wasn't worth while listening to that. However, I didn't lose any time; I spent those hours figuring up the price of cotton."—BERTHA CONDÉ, *What's Life All About?*

53. A concertmaster in the St. Louis Symphony, wondering if people generally would appreciate good music when they heard it, dressed like a tattered beggar and strolled through the streets of the city playing his violin. Although he looked like a beggar, he didn't play like one. To the violinist's satisfaction, not only did people appreciate his music, but many actually tried to help him secure work.

Appreciation of Nature

54. A man once said to Turner, the artist, "Mr. Turner, I never saw any sunsets like yours," to which the artist replied, "No, sir, but don't you wish you could?"

55. A friend of E. Stanley Jones in a small mission station in India said: "What a wonderful sunset, *especially for such a small place.*"

56. Some American tourists visited the Lake District with guidebooks and a guide. With a third of their attention they listened to what the guide said; with another third they read the guidebook; and with the remaining third they had an occasional squint at the scenery. After visiting the places which Wordsworth loved so much, one of them said to the guide, "I don't see anything very wonderful in your Lake District." But the guide said, "No, sir, but Wordsworth did."—LESLIE D. WEATHERHEAD, *The Transforming Friendship*

ARTIST

57. When a visitor in an artist's studio asked him why he stood on a pile of old canvasses while he worked, he replied: "My instructor once told me that an artist should stand on his past achievements."

58. He who works with his hands is a laborer. He who works with his hands and his head is an artisan. But he who works with his hands, his head, and his heart is an artist.—MARTHA PARKHILL AND DOROTHY SPAETH, *It's Fun to Make Things*

ASPIRATION

59. And ah for a man to arise in me,
That the man that I am
May cease to be.
—TENNYSON, "Maud"

60. William Blake once made a drawing of a little man standing at the foot of a ladder and reaching up to the moon crying, "I want, I want." Commenting on this drawing, Richard Roberts said: "Blake intended the drawing as a comment upon human nature. For him man was an insatiate, incarnate want, an embodied hunger."—HAROLD COOKE PHILLIPS, *Sails and Anchors*

61. On a mural Francis Scott Bradford has depicted the life of man. A heroic figure of man is painted as chained to the skyscrapers of his cities, rearing up, stretching his chains, peering onward into the stars and planets of the heavens. And the scroll inscribes the summary: "Man, though chained to earth, looks across time and space toward an unknown perfection which he may never reach but will forever seek."—ROLLO MAY, *The Springs of Creative Living*

62. Four men climbed a mountain to see the view. The first wore new and expensive shoes which did not fit, and he complained constantly of his feet. The second had a greedy eye and kept wishing for this house or that farm. The third saw clouds and worried for fear it might rain. But the fourth really saw the marvelous view. His mountaintop experience was looking away from the valley out of which he had just climbed to higher things.—HOWARD D. BARE

63. It is said of Jason Lee, the early

Methodist missionary to the great Northwest: "He fixed his hand upon the sky."

64.
I held it truth, with him who sings
　To one clear harp in divers tones,
　That men may rise on stepping-stones
Of their dead selves to higher things.
　　—TENNYSON, "In Memoriam"

65. "We cannot swing up a rope that is attached only to our belt," exclaims William Ernest Hocking.

66. There is an old legend of a prince who had a crooked back. Being very proud, he suffered mentally. One day he said to his most skillful sculptor: "Make a statue of me, but with a straight back. I would see myself as I might have been." When the perfect statue was finished, it was suggested that it be set up before the palace gate, but the prince said: "Place it in a secret nook in the palace garden where only I shall see it." The affair was soon forgotten, but every day the prince would steal away and look long and earnestly at the statue, and each time something seemed to set his blood tingling and his heart throbbing. Months passed, and people began to say: "The prince's back is not as crooked as it was," or "The prince seems much more noble looking than he used to be." Hearing this, the prince went again into the garden and stood before the statue, and behold, his back had become as straight as the statue's and his brow as noble—he was the man of the statue.—ROBERT JOHN CHRYSTIE

ATHEIST

67. John Buchan, one-time governor general of Canada, defined an atheist as "a man who has no visible means of support."

68. Harry Emerson Fosdick has defined atheism as a "theoretical formulation of the discouraged life."

69. A bomber crew, having bailed out of their badly damaged plane, salvaged a rubber raft, food, and water. On the sixth day, when their water supply gave out, one of them said, "Let us pray." On the seventh day they landed safely on a Malayan island. "I thought I was a Christian before I entered the Army," one of the crew told a reporter. "Now I know I am. One thing experience has taught me is this: there is no place on a rubber raft in the Pacific for an atheist."

AWARENESS

70. Some years ago a poor old man and his wife lived in a shack on the Oklahoma plains. One morning an engineer came up the path and asked if he could drill a test hole for oil under their kitchen floor. He found a gusher, tapped the oil out by the hundreds of barrels, and soon put that couple on Easy Street. One day the old man smiled and said reflectively: "But to think it was under our feet all the time."
—CARL KOPF, *Windows of Life*

71.
He searched the wide world over
To find a four-leafed clover
Which all the while had grown beside
　his door.
　　　　—AUTHOR UNKNOWN

72. Someone asked Thoreau where he managed to find so many arrowheads. By way of reply he simply stooped and picked one up.

73. A man visiting an art gallery spoke to the woman who was scrubbing the floors: "There are many beautiful pictures here." "I s'pose so, if a body has time to look up," the woman answered.

Awareness of Nature

74. A forest ranger was walking along a city street with his urban brother. "Do you hear that cricket?" the ranger said. When the brother could not hear it, the ranger leaned over and picked up a cricket which had been in a crack in the walk. The city brother was quite amazed. "It all depends on what your ear is trained to hear," the ranger added. Then he dropped a coin on the sidewalk and many busy persons stopped to look for it. Their ears had been trained to hear other noises than those of a cricket.—DONALD D. KENNEDY

75. Mark Hopkins once put this question to his class: "You would like to have the world, as much of it, at least, as you want. Would you be willing to have all that you want and be deaf? Perhaps you would. Would you be willing to have all that you want and be deaf and dumb? Probably not. Would you like to have all that you want in the world, and be deaf, dumb, and blind? Certainly not."

76.
If I have faltered more or less
In my great task of happiness;
If I have moved among my race
And shown no glorious morning face;
If beams from happy human eyes
Have moved me not; if morning skies,
Books, and my food, and summer rain
Knocked on my sullen heart in vain:—
Lord, thy most pointed pleasure take,
And stab my spirit broad awake.
　　　　—ROBERT LOUIS STEVENSON,
　　　　　"The Celestial Surgeon"

B

BABY

77. "God makes the world all over again," Jean Paul Richter used to say, "whenever a little child is born."

78. The story is told that during the gold rush days in California the men became desperately homesick for their wives and families. On one occasion the cry of a baby was heard in a theater. "Stop those fiddlers," one man said. "We haven't heard a baby's cry in months." The music stopped, and the men cheered as the baby continued to cry.

79. An old sailor who had seen all the wonders of the deep for forty years, and all the wonders of the world around the seven seas, was asked what in all his life had impressed him most. He answered, "The nails on a baby's fingers."

BAPTISM

80. A frontier preacher was busy digging a baptismal pool. "What is that for?" he was asked. "To baptize people," was the preacher's reply. "But there are no Baptists about here!" "No, but I'm digging this pool for the Baptists that are going to be about here."

81. A missionary reports that one native resisted baptism, saying: "I will wait and see just what this means in their lives." After many watchful weeks, the native said: "I, too, want to be baptized. I have watched those persons who were baptized, and it has made a dif-ference. I want Jesus to do for me what he has done for them."

82. When a Baptist was asked about baptism, he replied: "It's all right, but you musn't hang around the river too long."—E. STANLEY JONES, *The Way*

83. Harry Emerson Fosdick tells of a member of a New York City parish who said to his minister: "I have been a church member since I was baptized twenty-five years ago. Why has nothing vital happened to me in all that time?"

BEAUTY

84. Charles Kingsley said: "Never lose an opportunity to see anything beautiful. Beauty is God's handwriting."

85. An American wounded in action visited every possible attraction in Europe before returning to his native land. He explained his quest of the beautiful to a friend by saying: "You see, I am going blind. Not many months now. So I'm painting pictures on the canvas of my mind."

86. One spring morning in Japan when the cherry blossoms were out in their full splendor, a late snow fell and covered the whole landscape with a mantle of white, the delicate tints of the cherry blossoms against the whiteness of the snow making an unforgettable picture. On the morning in question, thinking of the loss of fruit, one Japanese gentleman wrote another a letter of sympathy and received an immediate reply which

said: "You have offered me a gross insult. You have written me a long letter and expressed sympathy, but you never mentioned the beautiful snow."—ROY L. SMITH, *Suburban Christians*

87. Alice Freeman Palmer, once president of Wellesley, spent some time in her youth teaching a Sunday-school class made up of small girls recruited from a city slum. One Sunday the idea came to her to ask those children, tragically dirty and unpromising, to find in their homes something beautiful, and then tell the other children about it the next Sunday. When the next Sunday came, one bedraggled little girl who lived in a particularly dirty tenement said slowly: "I ain't found nothing beautiful where I live except—except the sunshine on our baby's curls." Years later, long after Mrs. Palmer's untimely death, her husband was lecturing at a university in the West. He was entertained in a distinguished home, and his hostess told him eagerly that she had once been a member of Mrs. Palmer's Sunday-school class. She said: "I can remember that your wife once asked us to find something beautiful in our homes, and that I came back saying the only beautiful thing I could find was the sunshine on my sister's curls. But that suggestion your wife made was the turning point in my life. I began to look for something beautiful wherever I was, and I've been doing it ever since."— JAMES GORDON GILKEY

88. Hugh Martin in *The Parables of the Gospels* tells the story of a rather rough, uncultured man who fell in love with a beautiful vase in a shop window. He bought the vase and put it on the mantelpiece in his room. There it became a kind of judgment on its surroundings. He had to clean up the room to make it worthy of the vase. The curtains looked dingy beside it. The old chair with the stuffing coming out of the seat would not do. The wallpaper and the paint needed renewing. Gradually the whole room was transformed.

89. A scientist was studying with a microscope the purple heather on the hills of Scotland. A shepherd asked to see the heather under so powerful a lens. After looking the shepherd said: "Man, I wish I had never seen its beauty. These feet of mine have trampled on so many of them."—CHARLES H. PINCHBECK

90. Maude Royden Shaw, the English humanitarian, tells of happening in upon an illustrated lecture and seeing upon the screen what looked like a beautiful rose window only to learn that it was a magnified cross section of a spine of a lowly sea urchin.—HARRIS FRANKLIN RALL, *Christianity*

91. When Raphael's great picture "The Sistine Madonna" was first brought to Dresden, it was displayed in the castle in the presence of the king. It was brought into the throne room, but the most favorable spot in the room was occupied by the throne itself. The king, taking in the situation, pushed the throne aside, saying, "Make room for the immortal Raphael."—H. P. MYERS

92. A lady showed John Ruskin a valuable handkerchief she had intended to give to a friend. But an ugly blot was made where a drop of marking ink had fallen on it. Ruskin asked for it, and, when he returned it after a couple of days, he had made the blot the foundation for a lovely design. Where there had been a blot, there was now beauty, for it had been touched by the hand of a master.—WILLIAM J. HART

93. Once a man went to call at the place of business of one of his friends, a jeweler with a large clientele. The jeweler showed his friend a store of superb diamonds and other precious stones. Among them was a stone so lusterless that the friend said: "That one has no beauty at all." "Hasn't it?" asked the jeweler, lifting the stone from the tray and closing his fist over it. In a few moments, when he opened his hand, the stone glowed with all the splendor of the rainbow. "Why, what have you done to it?" asked the friend. The jeweler smiled. "That is an opal," he said. "It is what we call a sympathetic jewel. It needs only to be gripped with the human hand to bring out all its wonderful beauty."—J. C. MITCHELL

94. "When at sixteen I was vain because someone praised me, my father said: 'They are only praising your *youth*,'" Marie Stopes wrote. "'You can take no credit for beauty at sixteen. But if you are beautiful at sixty, it will be your own soul's doing. Then you may be proud of it and be loved for it.'"

95.
If of thy mortal goods thou art bereft,
And from thy slender store two loaves alone to thee are left,
Sell one, and with the dole
Buy hyacinths to feed thy soul.
—GULISTAN OF MOSLIH EDDIN SAADI

BEGINNING

96. "Life is full of ends," wrote Phillips Brooks, "but every end is a new beginning, and we are continually coming to the point where we close one chapter, but we always can turn and open a new and better and a diviner chapter."

97. "You certainly must have climbed out of the wrong side of the bed this morning," a mother said to her complaining daughter. In a few minutes the little girl went back into her bedroom. "What are you doing?" the mother asked. "I am getting out of the right side of the bed," the girl responded.

BELIEF

98. An unknown writer has put a new truth with an old adage: "If life is a comedy to him who thinks and a tragedy to him who feels, it is a victory to him who believes."

99. "A man lives," said Thomas Carlyle, "by believing something; not by debating and arguing about many things."

100. "Nothing is too big to be believed," Sir Oliver Lodge said, "and nothing is too good to be true."

101. When a young man told his minister that he never believed anything he could not understand, the minister said thoughtfully: "Then, sir, your creed would be the shortest of any man whom I ever knew."

102. A Negro preacher is said to have given the two essentials of the gospel as "believing it and behaving it."

103. When David Hume, the agnostic, was criticized for listening to John Brown, the Scotch minister, Hume said: "I don't believe all that he says, but he does. And once a week I like to hear a man who believes what he says."

104. Once when Mirabeau was listening to the sincere Robespierre, he leaned toward a friend and said: "That man will go far; he believes all he says."

105. Some people's faith has no more depth than that suggested by the White

Queen in *Through the Looking-Glass.* When Alice said that she couldn't believe that the queen was one hundred and one years, five months, and a day old, the queen said: "Can't you? Try again: draw a long breath, and shut your eyes."

BIBLE

106. Billy Sunday in a striking word picture said: "Twenty-nine years ago, with the Holy Spirit as my guide, I entered at the portico of Genesis, walked down the corridor of the Old Testament art galleries, where pictures of Noah, Abraham, Moses, Joseph, Isaac, Jacob, and Daniel hang on the wall. I passed into the music room of the Psalms, where the spirit sweeps the keyboard of nature until it seems that every reed and pipe in God's great organ responds to the harp of David, the sweet singer of Israel. I entered the chamber of Ecclesiastes, where the voice of the preacher is heard, and into the conservatory of Sharon and the lily of the valley, where sweet spices filled and perfumed my life. I entered the business office of the Proverbs and on into the observatory of the prophets, where I saw telescopes of various sizes pointing to far-off events, concentrating on the bright and morning star which was to rise above the moonlit hills of Judea for our salvation and redemption. I entered the audience room of the King of kings, catching a vision written by Matthew, Mark, Luke, and John. Thence into the correspondence room of Paul, Peter, James, and John writing their epistles. I stepped into the throne room of Revelation, where tower the glittering peaks, where sits the King of kings upon his throne of glory with the healing of the nations in his hand."

107. Outside one of the beautiful gateways of the magnificent mosque of St. Sophia, in Istanbul, there is a picture of an open Bible with this inscription: "The Lord said, I am the door; by me if any man enter in he shall be saved." The Mohammedans left this inscription when they took the beautiful temple from the Christians. They could see no reference here to Jesus Christ. Everything else that suggested Christianity was obliterated.

Belief in the Bible

108. François Voltaire, the French philosopher and satirist, expressed an elemental truth when he said; "If we would destroy the Christian religion, we must first of all destroy man's belief in the Bible."—S. A. CAMPBELL, *The Grit to Grapple with Life*

109. Ralph Connor writes of a sky-pilot on a western ranch and of how a cowboy in the audience began to quibble with him: "Of course that's in the Bible, ain't it?" "Yes," said the sky-pilot. "Well, how do you know it's true?" Before he could answer, a ranchman interrupted. "Look here!" he said in tones that would not brook denial. The cowboy looked. "Look here, young feller; how do you know anything's true? How do you know the pilot here's true when he speaks? Can't you tell by the feel? Can't you tell by the sound of his voice?"—GEORGE A. BUTTRICK, *Jesus Came Preaching*

Challenge of the Bible

110. William Jennings Bryan declared: "The Bible holds up before us ideals that are within sight of the weakest and the lowliest, and yet so high that the best and the noblest are kept with their faces turned ever upward. It carries the call of the Saviour to the remotest corners of the earth; on its pages are written the assurances of the present and our hopes for the future."—WIL-LIAM JENNINGS BRYAN, *In His Image*

111. John Hutton said: "The New Testament holds up a strong light by which a man can read even the *small print* of his soul."

112. When Olive Schreiner was a little girl, she got hold of a copy of the New Testament and began to read it. Before she got past the early chapters of Matthew, she rushed into her mother's room and said: "Oh, Mummy, look what I've found! Isn't it lovely? Now we can all live like this."—LESLIE D. WEATHERHEAD, *How Can I Find God?*

113. "What would you think if I should tell you that in ten minutes I could produce arguments that would utterly annihilate the Bible?" asked a skeptical friend. "About the same thing I would think if I saw a great gnat crawling up the side of Mount Washington, threatening to smash the whole thing with its weight," replied the believing friend.

Comfort of the Bible

114. When Sir Walter Scott was near death, he expressed a wish that his son-in-law should read to him. When asked what book he wished to have read, he said, "Need you ask? There is but one."

115. When a friend asked Johnny Bartek, the boy who had the New Testament on Rickenbacker's rubber raft adrift in the Pacific, what the New Testament did for him, Johnny said: "It kept us steady; we didn't lose our heads and crack up. It kept us sane." "What if the sea gull had not come?" the friend asked. "Then we would have died like men and not like cowards."

116. When a Scotch girl asked if she should read the Bible to her dying father, the old saint replied: "Na, na, lassie, I thatched my house before the storm began."—E. STANLEY JONES, *The Way*

Influence of the Bible

117. "The Bible," William Lyon Phelps said, "has been a greater influence on the course of English literature than all other forces put together."

118. When the missionaries in Nanking gave New Testaments to the Japanese soldiers, one Japanese official came to the missionaries, saying: "Please don't give our men any more New Testaments, for when they read this book, it takes the fight out of them—they don't want to fight any more."

119. A man of business came upon a native in Africa who was studiously bent over his Bible. "That book is out of date in my country," the man chuckled. "If it had been out of date here," the native returned, "you'd have been eaten long ago."

120. Thomas Jefferson, a serious student of the Bible, wrote: "I always have said and always will say that the studious perusal of the sacred volume will make better citizens, better fathers, and better husbands."—W. W. MOORE, *The Indispensable Book*

121. Theodore Roosevelt said of Abraham Lincoln: "He built up his entire reading upon his early study of the Bible. He mastered it; mastered it as later he mastered only one or two other books; mastered it so that he became almost a man of one book, who knew that book and instinctively put into practice what he had been taught therein."

122. Recently the chairman of a missionary meeting claimed that he was the founder of a flourishing Christian community in India, although he had never been out of England. To the amazed listeners he said that when he was five years old he wanted to give a penny to the missionaries but strongly objected to putting it in a brown box. He had no proof that it ever went abroad! The local minister was a friend of the family and also the friend of an Indian missionary. So the minister, to please the child, sold him a copy of the New Testament for his penny and directed the boy how to post it to the missionary in India, having first written on the flyleaf an inscription giving the name of the boy. The missionary gave it to a poor native who had walked miles through the jungle to procure a Testament, but who couldn't afford to buy one. Nothing was heard of the incident for twenty years. Then another missionary, preaching in a jungle village to people whom he thought had never previously heard the gospel message, noticed that his words were causing excited delight. Pausing in his preaching to ask questions, the preacher found that the people knew a great deal about Christ and that many were serving him. No preacher had ever been to the village before. The little Christian community had been born through the love and life of the native who had been given the Testament— the Testament which was sold for a penny to a child of five. —LESLIE D. WEATHERHEAD, *In Quest of a Kingdom*

123. Said an Indian Brahman to a missionary: "If you Christians in India, in Britain, or in America were like your book, you would conquer India in five years."

Inspiration of the Bible

124. Dwight L. Moody remarked, "I know the Bible is inspired because it inspires me."—W. W. MOORE, *The Indispensable Book*

125.

Whence, but from heaven could men, unskilled in arts,
In several ages born, in several parts,
Weave such agreeing truths? or how, or why
Should all conspire to cheat us with a lie?
Unasked their pains, ungrateful their advice,
Starving their gain, and martyrdom their price.
　　　—DRYDEN, *"Religio Laici"*

Interpretation of the Bible

126. John Wycliffe's rules for the interpretation of the Bible read:

It shall greatly helpe ye to understande Scripture,
If thou mark
Not only what is spoken or wrytten,
But of whom,
And to whom,
With what words,
At what time,
Where,
To what intent,
With what circumstances,
Considering what goeth before
And what followeth.

127. Henry Drummond on one occasion warned preachers against "killing the old doctrine and ostentatiously calling on their congregations to attend the funeral."—T. H. PATTISON, *Making of the Sermon*

128. An old Negro preacher, when shown a commentary prepared by a learned scholar, remarked, "Well, sir,

the Bible certainly do shed a lot of light on that book of yours."—ROBBIE TRENT, *Your Child and God*

Mother's Bible

129. Carl Sandburg in *Abraham Lincoln: The Prairie Years* recalls that Lincoln said to Mrs. Rankin in New Salem "that before he had learned to read as a boy, he had heard his mother saying over certain Bible verses day by day as she worked. He had learned those verses by heart; the tones of his mother's voice were in them."

130.
We search the world for truth. We cull
The good, the pure, the beautiful,
From graven stone and written scroll,
From all old flower-fields of the soul;
And, weary seekers of the best,
We come back laden from the quest,
To find that all the sages said
Is in the Book our mothers read.
　　　　　—WHITTIER, "Miriam"

131. "All that I have taught of art," wrote John Ruskin, "everything that I have written, whatever greatness there has been in any thought of mine, whatever I have done in my life, has simply been due to the fact that, when I was a child, my mother daily read with me a part of the Bible and daily made me learn a part of it by heart."

Neglect of the Bible

132. A small boy picked up a black book from the table, brushed off the dust, and asked: "Whose book is this?" "Why, son, that is God's book," the mother answered. The boy, noticing that the book was not used, said: "Maybe we should give it back to him. We don't have much use for it, do we?"

133. A little serving girl was in court one day as a witness and was asked by her mistress's lawyer whether the family had a Bible. "Yes, sir," the maid answered, "that's where we keep newspaper clippings."—ROY L. SMITH, *Suburban Christians*

134. One morning, so runs an old story, England woke up and found that the Bible was gone. Not only had the book itself been lost, but all traces of its influence and every note of its music had disappeared from life. The result was appalling. People did not know what the great writers were talking about. Shakespeare was almost unintelligible. Ruskin's works resembled an ancient tapestry. Everyday speech stammered and faltered. A change passed over the whole tone and temper of the nation. Life became hectic and vulgar. . . . Some fine high quality had taken its departure from life.—F. K. STAMM

135. Felix Riesenberg, librarian on the training ship "St. Mary" anchored at Hellgate, received a package of food from his mother. Wishing to hide it from shipmates who would hijack the precious stuff, he opened a cabinet where fifty dusty Bibles were kept. The Bibles had not been used for a long time, and Riesenberg thought that they would not be missed. So he threw the Bibles, one by one, through the porthole. In a few moments the captain rushed into the library asking for an explanation, for moving off with the tide through Hellgate were fifty Bibles. "I'm sorry," Riesenberg said, "I thought they would sink."

Popularity of the Bible

136. It has been estimated that more than 1,500,000,000 Bibles have been printed since Johann Gutenberg printed the first one more than five hundred years ago. The Bible sells more than 30,000,000 copies annually.

137. Over 2,500,000 copies of the English Revised Version of the Bible were bought or ordered by English speaking people within forty-eight hours of the announcement of its publication in 1885. The whole revised New Testament, which appeared in 1881, was cabled across the ocean and printed the next day in the Chicago *Tribune.*

Power of the Bible

138. "In Holland the people thought that the Bible must contain dynamite since the Nazis were so anxious to destroy it," W. A. Visser 'tHooft of the World Council of Churches said; "so they reopened its pages to find the dynamite—and they found it."

139. There is a story that when an East Indian prince visited Queen Victoria on business of state and asked her to tell him the secret of England's greatness and glory, she simply handed him a copy of the Bible with the words, "This is the secret of England's greatness."—W. W. MOORE, *The Indispensable Book*

140. "The New Testament is a wonderful instrument for purity and for holiness," writes Toyohiko Kagawa. "When you start a Bible movement, it means revolution, a quiet revolution against darkness and crime."

141. A little girl unwittingly expressed the challenge of the gospel when she said to her sister: "I tell you, the Bible does not end in Timothy; it ends in Revolutions."

142. An Indian boy whose zeal was better than his English wrote to E. Stanley Jones: "We are having a great rebible here."

Reading the Bible

143. Someone criticized Gipsy Smith: "I have been through the Bible forty times, and I never found what you have been preaching." To this Smith replied: "That might easily happen. What makes the difference is not how many times you have been through the Bible, but how many times and how thoroughly the Bible has been through you."

144. After imprisonment in the Bedford jail John Bunyan said: "I never knew all there was in the Bible until I spent those years in jail. I was constantly finding new treasures."

145. "Before . . . the anguish of my soul at my condition would break out upon me on a sudden," says Robinson Crusoe in Defoe's novel, "and my very heart would die within me to think of the woods, the mountains, the deserts I was in; and how I was a prisoner locked up with the eternal bars of the ocean in an uninhabited wilderness, without redemption. In the midst of the greatest composures of my mind, this would break upon me like a storm and make me wring my hands and weep like a child. But now I began to exercise myself with new thoughts; I daily read the Word of God and applied all its comforts to my present state. One morning, being very sad, I opened my Bible upon these words, 'I will never, never leave thee, nor forsake thee'; immediately it occurred that these words were to me. . . . 'Well, then,' said I, 'if God does not forsake me, of what ill consequence can it be or what matters it though the world should all forsake me, seeing on the other hand, if I had all the world and should lose the favor and blessing of God, there would be no comparison in the loss?' "

146. In his *Diary* entry for September 26, 1816, John Quincy Adams noted: "I have made it a practice for several years to read the Bible through in the course of every year. I usually devote to this reading the first hour after I rise every morning."

147. Abraham Lincoln in a letter to Joshua Speed said: "I am profitably engaged in reading the Bible. Take all of this book upon reason that you can and the balance upon faith, and you will live and die a better man."

148. Henry Ford once said that during World War I, Woodrow Wilson and he took a pledge to read a chapter of the Bible every day. "I have kept my pledge," Ford said, "and I understand that he did until his death."

149. Thomas Fuller in *Good Thoughts for Bad Times* wrote: "Lord this morning I read a chapter of the Bible and therein observed a memorable passage whereof I never took note before. Why now and no sooner did I see it? Formerly my eyes were as open, and the letters were as legible. Is there not a thin veil over thy word which is more rarefied by reading and at last wholly worn away?"

150. Edmund Burke, the greatest philosophical statesman that the British people ever produced, made a habit of reading a chapter in Isaiah before going to speak in the House of Commons. "Isaiah," he said, "possesses both the blaze of eloquence and the light of truth."—W. W. MOORE, *The Indispensable Book*

151. Henry Ward Beecher said that the greatest influence in his life was Charles Smith, a Negro who was a hired man on the farm which belonged to Beecher's father. "He did not try to influence me," Beecher said. "He did not know that he did it; I did not know it until a long time afterward. He used to lie on his humble bed and read the New Testament, unconscious that I was in the room. He would talk about it and chuckle over it. I had never heard the Bible really read before. It was a revelation and an impulse to me."

152. Henry Sloane Coffin has told of two Japanese women who visited a murderer under the sentence of death. After they had found him unresponsive, they laid a copy of the New Testament on the table and left. After the man had been executed, the following letter was found: "I was not sufficiently impressed to have any special belief in what I was reading. I put the New Testament on the shelf. A little later when I was tired of doing nothing, I took down the book again and began to read. This time I saw how Jesus was handed over to Pilate and tried unjustly and put to death by crucifixion. As I read this I began to think. I went on, and my attention was next taken with these words: 'And Jesus said: Father, forgive them, for they know not what they do.' I stopped. I was stabbed to the heart as if pierced by a five-inch nail. What did the verse reveal to me? Shall I call it the love of the heart of Christ? Shall I call it His compassion? I do not know what to call it. I only know that with an unspeakable grateful heart I believed."—*God Confronts Man in History*

Translations of the Bible

153. The most significant versions of the English Bible include: Wycliffe's version (1382), based upon the Latin Vulgate; Tyndale's version (1525-1531), based upon the Latin Vulgate

28

and the Greek text of Erasmus; Coverdale's Bible (1535), based upon Tyndale's version and the Latin Vulgate; the Rhemes and Douai version (1582-1610), the accepted Roman Catholic version, based on the Latin Vulgate; the King James version (1611), the work of fifty-four scholars under the authorization of King James I of England and based on Hebrew and Greek texts as well as the older English versions; the English Revised version (1881-1884), the work of English and American scholars, based on the most ancient copies of the original scriptures; the American Standard version (1900-1901), based on the English Revised version and using language preferred by the American members of the committee; and the Revised Standard version of the New Testament (1946), based on the American Standard version and the King James version.

154. When John Wycliffe in the fourteenth century translated the Latin Vulgate into English so that the common man might read the Bible, John Foxe wrote that some farmers "gave a load of hay for a few chapters of St. James or of St. Paul in English."

155. In the sixteenth century William Tyndale, English reformer and martyr, declared: "If God spare my life, I will cause a boy that driveth the plow shall know more of the Scripture than thou [a learned man] dost." Tyndale made his translation secretly in exile. When completed the translation was smuggled into England where copies were burned by order of the Bishop of London. Many plowboys got copies, however, before Tyndale was burned at the stake in 1536.

156. William Tyndale was working on his translation of the Old Testament at Antwerp when through the treachery of a spy, an agent of Henry VIII, he was arrested and taken to prison, where he languished for two years. Henry VIII insisted on his execution, and in 1536 he was chained to the stake, strangled, and finally burned. His last words were, "Lord, open the king of England's eyes." It is a remarkable fact that the year after his martyrdom the Bible was published throughout England by the command of this very English king and was appointed to be read by all of the people.

157. After being told of the modern translations of the Bible one particularly determined old deacon exclaimed: "If the King James version was good enough for St. Paul, why then it's good enough for me."

Understanding the Bible

158. Mark Twain is reported to have said: "Many people are troubled about the scriptures which are mysterious and hard to understand. I am most troubled about those which I can understand."

159. A Scotch preacher, after reading the morning scripture, said: "This is a difficult text; having looked it in the face, we will pass on."

Value of the Bible

160. Tolstoy said: "Without the Bible the education of the child in the present state of society is impossible."

161. Andrew Jackson in his last illness declared the Bible to be "the rock on which our republic rests."

162. "I believe a knowledge of the Bible without a college course," William Lyon Phelps said, "is more valuable than a college course without a knowledge of the Bible."

BIGOTRY

163. George Bernard Shaw in the preface to *On the Rocks* writes: "We are confronted with the growing perception that if we desire a certain type of civilization and culture we must exterminate the kind of people who do not fit into it."

164. David Harum said the "seven-day Babtists" were "so narrer in their views that fourteen of 'em c'n sit, side by side, in a buggy."

165. Over the door of the private library of Andrew Carnegie hung a motto that read:

He who cannot think is a fool;
He who will not think is a bigot;
He who dares not think is a slave.

166. One day Gandhi visited a Christian church in South Africa. He was stopped at the door by a man who said that the church did not welcome Negroes. He told Gandhi that there were other churches for the likes of him. Gandhi is said to have vowed that evening that he would never enter a Christian church again.

167. Galileo, before the "Holy Inquisition," was commanded to recant in these words: "But because I have been enjoined by this Holy Office altogether to abandon the false opinion which maintains that the sun is the center and immovable, and forbidden to hold, defend, or teach the said false doctrine in any manner, and after it had been signified to me that the said doctrine is repugnant with the Holy Scriptures, . . . I adjure, curse, and detest the said heresies and errors, . . . and I swear that I will never more in future say or assert anything verbally, or in writing, which may give rise to a similar suspicion of me."

168. When asked by his teacher why the Puritans came to this country, a small boy responded: "To worship in their own way and make other people do the same."

169. Caliph Omar ordered the destruction of the large Alexandrian library with these words: "Either these books conform to the Koran, or they do not. If they do, they are not needed; if they do not, they are positively harmful. Therefore, let them be destroyed."

BOASTING

170. When an American visiting in Scotland said that he came from God's own country, the Scotsman replied: "Then you must have lost your accent."

171. Lord Alfred Milner said: "The last thing which the thought of the British Empire inspires in me is a desire to boast—to wave a flag, or to shout 'Rule, Britannia.' When I think of it, I am much more inclined to go into a corner by myself and pray."

172. A little boy who had often heard his father speak of his part in the Civil War finally asked: "Father, did anyone help you put down the rebellion?"

BOOKS

173. "I ain't read many books," remarked the captain of a Gloucester fishing schooner. "Perhaps you might say I don't know much. But I comprehend a lot!"

174. "The debt which [man] owes to books is incalculable," wrote Thomas Macaulay; "they have guided him to truth; they have filled his mind with noble and graceful images; they have stood by him in all vicissitudes, comforters in sorrow, nurses in sickness, companions in solitude. These friendships are exposed to no danger from the occurrences by which other attachments are weakened or dissolved. Time glides on; fortune is inconstant; tempers are soured; bonds which seemed indissoluble are daily sundered by interest, by emulation, or by caprice. But no such cause can affect the silent converse which we hold with the highest of human intellects."

175. F. G. Peabody tells of a preface in a certain book which had this startling sentence: "The purpose of this book is that, being read, it may read you."

BOY

176. Grandmother was worried about her two grandsons who, she thought, were certainly lost. "Don't worry," grandfather said. "Where did you tell them not go to?" When grandmother looked in one spot which had been particularly forbidden, she found the boys.

177. A small boy who had two fingers bandaged was receiving much attention and sympathy. Finally he said: "Can't you see that I have three fingers on that hand that aren't hurt at all?"

178. "Why do you bow to that newsboy?" President Garfield was asked by a friend. "Because," the President answered, "no one knows what is buttoned up in that boy's jacket."

179. A doctor hesitated when a call for help came on a particularly inclement night, but his love of humanity was strong, and he went through a drenching rain to the home of a poor laborer. His services saved the life of a small child. Years later the doctor said: "I never dreamed that in saving the life of that child on the farm hearth I was saving the life of the leader of England." That child was Lloyd George, onetime British prime minister.

180. The deacons of the church had gathered together to discuss the progress of their work. "We love you, pastor," one of them said, "but don't you think you had better resign? There hasn't been a convert this year." "Yes," the pastor said, "it has been a dull year. Yet I mind me that one did come—well, Bobby Moffat. But he is so wee a bairn that I suppose it is not right to count him." Years later, when Robert Moffat came back from his years of missionary work in Africa, the king of England rose and uncovered in his presence.

181. When a small boy told his mother that he was eight feet tall, the mother questioned the boy's accuracy. The boy insisted: "I am, for I have just measured myself with this little ruler that I made."

BRIBERY

182. Neither bribery nor flattery would turn the heart of Savonarola, fifteenth-century Italian reformer, from truth as he perceived it. Lorenzo the Magnificent offered him rich gifts. The pope offered him a cardinalate. In his Lenten sermons of 1496, Savonarola said: "I desire neither hats nor mitres, be they great or small; I desire naught save that which thou hast given to thy saints; it is death, a crimson hat, a hat of blood that I desire." His last words from the gallows were: "The Lord hath suffered so much for me."

183. During the early days of the American occupation of Manila an American officer was put in charge of the city with orders to "clean it up." A Chinaman offered him $10,000 for a gambling concession. He was bluntly dismissed. The

next day he returned with an offer of $25,000, and the officer detailed an orderly to throw him out. The next day he returned with the offer of $50,000. The officer kicked him out but went to his superior and tendered his resignation. "What's the matter?" he was asked. "Is the Chinaman making it too hot for you?" "No," the officer replied, "but he is getting too near my price." —ELBERT RUSSELL, *More Chapel Talks*

BROTHERHOOD

184. One day when famine had wrought great misery in Russia, a beggar, weak, emaciated, all but starved to death, asked for alms. Tolstoy searched his pockets for a coin but discovered that he was without as much as a copper piece. Taking the beggar's worn hands between his own, he said: "Do not be angry with me, my brother; I have nothing with me." The thin, lined face of the beggar became illumined as from some inner light, and he whispered in reply: "But you called me brother—that was a great gift."— WESLEY BOYD

185. "In wounds and in misery," declares Rebecca of *Ivanhoe,* "the Gentile is the Jew's brother."

186.
There is a destiny that makes us brothers;
  None goes his way alone:
All that we send into the lives of others
  Comes back into our own.

I care not what his temples or his creeds,
  One thing holds firm and fast—
That into his fateful heap of days and deeds
  The soul of man is cast.[2]
    —EDWIN MARKHAM, "A Creed"

[2] Reprinted by permission of Virgil Markham. From *Poems of Edwin Markham,* Harper & Bros., 1950.

187. We need to realize that we are *not* our brothers' keepers, but we *are* our brothers' brothers.—BOYD M. McKEOWN

188.
No one could tell me where my soul might be;
I sought for God, but God eluded me;
I sought my brother out and found all three.
    —ERNEST CROSBY, "The Search"

189. There is an old Jewish legend concerning the place where the Temple was built. It relates that two brothers lived on adjoining farms; one was married and the other a bachelor. Their farms were of equal size, and at the harvest one farm was seen to be just as fruitful as the other. The wheat had been cut and was standing in sheaves in the fields. The married brother, sitting in his home thinking of his bachelor brother, said: "He is a lonely man. He has no wife, no children, no joy in life except what he buys. I think I will take some of my sheaves and put them over in his field tonight." It so happened that the bachelor was thinking of the married brother with his wife and children, and he said: "Brother has many mouths to feed, and I don't need all I have. I'll take some of my sheaves and put them in his field tonight." Secretly carrying out their plans they met face to face one dark night. The legend says that at the spot where they met the Temple was built, for there heaven was nearest earth.—CHARLES H. PINCHBECK

190. In his book *On the Edge of the Primeval Forest,* Albert Schweitzer tells of a typical African experience: "The operation is finished and in the hardly lighted dormitory, I watch for the sick man's awakening. Scarcely has he recovered consciousness when he stares about him and ejaculates again and again, 'I've no more pain! I've no more pain!' His hand feels for mine and will not let me go. Then I begin to tell him that it is the Lord Jesus who has told the doctor and his wife to come to the Ogowé. The African sun is shining through the coffee bushes into the dark shed, but we, black and white, sit side by side and feel that we know by experience the meaning of the words: 'And all ye are brethren.'"

191.
God, what a world, if men in street and
   mart
Felt that same kinship of the human
   heart
Which makes them, in the face of fire
   and flood,
Rise to the meaning of True Brotherhood.
      —ELLA WHEELER WILCOX,
       "True Brotherhood"

192. Eugene Debs, who went to prison because of conscientious principles against the first World War and of whom the warden said, "I have never known a finer Christian," once summarized his faith in mankind with these words: "Years ago I recognized my kinship with all human beings, and I made up my mind I was not one whit better than the meanest on earth. I said then and I say now that while there is a lower class, I am of it; while there is a criminal class, I am of it; while there is a soul in prison, I am not free."

193. On the bottom of the swimming pool in the YMCA at Monmouth, Illinois, the builders placed a beautiful tile emblem symbolic of the spiritual, mental, and physical nature of man. At the center of the familiar red triangle is the Bible opened at John 17:21. When a boy could not make out the wording, he swam to the bottom and read it. "It says John 17:21, but what is that?" he asked a man near by. "'That they all may be one,'" the man answered. The boy's reply was prophetic: "You sure have to go through a lot to find that out."—WARREN I. LYNES

194. "No man can believe in the brotherhood of man and be comfortable," wrote Studdert-Kennedy, chaplain to George V. "It is a doctrine that takes away all our cushions and leaves us with a cross."

195. When William Howard Taft was governor general of the Philippines, he tried to impress on his assistants and subordinates the idea that the United States was to play the part of big brother to the Filipinos. And American soldiers, with their rollicking humor, used to march through the streets of Manila singing:

He may be a brother of Big Bill Taft,
But he ain't no brother of mine.
   —W. H. P. FAUNCE, *Facing Life*

BURDEN

196. A woman climbed on a train and continued to hold her heavy burden as the train sped along the rails. A conductor, noticing her, said: "Madam, if you will set your burden down, the train will carry both you and it."

197. Into a cross-maker's shop one day came a man who wearily took down *his* cross from his shoulder and set it on the floor. "And what can I do for you?" asked the cross-maker. "I want to exchange my burden," said the man. "This one is too heavy for me to carry. I stagger under the load." "Very well," replied the cross-maker. "Take your pick of all these crosses and see which suits you best." So the man gladly set about trying them on. The first was very light—for a moment or two—but as he walked about, testing it, he concluded that it wouldn't do, for soon it became heavier than his old one. So he tried another, and another, and another, until at last he found one lighter than all the rest. "I can bear this one," he told the cross-maker. "May I have it?" "Very well," the cross-maker answered, "but that is the one you brought in with you."

198. Phillips Brooks used to say that he did not pray for a lighter load but for a stronger back.

199. When Napoleon saw certain of his soldiers force off the road a peasant woman carrying a large bundle so that they might pass, he ordered: "Respect the burden."

BUSINESS

200. Someone has characterized the modern businessman in this manner: "Business is no longer a part of American life; it is American life. The average businessman now devotes twenty-four hours a day to it. Before daybreak an alarm clock wrests him from his fitful slumbers. He gulps down business news along with his eggs and coffee. He plans business on his way to the office and spends his morning reading business, talking business, and dictating business. He keeps a business engagement for lunch and afterward rushes back to the office where all the afternoon he routes himself, schedules himself, and dispatches himself as though he were an express train. After everyone else has gone home, he wraps up his business and carries it home in a brief case. He arrives late, sits down to dinner, and throughout the meal stares glassily into space. He is conjuring up phantoms of business failure. Suddenly the telephone rings. It is a business acquaintance who wants advice on the stock market. Ten minutes later the poor man returns to the table too overwrought to eat, and begins to pour out his troubles to his wife. He spends the evening studying budgets, reports, and trade journals. Finally he turns wearily to bed. Bed is, he has learned from long experience, the best place in which to worry out a solution to business problems."

201. During an antislavery meeting in New York City a northern merchant called out to the speaker: Sir, we are not such fools as not to know that slavery is a great evil, a great wrong. . . . A great portion of the property of the Southerners is invested under its sanction; and the business of the North, as well as the South, has become adjusted to it. . . . We cannot afford, sir, to let you and your associates succeed in your endeavor to overthrow slavery."

202. Two bankers a few years ago were motoring downtown in New York. One said to the other: "Those who create wealth go down in the subway, between seven and eight; we who motor down, at nine, only take it away from one another."

C

CAUSE

203. After Wendell Phillips had given a lecture in Chicago, Henry Ward Beecher, who had attended, went to see his friend. Beecher found Phillips uncomfortable, uneasy, and dissatisfied with the lecture he had given. Finally Phillips said: "I know what the matter was. It was only a speech. I was not fighting for any needy cause; I was not defending any great truth. It was just words, words, words."

204. Lord Rosebery, writing on William E. Gladstone, said: "When he had convinced himself that a cause was right, it engrossed him, it inspired him with a certainty as deepseated and as impervious as ever moved mortal man. To him, then, obstacles, objection, the counsels of doubters, and critics were as naught; he pressed on with the passion of a whirlwind, but also with the steady persistence of some puissant machine."

CHALLENGE

205. A man endangered his own life to rescue a small boy from drowning. The boy said: "Thank you, sir, for saving me." The man replied: "That's all right, son. Just be sure you're worth saving."

206. A towering black man appeared at the door of a preacher's study one day on some trivial errand, and in the midst of the conversation that followed produced a tattered newspaper clipping from an over-stuffed wallet and handed it to the clergyman to read. It told the story of a Negro's rescue of a white girl from a band of ruffians and the subsequent honor paid him by a great city when the mayor and leading citizens presented him with a gold medal in appreciation of his heroism. Then thrusting his hand into an inside pocket, just over his heart, the huge fellow drew forth a little leather case and from it took the medal, handling it tenderly and with evident emotion. "Doctor," he said, "sometimes when the days go bad and it seems like I got more trouble than one poor soul can bear, I reach down in this pocket over my heart and feel of this medal and pray, 'Lord, help me be as good a man as those white folks thought I was the day they gave me this!'"—ROY L. SMITH, *Suburban Christians*

207. Dale Carnegie tells us that when William Paley, the English rector, was once challenged by an atheist to prove that there was a God, he replied: "If I were to tell you that those levers and wheels and springs made themselves," he said, opening the case of his pocket watch, "and fitted themselves together and started running on their own account, wouldn't you question my intelligence? Of course you would. But look up at the stars. Every one of them has its perfect appointed course and motion —the earth and planets around the sun, and the whole group pitching along at more than a million miles a day. Each star is another sun with its own group of worlds, rushing on through space like our own solar system. Yet there are no

35

collisions, no disturbance, no confusion. All quiet, efficient, and controlled. Is it easier to believe that they just happened or that someone made them so?"

CHANCE

208. Sir James Jeans says that it would take a hundred million years for a hundred thousand monkeys, pecking at random on a hundred thousand typewriters, to happen by chance upon the plays of Shakespeare.

209. Unable to make up his mind whether he should marry a young woman named Mary Ann Evans, Herbert Spencer decided that his decision should be determined by the flip of a coin. Heads he would marry her; tails he would not. Although friends had every reason for believing that he loved her and although they were well aware of her love for him, when the coin came down tails he left the woman who is known to us as George Eliot, one of England's great novelists.

210.
We do not what we ought
What we ought not, we do;
And lean upon the thought
That Chance will bring us through.
—Matthew Arnold,
"Empedocles on Etna"

CHARACTER

211. "Character," Dwight L. Moody has said, "is what you are in the dark."

212. Samuel Smiles in his book *Self-Help* wrote: "The crown and glory of life is character. It is the noblest possession of a man, constituting a rank in itself, and estate in the general good will; dignifying every station, and exalting every position in society. It exercises a greater power than wealth and secures all the honor without the jealousies of fame. It carries with it an influence which always tells; for it is the result of proved honor, rectitude, and consistency—qualities which, perhaps more than any others, command the general confidence and respect of mankind."

213. When a young man returned to his home from the war, his father asked him if the war had injured his character. "Of course not," the son exclaimed. "There are some things men with our name can be trusted to do."

214. When a soldier complained to a general that, while most of the officers wore the purple of the conquerors, a certain officer dressed plainly, the general said: "Never mind; he is purple within."

215. Someone has said: "When wealth is lost, nothing is lost; when health is lost, something is lost; when character is lost, all is lost!"

216. In the age of the atom these words of Thomas Edison are challenging: "What man's mind can create, man's character can control."

217. Charles Kingsley, English clergyman and novelist, when asked what kind of character he disliked most, replied: "My own."

CHEERFULNESS

218. "Cheerfulness," said William Makepeace Thackeray, "means a contented spirit, a pure heart, a kind and loving disposition; it means humility and charity, a generous appreciation of others, and a modest opinion of self."

219. A Boston newspaper once reported: "It was a dull rainy day when things looked dark and lowering, but

Phillips Brooks came down through Newspaper Row and all was bright."

220.
God, give me sympathy and sense
  And help me keep my courage high.
God, give me calm and confidence—
  And, please—a twinkle in my eye.[1]
  —MARGARET BAILEY, "Prayer"

221. When asked how he could be as cheerful as he was, one Negro remarked: "I have learned how to cooperate with the inevitable."

222. The hymn "Take the Name of Jesus with You" was written by Lydia Baxter, who, confined to her room as an invalid for many years, knew a joy and cheerfulness which was constant and contagious.

223. Norman Vincent Peale writes: "The man who says he is a Christian and who at the same time is fearful and gloomy and dripping with pessimism may be a Christian intellectually and ethically, but he hasn't much of it in his heart."—*Faith Is the Answer*

224. A newspaperman said to General von Hindenburg, "All your life, General, you have been a man of iron will and self-control. We would like to ask you for the secret of that fact and to inquire, for the help it may be to others, what you do when you feel yourself getting nervous." "I whistle," replied the great German. "But, sir, none of us has ever heard you whistle." "Is it possible?" replied the man of iron will, with feigned surprise. "Now that I come to think about it, neither have I."

CHILD

225. Francis Xavier, the great Jesuit missionary, exhausted by days and

nights of serving, said to his attendant, "I must sleep. If I do not, I shall die. If anyone comes—whoever comes—waken me not." He then retired to his tent, and his faithful servant began his watch. It was not long, however, till the pallid face of Xavier appeared at the door. "I made a mistake," he said to the watcher. "If a little child comes, waken me."—F. R. MILLER

226. The painting of "Cornelia and Her Jewels" in the National Gallery in London shows two women in conversation. One of them, having shown Cornelia her string of pearls, asks the mother of the Gracchi what her jewels are. Cornelia then embraces her two sons and says: "These are my jewels."

227. The father of William the Conqueror required his barons to swear allegiance to his young son when he left for the Crusades. When the barons scoffed, the father said: "He is little, but he will grow."

228. An anxious father pushed through the crowd of people that his son might meet the Marquis of Willingdon. "Well, son, I am delighted to meet you," the marquis said. The boy, looking up into his face, replied: "Yes, I knew you would be."

229. When Dwight L. Moody returned to a friend's house after conducting meetings in a town in England, the friend asked how many were converted that night. "Two and a half—two children and one adult. The children are giving their full lives to Christ, but the adult has but half of his life left to give."

230. Alistair Maclean in *High Country* tells of two English explorers who happened some time ago on an Egyptian tomb. "The tomb was shut by the iron silence of three thousand years. When they opened it, they found an exquisitely carved sarcophagus of a little child, and over it this inscription: 'Oh, my life, my love, my little one, would God I had died for thee!' They uncovered their heads and with dim eyes stepped into the light. Then they sealed the tomb and left love and death to their eternal vigil."

231.
The golf links lie so near the mill
  That almost every day
The laboring children can look out
  And see the men at play.
              —Sarah N. Cleghorn,
              "The Golf Links"

CHILD TRAINING

232. Socrates once said: "Could I climb to the highest place in Athens, I would lift my voice and proclaim: 'Fellow citizens, why do you turn and scrape every stone to gather wealth, and take so little care of your children to whom one day you must relinquish it all?'"

233. If we had paid no more attention to our plants than we have to our children," Luther Burbank said, "we would now be living in a jungle of weeds."

234. "How early can I begin the education of my child?" a woman asked Francis Wayland Parker, the educator. "When will your child be born?" he asked. "Why he is already five years old," she exclaimed. "My goodness, woman," Parker said, "don't stand here talking to me—hurry home; already you have lost the best five years."

235. "My son has just enrolled, and I hope you can keep an eye on him," said a father to the dean at a college. "My business has kept me away from home," the father admitted, "and, frankly, I don't seem to understand the boy. I hope you'll take a hand and straighten him out." The dean, somewhat irritated, said: "Sir, if you don't understand your son after nineteen years of being his father, I refuse to do in four years the job you should have done long ago."

236. When a mischievous young Negro lad had got into trouble, a wise old Negro commented to those who were trying to correct the boy: "You have just got to love him out of it."

237. When chided for the lack of faith of his sons, an earnest although impulsive father exclaimed: "I tells 'em to pray and they won't pray, and I tells 'em again to pray and they won't pray, and I knocks 'em down and they won't pray."

238. A little boy, asked what his name was, replied: "Willy Don't."—George B. Cutten

239. There is a story of a woman who said: "I guess I know how to bring up children. Haven't I lost thirteen?"

240. In ancient times there was a king whose son was unmanageable in spite of the efforts of many tutors. One day a tutor fastened a strip of royal purple to the boy's coat. "What is that for?" the boy asked. The tutor replied: "That is the emblem of your royalty." Afterwards when the boy showed signs of misbehavior, the slightest glance at the emblem would cause him to pull himself together and act like a prince.

241. A mother had asked her husband, who happened to be a statistician, to care for the children while she went shopping. When she returned, she found her husband exhausted by the experience. He handed her a record of the ordeal:

Dried the children's tears 14 times

Tied their shoes 16 times

Served drinks of water 22 times

Toy balloons purchased—3 per child

Average life of a balloon—12 seconds

Cautioned children not to cross the street 34 times

Children insisted on crossing the street 34 times

Number of Saturdays father will do this in the future—*none*.

—JAMES G. GILKEY, *Managing One's Self*

242. One of our leading university presidents tells us that one springtime he was in the north of Canada when the frost was breaking up and the roads were well-nigh impassable. He says that at one crossroad he saw this sign: "Take care which rut you choose; you will be in for the next twenty-five miles." —HARRY EMERSON FOSDICK, *Successful Christian Living*

CHRIST

243. He is tender and compassionate; but he is violent and uncompromising. He could make a child feel at home on his knee; but he could make his powerful enemies quail before him. He said that by him men would be judged; but he was meek and lowly in heart. He said the most awful things about sin that have ever been spoken; but he said the kindest things to sinners that human ears have ever heard. He asks from me my all, yet he gives himself to me utterly. He is the most knowable man who ever lived, yet no one has ever explained him. He asserts his authority at every turn, yet he withdraws from the applauding crowds. His joyous comradeship raises scandal, yet they call him Man of Sorrows. He raised from the dead, yet he deliberately chooses death. He has power such as none has ever had before or since, yet he ever knocks and waits and listens before he passes the low lintel of the human life awaiting the true low of the heart, the full allegiance of the will and concerned that no violence to our mental processes is ever demanded from us. He died two thousand years ago, yet to thousands he is a greater reality than their dearest friend, without whom joy would pass away from life and leave it cold and bleak and dead.—LESLIE D. WEATHERHEAD, *His Life and Ours*

244. Robert E. Speer has written in "What Jesus Does for Me" these words: "He gives me a clearer moral vision and the courage to try to live by that vision. He gives me the desire to work in the world as intensely as he worked. He kindles me, when I grow sluggish or indifferent, to a positive and aggressive antagonism to evil within and without. He gives me confidence in the truth and so helps me to rest, no matter what happens in the world, because I know that God and the truth must prevail. He counterbalances, as I cannot, the variable circumstances and unequal conditions of life and takes care of the excesses that are beyond me. He gives me grace and strength to try, at least, things that I know are impossible, and to attempt, first of all, the things that are hardest to be done. He helps me refuse to do good when I know that something better can be done. He helps me to keep on when I have to, even though I know I cannot. He saves me from the fret and killing of pride and vanity, and helps me to cease to care for the things that make people sick. He helps me to keep the central things clear and not to be fogged and broken down by the accessories and secondary things. He gives me a new and inward

living principle. I believe that he is this principle, and that there is another personality inside my personality that would not be there if it had not been for him and if it were not for him today."

245. Here is a man who was born in an obscure village, the child of a peasant woman. He grew up in another village, and that a despised one. He worked in a carpenter shop until thirty years of age, and then for three years he was an itinerant preacher. He never wrote a book. He never held an office. He never owned a home. He never had a family. He never went to college. He never put his foot inside a really big city. He never traveled, except in his infancy, more than two hundred miles from the place where he was born. He had no credentials but himself. While he was still a young man, the tide of popular opinion turned against him. His friends ran away. One of them betrayed him. He was turned over to his enemies. He went through the mockery of a trial. He was nailed upon a cross between two thieves. His executioners gambled for the only piece of property he had on earth, his seamless robe. When he was dead, he was taken down from the cross and laid in a borrowed grave through the courtesy of a friend. Nineteen wide centuries have come and gone, and today Jesus is the centerpiece of the human race and the leader of all human progress. I am well within the mark when I say that all the armies that ever marched, all the navies that were ever built, all the parliaments that have ever sat, and all the kings that have ever ruled, put together, have not affected the life of man upon this earth like this one solitary personality. All time dates from his birth, and it is impossible to understand or interpret the progress of human civilization in any nation on earth apart from his influence. Slowly through the ages man is coming to realize that the greatest necessity in the world is not water, iron, gold, food, and clothing, or even nitrate in the soil; but rather Christ enshrined in human hearts, thoughts, and motives.
—S. A. STUBER and T. C. CLARK, *Treasury of the Christian Faith*

246.
To be Himself a star most bright
To bring the wise men to His sight,
To be Himself a voice most sweet
To call the shepherds to His feet,
To be a child—it was His will,
That folk like us might find Him still.[2]
—JOHN ERSKINE, "Childhood"

247. What can I give Him
   Poor as I am?
If I were a shepherd,
   I would give Him a lamb;
If I were a wise man,
   I would do my part,—
But what I can I give Him,
   Give my heart.
—CHRISTINA G. ROSSETTI,
"What Can I Give Him?"

Antagonism Toward Christ

248. After the burning of a hundred heretics to the glory of God before the great cathedral in sixteenth-century Seville, Jesus appears to bring joy to the common people and consternation to the Grand Inquisitor in Dostoevsky's *The Brothers Karamazov*. The inquisitor, who has Jesus taken prisoner, asks Jesus why when he had the power fifteen hundred years before to perform miracles and mysteries he refused. Now the church has supplied that miracle, mystery and authority, and men are satisfied. The inquisitor does not wish Jesus to interfere with the work of the church. "Go," he says, "and come no

[2] Used by permission of the author.

more! Come not at all, never, never, never!"

249. During the Senate debate on the question of American participation in the League of Nations after World War I, Senator Henry Cabot Lodge declared that if Jesus Christ should come to the Senate chamber in person and ask the United States to join the League, he would still vote against it.

Attractiveness of Christ

250. A small boy, determined to draw a picture of Jesus, at last gave up his effort. "You haven't drawn Jesus," said his teacher. "No," said the small boy. "I couldn't make him beautiful enough."

251. Said Henry Drummond: "To become Christlike is the only thing in the whole world worth caring for; the thing before which every ambition of man is folly and all lower achievement vain."

252.

He wakes desires you never may forget;
  He shows you stars you never saw
    before;
  He makes you share with Him for-
    evermore
The burden of the world's divine regret.
          —Tennyson

253. "The strange thing about Jesus," said a Japanese student, "is that you can never get away from him."

254. Henry Sloane Coffin, commenting on Christ's call to the disciples, says: "His characteristic summons to disciples was not 'Copy me,' but 'Follow me.'"

Christ the Carpenter

255. Erasmus said: "By a Carpenter mankind was made, and only by that Carpenter can mankind be remade."

256. Beneath the chapel window at Stanford University which picture as the boy Jesus in the carpenter shop in Nazareth is this inscription: "The highest service may be prepared for and done in the humblest surroundings. In silence, in waiting, in obscure, unnoticed offices, in years of uneventful, unrecorded duties, the Son of God grew and waxed strong."

257.

The Carpenter of Galilee
  Comes down the street again,
In every land, in every age,
  He still is building men.
On Christmas Eve we hear Him knock;
  He goes from door to door:
"Are any workmen out of work?
  The Carpenter needs more."
          —Hilda W. Smith, "The Carpen-
                ter of Galilee"

Christ the Comforter

258. George Matheson prayed: "Son of man, whenever I doubt of life I think of thee. Thou never growest old to me. Last century is old. Last year is obsolete fashion, but thou art not obsolete. Thou art abreast of all the centuries, and I have never come up to thee, modern as I am."

259. The story is told by Hugh Macmillan in *The Daisies of Nazareth* of a highland shepherd on a lonely moor who had been infirm for many years and blind. He was so crippled with rheumatism that he could not stir from his seat beside his lowly peat fire. As he was sitting thus one day, a kindly visitor asked him whether the hours which he spent in this manner were not weary, and spoke of the blessedness of heaven. The old shepherd answered simply: "I know it well: I have been in heaven during the last ten years." He went on to explain to his visitor that since Jesus had entered his heart ten years before and had made his abode there, he had not felt the weariness as he had before.

—C. F. Andrews, *Christ in the Silence*

260.
In trouble then and fear I sought
  The Man who taught in Galilee;
And peace unto my soul was brought,
  And all my faith came back to me.

—Author Unknown

261.
'Twas August, and the fierce sun overhead
Smote on the squalid streets of Bethnal Green,
And the pale weaver, through his windows seen
In Spitalfields, look'd thrice dispirited.

I met a preacher there I knew, and said:
"Ill and o'er-worked, how fare you in this scene?"—
"Bravely!" said he; "for I of late have been
Much cheered with thoughts of Christ, *the living bread.*"

—Matthew Arnold, "East London"

262. When young Joseph Scriven lost by drowning the woman with whom he had made marriage plans, the youth emerged from months of bitterness and discouragement by writing a hymn which witnesses to a tender faith in Jesus as comforter and burden-bearer, "What a Friend We Have in Jesus."

263. A visitor to the Copenhagen Cathedral saw Thorwaldsen's "Kristus." A friend told him the story of the famous statue. When the artist had finished molding the plastic clay into a majestic "Kristus," he left it to dry and went home. That night a dense fog and mist rolled in from the sea, and when Thorwaldsen returned the next morning, he thought his masterpiece was ruined. The hands that had been held aloft to bless were now stretched out invitingly. The regal head was bowed low and looking down. But as he gazed, he saw a new "Kristus," different from his previous conception. This was a "Kristus" to worship. He said: "If you want to see his face, you must get down on your knees."

—Helen E. Springer

264. During a violent storm a little bird was hurled into Charles Wesley's room. When Wesley picked the bird up, he found him stunned but not dead. Holding the bird for a few moments Wesley calmed its fears and placed it on the window sill, from which in a few moments it flew away. Then Wesley sat down at his desk and wrote the hymn "Jesus, Lover of my soul, let me to thy bosom fly."

Compulsion of Christ

265. A man who had given his life to the ministry of suffering mankind in London was asked by a friend, "Why don't you run away from it all before you are broken by this inhuman burden?" "I would like to run away," was the reply. "I would like to run away from it all, but a strange Man on a cross won't let me."

266. "Thou canst not comprehend it," exclaimed Julian the Apostate in Ibsen's *Emperor and Galilean*, "thou who hast never been under the power of the God-Man. It is more than teaching that He spreads over the earth: it is witchcraft that takes the mind captive. They who have been under Him, I believe, can never get free."

Cross of Christ

267.

They borrowed a bed to lay his head
  When Christ the Lord came down;
They borrowed the ass in the mountain
    pass
  For him to ride to town;
But the crown that he wore and the
  cross that he bore
  Were his own—
The cross was his own.
  —AUTHOR UNKNOWN, "Borrowed"

268. Three large trees in a forest prayed that they might choose what they would be converted into when they were felled. One prayed to be made into a beautiful palace; the second to be a large ship and sail the seven seas; the third to stay in the forest and always point toward God. One day the woodman came and chopped down the first tree, but instead of a palace it was made into a common stable, wherein was born the fairest Babe in all creation. The second tree was made into a small ship that was launched on the Sea of Galilee, on the deck of which stood a tall young man who told the multitudes: "I am come that they might have life, and that they might have it more abundantly." The third tree was made into a cross, and to it men nailed that young man, the loveliest personality that ever walked the earth. Ever since then that cross has been pointing men to God. And so each prayer was answered.
    —MARVIN BAUER

269. John Bowring, who wrote "In the Cross of Christ I Glory," was a Christian layman who distinguished himself as a statesman, diplomat, British governor of Hong Kong, a member of Parliament, and a man of significant literary achievements. The hymn by which he is best remembered is the more interesting for it represents the devotion to Christ of a Unitarian. On his tombstone in Exeter are inscribed the words: "In the cross of Christ I glory."

270. A little girl, upon seeing for the first time a cross upon an altar, asked: "What's the plus sign doing on that table?"—DONALD H. TIPPETT

271. "The river [of history] moves on," writes Pierre van Paassen in *That Day Alone*, "but the Cross remains, now as then moving forward in stark reality. When the strong torture the weak, when the poor cry for bread, when the innocent languish in dungeons, when mothers go insane because they see their children die, when the outcasts roam a vague vision that recedes in the night, in the wilderness, when the soldiers go to battle, when those who sit in darkness pray for light, the Cross returns, and the head of the Man on the Cross sinks deeper on the tired breast."

272. "What is needed today is not adjusted personalities, but terribly unadjusted personalities, as Jesus was," writes Halford Luccock. "The cross is the eternal symbol of an unadjusted personality in an evil world."

273. When Émile Zola was condemned by his judges, his lawyer pointed to a crucifix and said: "Remember, gentlemen, that was once a closed case, too, but it was opened again."

274. Thomas à Kempis in his *Imitation of Christ* wrote: "Jesus hath many lovers of his kingdom, but few bearers of his cross. All are disposed to rejoice with him, but few to suffer sorrow for his sake. Many follow him to the breaking of the bread, but few to the drinking of his bitter cup."

275. Some American businessmen, visiting the "Passion Play," tried to lift the cross carried by Anton Lang, the actor who was then interpreting the role of Jesus. "Why must it be so heavy?" they asked Lang. "If I didn't feel the weight of it," Lang said, "I couldn't act my part!"

276. A native in Bechuanaland, on hearing the story of the cross, was deeply moved and said: "Jesus, away from there. That is my place."—LESLIE D. WEATHERHEAD, *A Plain Man Looks at the Cross*

Crucifixion of Christ

277. In Dürer's famous masterpiece "Descent from the Cross" one of the disciples is shown picking up the crown of thorns which had fallen from the bowed head of Christ, and is pressing his finger on a thorn in an effort to realize what it meant to wear it.

278. Rembrandt, the seventeenth-century Dutch painter, centered one of his paintings on the crucifixion. A careful observation of the figures in the shadows behind the cross will show that one of the men helping to crucify Jesus is Rembrandt himself. He was honest enough to admit that because of his own failures he was like those of old who put the master to death.

279. When told for the first time the story of the crucifixion, Clovis, king of the Franks, exclaimed: "If I had been there with my Franks, I would have avenged his wrong."

280. Describing the method of his work among the North American Indians, David Brainerd in his *Journal* noted: "I never got away from Jesus, and him crucified; and I found that when my people were gripped by this, I had no need to give them instructions about morality. I found that one followed as the sure and inevitable fruit of the other."

281. In 1840 Bishop Selwyn, who was a missionary among the cannibal Maoris of New Zealand, wrote: "I am in the midst of a sinful people, who have been accustomed to sin uncontrolled from their youth. If I speak to a native on murder, infanticide, cannibalism, and adultery, they laugh in my face and tell me I may think these acts are bad, but they are very good for a native, and they cannot conceive any harm in them. But on the contrary when I tell them that these and other sins brought the Son of God, the great Creator of the universe, from his eternal glory to this world to be incarnate and to be made a curse and to die —then they open their eyes and ears and mouths, and wish to hear more, and presently they acknowledge themselves sinners, and say they will leave off their sins."—LESLIE D. WEATHERHEAD, *A Plain Man Looks at the Cross*

282. In his drama *The Emperor and the Galilean,* Ibsen tells of a dream which Julian the Apostate had in which he fancied himself carried to another planet from which he looked down upon the earth where he had destroyed Christianity and rooted out the name of Jesus Christ. "But behold, there came a procession by me on the strange earth, where I stood. There were soldiers and judges and executioners at the head of it, and weeping women followed. And lo, in the midst of the slow-moving array was the Galilean— alive, and bearing a cross on His back. Then I called to Him, and I said, 'Whither away, Galilean?' and He turned His face to me and smiled and nodded slowly and said, 'To the place of the skull.'"

283. The choice between hate and love is considered by Studdert-Kennedy with these words: "The crucified Christ is looking down upon us with death in his bleeding hands and feet, but life is the light of his burning eyes, and demanding from us all—every individual man and woman—a choice between glory or force and wrath and fear. . . . He will not go away. I do not believe he will let us alone. He is going to drive us to a decision with his wounded hands. He will not let us have his world for a playground, a battlefield, a factory, or an empire any longer; we must give it to him. We must give it to him—or else there will be darkness over all the earth from the sixth hour until the ninth—and that may be a thousand years."

284. In "Good Friday" by John Masefield a peddler of lilies says to Christ:

Friend, it is over now, the passion, the
  tears, the pains,
Only the truth remains.[4]

Disciples of Christ

285. O Master, my Master!
    These sayings of Thine;
  Help me to make them
    Doings of mine.
        —AUTHOR UNKNOWN

286. W. Russell Maltby has said: "Jesus promised His disciples three things—that they would be entirely fearless, absurdly happy, and that they would get into trouble."

287. An old legend tells us that when Jesus returned to heaven he was asked by an angel: "What have you left be-

[4] From *Good Friday and Other Poems.* Copyright 1915, 1943 by John Masefield. Used by permission of the Macmillan Co., and The Society of Authors, London.

hind to carry out the work?" Jesus answered: "A little band of men and women who love me." "But what if they fail when the trial comes? Will all you have done be defeated?" "Yes," said Jesus, "if they fail, all I have done will be defeated." "Is there nothing more?" "No," said Jesus, "there is nothing more." "What then?" "They will not fail," said Jesus.—C. F. ANDREWS, *Christ in the Silence*

Christ the Example

288. "God never gave a man a thing to do concerning which it would be irreverent to ponder how the Son of God would have done it," wrote George MacDonald.

289. Sundar Singh of India was a man of noble birth. He renounced all connection with family and wealth to be a follower of Christ. His life was devoted to spreading the gospel, principally among his own people. He also traveled and lectured in the United States and in England, where his influence was greatly felt. While in England he had occasion to knock at the door of a home. A little child who answered his knock called: "Oh, mother, come quickly. Jesus is here."—MINNIE M. BASSETT

290.
O Son of Man, thou madest known,
Through quiet work in shop and home,
The sacredness of common things,
The chance of life that each day brings,
That Master workman, grant us grace
The challenge of our tasks to face;
By loyal scorn of second best,
By effort true, to meet each test.
        —AUTHOR UNKNOWN

Faith in Christ

291.
Not what, but *Whom*, I do believe,
  That, in my darkest hour of need,

Hath comfort that no mortal creed
To mortal man may give;—
Not what, but *Whom!*
For Christ is more than all the creeds,
And His full life of gentle deeds
Shall all the creeds outlive.

Not what I do believe, but *Whom!*
Who walks beside me in the gloom?
Who shares the burden wearisome?
Who all the dim way doth illume,
And bids me look beyond the tomb
The larger life to live?—
Not what I do believe,
But *Whom!*
Not what
But *Whom!* [5]
    —John Oxenham, "Credo"

292. Alfred Tennyson, walking in the garden with a friend, was asked what he thought of Jesus Christ. Pointing to some flowers Tennyson said: "What the sun is to these flowers, Christ is to my soul. He is the sun of my soul."

293. A teacher in New York City, Ray Palmer wrote "My Faith Looks Up to Thee" during his twenty-second year when sickness and poverty hounded him. Years later he said: "I gave form to what I felt by writing, with little effort, these stanzas. I recollect I wrote them with very tender emotion, and ended the last line with tears. I composed them with a deep consciousness of my own needs, without the slightest thought of writing for another eye, and least of all of writing a hymn for Christian worship."

Following Christ

294. Mr. Standfast in *Pilgrim's Progress* said: "I have loved to hear my Lord spoken of, and wherever I have seen the print of His shoe in the earth, there have I coveted to put mine also."

295. A traveler in the Near East asked a Turkish young man where he learned to speak English. "At Robert College," he answered. "And did you also learn to be a Christian there?" "Oh, no!" he replied. "I am not a Christian; I am only a humble follower of Jesus."—Elbert Russell, *More Chapel Talks*

296.
If Jesus Christ is a man,—
  And only a man—I say
That of all mankind I cleave to him,
  And to him will I cleave alway.

If Jesus Christ is a God,—
  And the only God,—I swear
I will follow Him through heaven and hell,
  The earth, the sea, and the air! [6]
    —Richard Watson Gilder,
     "The Song of a Heathen"

297.
White Captain of my soul, lead on;
I follow thee, come dark or dawn.
Only vouchsafe three things I crave:
Where terror stalks, help me be brave!
Where righteous ones can scarce endure
The siren call, help me be pure!
Where vows grow dim, and men dare do
What once they scorned, help me be true! [7]
    —Robert Freeman,
     "White Captain"

298. One day an old man went to Evangeline Booth, saying: "I was the lamplighter for your father when he held his first meeting under cover. I put up the wires and lighted the lamps. Your

[5] From *Selected Poems of John Oxenham.* Used by permission of Harper & Bros., publishers, and Erica Oxenham.

[6] Used by permission of Houghton Mifflin Co., publishers.

[7] Used by permission of Margery Freeman.

father placed his hand upon my head and said to me, 'My lad, always be a lamplighter for Jesus Christ.' I want you to know that I have always carried the light for my Lord."

299. When Wilfred Grenfell was a medical student in London, he accepted Dwight L. Moody's invitation to follow Christ. After completing his education he found his field of service on the bleak coasts of Labrador, where he became famous for his work. Fourteen years afterwards he called upon Moody in Boston. As they talked together, Dr. Grenfell said: "I want to thank you for leading me to know Christ." "That was fourteen years ago," responded Moody. "What have you been doing since?" "Doing!" exclaimed Dr. Grenfell. "I have been living and working that others may know Christ!" "Do you regret it?" asked Moody. "No," was Dr. Grenfell's quick reply. "The only regret is for the person who has once met Christ and then must hang his head when asked the question, 'What have you been doing since?'"—HALE THORNBERRY

God in Christ

300. Wrote Robert Gossip in *The Galilean Accent*: "Always Christians had thought, and hoped, and dreamed, and wondered about God. If only He were this, and ah, if He were really that! But at the Cross He breaks silence, the veil is rent from top to bottom, and they find themselves looking up into God's very face, seeing Him as He really is, hearing Him speaking, as it were, with His own very voice to very them. And what a wonderful message it is that comes through!"

301. Writes Solomon B. Freehof, distinguished Jewish preacher: "The consciousness of the presence of God has come to millions of men and women through Jesus. . . . He is still the living comrade of countless lives. No Moslem ever sings, 'Mohammed, lover of my soul,' nor does any Jew say of Moses, the teacher, 'I need thee every hour.' . . . He brought God near to men through his presence. He made the Divine personal for myriads of worshipers."—*What I Owe to Christ*

302. A Jewish rabbi has written: "You Christians possess one advantage over us. When we use the word 'God,' our listeners have a somewhat vague conception in their minds of righteousness and power combined in a Being who fills the universe. When you employ that word, your hearers think at once of the figure of Jesus of Nazareth."—HENRY SLOANE COFFIN, *God Confronts Man in History*

303. "Anything that one imagines of God apart from Christ," said Martin Luther, "is only useless thinking and vain idolatry."

304. John Morley, who was not a Christian, said: "If I believed that Jesus Christ was the Son of God and my Saviour, I would never write or talk anything else."

Greatness of Christ

305. Someone overheard a Negro on the street saying to another: "Jesus is the only Somebody you can't match." —E. STANLEY JONES, *The Way*

306. "The Galilean has been too great for our small hearts" were the words which H. G. Wells used to sum up the influence of Jesus upon human history in his *Outline of History*.

307. Napoleon said to General Bertrand: "I know men; and I tell you that

Jesus Christ is no mere man. Between him and every other person in the world there is no possible term of camparison. Alexander, Caesar, Charlemagne, and I founded empires. But on what did we rest the creations of our genius? Upon force. Jesus Christ founded his empire upon love; and at this hour millions of men would die for him."

308. Alfred Adler, a psychologist and a Jew, in answer to the question of a Los Angeles pastor, "What do you think of Jesus Christ?" said: "Whenever I hear his name, I stop for reverence to the greatest character of human history."

309. William Lyon Phelps wrote: "Jesus knew more about political economy than all the professors in all the colleges in the world, and he knew more about the human heart than Shakespeare. While I am not sure of many things, I am just as sure as that I stand here that Jesus is the greatest leader, the most absolutely right person the world has ever known."

310. Charles Lamb said: "If Shakespeare should come into this room, we would all rise; but if Jesus Christ should come in, we would all kneel."

311. Ernest Renan in his *Life of Jesus* wrote: "Jesus was the greatest religious genius that ever lived. His beauty is eternal, and his reign will never end. Jesus is in every respect unique, and nothing can be compared with him."

Hope in Christ

312. When World War II ended, the members of a certain church in Frankfurt, Germany, began repairing their bombed sanctuary. Among the objects to be restored was a statue of the Christ, which had been badly broken. All parts of the statue except the hands were found. After debating whether or not they should engage a sculptor to carve new hands, the members decided to leave the figure without hands. Under it they wrote: "Christ has no hands but our hands."

313. The English playwright and Nobel prize winner George Bernard Shaw has written: "I am no more of a Christian than Pilate was, or you are, gentle hearer; and yet, like Pilate, I greatly prefer Jesus of Nazareth to Amos or Caiaphas; and I am ready to admit that I see no way out of the world's misery but the way which would have been found by his will."

314. "Yes, life will work only one way," Leslie D. Weatherhead has declared, "and that is Christ's way. There is a precipice at the end of every other road. Broken, bruised, disillusioned, despairing, we know then that of ourselves and in ourselves there is no hope of finding anything but the hell of a great despair. 'Outside of God there is only death.' I wish I could persuade the reader of that before he finds it out for himself."

315. When someone was told that Clemenceau said that Woodrow Wilson talked like Jesus Christ at the peace conference following World War I, his comment was: "Would that it were true!"

Indifference Toward Christ

316. Anatole France in his story "The Procurator of Judea" describes Pilate as an old man reminiscing with an old friend, Laelius Lamia, about Judea. Subject after subject is discussed. Then Lamia mentions the crucifixion of Jesus. "Pontius, do you remember anything about the man?" After a thoughtful moment Pilate answers: "Jesus? Jesus— of Nazareth? I cannot call him to mind."

317. "What think ye of Christ?" Youth: Too happy to think—time enough. Manhood: Too busy to think—more money first. Maturity: Too anxious to think— worry over work. Declining years: Too aged to think—fixed habits. As death approaches: Too ill to think—weak and suffering. Death: Too late to think— the spirit has flown. Eternity: Forever to think—God's judgment day.

318.
Men overlooked a baby's birth
When love unnoticed came to earth;
And later, seeking in the skies,
Passed by a man in workman's guise.
And only children paused to stare
While God Incarnate made a chair.
—MARY TATLOW

Influence of Christ

319. "He has changed sunset into sunrise," Clement of Alexandria said of Christ.

320. Mark Rutherford, after a night in prison, said: "Last night Jesus came into my prison cell, and every stone shone like a ruby."

321. "In all the history of Christianity, whenever there has been a new emphasis upon Jesus," says E. Stanley Jones, "there has been a fresh outburst of vitality and virility."—WALTER R. BOWIE, The Bible

322. In front of Trinity Church in Boston stands a statue of Phillips Brooks. When the sculptor who was to make the statue received his commission, he went to the seminary in Virginia where the famous minister had studied; to Philadelphia, where he began his ministry; and to Boston, where he had made

such outstanding success, to try to discover the secret of his radiant life. He concluded that it was the way Phillips Brooks had been influenced by the power of Christ. When he made the statue, therefore, he placed behind the figure of the man a figure of Christ with arms oustretched in blessing over the minister's head.—HERBERT W. HAHN

323. In his letter of resignation as pastor of Plymouth Church, Brooklyn, Lyman Abbott said: "I see that what I had once hoped might be done for my fellows through schemes of social reform and philanthropy can only be done by the influence of Jesus Christ. There is no dynamo in reform save the cross of Jesus Christ."

324. "You don't really believe that yarn about Jesus turning the water into wine?" a friend said sneeringly to an old man who had sold furniture to buy liquor and had squandered his family's money to buy beer but now was a Christian. "I am an ignorant man," replied the convert; "I don't know about water and wine. But I know this—that in my house Jesus Christ has turned beer into furniture! And that is a good enough miracle for me."

Christ the King

325. One Palm Sunday in the city of Florence four hundred and fifty years ago Savonarola was preaching to a great multitude. Suddenly in the middle of his discourse he cried aloud: "It is the Lord's will to give a new Head to this city of Florence." For a moment he paused, keeping the people in suspense, and then he went on: "The new Head is Christ! Christ seeks to become your King." And at that the whole multitude were on their feet, shouting: "Long live Jesus, King of Florence!"

326. When Prince Oscar Bernadotte, brother of King Gustav of Sweden and a sincere Christian, was begged to speak to a great crowd gathered to see him, he said: "What have you come out to see? Is it that you wished to see the son of a king? Look well at me then, for that I truly am—a son of the father of your country, and a son of the King of kings."

Christ the Light

327. An inscription on the wall of a castle in Scotland reads: "When Jesus comes, the shadows depart."

328. In Holman Hunt's famous painting, "The Light of the World," the latch is on the inside of the door. One critic, when first viewing the painting, called the artist's attention to the missing latch. The artist said that the door represented man, who, when Christ knocked, must open himself.

329. When a small boy had seen Holman Hunt's great picture, "The Light of the World," he asked his father: "Daddy, why don't they let Jesus in?" The father answered: "I don't know." A moment later the small boy said: "Daddy, I know why they don't let Jesus in. They live in the basement, and they can't hear him knock."
—Joseph A. Smith

330. A child, after gazing thoughtfully at Holman Hunt's painting "The Light of the World," which portrays Christ knocking at a door, turned to his mother and asked: "Did he ever get in?"

331. A father showed his young son the picture by Holman Hunt of Christ standing at the door. "Isn't it about time that you opened your heart to him?" the father said. "It has never been closed to him," the boy answered.

The Living Christ

332. In a dialogue by John Masefield, English poet laureate, Pilate's wife says: "What do you think of his claims?" The centurion answers: "If a man believes something so much that he is ready to die for it, he is going to get others to believe it too." Pilate's wife asks: "Is he dead?" "No," replies the centurion, "he is not dead." "Where is he then?" again asks Pilate's wife. The centurion answers: "Let loose in the world, lady, where neither Roman nor Jew can stop his truth."

333. "Whenever Christianity has struck out a new path in her journey it has been because the personality of Jesus has again become living, and a ray from his being has once more illumined the world," comments an unknown writer.

334. Anton Reicha, the great conductor, was rehearsing his choir for a production of *The Messiah*. The chorus had sung through to the point where the soprano takes up the refrain, "I know that my Redeemer liveth." The technique of the soloist was perfect— faultless breathing, accurate note placing, splendid enunciation. When the final note died away, all eyes turned to Reicha for his approval. Instead he walked up to the singer with sorrowful eyes and said quietly: "My daughter, you do not know that your Redeemer lives, do you?" She flushed and replied: "Why, yes, I think I do." "Then sing it," cried the conductor. "Sing it so that all who hear you may know that you do know the joy and power of it." And he motioned the orchestra to play again. When the singer finished this time, the old master approached, saying: "You do know, for you have told me."—J. C. Mitchell

335.

I looked for Christ in the hidden skies,
A flaming vision to blind my eyes—
While Christ walked by with stumbling
    feet
Along with the men of Madison
    Street.[8]
      —RAYMOND KRESENSKY,
         "Christ on Madison Street"

336.

Shakespeare is dust, and will not come
To question from his Avon tomb,
And Socrates and Shelley keep
An Attic and Italian sleep.

They see not. But, O Christians, who
Throng Holborn and Fifth Avenue,
May you not meet, in spite of death,
A traveller from Nazareth.[9]
      —JOHN DRINKWATER,
         "To and Fro About the City"

337. "They may kill me if they please,"
said Savonarola, "but they will never,
never, never tear the living Christ from
my heart!"

Love of Christ

338. Zinzendorf asked John Wesley:
"Do you think it was self-denial for the
Lord Jesus to come down from heaven
to rescue a world? Was it self-denial?
No, it was love—love that swallows up
everything, and first of all self."

339. Said Henry George, the social reformer, to Cardinal Manning: "I loved
the people, and that love brought me to
Christ as their best friend and teacher."
"And I loved Christ," replied the cardinal, "and so learned to love the people
for whom he died."

340. A young artist had painted a picture of the Last Supper. He took it to

[8] Used by permission of the author.
[9] Copyright 1922 by John Drinkwater. Reprinted by permission of the Author's Estate.

Tolstoy for his criticism. After studying
it carefully the Russian writer pointed to
the central figure and said, "You do not
love him." "Why, that is the Lord
Christ," said the artist. "I know," replied
Tolstoy, "but you do not love him. If
you loved him more, you would paint
him better."

Message of Christ

341. "It is not difficult to see one vital
significance of Jesus Christ: he has
given us the most glorious interpretation of life's meaning that the sons of
men have ever had," writes Harry Emerson Fosdick. "The fatherhood of God,
the friendship of the Spirit, the sov-
ereignty of righteousness, the law of
love, the glory of service, the coming of
the kingdom, the eternal hope—there
never was an interpretation of life to
compare with that."—*Christianity and
Progress*

342. "Jesus came not to get men into
heaven, but to get heaven into men,"
says E. Stanley Jones, "not to get men
out of hell, but to get hell out of men."

343.

He said not,
   "Thou shall not be tempested,
   Thou shall not be travailed,
   Thou shall not be afflicted,"
But he said,
   "Thou shall not be overcome."
   —MOTHER JULIAN OF NORWICH

344. Robert Morrison of Glasgow said:
"The great word in the drift of life is
'may'; the great word in the life of
Christ is 'must,' and 'must' is the last
triumph of the will."

345. The three great words of Jesus,
George Jackson says, are *least, last,* and
lost. Jesus said: "The least should be
greatest, the last should be first, and the

lost should be found."—LESLIE D. WEATHERHEAD, *How May We Find Him?*

346. Matthew Arnold wrote: "Try all the ways to peace and welfare you can think of, and you will find that there is no way that brings you to it except the way of Jesus. But this way does bring you to it."

347. Said Adolf von Harnack: "Jesus Christ was the first to bring the value of every human soul to light, and what he did no one can ever more undo."

348. "Jesus Christ and his precepts are found to hit the moral experience of mankind; to hit it in the critical points; to hit it lastingly; and when doubts are thrown upon their really hitting it, then to come out stronger than ever." So wrote Matthew Arnold.

349. In a popular novel named *Queed* appearing a generation ago two of the engaging characters were an ex-prize fighter named Klinker and a little doctor who was Klinker's friend. One day Klinker asked his friend: "Doc, do you know what is the finest verse in Scripture? No? Well, I'll tell you. 'He spake of the temple of his body.' A dandy, ain't it? Do you know what I would do if I was a preacher? I'd go down to the corner of Third and Main streets next Sunday afternoon where them blackguards get together, and I'd preach them a sermon from that text."—ROBERT SPEER

350. The inscription on one of the frescoes at the eastern entrance of Rockefeller Center in New York City reads: "Man's ultimate destiny depends not on whether he can learn new lessons or make new discoveries and conquests, but on his acceptance of the lesson taught him close upon two thousand years ago."

351.
He spake of lilies, vines and corn,
  The sparrow and the raven,
And the words so natural yet so wise
  Were on men's hearts engraven;

And yeast and bread and flax and cloth
  And eggs and fish and candles.
See how the most familiar world
  He most divinely handles.[10]
                    —GEORGE A. BARTON

352. "They should have known that he was God," said Tertullian when speaking about the Pharisees and Christ. "His patience should have proved it to them."

Christ the Physician

353. When asked why he was going to Africa as a missionary doctor, David Livingstone said: "God had an only Son, and he was a missionary and a physician."

354. Samuel Rutherford once wrote to certain depressed and doubting souls, not arguing with them, but accepting the bleak facts as they had stated them. "Yes! you seem in a bad way. My advice is: 'Take you a house next door to the Physician, for it will be very singular if you should prove to be the very first he ever turned away unhealed.'"
—ARTHUR JOHN GOSSIP, *Experience Worketh Hope*

The Presence of Christ

355. The story is told of a Chinese Christian whose name was Lo. When he read Matt. 28:20, "Lo, I am with you alway," he thought Christ was speaking directly to him.

[10] Used by permission of Mrs. Katherine Barton Platt.

356. "Shall I tell you what supported me through all these years of exile among a people whose language I could not understand, and whose attitude toward me was always uncertain and often hostile?" asked David Livingstone. "It was this, 'Lo, I am with you always even unto the end of the world.'"

357. When the Russian police broke into a meeting of Christians, an officer took down the names of those present. When he had told the people that they must await their summons, he started to leave. "There is one name you have not got," an old man called. The officer checked his list and, finding that all present were accounted for, asked whose name was not on his list. "The Lord Jesus Christ!" called the old man. —JAMES S. STEWART, *The Strong Name*

358. F. W. Boreham tells the story of an old Scotsman who, when he was very ill, was visited by his minister. As the minister sat down on a chair near the bedside, he noticed on the other side of the bed another chair placed at such an angle as to suggest that a visitor had just left it. "Well, Donald," said the minister glancing at the chair, "I see I am not your first visitor." The Scotsman looked up in surprise, so the minister pointed to the chair. "Ah!" said the sufferer. "I'll tell you about the chair. Years ago I found it impossible to pray. I often fell asleep on my knees I was so tired. And if I kept awake, I could not control my thoughts from wandering. One day I was so worried I spoke to the minister about it. He told me not to worry about kneeling down. 'Just sit down,' he said, 'and put a chair opposite you. Imagine that Jesus is in it, and talk to him as you would to a friend.'" Then the Scotsman added: "And I have been doing that ever since.

So now you know why the chair is standing like that." A week later the daughter of the old Scot drove up to the minister's house and knocked at his door. She was shown into the study, and when the minister came in she could hardly restrain herself. "Father died in the night," she sobbed. "I had no idea death could be so near. I had just gone to lie down for an hour or two. He seemed to be sleeping so comfortably. And when I went back, he was dead. He hadn't moved since I saw him before, except that *his hand was out on the empty chair at the side of his bed.*" —LESLIE D. WEATHERHEAD, *The Transforming Friendship*

359. Justus, a disciple of Jesus in Lloyd Douglas' book *The Robe*, says to Marcellus, the centurion who had been in charge of the crucifixon: "I only know that he is alive—and I am always expecting to see him. Sometimes I feel aware of him, as if he were close by. . . . It keeps you honest. You have no temptation to cheat anyone, or lie to anyone, or hurt anyone—when, for all you know, Jesus is standing beside you." "I'm afraid I should feel very uncomfortable," Marcellus says, "being perpetually watched by some invisible presence." "Not if that presence helped you defend yourself against yourself, Marcellus. It is a great satisfaction to have someone standing by—to keep you at your best," Justus replies.

360. Leslie D. Weatherhead tells of a friend who once attended a Roman Catholic service in which the priest argued for the literal presence of Christ's body in the consecrated wafer on the altar. After the service the visitor talked with one of the worshipers and asked him if he believed all that the priest had claimed. The worshiper, who was an old man, said something like

this: "When I come to Mass, sir, I cannot follow what they do up at the altar. I just kneel down and think about Jesus. I think of that last week with his friends and the last supper; how he knelt in agony in Gethsemane; how they arrested him and all night tortured him; and how he died." And the old man's eyes filled with tears. "I get very near to Jesus then, sir, and when I go home I feel that he comes with me."
—*The Transforming Friendship*

361. The sculptor Charles Sargeant Jagger has an interesting account of his statue of Christ which now stands in a mission at Kelham, England. He tells that he repeatedly tried to imagine Christ, and as often failed; thus he came almost to the edge of despair. Then, he insists, the door opened, and Christ entered, saying, "Try again!" So he was able to carve the statue which has become a benediction.—GEORGE A. BUTTERICK, *Christ and Man's Dilemma*

362. A motto, once hung in many homes, read: "Christ is the Head of this house, the Unseen Guest at every meal, the Silent Listener to every conversation."

Resurrection of Christ

363. When a Mohammedan taunted a Christian by saying, "You Christians do not even have a tomb to which you can point, where your Jesus lies buried. We have the tomb of Mohammed in Mecca," the Christian replied, "That is just the point; your prophet is dead and lies buried; our Christ is risen and is with us always."

364. In *Jesus Manifest*, Dmitrii Merezhkovskii has written: "Belief in the resurrection of Jesus is the motive power of all Christian mankind. From what did this faith spring? From five or six remarkably vivid hallucinations? To

think so is just as absurd as to suppose that five or six sparks would make water boil in a huge caldron."

365. "Tell us why you believe that Jesus rose again," said two boys sneeringly to a man of known faith. "Well," was the answer, "one reason is that I was talking with him this morning."

366. R. W. Dale of Birmingham thought he had faith in Christ's resurrection and in a famous passage in his diary acknowledged that it was views he possessed, not news. When, during the making of a sermon in his study, views *became news*, he was so excited he couldn't keep still. He walked up and down his study saying: "Christ is living! Christ is living! At first it seemed strange and hardly true, but at last it came upon me as a burst of sudden glory; yes, Christ is living. It was to me a new discovery. I thought that all along I had believed it; but not until that moment did I feel sure about it."—LESLIE D. WEATHERHEAD, *The Eternal Voice*

Christ the Saviour

367. Sir James Simpson, the discoverer of the anesthetic properties of chloroform and one of the most prominent scientists of his generation, was asked by a friend to name the most wonderful discovery he had ever made, and quickly came this reply: "The greatest discovery I ever made was the discovery I had a Saviour."—WILSON O. WELDON

368. "Ah, Mr. Spurgeon," exclaimed an old lady whom Charles H. Spurgeon was visiting, "if Jesus Christ does save me, he shall never hear the last of it!"

369. Bishop McDowell put it this way: "We are saved by a Person and only a Person, and, as far as I know, by only one Person."

370. "There is only one piece of news I know," said a woman to Tennyson when the poet on a journey had arrived at her house and inquired if anything of note was happening. "There is only one piece of news I know: Christ died for all men." "Well," said Tennyson, "that is old news, and good news, and new news."

371. One of the old scholars told a story of a vagabond who fell ill in Lombardy and sought the aid of doctors. They discussed his case and finally said, "Let us try an experiment on this worthless creature." Then to their amazement from the sick man, lying in rags in the corner, came these words, "Will you call him a worthless creature for whom Christ died?"

Second Coming of Christ

372. An old Negro woman approached W. Leon Tucker one day and said: "I certainly enjoyed your sermon, especially what you said about the Comin' of the Lord. You know, I ain't lookin' for the *undertaker*. I'm lookin' for the *uppertaker*."

373. A Hindu said with sincerity to E. Stanley Jones: "Why do you preach on the second coming of Christ? He has already come—he is here—Gandhi."

Sinlessness of Christ

374. Gandhi, whose life became radiant with the teachings of Jesus although he never became a professing Christian himself, said: "The man to whom I owe most, the man to whom India owes most, is a man who never set his foot in India, and that man was Christ."

375. "Only once," wrote Alexander Whyte, "did God choose a completely sinless preacher."

Surrender to Christ

376. "Keep we our heads as high as we can," says John Middleton Murray at the close of his *Life of Jesus*, "they shall be bowed at the last."

377. Alexander Mackay wrote: "There is only one way of being truly Christian and of fulfilling in personal life the essential Christian mission; and that is by allowing ourselves to be conscripted utterly—body, mind and spirit, time, wealth and honor—by the Christ who, in Pascal's immortal saying, 'continues to agonize in the soul of His followers for the world's redemption.' "
—*That Other America*

378. In Henry van Dyke's story "The Lost Word" a young man named Hermas allows the name of Jesus to be taken from him in return for wealth and honor. After realizing the hopeless eternity that he faces, and having no name to thank for his blessings and no name to call up when death beckons his only child, Hermas welcomes the name of Jesus once more.

Trial of Christ

379. Three stairways approach the great doors of an old church in Rome. The two outer stairways are easily climbed but the one in the middle may be ascended on one's knees. This stairway, called the *Scala Santa*, is reputed to have been taken to Rome from Pilate's house and are the steps Jesus climbed to receive Pilate's condemnation.

380. "Pilate could wash his hands of Jesus," said W. Russell Maltby in *Christ and His Cross*, "but Jesus could not wash his hands of Pilate."

Universality of Christ

381. In a certain town in Austria there is a beautiful bridge over which at every few paces there are statues of Christ. There are twelve of them in all, each one representing Christ in relation to some particular business or profession. The herders and shepherds, as they cross the bridge, tarry for a moment before Christ the Good Shepherd; market gardeners and farmers, before Jesus the Sower; fishermen, before Christ stilling the tempest; the sick, before Christ the Healer; and so on. By stopping before their particular statue, men of each profession are reminded that Christ is their partner as they begin a new day's work.—CHARLES H. PINCHBECK

382. "Jesus was the only teacher tall enough to see over the fences that divide the human race into compartments," judged Frank Crane.

383. T. Z. Koo, who as secretary of the Y.M.C.A. in China walked eight hundred miles to get out of Japanese-controlled territory so that he could act as counselor to the Chinese delegation at the United Nations Conference in San Francisco in 1945, said: "There are differences in race, color, speech, and customs, and we can find clashing viewpoints beneath the surface in every land, but in Christ 'all things hold together.'"

384.
I lift my gaze beyond the night, and see,
　Above the banners of Man's hate unfurled,
The holy figure that on Calvary
　Stretched arms out wide enough for all the world.[11]
—JOHN HALL WHEELOCK, "1914"

[11] "1914" is reprinted with the permission of Charles Scribner's Sons from *The Black Panther* by John Hall Wheelock. Copyright 1922 Charles Scribner's Sons; renewal copyright 1950 John Hall Wheelock.

385. When E. Stanley Jones asked an earnest Hindu what he thought of Christ, the Hindu thoughtfully answered: "There is no one else who is seriously bidding for the heart of the world except Jesus Christ. There is no one else in the field."—*The Christ of the Indian Road*

Victory of Christ

386. Some years ago on a visit to Paris, Professor Jay William Hudson of the University of Missouri went to Napoleon's tomb at the twilight hour. He looked on the sarcophagus of Napoleon and then up to the figure of Christ on his cross, just visible in the rays of fading light coming through the stained-glass window above. "A question," he writes, "knocks at the door of your soul: Which, in the long stretch of centuries by which all things and all men are judged, was the more practically efficient, this Corsican or this Nazarene? . . . Over the tomb of the Corsican the traveler bends his head in melancholy meditation; up, up toward the life of the Nazarene the millions struggle with glad faces through the years."

387. Charles Rann Kennedy in his play *The Terrible Meek* describes the centurion as saying to Mary as she stands near the cross: "I tell you, woman, that this dead Son of yours, disfigured, shamed, spat upon, has built this day a kingdom that can never die. The living glory of him rules it. The earth is his and he made it. He and his brothers have been molding and making it through the long ages; they are the only ones who ever did possess it; not the proud, not the idle, not the vaunting empires of the world. Something has happened on this hill today to shake all the kingdoms of blood and fear to dust. The earth is his, the earth is theirs and they made it. The meek, the terrible

meek, the fierce agonizing meek are about to enter into their inheritance."

388. After World War I, George Bernard Shaw wrote: "The only man who came out of the war with an enhanced reputation for common sense was Jesus Christ. Though we crucified Christ on a stick, he somehow managed to get hold of the right end of it. . . . And if we were better men, we might try his plan."

389. The Mosque of Saint Sophia in Istanbul is a transformed Christian church. It was one of the most beautiful churches of the world. All the Christian inscriptions and symbols have been painted out and Moslem inscriptions and symbols put in their places. Standing under the great dome, one American could see that the figure of the ascending Christ with outstretched hands in blessing, which had been painted out, was coming back through the wearing off of the covering paint. The American turned to his friend and said: "He is coming back. You cannot blot him out. Through the accretions and daubs of the centuries he is coming back again. He shall yet reign. The future belongs to him."—E. STANLEY JONES, *Christ at the Round Table*

Witness of Christ

390. A man once criticized Dwight L. Moody for a grammatical error in one of his sermons. "I am using all the grammar I know for Jesus Christ. Are you?" Moody replied.

391. A woman of fashion in Boston was thunderstruck when a stranger, the zealous "Uncle John Vassar," besought her to accept Christ. She told her husband, who said indignantly, "If I had been there, I would have told him very quickly to go about his business." Her reply was emphatic: "If you had seen him, you would have thought he was about his business."—GEORGE A. BUTTRICK, *Christ and Man's Dilemma*

392. Ignatius, Bishop of Antioch, was called "Theophorus" (the God-bearer) because of his sanctity. When Emperor Trajan asked him why he had this surname, he replied: "Because I bore the Christ in my heart." Legend says that after his death as a martyr the name of God was found written on his heart in letters of gold.—J. PERRY COX

393. Hugh Latimer, the English martyr, in a sermon before the royal court said: "Latimer, Latimer, thou art going to speak before the high and mighty king, Henry VIII, who is able, if he think fit, to take thy life away. Be careful what thou sayest. But Latimer, Latimer, remember also thou art about to speak before the King of kings and Lord of lords. Take heed thou dost not displease him."

394. An American visiting in England was taken by his English friend to hear Charles H. Spurgeon. When they left the church the Englishman said: "Well, what do you think of him?" "Whom?" the American asked. "Why, Spurgeon, of course!" "Oh," replied the American, "to tell the truth, I was not thinking of Spurgeon. I was thinking of his Christ."

395. A woman devoted to Christ adopted once a peculiar method of shaming her Christian friends. She was found testifying to her faith before a wooden Indian in front of a cigar store. She was chided for the scene she created, and then defended herself by saying: "I would rather be a real Christian and talk religion to a wooden Indian than a wooden Christian who never talked religion to anyone."

396. Henry Drummond told of an American medical student in Edinburgh who tried to win an atheist. The two were great friends, but the American was a sincere Christian. Drummond himself had tried to win the atheist, but in vain. At last the American finished his course, packed his trunks, and got ready to return to the United States to start a practice. "Then," he told Drummond later, "I wondered whether a year of my life would be better spent in starting as a doctor in America or staying in Edinburgh to win that man for Christ. I have decided to stay." "Well," said Drummond, "it will pay you. You will get your man." It took eleven months, but after that time Drummond saw the two sitting together at a communion service. Before the one-time atheist left the university, he came to Drummond's room. Drummond said: "What do you want?" The man said: "I want to be a medical missionary."— LESLIE D. WEATHERHEAD, *Jesus and Ourselves*

397.
For me 'twas not the truth you taught,
  To you so clear, to me so dim,
But when you came to me, you brought
  A sense of Him.

And from your eyes He beckons me
  And from your heart His love is shed,
Till I lose sight of you and see
  The Christ instead.
          —AUTHOR UNKNOWN

Work of Christ

398. It was a Jew who brought the gospel to Rome; a Roman who took it to France; a Frenchman who took it to Scandinavia; a Scandinavian who took it to Scotland; a Scotsman who evange-lized Ireland; and an Irishman who in turn made the missionary conquest of Scotland. No people have ever received the gospel except at the hands of an alien.

399. When Julian the Apostate, sneering at Agathon, a Christian, said: "Tell me, Agathon, what has become of the Carpenter of Nazareth? Is he still around? Has he any work at all these days, your Carpenter? Are there still some little jobs coming his way at least?" the Christian answered: "Yes, Julian, the Carpenter of Nazareth is very busy these days. . . . He is nailing together a coffin for your empire." A few months later Julian was gone, but the Carpenter's influence was greatly increasing.

CHRISTIAN

400. Said Hugh Mackintosh of Edinburgh: "A genuine Christian ought to be as distinguishable amongst his fellows as a civilized man amongst savages; and what will mark him off will be something he has got from Jesus Christ, and which he could not possibly have got elsewhere."—*The Highway of God*

401. Edgar DeWitt Jones has given the following suggestions for a good Christian: "He should get religion like a Methodist; experience it like a Baptist; be sure of it like a Disciple; stick to it like a Lutheran; pray for it like a Presbyterian; conciliate it like a Congregationalist; glorify it like a Jew; be proud of it like an Episcopalian; practice it like a Christian Scientist; propagate it like a Roman Catholic; work for it like a Salvation Army lassie; enjoy it like a Negro."

402. "A Christian," someone has said, "is a man who, when he gets to the end of his rope, ties a knot and hangs on."

403. When John Bunyan described a Christian, he spoke of him as a man who put his fingers in his ears and ran on crying, "Life, Life, Eternal Life." When he was asked, "What are the things you seek, since you leave all the world to find them?" he replied, "I seek an inheritance, incorruptible, undefiled, and that fadeth not away: and it is laid up in heaven."

404. "Now that I am a Christian," said a new convert, "I feel much better when I feel bad than I did before when I felt good."

405. In his tract a Christian liberty Martin Luther said: "A Christian man is the most free lord of all, and subject to none. A Christian man is the most dutiful servant of all, and subject to everyone."

406. In a letter to his friend Donatus, Cyprian, bishop of the church at Carthage in the third century, wrote: "This is a cheerful world as I see it from my garden under the shadows of my vines. But if I were to ascend some high mountain and look out over the wide lands, you know very well what I should see: brigands on the highways, pirates on the sea, armies fighting, cities burning; in the amphitheatres men murdered to please applauding crowds; selfishness and cruelty and misery and despair under all roofs. It is a bad world, Donatus, an incredibly bad world. But I have discovered in the midst of it a quiet and holy people who have learned a great secret. They have found a joy which is a thousand times better than any pleasure of our sinful life. They are despised and persecuted, but they care not. They are masters of their souls. They have overcome the world. These people, Donatus, are the Christians—and I am one of them."

407. Wrote a second-century scholar: "What the soul is in a body, this the Christians are in the world. . . . Christians hold the world together."

408. The early Christians did not say in dismay, "Look what the world has come to," but in delight, "Look what has come to the world."

409. An old Negro, describing the difference between a good man and an evil man, said: "Though he fall, the good man does not waller."

410. "Now he wasn't what you'd call a good Christian," explained a Negro minister in the course of his funeral comments, "but he was what you'd call a respected sinner."

411. Dwight L. Moody met a man at his hotel one day and asked in his abrupt fashion: "My friend, are you a Christian?" The man, stiffening somewhat, replied: "What do you think?" Moody replied: "Not a red hot one."

412. When G. Campbell Morgan was speaking with Dwight L. Moody about the importance of the Bible in our national life, Moody said: "Oh, yes, the nation needs the Bible; but take it from me, the Christian man is the world's Bible, and in many cases a revision is necessary."

CHRISTIAN EDUCATION

413. When asked how he would typify Christian education, E. Stanley Jones said: "I would have a statue of a youth entering college, uncertain, uncouth, but eager. The first door he faces would lead to a room where all ways of life are studied. The next room would be a room where the Christian faith is studied; for I take it that, after studying the various ways, he would find that the universe backs the Christian way. Then there would be a third room, a little chapel where he would dedicate himself to this way. Then outside beyond these three rooms I would have another statue of the same youth, now emerging from his college course —facing away from the institution toward the rising sun, his face assured and confident, for two figures are beside him, Religion and Science, each with a hand upon his shoulder, and both pointing in the same direction toward the rising sun. And thus under the guidance of religion and science—two approaches to life—each corroborating the other, he goes forth to meet the day."— E. STANLEY JONES, *The Christ of the American Road*

414. "The only Christian thing about our colleges now," someone has said, "are their early endowments."

CHRISTIAN FELLOWSHIP

415. A Japanese airman shot down over Nanking was taken to a Chinese hospital. After some days he said to the nurses: "I am puzzled. I was told you were barbarians with no culture and we would have to give you ours. But you attend to me kindly and graciously— me, an enemy. What makes you do it?" "We are Christians," replied the nurses. "Christians?" exclaimed the airman. "Why, so am I! When I was sent over to bomb defenseless people, I felt I couldn't do it, so I dropped my bombs in an open field outside the city."— E. STANLEY JONES, *The Christ of the American Road*

416. Dr. William Axling tells of two Christian deacons, one a Chinese and one a Japanese, who met during the war between their peoples. Both had lost sons in the conflict. Without saying a word the Japanese put his hand on the shoulder of his Christian brother and said: "I understand."

417. Albert Schweitzer tells of a deaf man who never missed worship in his father's church. When asked why he, a deaf man who was unable to hear any of the service, was constantly in attendance, he replied: "The communion of the saints! The communion of the saints!"

CHRISTIAN LIFE

418. Charles E. Schofield said: "The Christian life is the outliving of the inliving Christ."

419. When a Hindu woman was converted, she suffered much persecution from her husband. When the missionary asked her what she did when her husband became angry, the native said: "Well, sir, I cook his food better; when he complains, I sweep the floor cleaner; and when he speaks unkindly, I answer him mildly. I try, sir, to show him that when I became a Christian I became a better wife and a better mother."

420. The epitaph marking the final resting place of General Gordon in St. Paul's Cathedral reads: "He gave his strength to the weak, his substance to the poor, his sympathy to the suffering, his heart to God."

Dedication to the Christian Life

421. When but six years of age Jane Addams was taken by her father to the then pioneer town of Freeport, Illinois. Sighting the squalor of the place, she remarked: "When I grow up to be a woman, I want to live in a big house near the poor people so I can help them." As a child she was beginning to "take it upon herself"—of which the fruitage was the splendid Hull House ministry in Chicago.—CLARENCE W. KEMPER

422. David Livingstone as a medical student determined to work in that part of the world where he was most needed. He planned to become a missionary to China, but the words of Robert Moffat of Africa, "From the hill where I live I can see the smoke of a thousand villages where no Christian has ever gone," challenged him to open new roads into the Dark Continent.

works for Pentecost

423. More than two hundred years ago in a little chapel on Aldersgate Street, John Wesley found his life's purpose. Afterwards he recorded his experience in his *Journal*: "About a quarter before nine, while [the reader of Luther's preface to the *Epistle to the Romans*] was describing the change which God works in the heart through faith in Christ, I felt my heart strangely warmed. I felt I did trust in Christ, Christ alone for salvation; and an assurance was given me, that he had taken away *my* sins, even *mine,* and saved *me* from the law of sin and death. I began to pray with all my might for those who had in a more especial manner despitefully used me and persecuted me. I then testified openly to all there what I now first felt in my heart."

424. Someone has suggested that man's prayer should be: "Lord, do not only count me—but count on me."

425.
I want to know the right, the true—
Some order of the scheme of things—
To be a part in some great plan
In which to lose, and losing, thus
To find myself.
—ANDREW W. SLEDD

Prayers for the Christian Life

426. Ignatius Loyola prayed: "Teach us, good Lord, to serve thee as thou deservest; to give and not to count the cost; to fight and not to heed the wounds; to toil and not to seek for rest; to labor and not to ask for any reward, save that of knowing that we do thy will; through Jesus Christ our Lord."

427.
Fronting my task, these things I ask:
To be true, this whole day through;
To be content with honest work,
Fearing only lest I shirk;
To see, and know, and do what's right;
To come, unsullied, home at night.
—AUTHOR UNKNOWN

Responsibilities of the Christian Life

428. E. Stanley Jones reports a conversation between two Hindus which he overheard. They were not Christians; they were orthodox Hindus. They were discussing how they ought to deal with the Moslems, also non-Christians. One of them proposed to use force, coercion, cruelty. But the other said: "No, we cannot do that. We must do our Christian duty by them."

429. Robert E. Lee, though the defeated general in the Civil War, is surely the most remembered military figure of that struggle. Something of the reason for his greatness is suggested by the following quotation from Lee's biography by Douglas S. Freeman: "What was his duty as a Christian and as a gentleman? That he answered by the sure criterion of right and wrong, and having answered, acted. Everywhere the two obligations went together: he never sought to expiate as a Christian for what he had failed to do as a gentleman, or to atone as a gentleman for what he had neglected as a Christian. He could not have conceived of a Christian who was not a gentleman."

430.
My business is not to remake myself,
But make the absolute best of what God
made.
  —Robert Browning,
    "Bishop Blougram's Apology"

431. To the words of the great philosopher Kant, "Act only on that law whereby thou canst at the same time will that it should become a universal law," Frank B. Fagerburg has added, "I must not do that which if all men should do would wreck human society."

432. E. Stanley Jones was pleading with a group of young people in India. "I wish you would stand up and tell me, if you will, why you are not Christians. Why will you not become Christians? What do you think of Christ? Why will you not follow him?" Then one young Indian answered, "Your Christ is wonderful, but you Christians are not like him."

Results of the Christian Life

433. A Cornishman, taunted by a visitor on the dearth of worldly pleasures in his country, answered quietly, "My lord, something over a hundred years ago a man named John Wesley came to these parts."—George A. Buttrick, *Christ and Man's Dilemma*

434. "He that does good to another," said Seneca, "does good also to himself, not only in the consequences, but in the very act; for the consciousness of well doing is, in itself, ample reward."

435. A Chinese proverb reads: "If there is righteousness in the heart, there is beauty in the character. If there is beauty in the character, there will be harmony in the home. If there is harmony in the home, there will be order in the nation. When there is order in

the nation, there will be peace in the world."

436. When a minister in a small community in Scotland made plans for a revival, a groceryman complained that he did not want a revival. "When we had the last one, I had to burn my bushel measure."

Rules for the Christian Life

437. General Booth's rules for Christian living are: (1) Consider your body as the temple of the Holy Spirit and treat it with reverence and care. (2) Keep your mind active. Stimulate it with thoughts of others that lead to doing something. (3) Take time to be holy with daily Bible reading and prayer. (4) Support the church of your faith. Mingle with others. (5) Cultivate the presence of God. He wants to enter your life and will as far as you let him. (6) Take God into the details of your life. You naturally call upon him in trouble and for the bigger things. (7) Pray for this troubled world and the leaders who hold the destinies of the various nations. (8) Have a thankful spirit for the blessings of God—country, home, friends, and numerous other blessings. (9) Work as if everything depended upon work, and pray as if everything depended upon prayer. (10) Think of death not as something to be dreaded, but as a great and new experience where loved ones are met and ambitions realized.

438. The following are the steps suggested by Alcoholics Anonymous for curing an addict: "(1) We admitted we were powerless over alcohol—that our lives had become unmanageable. (2) We came to believe that a Power greater than ourselves could restore us to sanity. (3) We made a decision to turn our wills and our lives over the care of

God *as we understood him.* (4) We made a searching and fearless moral inventory of ourselves. (5) We admitted to God, to ourselves, and to another human being the exact nature of our wrongs. (6) We were entirely ready to have God remove all defects of character. (7) We humbly asked him to remove our shortcomings. (8) We made a list of all persons we had harmed and became willing to make amends to them all. (9) We made direct amends to such people wherever possible, except where to do so would injure them or others. (10) We continued to take personal inventory and when we were wrong promptly admitted it. (11) We sought through prayer and meditation to improve our conscious contact with God *as we understood him,* praying only for knowledge of his will for us and the power to carry out that will. (12) Having had a spiritual experience as a result of these steps, we tried to carry this message to alcoholics and to practice these principles."—E. STANLEY JONES, *The Way*

439. Sir William Osler, one of the great physicians of modern times, told a group of students at Yale University in 1913: "Begin the day with Christ and his prayer—you need no other. Creedless, with it you have religion: creed-stuffed, it will leaven any theological dough in which you stick. Learn to know your Bible. . . . In forming character and in shaping conduct its touch has still its ancient power."

440. This is the recipe which Zane Grey, the author, once offered for greatness: "To bear up under loss; to fight the bitterness of defeat and the weakness of grief; to be victor over anger; to smile when tears are close; to resist disease and evil men and base instincts; to hate hate, and to love love; to go on when it would seem good to die; to look up with unquenchable faith in something ever more about to be. That is what any man can do, and be great."

441. The following words are from the pen of the Oriental philosopher Mencius who lived in the fourth century before Christ:

To dwell in the wise house of the
    world,
To stand in true attitude therein,
To walk in the wide path of men,
In success to share one's principles with
    the people,
In failure to live them out alone,
To be incorruptible by riches or honors,
Unchangeable by poverty,
Unmoved by perils or power:
These I call the qualities of a great
    man.

442.
To be honest, to be kind;
To earn a little and to spend a little
    less;
To make upon the whole a family happier for his presence;
To renounce when that shall be necessary and not to be embittered;
To keep a few friends, but those without capitulation,—
Above all, on the same grim conditions, to keep friends with himself—
Here is a task for all that a man has of fortitude and delicacy.
        —ROBERT LOUIS STEVENSON,
                "My Task"

443.
Four things in any land must dwell,
If it endures and prospers well:
One is manhood, true and good;
One is noble womanhood;

One is childlife, clean and bright;
And one, an altar kept alight.
—Author Unknown

444.
Sow a thought, reap an act;
Sow an act, reap a habit;
Sow a habit, reap a character;
Sow a character, reap a destiny.
—Author Unknown

445. William Penn suggested the trials and triumphs of the Christian faith when he wrote: "No pain, no palm; no thorns, no throne; no cross, no crown."

CHRISTIANITY

446. "Christianity," said Sherwood Eddy, "is not believing the impossible, but doing the incredible."

447. "Christianity combines the most absolute pessimism about man's unaided powers with an unquenchable optimism as to what—in God's hand—he may become," wrote Edward Burroughs.

448. "Christianity does not consist in abstaining from doing things no gentleman would think of doing," said Dick Sheppard, "but in doing things that are unlikely to occur to anyone who is not in touch with the spirit of Christ."

449. When a group of students asked Harnack what the Christian solution to a particular problem was, he replied: "Christianity provides no solutions—it provides a goal and power to move on toward that goal."

450. "We are losing our Christianity," declares Dean Inge of St. Paul's, London, "because Christianity is a creed for heroes, while we are mainly harmless, good-natured little people who want everybody to have a good time."

451. "It is this that made the future of Christianity," said Matthew Arnold, "its gladness, not its sorrow, . . . its drawing from the spiritual world a source of joy so abundant that it ran over upon the material world and transfigured it."

452. Henry P. Van Dusen has summarized the five major functions of the Christian movement: (1) custodian of the values of the past; (2) focal center for corporate life; (3) seedplot of creative, revolutionary forces in society; (4) spiritual confidant and sustainer and friend of ordinary folk; and (5) promise of the ultimate destiny of mankind's pilgrimage.—*Reality and Religion*

453. G. K. Chesterton once declared that "Christianity even when watered down is hot enough to boil all modern society to rags."

454. "Christianity has not failed," said Dean Inge. "It has never been tried."

Criticism of Christianity

455. In a pamphlet titled *Strong Meat*, Dorothy Sayers suggested: "It is startling to discover how many people there are who heartily dislike and despise Christianity without having the faintest notion what it is. If you tell them, they cannot believe you. I do not mean that they cannot believe the doctrine: that would be understandable enough, since it takes some believing. I mean that they simply cannot believe that anything so interesting, so exciting, and so dramatic can be the orthodox creed of the Christ."

456. When Sir Isaac Newton heard Halley the astronomer denouncing Christianity, he said: "Halley, when you speak of astronomy and mathematics, I will listen to you; but not when you talk of Christianity, for you have never tried it. But I have tried it and know it to be true."

457. As one considers the great advance made by Christianity during the present century, it is almost amusing to remember the words of Voltaire: "Ere the beginnings of the nineteenth century Christianity will have perished from the earth."

458. When Lispeth, a native Indian girl in Rudyard Kipling's "The Convert," fails to get comfort from an unsympathetic chaplain's wife, she turns against Christianity, saying:

To my own Gods I go.
It may be they shall give me greater ease
Than your cold Christ and tangled Trinities.[12]

459. The story is told of a shipwrecked mariner who, floating on a small raft in the South Seas, finally saw land. "Oh, thank God," he exclaimed as he saw a gallows on the shore, "I am in a Christian land."

Practice of Christianity

460. A missionary looked up a young native girl who had not come back for further instruction. The girl said: "I haven't learned yet to practice fully what I've been taught."—E. STANLEY JONES, *Abundant Living*

461. A minister in a new parish preached the same sermon three Sundays in a row. Finally one of the deacons called the young minister aside and reminded him of the fact that the same

[12] From *The Selected Prose and Poetry of Rudyard Kipling.* Copyright 1928 by Rudyard Kipling. Reprinted by permission of Mrs. George Bambridge, Doubleday & Co., Macmillan & Co., Ltd., London, and The Macmillan Co., Canada.

sermon was used for three Sundays. "I will preach a new sermon," the minister said, "when the people of my church start practicing the message of this one."

462. "By whose preaching were you converted?" a young man was asked. "Not by anyone's preaching, but by my mother's practicing," he answered.

463. A soap manufacturer, not a Christian, was talking with a minister. Said the soapmaker: "The gospel you preach hasn't done much good, for there's still a lot of wickedness and wicked people." The preacher made no immediate reply, but they soon passed a child making mud pies. He was exceedingly dirty. It was then the preacher's turn, and so he said: "Soap hasn't done much good in the world, I see; for there's still much dirt and many dirty people." "Oh, well," answered the manufacturer, "soap is useful only when it's applied." "Exactly," was the minister's reply; "so it is with the gospel we proclaim."

464. Samuel Taylor Coleridge wrote: "Do not talk to me about the evidences of Christianity. Try it. It has been eighteen hundred years in existence and has any one individual left a record like the following: 'I have given Christianity a fair trial. I was aware that its promises were made conditionally, but both outwardly and in my inward acts and affections I have performed the duties which it enjoins, yet my assurances of its truth have received no increase. Its promises have not been fulfilled. I repent me of my delusion.'"

465. Erasmus described Sir Thomas More with these words: "Elevation has not elated him or made him forgetful of his humble friends. He is always kind, always generous. Some he helps with money, some with influence. When he can give nothing else, he gives advice. He is Patron-General to all poor devils."

466. In the Boston Library there is the famous picture showing young Galahad approaching that high throne-seat which was said to rob a man of his life. The motto was carved on that chair: "He who sits herein shall lose himself." As Galahad moves forward, we can see the knights of the Round Table make the sign of the cross with their uplifted sword hilts. An angel draws aside the red coverlet from the chair. We can hear Galahad saying: "If I lose myself, I save myself."— GEORGE A. BUTTRICK, *Jesus Came Preaching*

467. After speaking with a group of natives about Jesus, a missionary asked how many knew this Man. The missionary was surprised when many said they knew him. Upon investigation he learned that a doctor had lived among them at one time and that the doctor had ministered to them without thoughts of self and personal rewards. "Yes," they said, "we knew him well."

468. A member of the congregation of one minister said: "If that man could not preach at all, the sermon of his countenance would be enough."

469. Of John of Austria, who lived when knighthood was in flower, it was said: "A true knight who fought for God, for honor, and for no reward."

470. Hervey Allen in *Anthony Adverse* describes Brother Francis in these words: "Brother Francis *is* a holy man. That is the trouble. He is not merely content to perform in the ritual of the Church. He is one of your complicated primitives, a man who has penetrated behind the scenery of religion, one who intends to live the story which the ritual is supposed to illustrate. You see he does not attack or interfere with the drama. That makes it a little difficult for his superiors. He does not provide them with an excuse to abolish him or thrust him out. On the contrary, as far as I can find out, he merely proposes to carry out their own precepts. That is, of course, profoundly embarrassing—to them. . . . Brother Francis and his kind are the men who have always made Christianity a dangerous religion. Just when the Church is about to be taken for a decorative and snugly-woven cocoon on a dead branch of the sacred tree, a place for a few fat slugs to hibernate where they have softly spun themselves in, pouf!—that cocoon bursts and the beautiful living psyche of Christianity emerges."

471. A rich man once invited Francis of Assisi to his home so that he might spy upon the saint's praying. All night long he heard him say, "My God and my All, my God and my All," and was so moved that forthwith he became a disciple.—GEORGE A. BUTTRICK, *Prayer*

472.
'Tis not the wide phylactery
  Nor stubborn fast, nor stated prayers,
That make us saints: we judge the tree
  By what it bears.

And when a man can live apart
  From works, on theologic trust,
I know the blood about his heart
  Is dry as dust.
      —ALICE CARY, "My Creed"

Supremacy of Christianity

473. Before Lewis D. Morse left for the mission field in India, he was asked by a group of students at Acadia College:

"What are you going to do about the religions of India when you reach the field of your work?" He answered: "If I find a religion in India that is better than Christianity, then I shall accept it and do my best to live up to it." Years later he went back to say: "I found no religion there, nor anywhere, that so meets human needs, and satisfies the hunger for God, as the truth of Jesus of Nazareth."

474. A young missionary wrote back to the church under which he was serving: "One does not know what Christianity is till he goes where it isn't."

475. T. R. Glover in *The Jesus of History* says that the reason the Christians conquered the pagan world was that the Christian "outlived, outthought, and outdied" the pagan.

CHRISTMAS
476.
It is Christmas in the mansion,
    Yule-log fires and silken frocks;
It is Christmas in the cottage,
    Mother's filling little socks.

It is Christmas on the highway,
    In the thronging, busy mart;
But the dearest, truest Christmas
    Is the Christmas in the heart.
            —Author Unknown
                "Christmas in the Heart"

477. Bethlehem, Pennsylvania, the "Christmas City," was named on Christmas Eve, 1741, by a group of Moravian settlers led by Count Zinzendorf who had met on the banks of the Lehigh River to sing carols.

478. A legend tells us that parishioners at a church in Mexico brought great quantities of flowers to the altar each Christmas. One day, while hundreds of people carried flowers to the cathedral, a little girl cried because she had none. A priest found her and asked the reason for her tears. "I have no flowers," she cried. The priest told her to pick a weed which grew near the roadside. The little girl wondered that the priest should tell her to pick a weed, but she did as she was told. When she placed the weed on the altar, the large green leaves glowed with a soft red light and was the most beautiful flower presented. Since that time, the legend says, the poinsettia plant has been the special flower of Christmas.

CHURCH
479.
A room of quiet . . . a temple of peace.
The home of faith . . . where doubtings cease.
A house of comfort . . . where hope is given;
A source of strength . . . to make earth heaven;
A shrine of worship . . . a place to pray—
I found all this . . . in my church today.
            —Cyrus E. Albertson

480. The Edinburgh Conference on Faith and Order of 1937 declared: "The Church is . . . the household of God, the family in which the fatherhood of God and the brotherhood of man is to be realized in the children of his adoption. It is the body of Christ, whose members derive their life and oneness from their one living Head."

481. The Church, Henry Sloane Coffin wrote in *Church and State in the Modern World,* must be (1) a fellowship of free persons under the law of Christ, (2) a redemptive fellowship, (3) a supra-national fellowship, (4) a supra-class fellowship, (5) a supra-racial fellowship, and (6) an eternal fellowship.

482. "Before I was born, my church gave to my parents ideals of life and love that made my home a place of strength and beauty," William H. Boddy wrote. "In helpless infancy my church joined my parents in consecrating me to Christ and in baptizing me in his name. My church enriched my childhood with the romance of religion and the lessons of life that have been woven into the texture of my soul. . . . In the stress and storm of adolescence my church heard the surge of my soul, and she guided my footsteps by lifting my eyes toward the stars. When first my heart knew the strange awakenings of love, my church taught me to chasten and spiritualize my affections. When my heart was seamed with sorrow, . . . my church drew me to the Friend of all the weary and whispered to me the hope of another morning, eternal and tearless. When my steps have slipped and I have known the bitterness of sin, my church has believed in me and . . . has called me back to live within the heights of myself. . . . My church calls me to her heart. She asks my service and my loyalty. She has a right to ask it! I will help her to do for others what she has done for me. In this place . . . I will help her keep aflame and aloft the torch of a living faith in Christ."

483. In Charles Rann Kennedy's drama *The Servant in the House* the bishop asks Manson to tell him about the Church. Manson replies: "I am afraid you may not consider it an altogether substantial concern. It has to be seen in a certain way, under certain conditions. Some people never see it at all. You must understand, this is no dead pile of stones and unmeaning timber. *It is a living thing*. . . . When you enter it you hear a sound—a sound as if some mighty poem chanted. Listen long enough, and you will learn that it is made up of the beating of human hearts, of the nameless music of men's souls—that is, if you have ears. If you have eyes, you will presently see the Church itself—a looming mystery of many shapes and shadows, leaping sheer from floor to dome. The work of no ordinary builder! . . . The pillars of it go up like the brawny trunks of heroes: the sweet human flesh of men and women is moulded about its bulwarks, strong, impregnable: the faces of little children laugh out from every cornerstone: the terrible spans and arches of it are the joined hands of comrades; and up in the heights and spaces there are inscribed the numberless musings of all the dreamers of the world. It is yet building—building and built upon. Sometimes the work goes forward in deep darkness: sometimes in blinding light: now beneath the burden of unutterable anguish: now to the tune of a great laughter and heroic shoutings like the cry of thunder. Sometimes, in the silence of the nighttime, one may hear the tiny hammerings of the comrades at work up in the dome—the comrades that have climbed ahead."

484. After a grueling battle with the African jungle, in constant fear of death by the savages, two explorers were amazed to see in the distance the white church spires of Uganda. With a sigh of relief they exclaimed: "Civilization at last."

485. Some years ago a little church on the coast of England was ruined by a hurricane. The congregation thought themselves unable to rebuild. Then one day a representative of the British Admiralty came to the clergyman to ask if they intended to reconstruct the church. The clergyman explained why they could not do it. "Well," said the representative of the British Navy, "if you do not rebuild the church, we will. That spire is on all our charts and maps. It is the landmark by which the ships of the seven seas steer their course."— HARRY EMERSON FOSDICK, *On Being Fit to Live With*

486. John Kelman said: "God pity the nation whose factory chimneys rise higher than her church spires."

487. Two persons were talking together before a large church which was being destroyed by fire. The first man spoke in a voice which could be heard above the noise of the firemen: "This is the first time I ever saw you at church." To this the second man responded: "This is the first time I ever saw the church on fire."

Church Attendance

488. Theodore Roosevelt listed nine reasons for going to church: (1) In this actual world a churchless community, a community where men have abandoned and scoffed at or ignored their religious needs, is a community on the rapid downgrade. (2) Church work and church attendance mean the cultivation of the habit of feeling some responsibility for others. (3) There are enough holidays for most of us. Sundays differ from other holidays in the fact that there are fifty-two of them every year. Therefore, on Sundays go to church. (4) Yes, I know all the excuses. I know that one can worship the Creator in a grove of trees, or by a running brook, or in a man's own house just as well as in a church. But I also know as a matter of cold fact the average man does not thus worship. (5) He may not hear a good sermon at church. He will hear a sermon by a good man who, with his good wife, is engaged all the week in making hard lives easier. (6) He will listen to and take part in reading some beautiful passages from the Bible. And if he is not familiar with the Bible, he has suffered a loss. (7) He will take part in singing good hymns. (8) He will meet and nod or speak to good, quiet neighbors. He will come away feeling a little more charitable toward all the world, even toward those excessively foolish young men who regard churchgoing as a soft performance. (9) I advocate a man's joining in church work for the sake of showing his faith by his works.

489. An unusual custom is observed in a small English chapel at evening service. At the end of each pew is a tall candlestick. When the family that customarily uses that pew is ushered in, the candle is lighted. When the family is not present, the pew remains dark. Obviously, the amount of light in the chapel is determined by the number of families present that evening.
—BRUCE R. BAXTER

490. There is a story of a French peasant in the Department of Arts who was accustomed once every day to lay aside his work and in his old blue smock and his wooden sabots to go to the cathedral for a quiet time and then return to his work. When asked what he did during his visit to the cathedral, he replied: "I look at Jesus, and Jesus looks at me."

491. When asked why he attended church, a deaf and dumb man wrote: "To show which side I'm on."

492. When Charles H. Spurgeon was speaking to a backslider about church attendance, he was unable to get the response he wanted. Then without speaking he took a pair of tongs and with them lifted a live coal out of the fireplace. Both men watched as the flame died and the coal became a dead, black cinder. "You don't need to say anything more," the man protested. "I'll be back in my place next Sunday."

493. "Went to church today," Robert Louis Stevenson wrote in his journal, "and was not greatly depressed."

494. "Do you expect the President to be in church today?" an early Sunday morning telephoner asked the rector of President Franklin D. Roosevelt's Washington church. "I cannot promise," the rector replied. "However, God will be there, and that will be incentive enough for a reasonably large attendance."

495. The fastest growing religious sect in America has been designated as the "Seventh-Day Absentists."

Closed Churches

496. In Cornwall the tiny church of St. Ennadoc stood in a little hollow among the sand hills—a lovely spot. And on Sundays people worshiped there, with the sound of breakers coming through the windows and mingling with the voices of men who offered God their simple vows, and women who prayed for husbands and brothers and sons gone out on the great sea. Then, slowly, attendances fell. One Sunday the door was not opened. Sand blowing against the window panes fell to the ground and slowly mounted against the walls. At length the sand crept up to the window sills, piled up and covered the windows, mounted higher and reached the roof. Only the stony finger of the spire, still pointing to the sky, reminded men and women of aspirations which once were theirs, of vows now ruined, of prayers now silent, and hope now dead.—LESLIE D. WEATHERHEAD, *A Shepherd Remembers*

497. One wonders at the implications behind the notice posted on the front door of a church one wintry morning: "Closed because of lack of heat."

498. The tragedy of churches which close for a summer vacation is illustrated by one church which had the name "Gateway to Heaven." Underneath the church name on the bulletin board were these words: "Closed for the summer."

Criticism of the Church

499. Someone has wisely said: "The Church has many critics but no rivals." ✓

500. Another critic of the Church has written a parody of a cherished hymn:

> Like a Freshman forum
>   Moves the Church of God;
> Brothers we are talking
>   Where the saints have trod.
> We are not decided
>   Whether we shall be
> One in deed or doctrine
>   Or futility.

501. The announcement of Sunday morning and evening sermon titles on the bulletin board of a certain church represented a sad commentary on twentieth-century religion:

> "The Church at Work"
> "Playing Second Fiddle"

502. A fitting inscription for many churches might be:

> Come weal,
> Come woe,
> My *status* is *quo*.

503.
Outwardly splendid as of old—
Inwardly sparkless, void and cold—

Her force and fire all spent and gone—
Like the dead moon, she still shines on.[13]
—WILLIAM WATSON,
"The Church Today"

504. Someone has described a typical American church in this manner: "The congregation is sleek and comfortable; the service is placid and graceful; there is a stir of busy-ness, particularly in the rooms at the rear of the auditorium—but it lacks the stir of great waters."

505. One critic of the church, an Englishman, described the average congregation as "the uninspiring spectacle of a docile and mild-mannered gentleman trying to persuade a docile company of people to be still more docile."—HALFORD LUCCOCK

506. In a recent novel a young man speaks to a clergyman concerning the failure of the church to meet the needs of modern youth: "You've been nice, padre, and so—I'll repay you. I'll give you something—something rare. Truth! A common man's truth that is precious, for it may bring you understanding of us. You say I am looking for something in which to have faith. It is true. I and millions like me. And now ask yourself why it is that we scorn to look for a focus of that faith in your church. Because your church has shown not the least understanding of the horrible morass in which we common men wade. So your churches are empty, and yet we go in our millions to cinema houses, theaters, football games. Why? Because by my eternal soul those things, warped and poor as they are, are nearer to God and the common man's need for him than your church with its timid fears. Your church has lived in terror for

[13] Used by permission of George G. Harrap & Co., Ltd.

generations. All the multiple and beautiful teachings of Christ you have thrown away because you know they would offend the rich and privileged. To cover the lack you have put into the Church of Christ the jewel-laden trappings and pomp he never knew and could never love. Give them up! Follow Christ once more! Rise up from your terror. Come back into our lives as we live them today. . . . We did not leave you. You left us. We are waiting for you to give the church back to us."

507. A small girl, not satisfied with the work that her church was doing, told her mother: "I guess I will draw out my money from the church and put it in the bank."

508. One Sunday when a family returned from the morning service, father criticized the sermon, daughter thought the choir's singing was atrocious, and mother found fault with the organist's playing. But the subject had to be dropped when the small boy of the family piped up, "But it was a good show for a nickel, don't you think, Dad?"—ROY A. BURKHART, *Youth and the Way of Jesus*

509. "The apostle Paul has too red a face," said a cardinal who was criticizing Raphael's celebrated frescoes. "He blushes," the painter said, "to see into whose hands the church has fallen."

Church Divisions

510. It is said that one day when Phillips Brooks was walking along the Maine shore at low tide, he observed little isolated pools on the broken coast which reminded him sorrowfully of the broken-up condition of Protestantism. Later on that day, however, as he looked out from his porch, a different picture greeted him. The little separated

pools were gone because the tide had come in. There is good reason today to believe that the tide is moving in on our Protestant disunity. — HAROLD COOKE PHILLIPS, *In the Light of the Cross*

511. Thomas Macaulay, the English historian, returned from the Orient saying: "In a country where people pray to cows the differences that divide Christians seem of small account."

512. Lloyd George, the British statesman, once remarked: "The church I belong to is torn in a fierce dispute. One section says that baptism is *in* the name of the Father, and the other that it is *into* the name of the Father. I belong to one of these parties. I feel most strongly about it. I would die for it in fact—but I forget which it is!"

513. When Isaac Casaubon, the great French scholar, was being shown the hall of the Sorbonne on the occasion of his first visit to Paris, his guide told him: "This is where the theologians have disputed for five hundred years." "Indeed," was the reply, "and pray, what have they settled?"

514.
You go to your church, and I'll go to mine,
But let's walk along together;
Our Father has built them side by side,
So let's walk along together.[14]
—PHILLIPS H. LORD,
"You Go to Your Church and I'll Go to Mine"

515.
Yes, we do differ when we most agree,
For words are not the same to you and me,

[14] From the *Seth Parker Hymnal*. Used by permission of the author.

And it may be our several spiritual needs
Are best supplied by seeming different creeds.
And, differing, we agree in one
Inseparable communion,
If the true life be in our hearts; the faith
Which not to want is death;
To want is penance; to desire
Is purgatorial fire;
To hope is paradise; and to believe
Is all of heaven that earth can e'er receive.
—HARTLEY COLERIDGE,
"Religious Unity"

Church of God

516. In the historic town of Annapolis Royal, Nova Scotia, there stands a small church edifice with a unique top piece on its spire. It is not a weather vane, nor a rooster, nor any of the various things found as decorative finish for church spires. Glistening there in the light is the form of a human hand, closed with the index finger pointing straight up. This meaningful symbol is carefully preserved with gold leaf and may be seen in full view at any angle of approach. There it has stood for many decades, giving its silent message to every passer-by.
—FREDERICK P. FREEMAN

517. "The church is with her back to the wall, you would think, to hear many church folks talk," W. Quay Rosselle once said. "But I think she has her face to the weeping wall when really she ought to have her back to the wall and her face toward God."

518. Karl Barth, the contemporary Swiss theologian, has said: "The freedom of the Gospel may be repudiated by men in the Church, may be trodden under foot. The Church may become desolate for centuries. But the Gospel itself remains free, so surely as God himself remains free! And though the Church be desolated, the true Church of God lives invisibly in those who 'have not bowed the knee to Baal,' but simply and joyfully confess the name of the Lord."—ADOLPH KELLER, *Religion and Revolution*

519. A visitor in Germany before the war reported seeing a church with a sign over the door which read: *Gott ist nicht hier* (God is not here).

520. A little boy, having been told that the church was God's house, asked: "When's he going to move in?"

History of the Church

521. A contemporary apologist for the church quotes Pericles' plea in behalf of Athens, "Think what she *may become* and be worthy of her." With equal appropriateness it might be said, "Think what the Church *has been,* and be worthy of her."—HENRY P. VAN DUSEN, *Reality and Religion*

522. An African writer of the third century, Cyprian, said: "He cannot have God for his Father who has not the Church for his mother."

523. At a Rotary Club meeting a businessman boasted that the company he represented was founded in 1874. The president, noting that date, asked if there was anyone representing an older firm than that. When a Christian minister arose, the men smiled before realizing that the clergyman was right.

524. Three hundred years ago the Church of Scotland took as its symbol the burning bush of Exodus, and as its motto the words, "Burned but not consumed."

525. On the wall of a seventeenth-century English church there is found this inscription: "In the year 1653 when all things sacred were throughout ye nation either demolished or profaned, Sir Robert Shirley, Barronet, founded this church; whose singular praise it is to have done the best things in the worst times and hoped them in the most calamitous."

Loyalty to the Church

526. Lardy Quinnet, a character in A. S. M. Hutchinson's novel *One Increasing Purpose,* says: "I went to church with my mother as a kid, I shall be buried by the Church; in between I am dashed if I scoff at the church."

527. In an appreciation of the Church, Charles Clayton Morrison has written: "I see through eyes that have been formed by it. My values have been given me by my participation in it. The God who has revealed himself in this community commands my supreme devotion. No other community that I know offers me a revelation of God comparable to that which Christ has given me through the community of which he is center and head."

528.
Then on memory's page I can see again
    The church by the side of the road;
And wherever I roam, it is guiding me home,
    The church by the side of the road.
                    —AUTHOR UNKNOWN

529. During the four years that John Wanamaker was postmaster general under President Harrison he traveled nearly 100,000 miles to be present each week in his home church. He said: "I have made it a rule of my life to be present in my regular place each Lord's day when in health and in the country, believing that we should not forsake the assembling of ourselves together. I could eat well and sleep well and yet be a very miserable man without the uplift that comes from attendance upon the divine ordinances."

530. When the bishop read the work of condemnation to Savonarola, "I separate thee from the Church militant, and from the Church triumphant," the martyr exclaimed: "From the Church militant—thou canst do that, but thou hast no power to separate me from the Church triumphant!"

Church Membership

531. "The New Testament knows nothing of unattached Christians," Archibald M. Hunter writes in *The Message of the New Testament.*

532. The late William Lyon Phelps, professor of English at Yale and a prominent Baptist layman, said: "I would rather belong to the Church than belong to any other organization or society or club. I would rather be a Church member than receive any honor or decoration in the world."—FRANK FRAGERBURG

533. Daniel Poling suggests the following reasons "Why I Should Join the Church":

1. I should belong to the church because I ought to be better than I am. Henry Ward Beecher once said: "The church is not a gallery for the exhibition of eminent Christians, but a school for the education of imperfect ones."

2. I should belong to the church because of what I can give to it and do through it, as well as because of what I may get out of it. The church is not a dormitory for sleepers; it is an institution of workers. It is not only a rest camp; it is a front-line trench.

3. I should belong to the church because every man should pay his debts and do his share toward discharging the obligation of society. Not only has the church been the bearer of the good news of personal salvation; it has been and is the supreme uplifting and conserving agency, without which "civilization would lapse into barbarism and press its way to perdition."

4. I should belong to the church because of memories—memories of things I can never forget, memories of faces that will never fade, memories of vows that are the glory of youth.

5. I should belong to the church because of hope—hope that lives when promises are dead, hope that paves the way for progress, hope that visions peace and social justice, hope for all time to come—and hope for eternity, the great hope that casts its anchor behind Jesus Christ.

6. I should belong to the church because of the strong men in it who need reinforcing, the weak men in it who need encouraging, the rascals in it who need rebuking. If I say that I am not good enough, my humility recommends me. If I sit in the seat of the scornful, my inactivity condemns me.

7. I should belong to the church—but not until I am ready to join a going concern; not until I am willing to become an active partner with Jesus Christ.

534. When Henry Ward Beecher was preaching at Park Street Church in Boston, someone asked him why it was that his church was so splendidly successful. His answer was: "I preach on Sunday, but I have 450 members who take up my message on Monday and preach it wherever they go."

535. Abraham Lincoln, though by nature religious and godly, was not a church member. When he was chided one day for not belonging to a church, he said: "If any church will write on its altar as the sole condition for membership the words of Jesus, 'Thou shalt love the Lord thy God with all thy heart, and with all thy soul, and with all thy mind, and with all thy strength, and thy neighbour as thyself,' that church will I join."

536. When a devoted old Negro applied for membership in a fashionable church, the minister told him to give added consideration to his desire to join. The old man said he would go home and pray about it. When the minister saw the Negro a few days later, he asked, "What did the Lord tell you to do?" "He told me it wasn't no use," said the Negro, adding, "He said: 'Ah been tryin' to get in that same church for ten years an' Ah still can't make it.'"

537. One day when Henry Ward Beecher was going for a drive the liveryman brought a fine-looking horse to the door. Beecher said: "That is a fine looking animal you have there, Sam. Is he as good as he looks?" Sam replied: "Boss, that horse is the best one in our stables. He will work any place you put him, and can do anything." Beecher smiled and with a note of humor in his voice remarked: "I wish to goodness he was a member of my church."—JACK E. JONES

538. A country minister in preaching a funeral sermon said: "The corpse has been a member of this church for twenty years."

539. "The chief trouble with the Church," said Emory B. Hunt, onetime president of Bucknell University, "is that you and I are in it."—CHARLES H. HEIMSATH, *Sermons on the Inner Life*

540. When a church member boasted to his pastor that he was a good Christian, the pastor said: "I don't see any prints of nails on your hands."

541. When a house girl asked for membership in Charles H. Spurgeon's Metropolitan Tabernacle in London, the minister asked for evidence of her change of heart. "I have none except that now I sweep under the mats and rugs in the house where I am employed," the girl said.

Neglect of the Church

542. A cultured lady, in defense of her family's cynical neglect of the church and all things religious, said to a friend: "I guess we have just outgrown the church."

543. Leslie D. Weatherhead writes: "I remember being in India when the Duke of Windsor, then Prince of Wales, came out to represent the king. Now, the Hindus and Mohammedans of India are deeply religious, though one may criticize their religion. Every day the devout went to their temples to offer prayer for the king's son. But they asked one question repeatedly about the prince: 'Why doesn't he ever go to church?'"—*In Quest of a Kingdom*

544. Artemus Ward, the great American humorist, said: "If you will show me a place where there ain't no meeting houses and where men don't pray, I will show you a place where people are slipshod and dirty, where gates are off the hinges, where old hats are stuffed in broken windows."

Task of the Church

545. A Negro church in Kansas City is reported to have the following church slogan: "Wake up, sing up, preach up, pray up, stay up, pay up, but never

give up or let up or back up or shut up until the cause of Christ in this church and in the world is built up."

546. "A church is not measured in greatness by the beauty of its architecture or the ability of its ministry," said John Bunyan, "but by the people who live truly and serve faithfully that for which it stands."

547. A French professor of economics is reported to have said: "It is not the function of the Christian Church to create a new civilization; it is the church's function to create the creators of a new civilization."

548. There is a timeless truth in Albert Einstein's comment on the stalwart Church in Nazi Germany: "Being a lover of freedom, when the revolution came in Germany, I looked to the universities to defend it, knowing that they had always boasted of their devotion to the cause of truth. But no the universities immediately were silenced. Then I looked to the great editors in days gone by who proclaimed their love of freedom; but they, like the universities, were silenced with a few short weeks. Only the Church stood squarely across the path of Hitler's campaign for the supression of truth. I never had any special interest in the Church before, but now I feel a great affection and admiration because the Church alone had the courage and persistence to stand for intellectual truth and moral freedom. I am forced thus to confess what I once despised I now praise unreservedly."

549. A recent cartoon pictures Uncle Sam, standing on the Ship of State, saying to the representatives of the Christian faith: "It is your business to keep off the Ship of State the barnacles of greed, selfishness, and dishonesty."

550. When a neighboring minister was once under fire, a professor said: "It is time now for me to join his church. The cause of justice is at stake."— CHARLES H. HEIMSATH, *Sermons on the Inner Life*

551. During the First World War, Marshal Foch stepped into a church, walked down the long aisle, and knelt at the altar. A poor peasant woman kneeling there recognized the great soldier and started to leave. The marshal said, "Remain—we are all equal here."

552. "If you take in that Negro as a member of the church, I'll leave," said one indignant churchgoer. To this another member said: "If you don't take him in, some of us will leave, for a church that is founded on a racial and class snobbery isn't worth staying in. Besides, if this member does go, then it will be no loss, for with that spirit he was never really in."

553. One modern has said: "The Church faces a generation which is trying to drink its way to prosperity, war its way to peace, spend its way to wealth and enjoy its way to heaven."

554. Willard L. Sperry writes: "The world seeks the church uncritically, habitually, at those times when life most matters. Parents who have drifted away from the church still bring their children back for baptism. Young people who profess to have outgrown religion still enter the church to be made man and wife. The last low whispers of the world's dead are not uniformly burdened with God's name, but the church is always requisitioned to speak that name over those dead. In obedience to some deep unreasoned prompting men seek

churches when life is most real."—*Reality in Worship*

555. "I am quite sure," writes E. Stanley Jones, "that I should not have survived as a young Christian had I not had the corporate life of the church to hold me up. When I rejoiced, they rejoiced with me. When I was weak, they strengthened me, and once when I fell—a rather bad fall—they gathered around me by prayer and love, and without blame or censure they lovingly lifted me back to my feet again."—*Victorious Living*

556. Thousands of visitors to New York City wish to see the Little Church Around the Corner. This church received its name in a most interesting manner. Back in 1871 Joseph Jefferson, an actor, went to a minister of a large church, asking that arrangements be made for the funeral of George Holland, another actor. But the minister said that his position as minister of a large and influential parish would not permit him to officiate at the funeral of an actor. He added, condescendingly, that there was a small church around the corner, the Church of the Transfiguration, where such a service might be held. When Jefferson found that minister willing to officiate, the actor raised his hand in a sincere and dramatic gesture and said: "May God bless this Little Church Around the Corner." Since that time not only has the church had many stage folk in its membership, but the marriage vows have been read to more than 100,000 couples at its altar.

557. "Come and have a round of golf on Sunday morning," said one friend to another. "Oh, no, I have to attend church," said the second. "Well," replied the friend, "I do not know what your religion is, but you keep it to yourself.

I have asked you to play golf half a dozen times, but you have never invited me to your church."

558. "Would it not be a great thing for all of us Christians in China to unite, and go out and double the number of Protestant Church Christians within the next five years?" a Chinese church leader asked John R. Mott. "How many are there now?" Mott asked. "Four hundred and thirty-five thousand," was the answer. "Well," said Mott, "It has taken over a hundred years to build in China a Christian Church of these dimensions, and do you now suggest the practicability of doubling that number in five years?" The answer, which Mott says he will never forget, was: "Why not?"

CITIZEN

559. The implication of these words by the ancient Greek Socrates is so modern it startles the reader: "I am a citizen, not of Athens or Greece, but of the world."

560. "If a man be gracious and considerate," Francis Bacon declared, "it shows that he is a citizen of the world, and that his heart is no island cut off from other lands but part of a vast continent. This of all virtues is the greatest, being of the character of God."

561. "A state can be no better than the citizens of which it is composed," wrote John Morley. "Our labor is not to mold states but to make citizens."

562. A delegate from Frederick, Maryland, signed his name to the Constitution with these words: "I am a citizen of the town of Frederick, of the county of Frederick, of the state of Maryland, and now I choose to be a citizen of the United States."

CLIMBING

563. God's Road is all uphill,
But do not tire,
Rejoice that we may still
Keep climbing higher.
—ARTHUR GUITERMAN
"A Poet's Proverb"

564. A group of people were climbing the Alps. Two men tried to go higher than the rest and were lost forever. Their friends said: "When last seen, they were going toward the heights."

565. An epitaph of a Swiss mountaineer reads: "He died climbing."

COMMUNION SERVICE

566. When friends in Scotland wrote to James Chalmers in the New Hebrides, asking if there was anything he would like them to send, he replied: "Send a communion set." At that time there was no church where he was, not even a convert; but he knew that there would be.

567. A minister was asked if he would allow Christ to preach in his pulpit. "Certainly," was the reply. "Would you allow him to administer the communion?" The clergyman hesitated. "I am afraid I couldn't, for he wasn't ordained."
—E. STANLEY JONES, *Christ at the Round Table*

568. When asked, during his exile, what the greatest experience of his life had been, Napoleon answered, "My first communion."

COMPANIONSHIP

569. A casual fellow traveler once said to John Wesley: "Young man, the Bible knows nothing of solitary religion. You must find companions or make them."
—HARRIS FRANKLIN RALL, *Christianity*

570. "Pray for me that I may come back alive," said a young soldier to a chaplain as he went out to cut wire in No Man's Land. "I will do more than that," said the chaplain. "I will go with you."

571. "Remember this always: there are only two classes of boys, good boys and bad boys," Theodore Roosevelt told his sons. "If you choose your companions among the good boys, you need not worry whether they are rich or poor, or who their fathers and mothers are."

572. When a boy, George Washington wrote in a book of maxims: "Associate yourself with men of good quality, if you esteem your reputation; for 'tis better to be alone than in bad company."

573. "Choose wisely your companions," William E. Gladstone cautioned a group of young men, "for a young man's companions, more than his food or clothes, his home or his parents, make him what he is."

574. An old adage reads: "Tell me whom you are with, and I will tell you what you are."

575. François de Bonivard, the prisoner of Chillon, was so in need of companionship during his long confinement that he made friends with a spider which crawled up the wall of his cell each day.

COMPASS

576. A seasoned Maine guide advised a traveler: "Always believe the compass."
—JOHN N. ALTHOUSE

577. When a man asked a clerk in a store for a compass, the clerk asked: "Do you want a compass to draw circles with or to go places with?"

COMPENSATION

578. "Some day an epic will be written about the law of compensation, the most dramatic thing in nature," William Beebe has written in *The Arcturus Adventure*. "The peacock, with his aristocratic, incomparable display of color, has only a wretched squawk of a voice. The nightingale, embodiment of glorious, soul-stirring song, has feathers of dullest russet and gray. And the albatross, master flying, walks awkwardly along the sand, moving as though each step brought him acute agony."

579. A spectator spoke to a man who was laying bricks for a great cathedral. "Isn't your brother a bishop?" the spectator asked. "Yes," the workman answered proudly. "Isn't this a funny world?" said the spectator. "Your brother a bishop and you a bricklayer. Things are equal, are they?" The workman stood erect. "That's not so," he said, "for my brother couldn't do this to save his life."

580. In the poem "Fable" by Emerson a squirrel says to a mountain:

If I cannot carry forests on my back,
Neither can you crack a nut.

581. An Irishman defined compensation in this way: "If you have one leg shorted than the other, the other is longer."—CHARLES LYON SEASHOLES, *For Times Out of Joint*

582. After working long and hard in a field where they had been told a treasure was buried two boys were "encouraged" by their father, who said: "After all, you have some gain from your effort; the digging itself was good exercise."

COMPLAINT

583. An Abrabian proverb reads: "I complained because I had no shoes until I met a man who had no feet."

584. One day fortune knocked on a fellow's door. But the fellow didn't hear it. He was over at his neighbor's telling a hard luck story.

585. When a friend complained to Charles Lamb that the world seemed "drained of all its sweets," Lamb replied: "Drained of its sweets? I don't know what you mean. Are there not roses and violets still in the earth, and the sun and moon still reigning in heaven?"

586. Laura E. Richards in *The Silver Crown* tells of a grumpy saint who did kind deeds with complaining. One day, meeting a poor woman with a heavy burden, he takes the burden upon his own back but scolds her for carrying so much. Another time he meets a lost child. He carries the child back through the snow to his home but scolds him for being lost.

COMPROMISE

587. When Rome had been humbled by Carthage, some members of the Rome Senate suggested that Rome seek some compromise. "Stop!" cried an old senator, leaping to his feet. "Remember this— Rome does not go to battle; Rome goes to war!"

588. "All government—indeed, every human benefit and enjoyment, every virtue and every prudent act—is founded on compromise and barter," said Edmund Burke in his famous speech on conciliation.

CONFIDENCE

589. During the most crucial period in the Civil War, when Lee's troops were

invading Pennsylvania, a cocksure civilian in Philadelphia telegraphed General Halleck in Washington offering his services as commander in chief of the Federal forces. He implied he could win the war in a week if he were only given the chance. General Halleck sent him this grim reply: "We already have five times as many generals as we want, but we are greatly in need of private soldiers. Anyone volunteering in that capacity will be very welcome. What do you say?"—JAMES G. GILKEY, *Managing One's Self*

590. When Nansen, the Arctic explorer, took his ship into the frozen North, tons of ice pushed against the ship. When asked if he were not worried for fear she would be crushed, the explorer said: "I feel perfectly calm. I know she can stand it. I watched every stick of timber and every piece of steel go into her hull."

591. It was confidence and not pride which led Stradivarius to say: "I make the best violin that can be made. It is impossible to make a better one."

592. During the cruel winter at Valley Forge during the American Revolution, when many of his troops threatened to desert, Washington shrewdly arranged a review of his ill-clad, rebellious regiments. As a particularly haggard and resentful group stood at attention before him, he drew himself up proudly and exclaimed: "I have great confidence in the men of Connecticut!"—JAMES GORDON GILKEY, *Managing One's Self*

593. From prison Martin Niemoeller addressed the following words to the members of his Berlin parish: "Let us thank God that he upholds me as he does and allows no spirit of despair to enter into Cell 448. Let the parish office

know that in all ignorance of what is coming I am confident, and that I hope to be ready when I am led along paths which I never would have sought for myself."

594. After a sign reading "Boy Wanted" was hung in a store window, a long line of applicants gathered at the door. One especially anxious fellow scribbled a note which he handed quietly to the examiner: "Don't do anything till you've seen me. I'm the last in the line, but I've sure got the goods."

CONSCIENCE

595. "Conscience," an unknown writer has said, "is not the law book in the courtroom, but the judge. It does not make the law, it enforces it."

596. Henry Sloane Coffin, returning from a visit to the Orient, wrote: "A keen-minded Chinese official, comparing the influence of Jesus with that of Confucius and Buddha and Lao-tse, once said to me in Peking: 'He seems to have the power to create a more delicate conscience.' "—WALTER R. BOWIE, *The Bible*

597. On the bell of the First Baptist Church of Providence, Rhode Island, are inscribed these words:

For freedom of conscience this town was
    first planted;
    Persuasion, not force, was used by
      the people;
This church is the oldest, and has not
    recanted;
    Enjoying and granting, bell, temple,
      and steeple.

598. William Penn in London Tower exclaimed: "My prison shall be my grave before I will budge a jot, for I owe my conscience to no mortal man."

599. "Man became the first implement-making creature not later than the beginning of the Ice Age, probably a million years ago," James H. Breasted, the archaeologist, has written. "At the same time he became the first weapon-making creature. For perhaps a million years, therefore, he has been improving those weapons; but it is less than five thousand years since man began to feel the power of conscience to such a degree that it became a potent social force."—*The Dawn of Conscience*

600.
Yet still there whispers the small voice within,
Heard through Gain's silence, and o'er Glory's din:
Whatever creed be taught or land be trod,
Man's conscience is the oracle of God.
      —BYRON, "The Island"

601. Socrates described a man's conscience as the wife from whom there is no divorce.

602. Stuart N. Hutchinson tells of a small boy who, having been told by his father that conscience is a small voice that warns against wrong, prayed: "O God, make the little voice loud."

603. "Conscience," said Huckleberry Finn, "takes up more room than all the rest of a fellow's insides."

604. When Mark Twain heard a squeak in his study, he turned around to find a wizened little pigmy sitting on his bookcase. "Who are you?" he asked. "I'm your conscience," answered the pigmy. "You have almost killed me, but I'm not dead yet."

605. In Hawthorne's *The Scarlet Letter* the story is told of a troubled conscience. For seven years Arthur Dimmesdale secretly suppressed a guilty conscience. But the day came when he could no longer endure the remorse of memory. He mounted the pillory in the market place and stood next to the girl he had wronged. To his townsmen he cried: "Stands anyone here who questions God's judgment on a sinner? Behold, behold a dreadful witness of it." He made his confession that he might rid himself of the pangs of a tortured conscience.

606. When politics had defeated his health measures in a Welsh mining town, the young doctor in A. J. Cronin's *The Citadel* sold his standards for money. So, after his wife's tragic death, he found in her purse snapshots of himself in those Galahad days, and letters of gratitude from impoverished miners, and other mementos that she had kept to remind herself of the man he might have been. He knew that his pain was only just. He shouted at himself in a drunken stupor that yet could not drug his conscience, "You thought you could get away with it. You thought you *were* getting away with it. But by God! you weren't."—GEORGE A. BUTTRICK, *Christ and Man's Dilemma*

CONSECRATION

607.
A picket frozen on duty,
    A mother starved for her brood,
Socrates drinking the hemlock,
    And Jesus on the rood;
And millions who, humble and nameless,
    The straight, hard pathway plod,
Some call it Consecration,
    And others call it God.[16]
      —WILLIAM HERBERT CARRUTH,
        "*Each in His Own Tongue*"

[16] Used by permission of Mrs. William H. Carruth.

608. "Perhaps you will be interested to know the origin of the consecration hymn 'Take My Life, and Let It Be,'" Frances R. Havergal wrote to her sister from Areley House, England, in February, 1874. "There were ten persons in the house, some unconverted and long prayed for; some converted, but not rejoicing Christians. He gave me the prayer: 'Lord, give me all in this house.' And he just *did!* Before I left the house everyone had got a blessing. The last night of my visit, after I had retired, the governess asked me to go to the two daughters. They were crying, etc. Then and there both of them trusted and rejoiced. It was nearly midnight. I was too happy to sleep, and passed most of the night in praise and renewal of my own consecration; and these little couplets formed themselves and chimed in my heart one after another until they finished with 'Ever, only, all for thee!'"

CONTENTMENT

609.
Ah, great it is to believe the dream
As we stand in youth by the starry stream;
But a greater thing is to fight life through,
And say at the end, "The dream is true!" [17]
—Edwin Markham, "The Dream"

610. A Scot nobleman, coming upon the gardener of his estate, said: "That's a very good coat you're wearing." Shaking the dust from his ragged coat, the gardener said that he begged to disagree. "Oh, no, I'm right," said the nobleman, "for it covers a contented spirit and a body that owes no man anything. That's more than most men can say of their coats."

[17] Used by permission of Virgil Markham.

611. An unknown writer has said: "A little is as much as a lot if it is enough."

612.
I was too ambitious in my deed,
And thought to distance all men in success,
Till God came on me, marked the place, and said,
"Ill-doer, henceforth keep within this line,
Attempting less than others"—and I stand
And work among Christ's little ones, content.
—Elizabeth Barrett Browning, "Content in Service"

613. One of the most unforgettable sentences in Defoe's novel is the one in which Robinson Crusoe says: "I do not possess anything I do not want, and I do not want anything I do not possess."

614. A motto which used to hang in many homes read: "The City of Contentment is in the State of Mind."

615. "To cease to rebel, to stop fighting back, to be content with half a loaf when you cannot have a whole one— these are hard lessons, but all of us must learn them," wrote Dr. Edward Livingston Trudeau, the physician who was a victim of tuberculosis. "I have found that the great word is Acquiescence."

CONVERSION

616. "I was so taken with the love and mercy of God," wrote John Bunyan of the day of his conversion, "that I knew not how to contain myself till I got home. I thought I could have spoken of his love to the very crows that sat upon the ploughed lands before me."

617. "I feel like a contemptible fine lady," said Elizabeth Fry before she was

converted, "all outside and no inside."
—E. Stanley Jones, *The Way*

618. Before his great spiritual experience which transformed the religious
life of England, John Wesley had gone
to Georgia as a missionary. "I went to
America to convert the Indians, but, oh!
who shall convert me?" he cried.

619. William D. Weyraugh has listed
eight things which account for John
Wesley's heart-warming experience in
Aldersgate on May 24, 1787: (1) The
Bible, which Wesley opened at these
words: "Whereby are given unto us exceeding great and precious promises,
that by these ye might be partakers of
the divine nature." (2) A friend who
had asked Wesley to go to St. Paul's.
(3) A great cathedral, where he entered and worshiped. (4) A choir which
was rendering an anthem based on Ps.
130: "Out of the depths have I cried
unto thee, O Lord." (5) A small group
of praying people in an upper room.
(6) A clergyman, for the message Wesley heard was written by Martin Luther.
(7) A layman—the person by whom
Luther's preface to the *Epistle to the
Romans* was read was probably a layman. (8) The power of the Holy Spirit,
for as Wesley listened the Holy Spirit
entered into his heart, and it was
"strangely warmed."

620. William Lecky the historian said:
"It was a national epoch when John
Wesley's heart was warmed in the
meetinghouse."

621. E. Stanley Jones, speaking of his
conversion, said: "As soon as the burden
rolled off and I became conscious that
Jesus was my personal Saviour, I felt a
sudden impulse and desire to throw my
arms around the world and to share the
experience with everybody else. A few

minutes before I had no such desire,
because I had nothing to share."

622. In *My Conversion,* Count Leo
Tolstoy wrote: "Five years ago faith
came to me: I believed in the doctrine
of Jesus, and all my life was suddenly
changed. I ceased to desire that which
previously I had desired, and on the
other hand, I took to desiring what I
had never desired before. That which
formerly used to appear good in my
eyes appeared evil, and that which used
to appear evil appeared good." Before
his conversion Tolstoy had acquired
fame and fortune through his great
writings. But he was unsatisfied. "I
fought duels," he wrote, "I gambled, I
wasted my substance wrung from the
sweat of peasants, punished the latter
cruelly, rioted with loose women, and
deceived men. Lying, robbery, adultery
of all kinds, drunkenness, murder, I
committed. Yet I was none the less considered by my equals a comparatively
moral man." His conversion, one of the
most dramatic of modern times, gave his
life a new purpose and meaning and, he
affirmed, an abiding satisfaction.

623. "I was once a wild thing on the
coast of Africa," said John Newton,
who wrote the hymn "How Sweet the
Name of Jesus Sounds," "but the Lord
caught me, and tamed me: and now
people come to see me like the lions in
the Tower. Doubt if the Lord can convert the heathen? Look at me!"

624. Alexander Whyte wrote: "I would
value above all that God can give me
in this world to see all my children
converted. I would rejoice to see their
conversion through any instrumentality
it pleased God to employ—a new minister, a passing evangelist, a good book
—but oh, if it pleases God, let me have
all my children's souls myself. Let them

all say in after years, 'It was my father that did it.' That would make my cup run over indeed."

625. All Russia became Christian with Emperor Vladimir. He desired to become a Christian but hesitated, for, as being beneath his dignity, he would not be baptized by the local clergy. He wanted the Patriarch of Constantinople to perform the ceremony—that would give the desired dignity. But to ask him to come to do it would be receiving a bounty at the hands of another. He decided that the only thing consonant with his honor would be to conquer Constantinople and compel the patriarch to baptize him. He would then stand as dictator and not as suppliant. That was actually carried out. Constantinople was captured and the Patriarch forced to baptize him. Then Russia became Christian.—E. STANLEY JONES, *The Christ of the Indian Road*

CONVICTIONS

626. Goethe once said, "Give me the benefit of your convictions if you have any, but keep your doubts to yourself, for I have enough of my own."

627. William Jennings Bryan spoke of a friend as having "no opinions—nothing but convictions."

CO-OPERATION

628. Marcus Aurelius said: "We are made for co-operation—like feet, like hands. . . . To act against one another, then, is contrary to nature."

629. In August, 1864, Abraham Lincoln gave up all hope of his own re-election. One day he came to his Cabinet with a sheet of paper that had been folded, and asked every member to sign it. Everyone did without knowing its contents. When, however, Lincoln was re-elected, they learned that what they had all agreed to was this: "It now seems altogether probable that this administration will not be re-elected. In that case it will become my duty so to co-operate with the president-elect as to save the Union between the election and the inauguration as he will have secured his election on such grounds that he cannot possibly save it afterwards."—ERNEST FREEMONT TITTLE, *A World That Cannot Be Shaken*

630. "You cannot sing an oratorio by yourself, I care not how splendid your voice may be. You must merge your own voice in the chorus," writes one discerning author. "You cannot render the *Fifth Symphony* by yourself, I care not how well you may play upon some single instrument. You must blend your efforts with those of an entire orchestra."

631. One day when Toscanini was conducting a rehearsal at the Metropolitan Opera House, a soprano soloist who was famous and temperamental objected to the maestro's many suggestions. "I am the star of this performance," she exclaimed. "Madame," Toscanini replied quietly, "in this performance there *are* no stars."

632. We ask the leaf, "Are you complete in yourself?" And the leaf answers, "No, my life is in the branches." We ask the branch, and the branch answers, "No, my life is in the root." We ask the root, and it answers, "No, my life is in the trunk and the branches and the leaves. Keep the branches stripped of leaves, and I shall die." So it is with the great tree of being. Nothing is completely and merely individual. —HARRY EMERSON FOSDICK, *The Meaning of Prayer*

633. When fighting during a certain war came to one small village, an old lady rushed out, brandishing an old broom handle as a weapon. "Grandma, you can't fight with that," said a young man. "But I can show which side I am on," was her quick reply.—WILSON O. WELDON

634. A visitor passing through an English war factory during World War II was startled to see at a lathe a man who bore a striking resemblance to the king. Greater was his astonishment to discover that it was the king. He found out that each day after his official duties were over, the king of England took his place in the factory and worked with his people.—HENRY F. POLLOCK

COURAGE

635. Woodrow Wilson said: "I had rather be defeated in a cause that will ultimately triumph than triumph in a cause that will ultimately be defeated."

636. Courage is armor
A blind man wears;
The calloused scar
Of outlived despairs:
Courage is Fear
That has said its prayers.[18]
—KARLE WILSON BAKER,
"Courage"

637. Two prisoners are in a cart headed for the guillotine in a scene from *A Tale of Two Cities* by Charles Dickens. The man, who has just found himself, is giving his life for a friend. A small girl near by has watched the man's courage and hopes that his strength will give her strength. "If I may ride with you," she ventures, "will you let me hold your hand? I am not afraid, but I am little and weak, and it will give me more

[18] Used by permission of the author.

courage." When the cart reaches the spot of execution, the little girl looks up into the man's face and says: "I think you were sent to me by Heaven."

638. When Martin Luther, having nailed his theses to the church door at Wittenberg, walked into the imperial council hall of Charles V to face the charge of heresy, an old knight touched him on the shoulder with his gauntlet, saying, "Little monk, you are taking a step the like of which neither I nor many a commander in our fiercest battles would take."—HARRY EMERSON FOSDICK, *On Being a Real Person*

639. A captain announced that men were needed for a particularly dangerous assignment. "Would those who are willing to volunteer take one step forward," he said. The entire company of men took one step forward. Looking up from the notice he had been reading, the captain said: "Is there no one who will volunteer?" "We have all stepped forward," one of the men explained.

640. Sir Walter Raleigh as he went to the scaffold said to his friends: "If you perceive any weakness in me, I beseech you ascribe it to my sickness rather than to myself."

641. Charles Denby, American Minister to China, estimated that more than fifteen thousand Protestant Chinese Christians were killed in the Boxer Rebellion, and that of those thus tested, only 2 per cent renounced their faith to save their lives.

642. Toyohiko Kagawa on one occasion called together a little group of missionaries and said: "Brethren, I'm on my way to prison. I know very well that if I persist in the course I am taking,

I shall be sent to jail and perhaps worse, but I will not turn back!"

643. Wendell Phillips, the great abolitionist, was severely criticized for the stand he took toward human slavery. Before he would leave for a lecture, his wife, an invalid who could not accompany him, would bid farewell with these words: "Now, Wendell, don't you shilly-shally."

644. Admiral Drake, standing on his quarter-deck before an engagement, was observed to shake, whereupon he remarked: "My flesh trembles at the many dangers into which my resolute heart will lead me."

COURTESY

645. An old man arrived late at the Olympic games at Athens. All the seats were occupied. He passed the Athenian section and was laughed at. He went on to where the Spartans sat. Like one man they all arose to offer him a seat. The Athenians, seeing this, raised a loud cheer. "Ah," said the aged stranger, "the Athenians admire that which is good, but the Spartans practice it."—CLIFFORD C. GREINER

646. While driving in his carriage one day President Lincoln returned greetings with an old Negro who had saluted the chief executive. "Why," questioned a friend, "did you tip your hat to that old darky?" "I have never wished," replied the President, "that anyone should be more courteous than I."

647. Robert E. Lee was once seated in a train when a poor woman entered. Every seat was filled, many of them with his officers and soldiers. Not one moved until she reached the end of the car where Lee was seated. He gallantly arose and led her to his seat. Whereupon everyone in that car leaped to his feet to offer him a place. "No, gentlemen," was the answer, "if you cannot give your seats to an old woman, you cannot give them to me."

648.

How sweet and gracious, even in common speech,
Is that fine sense which men call Courtesy!
Wholesome as air and genial as the light,
Welcome in every clime as breath of flowers,
It transmutes aliens into trusting friends,
And gives its owner passport round the globe.

    —JAMES T. FIELDS, "Courtesy"

COVETOUSNESS

649. Francis Xavier once said that he had heard thousands of confessions but never one of covetousness. It is a sin we never mention.

650. In 1918, near the end of the First World War, an American bishop said that it was his judgment that we were near the end of the war. Later at his hotel he met a woman who had heard his sermon. "I hope the war will not end so soon," she said. "My husband is making a million dollars a month in munitions." "Madam," said the bishop, "you deserve a special hell built for you."—COSTEN J. HARRELL, The Way of the Transgressor

651. A man once said to his neighbor: "Neighbor, you are so tightfisted God himself couldn't pry your hand open to put a blessing in it."

COWARDICE

652. One of the first responsibilities which George Washington faced when he assumed command of the American forces was to order the court-martial of Captain John Callender, an officer of the Massachusetts militia who was charged with cowardice at the Battle of Bunker Hill. "It is with inexpressible concern," Washington wrote, "that the general upon his first arrival in the army should find an officer sentenced by a General Court Martial to be cashiered for cowardice—a crime of all others the most infamous in a soldier, the most injurious to an army, and the last to be forgiven." After this judgment was passed, Callender re-enlisted in the army as a private. At the Battle of Long Island he was so distinguished for courage that Washington revoked the sentence and restored him to his rank.

653. "If the good Lord has given a man a cowardly pair of legs," Lincoln said when a young soldier who had been absent without leave was brought to him, "it is hard to keep them from running away with him."

654. It is said that just before a battle Marshal Ney found his knees trembling. Looking scornfully down at them, he exclaimed: "Shaking are you? Well, you would shake a whole lot more if you only knew where I am going to take you in the next half hour."

655. When Marshal Foch found an officer punishing a French corporal for showing fear in battle, the marshal said: "None but a coward dares to boast that he has never known fear."

CREED

656. Bishop Wilberforce and Thomas Carlyle were talking one day about the deep things of life, and Carlyle said: "My lord, have you a creed?" "Yes," the bishop replied, "and the older I grow, the firmer that creed becomes under my feet. There is only one thing that staggers me." "What is that?" Carlyle asked. "The slow progress that that creed seems to make in the world," was the bishop's answer. After a moment of silence Carlyle made this wise remark: "Yes, but if you have a creed, you can afford to wait."

657.
Faithfully faithful to every trust,
  Honestly honest in every deed,
Righteously righteous and justly just;
  This is the whole of the good man's creed.
                    —AUTHOR UNKNOWN

658.
And so the Word had breath, and wrought
  With human hands the creed of creeds
In loveliness of perfect deeds,
More strong than all poetic thought.
        —TENNYSON, "In Memoriam"

659. Augustine's personal creed was: "A whole Bible for my staff, a whole Christ for my salvation, a whole Church for my fellowship, and a whole world for my parish."

660. "Here is my creed," said Benjamin Franklin. "I believe in one God, creator of the universe. That he governs it by his providence. That he ought to be worshiped. That the most acceptable service we render him is doing good to his other children. That the soul of man is immortal and will be treated with justice in another life respecting its conduct in this."

661. The motto of Moses Mendelssohn, German Jewish philosopher, is succinct and suggestive: "To love the beautiful, to desire the good, to do the best."

662. Norman MacLeod of the Barony of Glasgow, a friend and confidant of Queen Victoria, summed up the meaning of religion for him in one sentence: "There is a Father in heaven who loves us, a Brother Saviour who died for us, a Spirit who helps us to be good, and a Home where we shall all meet at last."

663. William Ellery Channing described these words as "My Symphony": "To live content with small means; to seek elegance rather than luxury, and refinement rather than fashion; to be worthy, not respectable, and wealthy, not rich; to study hard, think quietly, talk gently, act frankly; to listen to stars and birds, to babes and sages, with open heart; to bear all cheerfully, do all bravely, await occasions, hurry never; in a word, to let the spiritual, unbidden, and unconscious, grow up through the common—this is to be my symphony."

664. The late William L. Sullivan in his autobiography, *Under Orders,* wrote: "So at the end of the long journey I have come to this: the first article of my creed is that I am a moral personality under orders."

665. "My message has been very simple," wrote Joseph Fort Newton. "To live well we must have a faith fit to live by, a self fit to live with, and a work fit to live for—something to which we can give ourselves and thus get ourselves off our hands. We cannot tell what may happen to us in the strange medley of life. But we can decide what happens in us—how we take it, what we do with it—and that is what really counts in the end. How to take the raw stuff of life and make it a thing of worth and beauty—that is the test of living.

Life is an adventure of faith, if we are to be victors over it, not victims of it. Faith in the God above us, faith in the little infinite soul within us, faith in life and in our fellow souls—without faith, the plus quality, we cannot really live."

666. On his deathbed Voltaire was denied absolution by a priest because he refused to subscribe to the Catholic theology in its entirety. Voltaire answered: "I adore God. I love my friends. I do not hate my enemies. I abhor superstition."

667.
To keep my health!
To do my work!
    To live!
To see to it I grow and gain and give!
Never to look behind me for an hour!
To wait in weakness and to walk in
    power.
But always fronting onward toward the
    light,
Always and always facing toward the
    right,
Robbed, starved, defeated, fallen, wide
    astray—
On with what strength I have
Back to the way!
—CHARLOTTE P. GILMAN, "Resolve"

668. E. Stanley Jones has summarized world philosophies in this manner: Greece said, "Be moderate—know thyself"; Rome said, "Be strong—order thyself"; Confucianism says, "Be superior—correct thyself"; Shintoism says, "Be loyal—suppress thyself"; Buddhism says, "Be disillusioned—annihilate thyself"; Hinduism says, "Be separated—merge thyself"; Mohammedanism says, "Be submissive—assert thyself"; Judaism says, "Be holy—conform thyself"; modern materialism says, "Be industrious—enjoy thyself"; modern dilettanteism says, "Be broad—cultivate thyself"; Christianity says, "Be Christlike—give thyself."—*The Christ of the Indian Road*

669. One minister, unable to accept much of the orthodoxy of his church, explained his solution in this way: "I get around the difficult points; I make the choir chant the creed."

CRITICISM

670. "It is literally true that in judging others we trumpet abroad our secret faults," writes J. A. Hadfield in *Psychology and Morals*. "Allow any man to give free vent to his feelings about others, and then you may with perfect safety turn and say, Thou art the man."

671. Mrs. Henry Nelson Weiman has said: "People must earn the right to criticize."

672. John Ruskin once defined a critic as "one who cannot paint."

673. A man complained that he had but one talent. "What is that talent?" asked an interested friend. "The talent of criticism." "Well," advised the friend, "I should suggest that you do with that talent what the man of one talent in the parable did. Criticism may be useful when mixed with other talents, but those whose only ability is to criticize might as well be buried, talent and all."

674. A visitor in an art gallery was criticizing many of the masterpieces. "I do not care for your pictures," he said to the man in charge. "Sir," was the reply, "it is our visitors and not our pictures that are on trial."

675. It happened once that upon his first visit to the Sistine Chapel a tourist could see nothing admirable in Michel-

angelo's frescoes. Nor did he hesitate to "snarl his displeasure." However, he decided, quite wisely, that perchance the judgment of the race was right, and his wrong. He therefore kept returning to those works of art until the beauty they embodied was born anew in him. He then began to see their deeper meaning.—HAROLD COOKE PHILLIPS, *Sails and Anchors*

676. When, following the Civil War, Robert E. Lee was president of Washington College, a professor criticized Grant. "Sir," Lee remonstrated, "if ever I hear you speak again in my presence disrespectfully of General Grant, either you or I will sever his connection with this institution."

677. "It was my custom in my youth," says a celebrated Persian writer, "to rise from my sleep, to watch, pray, and read the Koran. One night, as I was thus engaged, my father, a man of practiced virtue, awoke. 'Behold,' said I to him, 'thy children are lost in irreligious slumbers, while I alone wake to praise God.' 'Son of my soul, said he, 'it is better to sleep than to wake to remark the faults of thy brethren.'"

678. Said the minister at the funeral of a man who was widely known for his troublesomeness: "Well, I can say one good thing about him. He wasn't always as mean as he was sometimes."

679. Thomas Carlyle addressed these words to the Frenchman Voltaire: "Have you only a torch for destruction? Have you no hammer for building?"

680. After Sir Isaac Newton had published his law of gravitation, one of his critics exclaimed: "This crazy mathematician will not have twenty followers in his lifetime." The critic's judgment

was right, but another generation responded enthusiastically to Newton's theory.

681. There is an old story of a woman who made artificial fruits so perfectly that people could not tell them from the real fruit. But she had some critics who would find fault with the shape of the fruit, the color, and other things. One day as the critics stood before a table on which she had placed several pieces of fruit, they criticized particularly one apple. When they had finished, the woman picked up the apple, cut it in half, and began to eat it, for it was a real apple.—HOMER H. ELLIOTT

682. When a student of Whistler brought for the artist's criticism a picture of a woman holding a candle, the master made one comment: "How beautifully you have painted the candle!"

683. Harry Emerson Fosdick tells of the cowboy, enraged at the villain in a cinema, who began shooting at the screen where the figures moved instead of at the projector where they originated.—*On Being a Real Person*

684. When a friend brought a painting to Sir Joshua Reynolds, the latter was asked to appraise it. Wanting to be considerate, Sir Joshua said: "The composition is good; the coloring is admirable, but—" He hesitated, then, snapping his fingers, said: "It wants *that!*"

685. An ambitious young author took a manuscript to George Bernard Shaw for criticism. While the youth read his writing, Shaw dozed and then fell asleep. The youth remonstrated, saying that he had come for Shaw's comments. "My dear boy," Shaw said, "sleep is a comment."

686. The story is told of a woman who never criticized another person. Some of her friends, wishing to tempt her, began speaking about a good-for-nothing character. "Well," said the woman at length, "he is a good whistler. At least we can give him credit for that."

687. In a letter to a friend Benjamin Franklin showed the following attitude toward the many censures he received in his public life: "Such censures I have generally passed over in silence; conceiving when they were just that I ought rather to amend than defend; and when they were undeserved that a little time would justify me. Splashes of dirt thrown upon my character I suffered while fresh to remain. I did not choose to spread by endeavoring to remove them, but relied on the vulgar adage that they would all rub off when they were dry."

CROSS

688. Some years ago E. Stanley Jones said: "All my life I have borne a cross. Recently that cross was lifted. Now I find myself praying for another cross, because my cross has made me what I am today."

689.
I made the cross myself whose weight
   Was later laid on me.
This thought is torture as I toil
   Up life's steep Calvary.

To think mine own hands drove the
   nails!
   I sang a merry song,
And chose the heaviest wood I had
   To build it firm and strong.

If I had guessed—if I had dreamed
   Its weight was meant for me,

I should have made a lighter cross
　　To bear up Calvary!
　　　　　—ANNE REEVE ALDRICH,
　　　　　"A Little Parable"

690. "What do you see in life?" a spiritual teacher asked a woman who came to him for counsel. "I suppose I see what everyone sees—a question mark written large across the horizon," she answered. "Don't see a question mark. See a cross," was his wise and searching reply.

691. On the outskirts of London there stands a white cross. One day in the heart of the city a policeman heard a little boy crying as if his heart would break. Presently he found the child and asked: "What's the matter, my boy? Can I help you?" "Oh," replied the child, "I am lost." "Well, don't cry. We can fix that," said the officer, adding, "Where do you live?" "If you will take me to the hill where the white cross stands, I can find my way," the boy answered.

692. George Buttrick in his book *Prayer* writes that the carpenters who belonged to the early guilds chose as their motto these words of Jesus, "I am the door." Therefore they decided to make all doors so that the two smaller upper panels and the two larger lower panels would form a cross, and this custom has come down to our own times.

693. The Russian cross has two crossbars, one rather oblique. The reason is thought to be this: A priest said to his flock, "You will not obey the cross; you will not live right; so I take the cross out of the church." He did. But there was such an outcry that he brought back

the cross, "canceled." "I bring it back to you, but I bring it back with a line drawn through it, for you have canceled the cross."—E. STANLEY JONES, *Abundant Living*

694. A missionary to Ethiopia found crosses everywhere—on trees, scratched on rocks, on the huts. When he asked what they meant, one man said he did not know: "Our fathers made them, and we make them."—ARTHUR C. BALDWIN

695. Florence Converse has a story, "Crux Ave, Spes Unica," in which Mr. Budget, blueprint in hand, proposes to take down an old cross as a thing out of date and unsightly. He intends to erect in its place a short-wave radio station, to broadcast a modern religion with no cross in it. The wrecking crew tries with ropes, ladders, and tools to pull the old cross down—warning a poor "lunatic," the only sane man on the scene, not to let it fall on him. Having failed to pull it down, they try to dig it up, but that fails too. The "lunatic" tells them why: "They can't pull it over. They can't dig it up. It's from the beginning. It's the core of Creation."—JOSEPH FORT NEWTON, *His Cross and Ours*

696.
Three workmen fashioning a cross
　　On which the fourth must die!
Yet none of any other asked
　　"And why? And why? And why?"
Said they: "This is our business,
　　Our living we must earn;
What happens to the other man
　　Is none of our concern!" [19]
　　　　　—CLYDE McGEE, "Cross Makers"

[19] Used by permission of Betty McGee.

D

DARKNESS

697. A small Indian boy, sitting with his father near a campfire, said: "What does the fire eat, Father?" The father answered: "It eats the forest, dark and tall, but most of all it feeds on the darkness of the night."

698. The coal mines at Sydney, Cape Breton, run out several miles under the ocean. Horses are used in these mines. After a time spent under ground they become blinded if brought to the surface, so they are kept at their undersea work as long as they can work.—AVERY ALBERT SHAW, *The Tent and the Sky*

DAY

699. Two travelers, one a veteran and the other a novice, were climbing in the Pyrenees. At night they were caught on one of the peaks and had to sleep upon a ledge. Toward morning a storm came up, and the howling wind wailed fiercely among the heights. The frightened novice awakened his friend and said, "I think it is the end of the world!" "Oh, no," said the veteran, "this is how the dawn comes in the Pyrenees!"
—HILAIRE BELLOC

700.
Listen to the Exhortation of the Dawn!
Look to this Day!
For it is Life, the very Life of Life.
In its brief course lie all the
Verities and Realities of your Existence:
  The Bliss of Growth,
  The Glory of Action,
  The Splendor of Beauty,

For Yesterday is but a Dream,
And Tomorrow is only a Vision:
But Today well-lived makes
Every Yesterday a Dream of Happiness,
And every Tomorrow a Vision of Hope.
Look well therefore to this Day!
Such is the Salutation of the Dawn!
—*Based on the Sanskrit ca.* 1200 B.C.

701. "Each new day is an opportunity to start all over again, . . . to cleanse our minds and hearts anew, and to clarify our vision," wrote Oliver Wendell Holmes. "And let us not clutter up today with the leavings of other days."

702. "Let every dawn of morning be to you as the beginning of life," said John Ruskin, "and every setting sun be to you as its close; then let every one of these short lives leave its sure record of some kindly thing done for others, some goodly strength or knowledge gained for yourself."

703. A Knight's Prayer in the Children's Corner of Chester Cathedral reads: "My Lord, I am ready on the threshold of this new day to go forth armed with thy power, seeking adventure on the high road, to right wrong, to overcome evil, to suffer wounds and endure pain if need be, but in all things to serve thee bravely, faithfully, joyfully, that at the end of the day's labor, kneeling for thy blessing, thou mayst find no blot upon my shield. Amen."

704. "For my own part," wrote William Lyon Phelps, "I live every day as if this

were the first day I had ever seen and the last I were going to see."

705. So here hath been dawning
Another blue day:
Think, wilt thou let it
Slip useless away?
—Thomas Carlyle, "Today"

706. So brief the hour
For work or play,
Why grieve the night
Or waste the day?
—Frances M. Lipp

DEATH

707. I am standing upon the seashore. A ship at my side spreads her white sails in the morning breeze and starts for the blue ocean. She is an object of beauty and strength, and I stand and watch her until at length she is only a ribbon, or white cloud, just where the sea and sky come to mingle with each other. Then someone at my side says: "There! She's gone!" Gone where? Gone from my sight—that is all. She is just as large in mast and hull and spar as she was when she left my side, and just as able to bear her load of living freight— to the place of destination. Her diminished size is in me, not in her; and just at the moment when someone at my side says: "There! She's gone!" there are other voices ready to take up the glad shout, "There she comes!" And that is dying.

708. When asked why he made nothing of death, Pionius of Smyrna replied: "We are bent not upon death but upon life."

709. When death had brought grief to the home of Thomas Carlyle, a friend opened the Bible and read the words, "Let not your heart be troubled. In My Father's house are many mansions."

"Aye," muttered Carlyle, "if you were God, you had a right to say that; but if you were only a man, what do you know any more than the rest of us?"— James S. Stewart, *The Strong Name*

710. There stands in one of the great art galleries a big bronze bas-relief called "The Sculptor and the Angel of Death." It is the figure of a young, ambitious sculptor busy at a block of marble. He had already released from it the fine face of a figure that he eagerly aspires to set free. The worker with his carefully placed chisel is ready to strike with his uplifted mallet when the Angel of Death, who has suddenly appeared, touches him to stop, and with a look of surprise and dismay the unfinished thing must be left so.—M. S. Rice, *The Distinction of the Indistinguished*

Attitude Toward Death

711. When during World War I, Sir Harry Lauder, the great Scot comedian, heard that his son had been killed in France, he said: "In a time like this there are three courses open to a man. He may give way to despair, sour upon the world, and become a grouch. He may endeavor to drown his sorrow in drink or by a life of waywardness and wickedness. Or he may turn to God."

712. The last words of Jean Valjean in Victor Hugo's *Les Miserables* were: "Children, I can no longer see clearly. Think of me a little. I know not what is the matter with me, but I see light."

713. When O. Henry, the short-story writer, was dying on June 5, 1910, he whispered to someone near him: "Turn up the light. I don't want to go home in the dark."

714. John Wesley in his *Journal* gives this record of his mother's death: "From three to four the silver cord was loosing, and the wheel breaking at the cistern; and then the soul was set at liberty. We stood round the bed and fulfilled her last request: 'Children, as soon as I am released, sing a psalm of praise to God.'"

715. Shortly before his death a friend said to Henry Thoreau: "Have you made your peace with God, Henry?" To this Thoreau replied: "I don't know that we ever quarrelled."

Fear of Death

716. Friends advised Caesar to take certain measures for the protection of himself. "He who lives in the fear of death," Caesar said, "every moment feels its torture; I will die but once."

717. A survivor of the *Lusitania* reported that Charles Frohman, who was drowned, said: "Why should we fear death? It is life's finest form of adventure."

718.
Death stands above me, whispering low
  I know not what into my ear;
Of his strange language all I know
  Is, there is not a word of fear.
        —WALTER SAVAGE LANDOR,
        "Death Stands Above Me"

719. After the death of Alexander the Great one of his generals, Ptolemy Philadelphus, inherited Egypt and lived his life amid wealth and luxury. As he grew old, he was haunted by the fear of death and even sought in the lore of Egyptian priests the secret of eternal life. One day, seeing a beggar lying content in the sun, he murmured: "Alas, that I was not born one of these!"
—CECIL F. WILSON

Death a Pilgrimage

720. The epitaph on the grave in Canterbury, England, of Henry Alford, writer of the hymn "Ten Thousand Times Ten Thousand" is: "The inn of a pilgrim journeying to Jerusalem."

721. Christmas Evans, great Welsh preacher, when at the point of death, bade farewell to his friends and turning his head exclaimed, "Drive on! Drive on!" as if he saw Christ's chariot come for him.

722. On a simple gravestone in Kenya, South Africa, is this inscription: "Lord Baden-Powell, Chief Scout of the World. Born February 22nd, 1857, died January 8th, 1941." Underneath is a circle with a dot in the center, which is the scout sign for "I have gone home."

723.
The grave itself is but a covered bridge
Leading from light to light, through a
  brief darkness.
—LONGFELLOW, "The Golden Legend"

Preparation for Death

724. After a group of soldiers had been entertained in London, one man stood to thank the hosts of the evening. Then, almost as an afterthought, he added: "We are soon crossing to France and to the trenches, and very possibly, of course, to death. Will any of our friends here tell us how to die?"

725. John Huss, the fourteenth-century Bohemian religious reformer, was called before the Council of Constance. In the presence of both pope and emperor Huss was advised to submit. "If you do this," one of the cardinals said, "you will best consult your safety and your standing." Without consideration for his safety or standing he remained firm to the truth as he saw it. From prison

he later wrote: "I write this in prison and in chains, expecting tomorrow to receive sentence of death, full of hope in God that I shall not swerve from the truth, nor abjure errors imputed to me by false witnesses. . . . In the truth which I have proclaimed according to the gospel of Jesus Christ . . . I will, this day, joyfully die."

726. Shortly before his death Augustine begged one of his disciples to paint on the wall opposite his bed the words of the thirty-second psalm: "Blessed is he whose transgression is forgiven, whose sin is covered. Blessed is the man unto whom the Lord imputeth not iniquity." And gazing upon these words, he died.

727. A twenty-two-year-old Dutch patriot wrote the following letter to his parents before he was executed by a Nazi firing squad for the crime of trying to escape with his three companions to England and join the Dutch forces there: "In a little while at five o'clock it is going to happen, and that is not so terrible. . . . On the contrary, it is beautiful to be in God's strength. God has told us that he will not forsake us if only we pray to him for support. I feel so strongly my nearness to God I am fully prepared to die. . . . I have confessed all my sins to him and have become very quiet. Therefore do not mourn but trust in God and pray for strength. . . . Give me a firm handshake. God's will be done. . . . Greet everybody for the four of us. . . . We are courageous. Be the same. They can only take our bodies. Our souls are in God's hands. . . . May God bless you all. Have no hate. I die without hatred. God rules everything."—*This Week*

728. When asked how he felt, Benjamin Parsons during his last illness is reported to have said: "My head is resting very sweetly on three pillows—infinite power, infinite wisdom, and infinite love."

729. Bishop Joseph Lightfoot, during the last moments of his life, was asked by his chaplain what he was doing. "I am feeding on a few great thoughts," the bishop said.

730. The grave of Dr. Elisha Mitchell, who lost his life trying to scale the highest peak in the Blue Ridge Mountains of North Carolina, is marked with these words: "He reached the heights to rest in peace."

DECISION

731. Whenever Robinson Crusoe had an important decision to make, he would write down two columns of reflections and reasons why he should and why he should not do that certain thing. One column was for and the other column was against the course to be chosen. After a while he would look over his thoughts, thus lined up like soldiers for his inspection, and the right decision would come to the fore.

732. Traveling through the archipelago of southern Alaska, one passes first around Cape Decision before he finds himself at Christian Sound.

733. These are the words of Marshal Foch, spoken at one of the most critical moments of World War I: "My right has been beaten back. My left is periled. My center is wavering. The situation is ideal. I attack."

734. Henry Drummond's suggestions for decisive Christian living were: (1) Pray. (2) Think. (3) Talk to wise people, but do not regard their decision as final. (4) Beware of the bias of your

own will, but do not be too much afraid of it. God does not necessarily thwart a man's nature and likings, and it is a mistake to think that his will is in the line of the disagreeable. (5) Meanwhile do the next thing, for doing God's will in small things is the best preparation for doing it in great things. (6) When decision and action are necessary, go ahead. (7) Never reconsider the decision when it is finally acted upon. (8) You will probably not find out till afterwards, perhaps long afterwards, that you have been led at all.

DEDICATION

735. Winifred Holtby in *Letters to a Friend* tells of a dedication service for a fellow student who was going to China as a missionary. "It must be nice," she wrote, "to decide to dedicate oneself to one particular form of service as she did when she was about twelve, and then train, prepare, and go and do it. And on your going, to have eight hundred people to pray over you and say that you do right. There is a satisfactory definiteness and conviction there about things. . . . The difficulty is to what can one dedicate oneself. I am blown about by a wandering wind of great pity and sorrow and desire, while my weakness and self-indulgence and timidity keep me tied to earth."

736. When Francis Asbury left for America, he made this entry in his diary: "Whither am I going? To the new world! What to do? To gain honor? Not if I know my heart! To get money? No! I am going to live to God and to bring others so to do."

737. In the year 1623 an English farmer thought: "The world needs a man, a good man, a great man, a strong man."

He seemed to hear a voice saying, "Thou art the man." That evening this person, Oliver Cromwell, was reading from the fourth chapter of Philippians. He later said: "I came to the thirteenth verse where Paul saith, 'I can do all things through Christ which strengtheneth me.' Then faith began to work and my heart to find comfort and support, and I said to myself, 'He that was Paul's Christ is my Christ too,' and so I drew water out of the wells of salvation." In London, Cromwell later became leader of the Puritan Commonwealth Government.

DEED

738. "Cast thy word, thy deed, into the ever-living, ever-working present," challenged Thomas Carlyle.

739.

I spoke a word,
And no one heard;
I wrote a word,
And no one cared,
Or seemed to heed;
But after half a score of years
It blossomed in a fragrant deed.

Preachers and teachers all are we,—
Sowers of seeds unconsciously.
Our hearers are beyond our ken,
Yet all we give may come again
With usury of joy or pain.
We never know
To what one little word may grow.
See to it then that all your seeds
Be such as bring forth noble deeds.[1]
—JOHN OXENHAM, *"A Little Word"*

DEFEAT

740. In his *Life of Woodrow Wilson,* Josephus Daniels writes: "Wilson never

[1] Used by permission of the author's daughter, Erica Oxenham.

knew defeat, for defeat never comes to any man until he admits it. Not long before the close of his life Woodrow Wilson said to a friend: 'Do not trouble about things we have fought for. They are sure to prevail. They are only delayed.' With the quaintness which gave charm to his sayings, he added: 'And I will make this concession to Providence—it may come in a better way than we propose.'"

741. When he was defeated for reelection to the Senate, Albert J. Beveridge determined that he would not despair. He plunged into the writing of *John Marshall* and then turned to the writing of *Abraham Lincoln*. These volumes will be read by the lovers of biography for years to come, and through them he will be remembered longer than if he had served out his life in legislature.

742.
Not in the clamor of the crowded street,
   Not in the shouts and plaudits of the throng,
But in ourselves are triumph and defeat.
   —LONGFELLOW, *"The Poets"*

DEMOCRACY

743. "Democracy is not simply politics, election by a majority, government by a parliament," said Harry Emerson Fosdick. "It is also the conviction that there are extraordinary possibilities in ordinary people and that if the doors of opportunity are thrown open wide enough surprising consequences will come from unlikely sources."

744. W. W. Charters has summarized the characteristics of the democratic pattern of life in this manner: (1) respect for the dignity and worth of the individual human personality; (2) open opportunity for the individual; (3) economic and social security; (4) the search for truth; (5) free discussion; freedom of speech; freedom of the press; (6) universal education; (7) the rule of the majority; the rights of the minority; the honest ballot; (8) justice for the common man; trial by jury; arbitration of disputes; orderly legal processes; freedom from search and seizure; right to petition; (9) freedom of religion; (10) respect for the rights of private property; (11) the practice of the fundamental social virtues; (12) the responsibility of the individual to participate in the duties of democracy.—*Heirs of Democracy*

745. William Pierson Merrill in his book *Christian Internationalism* says: "The early Christian churches were the first truly democratic communities in the world."

746. Thomas Mann, the novelist, has defined democracy as the political expression of Christianity.

DESIRE

747. "There are two tragedies in life," wrote George Bernard Shaw. "One is not to get your heart's desire. The other is to get it."

748. Sociologists speak of the four fundamental needs each person must have in order to be at peace. These are called Thomas' Four Wishes and are the wishes for security, new experience, recognition, and response.

749. A young woman who has traveled the world over for an international organization, and who has had unusual opportunity to make friends in many lands, was asked what common wants she found in people wherever she went. "Everywhere," she replied, "I find people having three great wants. First, they want some degree of physical comfort—

food, freedom to move about, shelter. Second, they want the approval of their fellows. And third, they want some assurance as to what life means."—LOIS H. FLINT, *Learning to Live*

750. Edgar Sheffield Brightman told a group of high school students: "Everybody wants something. The practical man is the man who knows how to get what he wants. The philosopher is the man who knows what man ought to want. The ideal man is the man who knows how to get what he ought to want."

751. There are two ways of growing rich: adding to our possessions or simplifying our wants. By the latter process our essential riches are greatly increased.—AVERY ALBERT SHAW, *The Tent and the Sky*

752. William J. Hutchins, president of Berea College, tells of a man who visited the mountain store and saw a bunch of bananas for the first time. The storekeeper said, "Try one." The answer was abrupt, "No, I ain't going to." "Why not?" asked the storekeeper. The mountaineer replied, "I got so many tastes now I can't satisfy, I ain't goin' to add another one."—G. BROMLEY OXNAM, *Preaching in a Revolutionary Age*

DESPAIR

753. One day when Luther was downcast and despairing, his wife came into the room, saying: "Have you not heard the news? God is dead!" Luther told his wife not to blaspheme. Then she said: "And if God is not dead, what right have you, his servant, you a Christian man, to be so downcast and depressed?"

754. Robert Cushman, one of the Pilgrims who sailed on the "Mayflower" in 1620, wrote to a friend just before the ship left Holland: "If we ever make a plantation in the new world, God works a miracle! Specially considering how scant we shall be of victuals, and most of all ununited amongst ourselves. If I should write you of all the things which promiscuously forerun our ruin, I should overcharge my weak head and grieve your tender heart. Only this I pray you. Prepare for evil tidings of us every day. Pray for us instantly. I see not in reason how we shall escape."

755. The Duke of Wellington is reputed to have said just before his death: "I thank God that I shall be spared from seeing the consummation of ruin that is settling in around us."

756. "I tell you it's no joke to paint a portrait!" said William Morris Hunt, famous portrait painter. "Into the painting of every picture that is worth anything there comes, sometime, this period of despair!"

757. General Washington, writing from Valley Forge to the President of the Continental Congress in January, 1778, reported that only 572 troops were fit for duty. "Unless there is a great and capital change, this army must inevitably be reduced to one or other of these three things: starve, dissolve, or disperse in order to obtain subsistence in the best manner they can." Nearly 3,000 of the 17,000 men then in camp were unfit for duty because they were barefoot and otherwise naked, he added.

DETERMINATION

758. Day after day during his voyage to America, Columbus made the following determined entry in his diary: "This day we sailed on."

759. Something of the reason for Thomas Edison's success is explained by an ex-

perience in his childhood. "One day," Edison wrote, "I overheard the teacher tell the inspector that I was 'addled,' and it would not be worth while keeping me in school any longer. I was so hurt by this last straw that I burst out crying and went home and told my mother." But instead of becoming discouraged, he became determined, and no person after that day had reason to speak of Edison in that manner.

760. Realizing the difficulties which his students faced, General Samuel Chapman Armstrong, founder of Hampton Institute, the first school for Negroes to be organized after the Civil War, told them: "Once there was a woodchuck. Now, all of you know that woodchucks can't climb trees. But one day this woodchuck was chased by a dog. He ran as fast as his short legs could carry him across the fields until he came to a tree. 'If I can only get up that tree,' he said to himself, 'I'll be safe.' He *had* to get up there, so he did. Overcoming handicaps is a matter of doing what often seems impossible."—Norris L. Tibbetts

761. Admiral Robert Peary wrote: "The determination to reach the Pole had become so much a part of my being that, strange as it may seem, I long ago ceased to think of myself save as an instrument for the attainment of that end."

762. After reading of Admiral Peary's struggles to reach the North Pole, a boy wrote in his diary: "I have decided to be the first man to reach the North Pole." Years later this person was not only the first man to fly over the North Pole but the first person to fly over the South Pole as well. His name, of course, is Richard E. Byrd.

763. In 1865 Charles Steinmetz was born in Breslau, Germany. The boy in- herited a spinal weakness which had plagued the lives of both his father and grandfather. While he was a baby, Steinmetz' mother died. He soon thereafter learned that his deformed body could never be straightened. While in the university he was accused of radicalism and had to leave Germany for Switzerland. In 1889, he arrived in New York, having traveled in the steerage of an immigrant liner. Poor, friendless, hunchbacked, this youth rose through determination to the position of world leadership in electrical research and engineering. Of him Archer Wallace has written: "This deformed hunchback had the mind of an angel and the soul of a seer."

764. An automobile careened around a bend in a road in the Ozarks and hit a preacher who was riding his horse to a pastoral call. The young man was hopelessly injured. The doctor, not wishing to cause further pain, ordered a tent be raised over the young man so that he might die in peace. But the youth had an indomitable will and he did not die. He remained in the tent for some time and while there he began to write a novel. The book was *When a Man's a Man*, and the author, who became one of the most widely read men of his day, was Harold Bell Wright.

765. In 1893 Robert Louis Stevenson wrote to a friend: "For fourteen years I have not had one day of real health. I have wakened sick and gone to bed weary, and yet I have done my work unflinchingly. I have written my books in bed and out of bed, written them when I was worn by coughing, written them during hemorrhages, written them when my head swam for weakness. I have now done this for so long that it seems to me I have won my wager and recovered my glove! But the battle still

goes on—ill or well is a trifle so long as it goes."

766. Nelson, when signaled at Copenhagen to withdraw from the fight, clapped the telescope to his blind eye and vowed he could see no signal.

767. Thomas Edison once said: "When everybody else is quitting on a problem, that is the time when I begin."

768. Pierre Curie—in the film story *Madame Curie*—exclaims after the 487th experiment fails: "It can't be done; it can't be done! Maybe in a hundred years it can be done, but never in our lifetime." To this his wife replies: "If it takes a hundred years, it will be a pity, but I dare not do less than work for it so long as I have life."

769. "O God," prayed a member of the Westminster Assembly long ago, "we beseech thee to guide us aright, for we are very determined."

770. When Napoleon found Moscow burned before him and his supplies fast running out, he faced round westward to begin the long retreat to Paris and summoned the man he could count on best, the brave Marshal Ney. "I appoint you, my Marshal," he said, "to command the rear guard. You are to keep the Russians back from the main body of my army. You are to be the breakwater between us and the deluge. You are to block their advance at any price, till I extricate my men from this trap of death and get them home to France." And Marshall Ney promised that he would do it. He drew his troops into lines and slowly, grimly they began to fight the way back, taking on themselves the full weight of the Russian march of death, enduring indescribable things from wounds and frost and famine.

So the terrible days and nights were past. And then, it is said, one day long afterward when some officers were playing cards in their quarters in Paris, the door of the room opened, and there stood before them the most dishevelled figure they had ever seen, old and bent and emaciated, his clothing tattered, his hands trembling, and lines of terrible suffering carved deep into his features. "Who are you?" they cried. But suddenly to one of them there came a flash of recognition. "Why," he exclaimed, springing to his feet, "it's the marshal! It's Marshal Ney!" "Tell us, Marshal," they said, "tell us—for we have been wondering—where *is* the rear guard?" And the bent, broken figure squared his shoulders a moment and looked them in the face: "Sirs, *I am* the rear guard!" And it was a fact. He alone had seen it through.—JAMES S. STEWART, *The Gates of New Life*

771. A visitor to the Hermitage many years after Andrew Jackson's death asked an old Negro who had known the president if Jackson had gone to heaven. The old man responded quickly: "If he sot his head that way, he did."

DEVIL

772. After seeing Guido Reni's famous painting in the Louvre which shows Michael with his foot on Satan's throat, William James said: "The world is all the richer for having a devil in it, *so long as we keep our foot upon his neck.*"

773. One night Thomas Carlyle took Ralph Waldo Emerson through the dark streets of one of London's worst sections and commented: "Do you believe in the devil now?"

DEVOTION

774. "We are not devout," wrote Jean Grou in the eighteenth century, "just because we are able to reason well about the things of God, nor because we have grand ideas or fine imaginations about spiritual matters, nor because we are sometimes affected by tears. Devotion is not a thing which passes, which comes and goes, as it were, but it is something habitual, fixed, permanent, which extends over every instant of life and regulates all our conduct."—Douglas V. Steere, *Prayer and Worship*

775. Francis of Sales wrote: "Devotion is simply the promptitude, fervor, affection, and agility which we have in the service of God: and there is a difference between a good man and a devout man; for he is a good man who keeps the commandments of God, although it be without great promptitude or fervor; but he is devout who not only observes them but does so willingly, promptly, and with a good heart."

DIFFICULTY

776. "The pessimist sees the difficulty in every opportunity," wrote L. P. Jacks. "The optimist, the opportunity in every difficulty."

777. The following story is told by W. M. Clayton: "Some years ago I met at a little watering place in Belgium an old man who told me he had for many years been a professional Swiss mountain guide. One thing he said to me I never have forgotten. We had been talking about the heights of mountains in Asia and North and South America in comparison with those of his native Switzerland when he remarked, more or less apropos of nothing: 'Remember this, young man. A mountain is never so high as from the bottom.' For a moment I stared at him, and he went on: 'When you stand at the base of a mountain you have never before climbed and looking up, contemplate the dangers

and difficulties and calculate the hidden ones while appraising those plainly to be seen—well, then that mountain looks *high*. But when you have actually scaled it and have overcome its difficulties and dangers, you begin to think it was not so very terrible after all, and even though you know how high it is in feet, still you are not so impressed as you were at the base.' "

778. "The battle of life is in most cases fought up hill," declared Edmund Burke, "and to win it without a struggle were perhaps to win it without honor. If there were no difficulties, there would be no success; if there were nothing to struggle for, there would be nothing to be achieved. Difficulties may intimidate the weak, but they act only as a wholesome stimulus to men of resolution and valor. All experience of life, indeed, serves to prove that the impediments thrown in the way of human advancement may, for the most part, be overcome by steady good conduct, honest zeal, activity, perseverance, and, above all, by a determined resolution to surmount difficulties and to stand up manfully against misfortune."

779. Giacomo Carissimi, when praised for the ease and grace of his melodies, exclaimed: "Ah! you little know with what difficulty this ease has been acquired."

DIRECTION

780. An Arkansas native had come to town for groceries, which the clerk was wrapping up in a newspaper. "Don't tear that paper," warned the native. "I want the gals to read it to me when I get home. No, I never learned to read. But I can figger! When I come to a signpost along the road, I can tell how far, but I don't know where to."—Paul E. Johnson, *Who Are You?*

781. Margaret T. Applegarth tells the story of a man who wanted to walk to Smithville. Reaching a signpost he was annoyed to see that while one arm pointed to a smooth, delightful road the other, marked "Smithville," pointed up a rough, steep path. Suddenly he had a happy thought. He climbed up, changed the signs around and set forth happily; but though he walked and walked, he never reached Smithville.

782. "He who chooses the beginning of a road chooses the place it leads to," Harry Emerson Fosdick has said.

783. A picture was once painted by a great artist who set the scene in a night background. Across the dark waters of a lonely lake a solitary man could be seen rowing a small boat. A high wind churned the waters of the lake into white-crested billows which raged around the little skiff. Above was a dark and angry sky. But through the blackness there shone one lone star. Upon this the rower fixed his gaze—and on through the storm he rowed. He was undismayed by the midnight blackness. Beneath the picture the artist had written: "If I lose that, I am lost."— W. HARRY FREDA

784. Bernard C. Clausen tells of an old sea captain who used to navigate his ship by stars painted on the ceiling of his cabin.

785. A deacon wanted to speak tactfully to a student who had supplied in the church. "I'll put my remarks in the form of a parable," the deacon smiled. "I recollect Archie Tucker's first deer hunt. He was kind of green. He followed the deer all right, but he followed it all day in the wrong direction."

DISCONTENTMENT

786. In the play made from Dostoevski's book *The Brothers Karamazov* the plot shows the dangers that arise from a disbelief in God, religion, and sin. The old rascal and roue, Feodor, asks Ivan, his philosophical son, if there is or is not any God, or immortality. Ivan answers, there is no God and not even a shred of immortality to hope for. "Why, then—why, then—Ivan! Everything is permissible," Feodor exclaims. "Yes, Father, everything is permissible," Ivan answers. "Sh! We won't talk about it. We will keep that to ourselves, dear boy," says Feodor. The drunken libertine appreciated better than did his intellectual son the consequences of such a belief. That hardened sinner knows more about the enormity of evil than the theorist.—EDWIN A. McALPINE, *Old and New Books as Life Teachers*

787. Gordon Graham wrote concerning discontent: "There are two kinds of discontent in this world; the discontent that works, and the discontent that wrings its hands. The first gets what it wants, and the second loses what it has. There's no cure for the first but success; and there's no cure at all for the second."

DISCOURAGEMENT

788. When asked what his most cherished tool of evil was, the devil said: "Discouragement. I can pry open and get inside a man's consciousness with that when I could not get near him with any of my other tools; and when once inside, I can use him in whatever way suits me best. It is much worn because I have used it on nearly everybody, yet few know that it belongs to me."

789. When a friend asked Douglas Haig during a particularly trying period in World War I if he was discouraged,

he replied: "Discouraged! A Christian man has no right to be discouraged in the same world as God."

790. The following story is often told of Edwin Booth: On an especially stormy night the audience in the theater numbered only a few rain-spattered men who remained in seats near the back of the house. When a discouraged cast pleaded with Booth that the play should be postponed, the great actor said, "No. We shall go on. Remember the king sits in every audience. Play to *him*." In the hours which followed Booth presented one of the finest performances of his honored career. A day or two later the king sent for Booth and made public the actor's words to his cast. Although Booth had been unaware of the fact, one of the men in the shadows of the last row of the theater on that stormy night had been none other than the king himself.

791. Robert Millikan has quoted a famous physicist who in 1893 said that all the great discoveries in physics had already been made and that future progress was to be looked for, not in bringing to light qualitatively new phenomena, but rather in making more exact quantitative measurements upon old phenomena. Millikan adds that it was after this speculation that the great modern discoveries of X rays, radioactivity, and the electron were made.

DISHONESTY

792. John Ruskin wrote that in one corner of a Venetian church he found the statue of a doge. The side toward the audience was elaborately finished; the side toward the corner was left rough. On the public side the forehead was carefully wrinkled, the cap beautifully chased, the ermine robe scrupu-

lously imitated; on the dark side the marble was unwrought. "Now," said Ruskin, "comes the very gist and point of the whole matter. This lying monument is at least veracious, if in nothing else, in its testimony to the character of the sculptor. He was banished from Venice for forgery in 1487."—HARRY EMERSON FOSDICK, *The Manhood of the Master*

793. The story goes that Sir Christopher Wren ran out of money near the end of the building of St. Paul's Cathedral in London. So he found it necessary to make the massive columns mere shells, filled with waste and rubbish. They were imposing looking, seemingly solid enough to last for centuries, but time told the story. The walls began to crack, and the dome tilted, and the sham was exposed.—WILLIAM E. PHIFER, JR., *The Cross and Great Living*

794. Some have called the disaster of crumbling buildings following the San Francisco earthquake an act of God, but a distinguished architect, after investigating the tragedy, reported: "Dishonest mortar was responsible for nearly all the earthquake damage in San Francisco."

795. According to an old legend a king ordered an architect to build him a palace. The architect, though bearing a good name, was dishonest. He erected a building which had a stately appearance but was made of shoddy material. When it was completed, the king said: "I have long meant to reward you for your excellent work. The palace is yours. Abide in it as long as you live."

DOUBT

796. When asked if he had ever been lost in the forest, Daniel Boone observed: "Never lost, but once in a while bewildered."

797. "Never be afraid of doubt," suggested Samuel T. Coleridge, "if only you have the disposition to believe."

798. "If you pray for bread and bring no basket to carry it," Dwight L. Moody used to say, "you prove the doubting spirit which may be the only hindrance to the boon you ask."

799. Charles H. Spurgeon said wisely: "It is never worth while to make rents in a garment for the sake of mending them, nor to create doubts in order to show how cleverly we can quiet them."

800. When Clarence Darrow said in a debate: "They tell me there is a God; but I have never seen him, I have never touched him, I have no personal acquaintance with him," Roy L. Smith replied: "It is credibly reported that Mr. Darrow has a mind; but I have never seen it, I have never touched it, I have no proof of it at all."

801. A student told Benjamin Jowett, master of Balliol College, that he found no positive evidence of the existence of God. "If you do not find God by five o'clock this afternoon," Jowett advised, "you will leave this college!"

DUTY

802. Robert Louis Stevenson told the story of a ship at sea in a time of storm. The passengers were in great distress. After a time one of them, against orders, went up on deck and made his way to the pilot. The seaman was at his post of duty at the wheel. When he saw the man was greatly frightened he gave him a reassuring smile. Then the man turned and went back to the other passengers

with such words of comfort as these: "I have seen the face of the pilot and he smiled. All is well."—ROBERT H. RIDLEY

803. The inscription on the statue of Robert E. Lee in the Hall of Fame reads: "Duty then is the sublimest word in our language. Do your duty in all things. You cannot do more. You should never wish to do less."

804. "Do the duty which lies nearest thee which thou knowest to be a duty," said Thomas Carlyle. "Thy second duty will already have become clearer."

805. "My duty I myself must do," said Josiah Royce. "Not even God can do it for me."

806. Andrew Carnegie suggested: "Do your duty and a little bit more, and you will always have success."

807.
The world is full of beauty,
  As other worlds above;
And if we did our duty
  It might be full of love.
—GERALD MASSEY

808.
So nigh is grandeur to our dust,
  So near is God to man,
When Duty whispers low, *Thou must*,
  The youth replies, *I can*.
—EMERSON, *"Voluntaries"*

809. When a young man asked the Duke of Wellington whether he did not deem it useless to attempt to convert India, the general replied sternly: "What are your marching orders, sir?"

810. It is said that a woman once called on the great Phillips Brooks, telling him that she had just returned from the Orient with a new religion which was to transform the world. "How did you

get through the customs office?" inquired the preacher. "Why, Dr. Brooks, you do not understand," the woman explained. "This is a new religion, and certainly the customs office has no interest in any such thing." "Oh, I see," the good man answered; "it has no duty connected with it."—ROY L. SMITH, *Suburban Christians*

811. In a heavy fog a great ocean liner came too near the New England coast, and the gale blew her on the rocks and pounded her mercilessly. But fortunately there was the Coast Guard. These men arrived and surveyed the situation. The group was under the command of a veteran captain, but there were several new members. One of these, with white face, said to the leader: "Sir, the wind is offshore, and the tide is running out. Of course we can go out, but what good will it do? Against the wind and the tide we cannot come back." But the captain replied: "Launch the boat. We have to go out. *We do not have to come back.*" —G. RAY JORDAN

E

EASTER

812. Bliss Perry declared: "Easter begins, like all deep things, in mystery and ends, like all high things, in courage."

813. On Easter, 1945, the Germans and the Allies on the Italian front, located four hundred yards apart, joined in the same Easter services. Germans who were in sight of the field altar withheld their fire while Protestant and Roman Catholic services were held and broadcast to German troops in the sector. Chaplain Reiboth of Seward, Nebraska, read the Easter story in German and in English; while Chaplain Crowley of Syracuse, New York, in his Easter message said: "A happy Easter. As an American chaplain I greet Protestants and Catholics in the German army. We have been instructed to love all men, even our enemies. Today is Easter Day—the day of Christ's triumph. Christ died and rose for all men, the Germans and the Americans alike, therefore I wish you also on behalf of my soldiers a happy Easter."

EDUCATION

814. "Whom, then, do I call educated?" asked Socrates. "First, those who control circumstances instead of being mastered by them; those who meet all occasions manfully and act in accordance with intelligent thinking; those who are honorable in all dealings, who treat good-naturedly persons and things that are disagreeable; and, furthermore, those who hold their pleasure under control and are not overcome by misfortune; finally those who are not spoiled by success."

815. "Education does not mean teaching people what they do not know," wrote John Ruskin. "It means teaching them to behave as they do not now behave."

816. When passed through the prism of human experience, the white light of the comprehensive statement "I live" reveals a beautifully illuminating spectrum. No one has really learned to live until he can convincingly say to himself the eleven great verbs of life: I am, I think, I know, I feel, I wonder, I see, I believe, I can, I ought, I will, I serve. Education, in both life and religion, is but the process of learning through experience the meaning of these fundamental verbs of life and acquiring the personal power of each:

I *am*—the power of self-knowledge
I *think*—the power to investigate
I *know*—the power to master facts
I *feel*—the power to appreciate, to value, to love
I *wonder*—the spirit of reverence, curiosity, worship
I *see*—the power of insight, imagination, vision
I *believe*—the power of adventurous faith
I *can*—the power to act and the skill to accomplish
I *ought*—the power of conscience, the moral imperative

I will—will power, loyalty to duty, consecration

I serve—the power to be useful, devotion to a cause.

—GEORGE WALTER FISKE, *The Recovery of Worship*

817. The first-year students in an ancient academy were called wise men; the second-year students were called philosophers; the third-year students were called disciples, learners.

818. "The secret of education," Emerson said, "lies in respecting the pupil."

819. "We come to college not to prepare to make a living but to learn to live a life" is the way one college student expressed his desire for higher education.

820. Over the arch to the entrance of the University of Virginia are these words: "Pass through this gateway and seek the light of truth, the way of honor, the will to work for men."

821. After the Civil War, General Robert E. Lee was offered much money for the use of his name. It was a good name, but it was not for sale. Instead he became president of a small college which had been ravaged by the war. "I have led the young men of the South in battle," he said; "I intend to give the remaining years of my life in training them to do their duty in the time of peace."

822. A few years ago in New York City a man died who had something of a record as far as formal education was concerned. When he was very young he received a bequest which offered him an allowance of two thousand dollars a year for as many years as he might wish to remain in school. With that opportunity he could not resist the temptation of continued schooling. When he died at the age of seventy-eight, he was still attending classes. He had secured eleven degrees in as wide a variety of subjects as medicine, business, law, economics, accounting, and engineering. One wonders if he had time with such an opportunity offered to put that knowledge to some use.

823. A young child conscious of the new knowledge she had learned in school, wistfully asked her mother, "Do I know now as much as I don't know?"

824. "Your brain shouldn't be a cold-storage chamber," an old schoolmaster of Ernest Raymond's used to say to his class, "but a powerhouse."

EFFORT

825. "O Lord," wrote Leonardo da Vinci in his notebook, "thou givest us everything, at the price of an effort."

826. "If you care enough for a result," wrote William James, "you will most certainly attain it. If you wish to be rich, you will be rich; if you wish to be learned, you will be learned; if you wish to be good, you will be good."

827. Benjamin Franklin in *Poor Richard's Almanac* wrote: "The man who does things makes many mistakes but he never makes the biggest mistake of all—doing nothing."

828. Writing concerning Henry Irving, the great Shakespearean actor, Ellen Terry said: "Henry Irving at first had everything against him as an actor. He could not speak; he could not walk; he could not *look*. He wanted to do things in a part, and he could not do them. His amazing power was im-

prisoned, and only after long and weary years did he succeed in setting it free."

829.
Before God's footstool to confess
   A poor soul knelt and bowed his head.
"I failed," he wailed. The Master said,
"Thou did'st thy best—that is success."
       —AUTHOR UNKNOWN

830. A man, discouraged by his failure to accomplish a certain worthy task, dreamed that an angel placed him before a rock, giving him a hammer and saying: "Pound and keep on pounding." The man wept because he could not break the rock. "Why do you weep?" asked the angel. "Because I cannot break the rock." "But," said the angel, "you have nothing to do with the results. Pound and keep on pounding, whether you break the rock or not."

831. When Lincoln was one day severely criticized, he said: "I do the very best I know how—the very best I can; and I mean to keep doing so until the end. If the end brings me out all right, what is said against me won't amount to anything. If the end brings me out wrong, ten angels swearing I was right would make no difference."

832. When a German officer told the Duke of Wellington of a feat by German soldiers and asked: "Could an equal number of British soldiers do that?" Wellington replied: "I don't know, but I do know that half that number would try."

833. A lad sat listening to a man forcefully quoting Kipling's poem "If":

If you can keep your head when all
   about you
Are losing theirs and blaming it on you,
If you can trust yourself when all men
   doubt you,
But make allowance for their doubting
   too;
If you can wait and not be tired by
   waiting,
Or being lied about, don't deal in lies,
Or being hated, don't give way to hating,
And yet don't look to good, nor talk too
   wise.[1]

At the close the lad said, "But what if you can't?"

834. A small boy had tried desperately to stand up on his ice skates. A lady who had watched him for some time asked why he didn't take off the skates and go home. "But I didn't get these skates to give up with. I got them to learn how," the boy protested.

835. In Lloyd Douglas' *Magnificent Obsession* a medical student was described as being criticized by the dean for poor scholarship. "Well, I'm doing average work, aren't I?" the boy protested. "Yes," said the dean, "but do you want to be an average doctor?"

836. There is a legend of a comfort-loving man who died and was borne to the other world where every wish was gratified. No effort, no struggle was required of him. He became bored and said: "I can't stand this everlasting bliss any longer. I want to feel there are things I cannot have. I want to go to hell." The attendant replied: "And where do you think you are sir?"— HARRY O. RITTER

837. Leo Tolstoy in his essay *Labor and*

[1] From *Rewards and Fairies* by Rudyard Kipling. Copyright 1910 by Rudyard Kipling. Reprinted by permission of Mrs. George Bambridge, Doubleday & Co., Macmillan & Co., Ltd., London, and The Macmillan Co., Canada.

Luxury suggests that to be complete personalities, men must enjoy four employments: employment of muscle in some hard labor; employment of fingers and hands in some form of skill; employment of mind and imagination; and employment of the faculty of fellowship.

ENCOURAGEMENT

838. A little boy who loved music was bitterly disappointed because he could neither play nor sing. One day he told his disappointment to Amati, the violin-maker, who said: "Come into the house and you shall try. The song in the heart is all that matters, for there are many ways of making music. Some play violins, some sing, some paint pictures, some carve statues, while others till the soil and grow flowers. Each sings a song and helps to make the music of the world. You can make music too." It was this encouragement which stimulated Antonio Stradivarius to become the world's greatest violinmaker.—MARY BETH FULTON

839. When Sir William Osler was a young man in medical school in Montreal, he was much discouraged about his future career. But, fortunately, one day he chanced to read these words of Carlyle: "Our main business in life is not to see what lies dimly at a distance but do what lies clearly at hand." These words struck Osler like a revelation. He went about repeating them to himself, quoting them to his friends, and writing them in his notebook.—J. MACK WILLIAMS

840. Next to a very narrow road leading to the "Cave of the Winds" near Colorado Springs, Colorado, is a sign which has encouraged many an apprehensive motorist: "You can do it as millions of others have."

841. Demosthenes came very near being lost to the world. At his first attempt to make a speech the whole crowd hissed him, and he was going to give up in despair, when someone who had heard him put new courage into him by saying that he spoke a little like Pericles. He tried a second time, and again the people hissed him. But as he was going away in utter despair, he was encouraged by one of the most successful actors of the day, who put a new heart in him. The world owes Demosthenes to these two men who spoke a word of cheer to a discouraged brother.

842. When Thomas Edison first invented the phonograph, its low tones were muffled and its high tones were harsh. Thereupon he employed a man to improve this situation. After two years of fruitless experimenting the man, completely discouraged, went to the great inventor and said: "Mr. Edison, I have spent thousands of your dollars and two years of my life and have accomplished nothing. Surely if there were a solution to this problem, I would have found it by now. I wish to resign." Edison looked him straight in the eyes and said: "George, I believe that for every problem God has given us he has a solution. We may not find it, but some day someone will. Go back and try a while longer."
—ROY W. PFAFF

843. The following verses by the Greek poet Theodoridas represent the inevitable desire of men to conquer where others have failed:

A shipwrecked sailor buried on this coast bids you set sail.
Full many a gallant ship, when this was lost, weathered the gale.

ENDURANCE

844. Although the Pilgrim Fathers experienced one of the most treacherous winters imaginable during their first months in New England, it is challenging to note that not one of those who survived expressed a desire to return to England when the "Mayflower" returned in the spring.

845. A trainer of a prize fighter was asked: "What is the difference between a good fighter and a great one?" He replied: "When the going gets tough, a great one lasts five minutes longer."

ENEMY

846. Edward Everett Hale toward the end of his life said: "I do not think anybody in the world ever had so many friends as I have had. However, I once had an enemy, a determined enemy, and I have been trying all day to remember his name."

847. "My soul is too glad and too great to be at heart the enemy of any man," wrote Martin Luther.

848. Antoine de Saint Exupéry in his *Wind, Sand and Stars* pictures Leo from the trenches in Spain calling out across eight hundred yards of no man's land to his "enemy" one night: "Hi, Antonio! Are you asleep? Antonio, it's me, Leo." Then the answer came: "Quiet! Go to bed! Time to sleep." But Leo calls again: "Antonio, what are you fighting for?" "Spain," is the answer. "And you?" Leo answers: "The bread of my brothers." After a pause one says: "Good night, friend." "Good night, friend," the reply is returned.

ENTHUSIASM

849. John Robert Seeley in *Ecce Homo* wrote: "No virtue is safe that is not enthusiastic."

850. William Lyon Phelps asked William R. Harper, onetime president of the University of Chicago, at the end of a long lecture day: "How do you keep so enthusiastic so late in the day, especially after teaching a subject as dry as Hebrew?" "Well," Dr. Harper replied, "if I have no enthusiasm, then I create it."

851. "What makes it possible for you to work so hard?" a white man asked his colored friend. "Well, 'tis dis way," was the answer. "I sticks de match ob enthusiasm to de fuse ob yenergy—and jes natchurally explodes, I does."

852. "Get on fire for God," John Wesley said, "and men will come to see you burn."

853. E. Stanley Jones tells of a young Burmese who left his Ashram group saying: "I came here a flickering torch, but I go away a flaming torch."

854. A painter who had more enthusiasm than ability saved his money and journeyed to Florence, where he was found one day before one of the supreme paintings of the world. Contritely he said to himself, "I too am a painter."

ETERNITY

855. Lorado Taft, an American sculptor, said of his profession: "What we sculptors need is to get back into our work the hint of eternity."

856. "He who has no vision of eternity," said Carlyle, "has no hold on time."

857. In his later years John Jay, first chief justice of the U.S. Supreme Court, used to say: "I have a long life to look back upon and an eternity to look forward to."

EXAMPLE   858-867

EVANGELISM

858. When criticized because of the evangelistic methods he used, Dwight L. Moody said: "I like my way of doing it better than your way of *not* doing it."

859. John Gossip, of England, tells this story: "Years ago in Glasgow I was hurrying to a meeting in a distant part of the city one Sunday morning before the cars began, and noticed what was then quite a new thing, the pavements chalked at intervals with invitations to a hall. I stopped a policeman and asked what it meant. 'These are socialists,' he said, 'and since very early morning they have been out and about, inviting the whole universe to a little place that will hold scarcely anyone. Believe me, sir, I disagree with them, but men so much in earnest as they are, are sure one day to sweep the city. What can hold them? What can keep them down?' and then he added: 'Why are you ministers not out and at it too? You have a case far better and more glorious. If you would only work for it as these men do for theirs, why, you would sweep the world.'"

EVIL

860. "This is a good universe," said Thomas Carlyle. "There is no permanent place in it for evil. Yea, it would seem as if God and man and the universe itself were opposed to evil. Evil may hide behind this fallacy and that, but it will be hunted from fallacy to fallacy until there is no more fallacy for it to hide behind."

861. Theodore Roosevelt at the ground breaking for the National Cathedral at Washington, D.C., said: "The times are evil; that is, there is much that is evil in them. It would be to our shame and discredit if we failed to recognize that evil; if we wrapped ourselves in a foolish optimism and failed to war with heart and strength against the evil. It would be equally to our discredit if we declined to strive for good because we feared the strength of evil. There is much evil. There is much good, too."

862. When Robert Owen summarized the fundamental evils of the world as religious perplexities, money difficulties, disappointment in love, intemperance, and anxiety for offspring, Emerson said: "You are very external in your evils, Mr. Owen. Let me give you some real mischiefs: living for show, losing the whole in particulars, indulgence of vital powers in trivialities."

863. "King Zeus," prayed the pagan Plato, "grant us the good whether we pray for it or not, but evil keep from us though we pray for it."

864. Socrates just before his death spoke to his accusers: "Wherefore, O judges, be of good cheer about death, and know this of a truth—that no evil can happen to a good man, either in life or after life."

EXAMPLE

865. Tertullian, one of the great church fathers, said that he and most of the converts who came out of paganism in his day were won to Christ, not by books or sermons, but by observing how Christians lived and died.

866. A Mohammedan said to E. Stanley Jones: "Our religion teaches us to fight, while yours teaches you to conquer by love. You should, therefore, show us a better example."

867. "People seldom improve when they have no model but themselves to copy," Oliver Goldsmith said.

868. "Tell me," a peasant said to Francis of Assisi, "art thou Brother Francis?" When Francis assented, the peasant said: "Try then to be as good as thou art of all folk held to be, seeing that many have faith in thee; and, therefore, I admonish thee that in thee there be nought save what men hope to find therein."

869. When Russell Conwell left Yale University to fight in the Civil War, a youthful admirer, Johnny Ring, was allowed to go along as Conwell's orderly. Conwell, then an unbeliever, made fun of Johnny's habit of reading his Bible and praying each night. One day after a surprise Confederate attack Conwell's men had to make a hasty retreat. Only after they had set ablaze a bridge they had crossed did Conwell realize that he had left his sword behind. Johnny ran back across the bridge, rescued the sword, but was so severely burned that he died a few days later. Conwell, near the body of his young friend, vowed that henceforth he would live two lives: one for himself and the other for Johnny Ring. His famous lecture "Acres of Diamonds" earned several millions of dollars. All of this was given to a hospital and a university which he founded.

870. Returning from a visit with Féne-lon, the archbishop of Cambrai, Lord Chesterfield said: "If I had stayed another day in his presence, I am afraid I would have become a Christian, his spirit was so pure, so attractive and beautiful."

871. While a missionary was giving an address to some Hindu ladies, one of them got up and walked out. After a short absence she returned and listened more intently than before. At the close the missionary asked her if she left because she was not interested. The Hindu replied: "Oh, yes, I was so interested in the wonderful things you were saying that I went out to ask your carriage driver whether you really meant it and whether you lived it at home. He said you did, so I came back to listen again."

872. Pompilia said of Caponsacchi:

Through such souls alone
God stooping shows sufficient of his light
For us i' the dark to rise by. And I rise.
—BROWNING, *The Ring and the Book*

873. "Do you know the Father?" Thomas Erskine of Linlathen asked a shepherd. The shepherd, taken aback, said nothing; but the wonderful tone and personality of the questioner made so deep an impression upon his mind that he could not get past the question put to him, nor dismiss it from his mind, with the remarkable result that, meeting Erskine many years afterward, the shepherd recognized him at once and said: "I know the Father now."—FRED-ERICK K. STAMM, *In the Shadow of the Cross*

874. Leslie D. Weatherhead tells of a rather pompous missionary bishop who visited an Indian community to examine candidates for baptism. The candidates were gathered together by the missionary, whom we will call Mr. Murray. The bishop asked the first native: "What is it to be a Christian?" Expecting a theological answer of some sort he was surprised to hear the candidate exclaim: "To live like Mr. Murray."—*In Quest of a Kingdom*

875. When Red Jacket, the great orator of the Iroquois, was urged to become a Christian, he told the missionaries that the Christians must prove their faith first. "Go, then, and teach the whites. Select, for example, the people of Buf-

falo. We will be spectators and remain silent. Improve their morals and refine their habits. Make them less disposed to cheat the Indians, to make them drunk, and to take from them their lands. Let us know the tree by the blossoms, and the blossoms by the fruit. When this shall be made clear to our minds, we may be more willing to listen to you. But until then we must be allowed to follow the religion of our ancestors."

EXPERIENCE

876. "Experience is like a costly comb given to a man whose hair is gone," reads a Turkish proverb.

877. "Experience," says Aldous Huxley, "is not what happens to a man; it is what a man does with what happens to him. It is a gift for dealing with the accidents of existence, not the accidents themselves."

878. Robert Browning one day was telling some people that he had once met Shelley. "And what else? What else happened to you on that outing?" they asked. "What else?" he cried, taken aback. "I tell you I saw Shelley, and, of course, in view of that, everything else just faded from my mind."—FREDERICK KELLER STAMM, *The Conversations of Jesus*

879. When Walpole accused William Pitt of being young, Pitt replied in words which will ever ring in Parliamentary history: "The atrocious crime of being a young man which the honorable gentleman has with such spirit and decency charged upon me, I shall neither attempt to palliate nor deny; but content myself with wishing that I may be one of those whose follies may cease with their youth, and not of that number who are ignorant in spite of experience."

EXPRESSION

880. "It is a law of the mind," writes E. Stanley Jones, "that that which is not expressed dies. All expression deepens impression. As someone has put it, 'Impression minus expression equals depression.' Our churches are filled with spiritual depression because there is so little spiritual expression."

881. Epictetus claimed: "I cannot give credence to a philosopher who professes to have found the secret of high living, and the power to conquer evil, if he speaks without animation, in a hang-dog fashion, with the face of a condemned man on his way to execution, and a moustache drooping in such a melancholy fashion that it seems to reach down to his knees. He does not look like a conqueror to me."

882. An old mountaineer was persuaded to leave his mountain home and live with his daughter in the city. Several weeks later, expressing his dissatisfaction, he returned to his own property. When asked why he returned, he said: "I just had to have something to lean my eyes against."

F

FACE

883. A Japanese woman, looking at the radiant faces of the girls in a mission school, asked the teacher if they took only pretty girls to be educated. "No," replied the missionary, "we take all the girls who come to us." "But," continued the Japanese mother, "all your girls seem to be pretty. What do you do to them?" "We teach them soul culture," smiled the teacher. Thoughtfully the mother said, "I do not want my daughter to become a Christian, but I shall send her to your school to get that look on her face."—R. BALLARD PEARSON

884. An old saying suggests: "The gods we serve write their names on our faces."

885. "When you speak of heaven," Charles H. Spurgeon told a group of seminary students, "let your face light up and be irradiated with a heavenly gleam. Let your eyes shine with reflected glory. And when you speak of hell—well, then your everyday face will do."

FAILURE

886. "The most important of my discoveries have been suggested to me by failures," said Sir Humphry Davy, the English chemist.

887. Eleven hundred unsuccessful experiments didn't mean failure to Edison. He said rather: "I found out eleven hundred ways how not to do things."

888. Longinus wrote: "In great attempts it is glorious even to fail."

889. Leonardo da Vinci raised himself slightly from his deathbed as the king entered his room, and said "that he had offended God and man in that he had not labored in art as he ought to have done."

890. A young woman leaped from an airplane, leaving this note behind: "I have had nothing but discord. I long for harmony. Perhaps I shall find music where I go."

891. Only a slender slab in Princeton Cemetery marks the grave of Aaron Burr. He was buried according to his request at the feet of his father and grandfather, both of whom were presidents of Princeton University. Some efforts were made soon after his death to procure a monument, but the project failed. For two years the spot where he lay was unmarked. One morning it was discovered that a small, inexpensive monument had been placed during the night over his remains. No one in the town saw the monument erected or knew anything about it.

892. When asked in an examination at the United States Naval Academy, "Why did the Spanish Armada fail?" one student wrote: "Because of three ships—leadership, marksmanship, and seamanship."

893. A visitor in India reported seeing on the signboard of a professional man the words: "B. A. failed." That meant he had gone as far as the examination for the degree but had failed to pass. It was viewed as a matter of distinction, not shame.—GEORGE W. RIDOUT

FAITH

894.
Faith is not merely praying
Upon your knees at night;
Faith is not merely straying
Through darkness to the light.

Faith is not merely waiting
For glory that may be.
Faith is not merely hating
The sinful ecstasy.

Faith is the brave endeavor,
The splendid enterprise,
The strength to serve, whatever
Conditions may arise.
—S. E. KISER, "Faith"

895. Says Dean W. R. Inge: "Faith is an act of self-consecration in which the will, the intellect, and the affections all have their place. It is the resolve to live as if certain things are true and we shall one day find out for ourselves that they are true. The process of verification begins as soon as we have honestly set out to climb. We ourselves change, and the world changes to our sight. The landscape opens out more and more as we get farther up the hill."

896. William James quoted a friend as saying: "As the essence of courage is to stake one's life on a possibility, so the essence of faith is to believe that the possibility exists."

897. A beautiful old allegory pictures Knowledge as a strong, handsome knight making his way over the great tableland of the earth. With each step he tests and makes certain of the ground beneath his feet. Beside him and just above the ground moves the white-winged angel Faith. Side by side they go until they come to the verge of a vast precipice. Here the path stops suddenly, and Knowledge can go no further. But the white-winged angel rises majestically from the ground and moves on across the chasm, leaving her companion behind.—MRS. RAY B. STRANG

898. Every personal confession of faith must begin, as does the famous Apostles' Creed, with the pronoun "I."

899. "Act on what faith you have," said Dr. Wilfred Grenfell. "Don't worry about what you haven't."

900. "Live *by* faith till you *have* faith," Peter Boehler said to John Wesley.

901. After facing much trouble a man was asked: "How is the outlook?" To this he answered: "The *outlook* is dark, but the *uplook* is wonderful."

902. Nothing before, nothing behind;
The steps of faith
Fall on the seeming void, and find
The rock beneath.
—JOHN G. WHITTIER,
"My Soul and I"

903.
In every seed to breathe the flower,
In every drop of dew
To reverence a cloistered star
Within the distant blue;
To wait the promise of the bow,
Despite the cloud between,
Is Faith—the fervid evidence
Of loveliness unseen.[2]
—JOHN B. TABB, "Faith"

[2] Reprinted by permission of the publisher, Dodd, Mead & Co., from *The Poetry of Father Tabb*.

904. Shortly before his assassination Lincoln, considering the four difficult years which he had passed through, said: "I have not controlled events. I would rather say that events have controlled me. But I have met them all with this faith."

905. Dwight L. Moody once said: "I suppose that if all the times I have prayed for faith were put together, it would amount to months. I used to say, 'What we want is faith; if we only have faith we can turn Chicago upside down,' or rather right side up. I thought that some day faith would come down and strike me like lightning. But faith did not seem to come. One day I read in the tenth chapter of Romans, 'Faith cometh by hearing, and hearing by the Word of God.' I had closed my Bible and prayed for faith. I now opened my Bible and began to study, and faith has been growing ever since."

906. One day Wendell Phillips, the abolitionist, met a devout Negro woman. When he marveled at her faith, she said: "I would give you some to take home with you, if you had anything to put it in."

907. The story is told of a man who stretched a strong cable across Niagara Falls, then pushed a wheelbarrow before him as he walked over the cable. A large crowd had gathered to watch him. The people almost held their breath. At last he was safely over, and the crowd cheered and cheered. Then he announced that on the morrow he would push a man over the cable in the wheelbarrow. Many said, "It cannot be done. He can never do it." Nevertheless, a large crowd gathered the next day and waited expectantly to see what would happen. Again it was expressed, "He cannot do it. I know it cannot be done." But a boy was heard to say, "Yes, he can do it; I know he can do it; he has a steady eye." Just then a man stepped up to the boy and said, "Do you really believe it can be done?" The boy answered, "Yes, I am sure he can do it." Then the man said: "I am glad to hear you say that, for I am the man who is going to push the wheelbarrow, and as yet I have not found a man who is willing to ride in it. Come on, let us go."

Faith in God

908. "The only faith which makes a Christian," said Martin Luther, "is that which casts itself on God for life or death."

909. Dr. David Seabury, the famous clinical psychologist, says of the many mental cases he has treated: "I have never been able to bring a man back to sanity and right thinking until I have brought him first to faith in God."

910. George Macdonald in *Robert Falconer* wrote: "This is a sane, wholesome, practical, working faith: first, that it is a man's business to do the will of God; second, that God takes on himself the special care of that man; and third, that therefore that man ought never to be afraid of anything."

911. "To believe that this terrible machine world is really from God," George Tyrrell said, "in God, and unto God, and that through it and in spite of its blind fatality all works for good—that is faith in long trousers."

912. "I bless myself and am thankful," declared Sir Thomas Browne, "that I never saw Christ or his disciples. I would not have been one of those Israelites that passed the Red Sea; nor one of Christ's patients, on whom he wrought his wonders: then had my faith been thrust upon me: nor should I enjoy the greater blessing pronounced to all that believe and saw not."

913. When John G. Paton, first missionary to the cannibals of the South Sea islands, was translating the New Testament into their language, he could not find an adequate equivalent for the word faith. One day a runner came into his tent out of breath and, with an exclamation, sank down upon his bamboo couch. Paton leaped to his feet crying, "That's it! That's it!" He asked the native to repeat the word. It meant that the native was casting his weight upon the bamboo couch. Paton said: "That's what faith in Christ is; it means to cast yourself upon Jesus Christ for reconciliation, for forgiveness, for redemption, for peace, and for everlasting life."

Inner Faith

914. "Man must be arched and buttressed from within," said Marcus Aurelius, "else the temple wavers to the dust."

915. Peter Forsythe wrote: "Unless there is *within* us that which is *above* us, we shall soon yield to that which is *about* us."

916. Maurice Maeterlinck, the Belgian poet and dramatist, tells of an old mansion in Europe with this motto carved on one of the beams: "Within me there is more."—PAUL E. SCHERER, *For We Have This Treasure*

917. A gentleman came to John McNeill saying that he had heard that the church was in debt and that he wished to help. He left a blank check and told the minister to fill in the amount. The minister, underestimating the good will

of the stranger, wrote in one half the sum of the church's indebtedness. Later the man returned, signed the check without looking at the figure, said he had always wanted to do something for God's work, and left. The stranger's heart was larger than the minister's faith.

Loss of Faith

918. One of Yale's foremost teachers of a generation ago began his career with a glowing religious faith and entered the ministry. When called from a pastorate to a chair of economics and social science, he considered himself a Christian believer. But as the years went by and he ceased to take any active part in religious efforts, he found himself slipping into less devout modes of thought and finally lost all religious interest. In explaining the change which had come over him he said: "I never consciously gave up a religious belief. It was as if I had put my beliefs into a drawer, and when I opened it, there was nothing there at all."—HENRY SLOANE COFFIN, *What Men Are Asking*

919. In prison Thomas Cranmer, Archbishop of Canterbury in the sixteenth century, recanted his faith. "Sign that document or die," he was instructed as he received the recantation notice. He signed but suffered great remorse for his failure to continue in faith. Later, in spite of the recantation, he was led out to die. He thrust his right arm first into the flames. "This unworthy hand," he said, "this which hath sinned, having signed the writing, must be the first to suffer," and he held it there till it was blackened and consumed; then he plunged into the martyr pyre himself.

920. James A. Froude, the English historian, wrote in his *Nemesis of Faith*: "When I go to church, the old church

of my old child days, when I hear the old familiar bells, with their warm, sweet heart music, and the young and old troop by along the road in their best Sunday dresses, old well-known faces and young unknown ones which by and by will grow to be so like them; when I hear the lessons, the old lessons, being read in the old way, and all the old associations come floating back upon me, telling me what I too once was, before I ever doubted things were what I was taught they were; oh, they sound so sad, so bitterly sad! The tears rise into my eyes; the church seems full of voices, whispering to me 'Infidel, Infidel, Apostate'; all these believing faces in their reverent attention glisten with reproaches, so calm they look, so dignified, so earnestly composed. I wish—I wish I had never been born."

Need of Faith

921. Justice Oliver Wendell Holmes at eighty said: "It is faith in something, enthusiasm for something, that makes life worth living."

922. H. Wheeler Robinson has told of a man, both skeptic and anarchist, who entered a church in Paris during the singing of the Mass: "Lamb of God, who takest away the sins of the world." The anarchist, pierced by a truth deeper than his arguments, exclaimed: "Oh, God! what a dream. If only He could!"
—GEORGE A. BUTTRICK, Christ and Man's Dilemma

923. "As human beings," says Harry Emerson Fosdick, "we are so made that we cannot help living in two worlds, the 'is' and the 'ought,' the actual and the possible, the factual and the ideal. Now the power which reaches out into the 'ought' and transforms it into the 'is,' which lays hold upon the possible and of it makes the actual, is creative faith."

Results of Faith

924. "A little faith will bring your soul to heaven," said Dwight L. Moody, "but a lot of faith will bring heaven to your soul."

925. Someone, while visiting in Scotland, found Purdy, an old family retainer, with fortune gone and home devastated by the years, still holding steady his faith in God. "How did you do it, Purdy?" he was asked, and this was his answer: "You see the outworks. For years they have lain in ruins. But that castle has always stood. So with me. When I lost all my savings, when I saw my Jim suffering, when Tom didn't come back from the war—well, as you might say, the outworks were stormed; but, sir, I've kept the castle. I haven't surrendered my faith, and hardness and bitterness have never got inside. And if they do, sir, it will be my fault."
—ROY A. BURKHART, Youth and the Way of Jesus

926. When George Fox was arrested by the soldiers of King Charles, they could not bend his spirit or make him deny his faith. They said of him: "He is as stiff as a tree, and as pure as a bell."

927. When William and Mary College, the oldest college in America, was closed in 1881, probably as a result of the financial struggle following the Civil War, President Benjamin Ewell for seven long years rang the bell each morning. The bell ringing, which typified the president's faith, was at last rewarded when the college reopened its door to students.

928. When Bishop William S. Lewis asked a young Chinese why, having refused a splendid position with the government, he offered himself as a Christian preacher, the youth said: "During the Boxer uprising I lived in an inland village where there was a temple for devil worship. The Christians were led by the soldiers to that temple and ordered to renounce their religion and bow before the devil image or be executed. I saw 163 of my townsmen walk by the devil god with heads erect, when a little bow would have saved their lives—then out to a great beam over which they placed their heads for the swift stroke of the executioner's sword that sent their heads rolling in the dust. My father was one of that number. It was the unshaken integrity of their faith that thrilled me and gave me a longing for the new life. I must go back and tell my fellow townsmen of Christ, who loves them, and of his power to save."

929. "Just as I Am, Without One Plea" was written by Charlotte Elliott, who was an invalid for more than fifty years. Often as she watched those about her busy with many important tasks she became discouraged. But her faith helped her to rise above despair. This hymn is a testament of the faith she had which gave meaning to her sheltered life.

930.

I know no deeper doubt to make me
  mad,
I need no brighter love to keep me pure.
To me the faiths of old are daily bread;
I bless their hope, I bless their will to
  save.
    —AUTHOR UNKNOWN,
      "What Riches Have You"

FAME

931. Our great monuments are always to the heroes of the battlefield. France built a great tomb for Napoleon. Close by is a relatively insignificant statue erected to Louis Pasteur, who gave his life constructively to save men.—HAROLD COOKE PHILLIPS, *In the Light of the Cross*

932. Henry Ward Beecher declared: "I would rather have written that hymn of Wesley's, 'Jesus, Lover of My Soul,' than to have the fame of all the kings that ever sat on the earth. It is more glorious. It has more power in it. That hymn will go on singing until the last trumpet brings forth the angel band; and then, I think, it will mount up on some lip to the very presence of God."

FAMILY

933. Writing to his sister during an election, Theodore Roosevelt said: "As I went up the White House steps, Edith came to meet me at the door, and I suddenly realized that, after all, no matter what the outcome of the election was, my happiness was assured—that even though my ambition to have the seal of approval put upon my administration might not be gratified, my happiness was assured—for my life with Edith and my children constitutes my happiness."

934. After visiting the home of Herbert Spencer, John Fiske wrote to his wife: "I showed Spencer the little picture of our picnic wagon with the children inside. When I realized how lonely he must be without any wife and babies of his own, and how solitary he is in all his greatness, I had to pity him. Then as I watched him studying that picture and gazing at our children's faces, I said to myself, 'That wagonload of youngsters is worth more than all the philosophy ever concocted, from Aristotle to Spencer inclusive!' "—HARRY EMERSON FOSDICK, *The Hope of the World*

935. Sir Ernest Shackleton, in describing the break for safety which he and his companions made when they were attempting to return from the expedition to the South Pole, tells that he was profoundly impressed with the things his companions considered important, as contrasted with those which they threw away. The money out of their pockets they put to one side. Even food in their knapsacks they threw away. But the things they did not leave were the pictures of loved ones and letters from home. These they carried with them; and in moments when it seemed as though the body needed food, the soul would feed on the intangible inspirations that come from love.—ALBERT W. BEAVER

936. During the long months while he was confined in the Bedford jail, John Bunyan wrote *Pilgrim's Progress,* one of the great devotional books in English. While he wrote he was particularly worried about his family. In one of his letters he wrote: "The parting from my wife and children hath been as pulling of the flesh from the bone; and that not only because I am somewhat too fond of these great mercies, but also because I have often brought to my mind the thought of the hardships, miseries, and wants my poor family will be like to meet should I be taken from them. Especially my poor blind child, who lies nearer my heart than all else. The thought of what my blind one may undergo almost breaks my heart to pieces."

937. A small boy and his sister had quarreled most of the day. Finally the little girl, wishing to stop the squabbling, said: "Now let's act like we are brother and sister."

FAMILY WORSHIP

938. J. Edgar Hoover has said: "If there is to be peace and happiness in our homes, then we as a nation must return to God and to the practice of daily family altars."

939. In the preface of his *Covenant Prayer,* Bishop Coxe tells of visiting an old feudal castle in England, so old that one of its towers dated back to the days of King John. When the bishop went down to breakfast, he found the young owner of the castle, his family and servants, assembled for morning prayer, conducted by the head of the family. As the bishop lifted his eyes, he noticed high overhead a massive beam that spanned the grand old hall and bore in old English the following inscription:

"That house shall be preserved and
   never shall decay,
Where the Almighty God is worshipped
   day by day. A.D. 1558."
           —ROBERT H. RIDLEY

940. John G. Paton, missionary to the New Hebrides, tells how as a boy he used to crouch outside his father's bedroom to hear him pray. God was so real to his father that he became real to the boy listening outside also. Paton says that if everything else in religion were by some accident blotted out, his soul would go back to those days of reality. He tells us that for sixty years his father kept up the practice of family prayer. "None of us," he writes, "can remember that one day passed unhallowed thus. No hurry for business or market, no arrival of friends or guests, no trouble or sorrow, no joy or excitement ever prevented us from kneeling around the family altar while our high priest offered himself and his children to God." And Doctor Paton's father, it may be remembered, was a farm laborer.—Leslie D. Weatherhead, *The Eternal Voice*

941. John Buchan, onetime governor general of Canada, in his autobiography, *Pilgrim's Way*, recalled family prayers during his childhood: "It was the custom to return from church through the fields, which lay yellow in the sunset. While our elders cast a half-ashamed sabbatical eye over the crops of meadow hay and the kyloes in the pastures, we children, feeling the bonds of the Sabbath ritual slackening, were hard at work planning enterprises for the morrow. Then in the dusky parlour, with its comforting secular aroma of tobacco, my grandfather read chapters of both Testaments and a lengthy prayer from some forgotten *Family Altar*. I did not follow one word, for my thoughts were busy with other things. He read in a high liturgical manner, his voice rising and falling in reverent cadences. It seemed to us children a benediction on the enforced leisure of the day and a promise of a new and glorious week of wind and sun."

942. "Ike" Hoover, chief usher in the executive mansion, gives an interesting glimpse of President Benjamin Harrison's term in the early nineties in his book *Forty-two Years in the White House*: "Immediately after breakfast the family would retire to the upper floor and be closeted in one of the upper rooms for a half hour of prayer. The entire atmosphere of the household would be supercharged with religious feeling during this time. Until the ceremony had been completed, one could not go about one's daily duties without a feeling that prayer was being disturbed."

943. A prayer which Robert Louis Stevenson wrote for the morning devotions of his household in the South Sea Islands reads: "The day returns and brings us the petty round of irritating concerns and duties. Help us to play the man. Grant us courage to endure the lesser ills unshaken."

944.
Seven Reasons for Family Worship
1. It will enrich the life of the family and make the home fit for the presence of the Unseen Guest.
2. It will encourage tolerance and understanding, and put faith in the place of friction.
3. It will bring across the threshold an Infallible Guide for the youth of the home, to give their lives meaning and direction.
4. It will send us forth to the day's work in utter cheerfulness, dedicating the day to the glory of God.
5. It will so strengthen us against suffering, sorrow, and frustration that nothing the world can do to us can hurt us.
6. It will reinforce the work of church and church school, give us a Christ for *all* the week.
7. It will bring the consciousness of a family unity in God, a new dependence on his fatherhood, a new sense of the wider unity and brotherhood of man.

FATHER

945. "It is not flesh and blood," wrote Johann Schiller, "but the heart which makes us fathers and sons."

946. Wrote William Wordsworth in *Ecclesiastical Sonnets*:

Father!—to God himself we cannot give
A holier name.

947. Thomas Carlyle, thinking of his home in Ecclefechan, said: "Thank heaven, I know and have known what it is to be a son and love a father as spirit can love spirit. God give me to live to my father's honor and his!"

948. When Hector of Troy heard the call to battle, he went to bid farewell to Andromache and his infant son. He was ready for the fray, armed and helmeted. As he drew near the baby, the child cried out and shrank away, frightened by the waving plume. Hector smiled and, laying aside the helmet, took his son and kissed him fondly. Instantly the child's fears were allayed. This was no warrior—this was his father.—WILLIAM E. PHIFER, JR., *The Cross and Great Living*

949. "By profession I am a soldier and take pride in that fact," said General Douglas MacArthur. "But I am prouder, infinitely prouder, to be a father. A soldier destroys in order to build. The father only builds, never destroys. The one has the potentialities of death; the other embodies creation and life. And while the hordes of death are mighty, the battles of life are mightier still. My hope is that my son, when I am gone, will remember me not from the battle, but in the home, repeating with him one simple daily prayer, 'Our Father which art in heaven.'"

950. During a violent storm at sea a passenger asked a small boy if he was afraid. "No, I am not," was the answer. "I have my eyes on that little window, and through the window I can see the bridge, and on that bridge I can see my father. He will get us to shore safely."

951. A son speaks: At eleven years: "My parents are grand. They know simply everything." At sixteen: "Really and truly, my parents are not quite so grand as I used to think. They don't know everything." At nineteen: "Although my parents think they are always right, they really know very little compared with what I know already." At twenty-two: "My parents do not understand young people; they have nothing in common with the young generation." At thirty: "To tell the truth, my parents were right in many things." At fifty: "My parents were wonderful people. They had a clear mind and always did the necessary thing at the right moment. My beloved parents."

Father's Concern

952. A father and a son, both bearing the same name, were taken prisoners during the French Revolution. One day when the son's name was read among those called to die, the father answered the name and took his son's place.

953. A boy returned from the European war saying that the thing that had helped him most during the long months of fighting was the remembrance of his father's hand on his shoulder when the father, unable to speak, had seen him off from New York.

954. When a father overheard one of his sons say, "If you do that, father won't love you," he approached his children with these words: "I shall always love you. When you do what is right, I love you with a glad heart, and when you do what is wrong, I still love you, but with a heart full of sorrow."

955. Horace Mann, speaking at the opening of a reformatory for boys, said that if only one boy was saved from ruin, it would justify all the cost and labor of establishing the institution. Afterward a friend asked the eminent educator if he had not exaggerated a little. "Not if that boy was my son," was the reply.—H. J. SINCLAIR

956. A father who was discussing his wayward son with a friend received this reply: "If he were my son, I would kick him out." The father answered: "Yes, if he were your son, so would I. But he isn't your son; he is my son, and I can't do it."

Father's Example

957. One winter day a man found it necessary to go to see a neighbor who lived beyond a steep and rugged mountain. He had climbed the dangerous trail for some minutes through the drifted snow and along the edge of a precipice when he heard a voice call: "Be careful, daddy. I'm walking in your steps."

958. When Quentin Roosevelt was in the 94th Aero Squadron on the Western Front during World War I, an observer said: "I am a friend of your father's. I have come here especially to tell you how millions of Americans back home appreciate the splendid ways in which the sons of Theodore Roosevelt are acquitting themselves in this conflict." "Well, you see," Quentin replied, "it's up to us to practice what father preaches. I'm Roosevelt's son. It's up to me to live like a Roosevelt."

959. When a little boy said an ugly word, he looked sheepishly at a man who stood near by. The man told the boy that the use of the word wouldn't hurt him and that he should learn to say whatever he wished. The little boy was puzzled for a moment and then said: "If you were my father, you would not say that."

Father's Neglect

960. When a young man had been given a prison sentence, the judge reminded him of the distinguished career of his father, a famous lawyer. "When I went to him for advice or companionship," the youth recalled, "he would look up from a book on the law of trusts and say, 'Run away, boy. I am busy.' My father finished his book, and here I am."

961. A famous and busy member of the English House of Lords is reported to have met his small son playing in Hyde Park and said: "By Jove, child, I've seen you before somewhere!"

FEAR

962. In his book *The Conquest of Fear*, Basil King writes: "When I say that during most of my life I have been the prey of fear, I take it I am expressing the case of most people. I cannot remember a time when dread of one kind or another was not in the air. In childhood it was the fear of going to bed; later it was the fear of school; still later it was the experience of waking in the morning with a feeling of dismay at the amount of work that had to be done before night. In some form or other fear dogs every one of us. The mother is afraid for her children; the father is afraid for his business; most of us are afraid for our job. There is not a home or an office, a school or a church, in which some hangdog apprehension is not eating at the hearts of the people who go in and out. I am ready to guess that all the miseries wrought by sin and sickness combined would not equal those we bring on ourselves through fear. We are not sick all the time. We are not sinning all the time. But most of us are always afraid—afraid of something or somebody."

963. Angelo Patri once said: "Education consists in being afraid at the right time."

964. Napoleon, when an artillery officer at the siege of Toulon, built a battery in such an exposed position that he was told he would never find men to man it. So he put up a sign reading: "The battery of men without fear." After that there were always more volunteers than were needed.

965. An Arab folk tale relates that Pestilence once met a caravan upon the desert way to Bagdad. "Why," asked the Arab chief, "must you hasten to Bagdad?" "To take five thousand lives," Pestilence replied. Upon the way back from the City of the Caliphs, Pestilence and the caravan met again. "You deceived me," the chief said angrily. "Instead of five thousand lives you took fifty thousand." "Nay," said Pestilence. "Five thousand and not one more. It was Fear who killed the rest."
—Maurice Duhamel, *We Are Not Afraid*

966. Charles H. Spurgeon told of a minister who made up a generous purse of money to pay a widow's rent, but when he knocked at her door there was no answer. Later when the widow was told who visited her, she said: "I thought it was the man who came to collect the rent."

967. John Wesley had always thought he was a true Christian until one day his ship was caught in a storm in the Atlantic and fear got hold of him. The people on board, he noticed, who were not terror-stricken were a little group of Moravian missionaries. And when the storm abated, "Were you not afraid?" Wesley asked one of them. "Afraid?" said the Moravian. "Why should I be afraid? I know Christ!" And then looking at Wesley with disconcerting frankness, "Do *you* know Christ?" he asked. And at that Wesley for the first time in his life realized that he did not.
—James S. Stewart, *The Gates of New Life*

968. "Fear not to sow because of the birds" is the legend below a beautiful stained-glass picture of the sower.

969. Preston Bradley in his book *Mastering Fear* wrote: "To banish fear you must look within your mind, find the cause of your fear and worry and lack of self-confidence. Then you must train your mental habits to a new point of view. This means substituting faith for fear, a courageous outlook for a lack of self-assurance, a positive attitude toward life for a negative. Fear becomes ingrown only when the fear-bringing situation is not examined and penetrated."

FELLOWSHIP

970. "O God," prayed George Fox, founder of the Quakers, "I pray to be baptized into a sense of all conditions that I might be able to know the needs and feel the sorrows of all men."

971. John Bunyan in his farewell sermon said: "Dost thou see a soul that has the image of God in him? Love him, love him; say, 'This man and I must go to heaven together one day.'"

972. John Fawcett, pastor of the Baptist church in Wainsgate, Yorkshire, was about to deliver his farewell sermon and leave his parish for a larger work. The members of his church showed such signs of devotion that at the last moment he determined not to go but to remain with those who loved and needed him. When he returned to his pulpit and announced his decision to stay with them, he gave them the hymn of Christian fellowship, "Blest Be the Tie That Binds." Fawcett continued as pastor in Wainsgate for the rest of his life.

973.
And how to build a better world?
    Well, not by chart or plan,
Unless we start to teach the boy
    To be a better man.
For all our dreams of nobler things
    Will meet the same old fate,
Unless we turn to fellowship,
    And do away with hate.[3]
        —EDGAR A. GUEST,
            "The Better World"

974.
'Tis the human touch in this world that counts,
    The touch of your hand and mine,
Which means far more to the fainting heart
    Than shelter and bread and wine;
For shelter is gone when the night is o'er,
    And bread lasts only a day,
But the touch of the hand and the sound of the voice
    Sing on in the soul alway.
        —SPENCER MICHAEL FREE,
            "The Human Touch"

975. Hugh Walpole's blind hero of *Blind Man's House*, who almost wrecks the happiness of his home because of his pride and aloofness, but who finally sees it, expresses it in these words: "I have learned this lesson of our interdependence, the lesson all mankind must learn. No one of us can move any more, or sigh, or sneeze, or cough, or whisper without disturbing the rest of us. Until we learn this fellowship, generous and

[3] Copyright and used by permission of the author.

understanding, of all living men upon the earth, there will be no peace."

FORGETFULNESS

976. Themistocles the Greek philosopher said: "Teach me the art of forgetting; for I often remember what I would not, and cannot forget what I would."

977. When hurt by a man named Lampe, the philosopher Kant wrote on his memorandum pad: "Remember to forget Lampe."

978. Norman Duncan in his book *Doctor Luke of Labrador* tells how Wilfred Grenfell's mother on his birthday took him upon her lap, saying: "Look in your mother's eyes, lad, and say this after me: My mother looked upon my heart and found it brave and sweet, willing for the day's work, and harboring no shameful hope." Then, after a moment's thought, she added: "Ah, but you will forget." "No, no," cried Grenfell, "I'll not forget."

FORGIVENESS

979. Forgiveness is the perfume of the violet on the heel that crushed it.

980. There is an old story of a pious deacon who, goaded apparently beyond endurance by the persistent malice of an enemy, publicly vowed to "kill him." It came to the ears of his enemy, who waited sardonically to see what the good and harmless old fool would do. Actually the deacon sought out every opportunity to do his enemy good. This was at first a source of merriment and some slight annoyance; but when at last the deacon rendered costly and sacrificial service to his adversary, risking his life to save the man's wife from drowning, the deadlock between the

two was broken and a new relationship set up. "All right," said the man, "you've done what you said you'd do, and I admit it. You've killed me—or at least you've killed the man that I was. Now, what can I do for you?"—WALTER MARSHALL HORTON, *Our Christian Faith*

981. In Alberta, Canada, there is a city called Wetaskawin, meaning "The Hills of Peace," which got its name in this way: When the first missionaries came to that province, they were fiercely opposed by a young chief of the Cree Indians named Maskepetoon, who waged savage war against the Blackfeet. Eventually Maskepetoon became a Christian. Shortly afterwards his father was murdered by one of the Blackfeet. Maskepetoon rode into the enemy camp and demanded that the murderer be brought forth to him. When this was done, he said: "You have killed my father. Now *you* must be my father. You shall ride my best horse and wear my best clothes." Whereupon the old man exclaimed: "My son, you have killed me!"—DORIS BURKE

982. When the books of a certain Scotch doctor were examined after his death, it was found that a number of accounts were crossed out with a note: "Forgiven—too poor to pay." But the physician's wife decided that these accounts must be paid, and proceeded to sue for the money. The judge asked one question: "Is this your husband's handwriting?" When she replied that it was, he said: "Then there is no tribunal in the land that can obtain this money when he has written the word 'Forgiven.'"—EMERY PARKS

983. One day when Dr. Walter Rauschenbusch, the prophet of the social gospel, was crossing the street in Rochester, New York, he was hit by a trolley car. When the motorman began to explain that he had sounded the gong, Rauschenbusch stopped him: "I am very sorry that I crossed the street in front of you, but you see, I am deaf, and I did not hear you approaching." He then reached into his pocket and took out a five-dollar bill and gave it to the motorman, saying, "Take this as a gift and forgive me."

984. Comus, a Duke of Florence, had a saying that indicated the limitations of his religion: "You shall read that we are commanded to forgive our enemies, but you never read we are commanded to forgive our friends."

985. During the afternoon preceding his assassination Lincoln signed a pardon for a soldier sentenced to be shot for desertion, remarking as he did so: "Well, I think the boy can do more good above the ground than under the ground."

986. The Norwegian writer Johan Bojer in *The Great Hunger* tells of a man whose little child was killed by a neighbor's dog. Revenge would not long satisfy this man, so he found a better way to relieve the agony of his heart. When a famine had plagued the people and the neighbor's fields lay bare and he had no corn to plant for next year's harvest, the troubled father went out one night and sowed the neighbor's field, explaining: "I went and sowed seed in my enemy's field that God might exist."

987. Before his death Frederick the Great was told that he should forgive his enemies. "Dorothy," he said to the queen, "write to your brother that I forgive him all the evil he has done me; but wait till I am dead first."

988. Said David Deans to his daughter after her sister had disgraced the family in Walter Scott's *Heart of Midlothian:* "She went out from us because she was not of us; let her gang her gait. The Lord kens his time. She was a bairn of prayers and may not prove a castaway. But never more let her name be spoken between you and me."

FORWARD

989. Christian in Bunyan's *Pilgrim's Progress* says: "I must venture. To go back is nothing but death; to go forward is fear of death and everlasting life beyond it. I will yet go forward."

990. "I am willing to go anywhere," Livingstone said as he left for Africa, "provided it be forward."

FOUNDATION

991. Harkness Tower at Yale University is of exquisite grace and beauty. There is one stone in the lower part of the structure which is different from any other in the building. It bears an inscription which states that it is a part of the bedrock on which the tower stands, and that it is set there to be a visible witness of the invisible foundations and to bear testimony to the truth that the things which are not seen are eternal.

992. An old Greek was approached by a visitor who said: "I observe your old and happy life. How do you attain it?" The old philosopher replied: "You see also the fine trees and orchards I possess. Well, I have them because I planted them as a young man. So in youth I laid the foundations of my life. I did not wait until I was old to begin to build for this day."—Fred R. Chenault

FREEDOM

993. Jan Masaryk, Czechoslovak statesman, once told an American audience: "Raised in liberty, most Americans accept their freedom as a matter of course. Sometimes it seems to me you free people don't realize what you've got. . . . You can wake up in the morning free to do as you choose, to read what you wish, to worship the way you please, and to listen to a lovely piece of music."

994. A missionary who returned to America after a long imprisonment in a Japanese camp was asked what he thought about during his confinement. His answer was, "I spent such time as I had to think wondering whether I would be worthy of freedom when I got it."

995. Garibaldi's challenging words to his soldiers were: "Soldiers, what I have to offer you is fatigue, danger, struggle, and death; the chill of the cold night in the free air, and heat under the burning sun; no lodgings, no munitions, no provisions, but forced marches, dangerous watch posts, and continual struggle with bayonets against batteries. Those who love freedom and their country may follow me."

996. "My Lords, greater than armies is goodness; greater than swords is freedom. Scotland! Scotland! lift up thy banner and be free," challenged John Knox in the sixteenth century.

997. Narodny said of Russia: "I am nothing; personal success, happiness, they are nothing; exile, Siberia, the czar's bullet, they are nothing; there is just one thing, that Russia must be free."

998. A parable by Rabindranath Tagore, Nobel prize poet, reads: "I have on my table a violin string. It is free to move in any direction I like. If I twist one end, it responds; it is free. But it is not free to sing. So I take it and fix it into my violin. I bind it, and, when it is bound, it is free for the first time to sing."

999. Mark Twain tells a quaint story of the man who spent years in prison, only to walk out one morning when he discovered that the doors had never been locked.

FRIENDS

1000. Speaking to a graduating class at the University of Chicago several years ago, Chancellor Robert M. Hutchins said: "My experience and observation lead to me warn you that the greatest, the most insidious, the most paralyzing danger you will face is the danger of corruption. Time will corrupt you. Your friends, your wives or husbands, your business or professional associations will corrupt you; your social, political, and financial ambitions will corrupt you. The worst thing about life is that it is demoralizing. . . . Believe me, you are closer to the truth now than you ever will be again. . . . Take your stand now before time has corrupted you. Before you know it, it will be too late."

1001. "I didn't find my friends," said Ralph Waldo Emerson. "The good God gave them to me."

1002. An English publication offered a prize for the best definition of a friend. Among the thousands of answers received were the following: "One who multiplies joys, divides grief, and whose honesty is inviolable." "One who understands our silence." "A volume of sympathy bound in cloth." "A watch which beats true for all time and never runs down." The winning definition read:

"A friend is the one who comes in when the whole world has gone out." —EDGAR DEWITT JONES, *Blundering into Paradise*

1003. "I will not say that I am loyal or that Your Majesty is gracious," Alfred Tennyson wrote to Queen Victoria, "for those are terms used or abused by every courtier, but I will say that during our conversation I felt the touch of that true friendship that binds human hearts together whether they be kings or cobblers."

1004. When Michael Pupin was asked by immigration officials if he had any friends in America, he named Benjamin Franklin, Abraham Lincoln, and Harriet Beecher Stowe. The officials let him in; they were sure that a boy who was familiar with such people would make his way.—WALTER DUDLEY CAVERT, *Remember Now . . .*

1005. "Is it true that all the people in the world could get into the state of Texas?" a man asked. "Yes," someone replied, "if they were *friends*."

1006. When the king of Belgium wished to honor Herbert Hoover for his humanitarian services to the Belgians after World War I, Hoover refused, saying: "You have stood at the gateway of civilization and held back the tide of aggression, while we have only shared with you what we had to give. For that one does not ask honors." But the king, wishing to recognize Hoover's personal helpfulness, created a new order to which only one man belonged. The title was "Friend of the Belgian People."

1007. When George V was visiting the front lines during World War I, he overheard a wounded New Zealander speaking to a companion: "Who is that man? Where have I seen him before? Or where have I seen his picture?" When the king moved nearer the wounded man's cot, the soldier in a flash of recognition realized the identity of his visitor. Reaching out his hand, he exclaimed to the beloved monarch: "I've heard of you, sir—put it there!"

1008. When Emerson was an old man with failing mental powers, he stood by the grave of Longfellow. "The gentleman who lies here was a beautiful soul, but I have forgotten his name." The impression of his friend's life was stronger than the remembrance of his friend's name.

1009. Jonathan Swift, author of *Gulliver's Travels*, was generally pessimistic about human nature. In a letter to Alexander Pope he wrote: "I hate and detest that animal called man, although I heartily love John, Peter, Thomas, and so forth."

1010. "Every man," Henry Ward Beecher said, "should keep a fair-sized cemetery in which to bury the faults of his friends."

1011.
He who has a thousand friends has not
  a friend to spare,
And he who has one enemy shall meet
  him everywhere.
—ALI BEN ABU TALEB (A.D. 660)

Importance of Friends

1012. "What is the secret of your life? Tell me, that I may make mine beautiful, too," said Elizabeth Barrett Browning to Charles Kingsley. "I had a friend," was the simple reply.

1013. When Abraham Lincoln was first talked about as a possible candidate for the presidency, many people in his party said: "Why Lincoln? He has no influence; he has won no high political honors; he has no money; in fact, he hasn't much of anything but a lot of friends."

Loss of Friends

1014. Sir Walter Raleigh, onetime courtier to Queen Elizabeth, was sentenced to be executed on a trumped-up charge. A few hours before the end he wrote to his wife: "To what friend to direct thee, I know not, for all mine have left me in the true time of trial."

1015. The Maréchal de Villars, taking leave of Louis XIV, exclaimed, "Defend me from my friends; I can defend myself from my enemies."—GEORGE A. BUTTRICK, *Prayer*

Loyalty of Friends

1016. Leslie D. Weatherhead tells of two soldiers who became fast comrades during World War I. When, after an unsuccessful night sortie, one of them was missing, the second youth heard a cry from no man's land. His commanding officer granted permission for a rescue attempt, but added: "It's not worth it. Your friend is probably dead by this time, and you will throw your life away." The attempt was immediately made. When, some time later, the rescuer returned, he was dragging the body of his dead comrade, and he himself was mortally wounded. Looking up to his commanding officer he said with joy: "Sir, it *was* worth it. When I reached him, he looked up and said to me, 'I knew you'd come.'"

1017. A very beautiful custom in some parts of the South Sea Islands is that when two men become deeply attached to each other they exchange names, and each is known by the name of the other for the rest of his life. Such an exchange of names—one speaking in another's name—whether in marriage or friendship, implies a sacred tie of absolute unity, absolute love.—GLENN CLARK, *The Soul's Sincere Desire*

Need of Friends

1018. Channing Pollock told of the man who confessed to him: "I'm a lucky man! I'm making a thousand dollars a day! So what? I haven't a friend in the world. It's a living death."

1019. A young man far from home and without money wired his father: "I am in the big city without money or friends. What shall I do?" The father wired back: "Make some friends at once."

1020. While Carl Kopf was watching police grappling for the body of a person who had jumped from Harvard Bridge, a child asked why the woman had jumped. Kopf ventured: "Maybe she had no work and nothing to eat. Or maybe she had no friends and was lonesome." "Well," the child said, "she won't find any friends in the river." —CARL KOPF, *Windows on Life*

FUTURE

1021. "In the convex driving mirror she could see," writes Jan Struther in *Mrs. Miniver*, "dwindling rapidly, the patch of road where they had stood; and she wondered why it had never occurred to her before that you cannot successfully navigate the future unless you keep always framed beside it a small clear image of the past."

1022. Excellent advice for those who fear the future was given by a superintendent of a telephone company who was instructing young men in pole climbing. "Do not look straight up or down," he cautioned, "but just a little ahead of your highest hand."

1023. An editor about to be beheaded during the French Revolution said: "It is too bad to take off my head. I wanted to see how this thing was coming out."

G

GARDEN

1024.

A garden is a lovesome thing, God wot!
  Rose plot,
  Fringed pool,
Ferned grot—
  The veriest school
Of peace: and yet the fool
Contends that God is not—
Not God! In gardens! When the eve is
  cool?
  Nay but I have a sign;
  'Tis very sure God walks in mine.
    —THOMAS EDWARD BROWN,
            "My Garden"

1025. William S. Abernethy in his book *Left-Handed Folks* tells of an old German university professor who spoke often of his garden. Some of his students were curious to see it. When they found it, they were amazed that it was very small. "The flowers are beautiful," one student said to the professor, "but your garden is so small." "True," exclaimed the old man "but see how high it is."

1026. In the heart of the city of London there is a quiet garden adjoining the spot where John Wesley was brought into full assurance of salvation. The garden has a sundial bearing this inscription: "This ancient burying-ground was converted into a garden by the vote of the parish vestry."

GENEROSITY

1027. In the cloister wall of the Chicago Theological Seminary is set a famous cornerstone taken from an early Christian chapel of the fourth century located near Hebron, south of Jerusalem. The Greek inscription translates: "This new building was made possible by the generosity of Stephanus, the brilliant and famous physician of the royal house."

1028. "The largeness of Nature and of this nation were *monstrous*," wrote Walt Whitman in the preface of *Leaves of Grass*, "without a corresponding largeness and generosity of the spirit of the citizen."

GIVING

1029. The epitaph of Robyn of Doncaster, who died in 1579 at Doncaster, Yorkshire, England, reads:

> That I spent that I had;
> That I gave that I have;
> That I left that I loose.

1030.

The Holy Supper is kept, indeed,
In whatso we share with another's need;
Not what we give, but what we share,—
For the gift without the giver is bare;
Who gives himself with his alms feeds
  three:—
Himself, his hungering neighbor, and
  me.
    —JAMES RUSSELL LOWELL,
      "The Vision of Sir Launfal"

1031. A surgeon, having just amputated the shattered arm of a young French soldier, said: "I am sorry that you had to lose your arm." "I did not lose it," the soldier protested. "I gave it."

1032. When the Liberty Loan slogan "Give until it hurts" was announced during World War I, a businessman remarked: "It should read, 'Give until it makes you rejoice.'"

1033. "The Golden Ladder of Giving" by Maimonides, a Jewish scholar of the twelfth century, includes the following eight steps: (1) To give reluctantly, the gift of the hand, but not of the heart. (2) To give cheerfully, but not in proportion to the need. (3) To give cheerfully, and proportionately, but not until solicited. (4) To give cheerfully, proportionately, and unsolicited, but to put the gift into the poor man's hand, thus creating shame. (5) To give in such a way that the distressed may know their benefactor, without being known to him. (6) To know the objects of our bounty, but remain unknown to them. (7) To give so that the benefactor may not know those whom he has relieved, and they shall not know him. (8) To prevent poverty by teaching a trade, setting a man up in business, or in some other way preventing the need of charity. This is the highest step in charity's Golden Ladder.

1034. When an old blind sewing woman in France gave twenty-five francs for missions, a friend told her that she had given more than she could afford. "No," said the woman. "The women who work with me spend twenty-five francs each for oil for their lamps. I am blind and need no lamp, so I can give my francs to light other lives."

1035. John Wesley is said to have preached a sermon which had three significant points: (1) "Get all you

can." To this an old miserly fellow said, "Amen." (2) "Keep all you can." The same man said, "Amen," again. (3) "Give all you can." Then the rich but selfish man said, "What a shame to spoil a good sermon."

1036. A missionary persuaded a London merchant of the great needs of his field. The merchant gave the missionary a check. In the morning the merchant learned that his business had suffered a heavy financial loss. Regretfully the missionary returned the check when the merchant requested it. Soon thereafter the missionary received a larger check. The merchant, who had torn up the first check, wrote: "God is teaching me that I must give while I can."—EGBERT W. SMITH, *The Desire of All Nations*

1037. In the Tate Gallery in London there is a famous painting by Watts entitled *"Sic Transit Gloria."* It is just the body of a man stretched on a bier, with a robe thrown over it. As one looks at it he notices the little touches the artist has given it. There is a half-open book. The man must have been a lover of literature. The lyre near by tells us he loved music and was charmed by it. The sword and ermine robe show us that he was a warrior and a statesman. The feather of a peacock hints at the lighter side of life, vanity and romance. On the edge of the canvas the artist has inscribed these words, letting the man tell us what he has learned too late: "What I spent I had; what I saved I lost; what I gave I have."—FREDERICK KELLER STAMM, *The Conversations of Jesus*

1038. A small boy asked his father for money for the church offering. The father said he had only a penny in change. "But I can't put just a penny in the collection," the little boy said,

"You don't want me to look cheap to the Lord, do you?"

1039. Louis XI of France once made out a deed in which he gave the province of Boulogne to the Virgin Mary but expressly stated that all the income and revenues should forever be paid to himself and his heirs. He gave everything for his religion but did it in such a way that he made no personal sacrifice.—WALTER DUDLEY CAVERT, *Remember Now* . . .

1040. A beggar at the end of the day heard the cry, "The king comes!" Expecting a princely gift from the king, the beggar was astounded when he extended his cup to have the king stop his great white charger and ask, "What gift have *you* for the king?"—FRANK FAGERBURG

GOAL

1041.
The man who seeks one thing in life, and but one
May hope to achieve it before life be done;
But he who seeks all things wherever he goes,
Only reaps from the hopes which around him he sows
A host of barren regrets.
    —OWEN MEREDITH, "One Thing"

1042. "No man has gone so far," said Oliver Cromwell, "as he who does not know where he is going."

GOD

1043. It is said that when the Shorter Catechism was being prepared by the Westminster Assembly of divines a grave perplexity arose as to the proper definition of God. One of the younger men was asked to pray for guidance. He began in this manner: "O God, thou who art a spirit infinite, eternal, and unchangeable in thy being, wisdom, power, holiness, justice, goodness, and truth"; and those words were incorporated as furnishing the best definition of God.

1044. "God is he without whom one cannot live," was Leo Tolstoy's definition of God.

1045.
God is in all that liberates and lifts,
In all that humbles, sweetens, and consoles.
    —JAMES RUSSEL LOWELL

1046. Lawrence of Arabia has said that an Arab sheik, after hearing the Western scholar recount the wonders revealed by the telescope, said: "You foreigners see millions of stars, and nothing beyond. We Arabs see only a few stars—and God."

1047. Christopher Morley in *Inward Ho!* writes: "I had a thousand questions to ask God; but when I met him, they all fled and didn't seem to matter."

1048. Franz Joseph Haydn told Caprani that at the thought of God his heart leaped for joy and he could not help his music doing the same.

1049. "The older I grow," said Thomas Carlyle, "and now I stand upon the brink of eternity, the more comes back to me the sentence in the catechism which I learned when a child, and the fuller and deeper its meaning becomes: 'What is the chief end of man? To glorify God and enjoy him forever.'"

1050. John Henry Newman, after considering a world with no trace of God, concluded that it would be "just as if I were to look into a mirror and not see my face."

1051. In *The Evening Altar,* Carl Petty told of a Hindu student who, when asked what impressions he had received during a visit in America, replied: "I take it from what I heard that God is a Caucasian, an American, a Baptist, and a Republican."

1052. Over a fireplace at Princeton University is a motto written by Albert Einstein which reads: "God is a scientist, not a magician."

1053. "What are you doing, Annabel?" asked her mother. "I'm making a picture of God." "Oh, but you can't do that! Nobody knows what God looks like." "Well," said the girl, "when I get through, they will!"

1054. Early American Indians called their god "Gitchie Manitou," meaning "The Unclaimed Spirit."

Belief in God

1055. Said Unamuno, a Spanish philosopher: "If you ask me how I believe in God, how God creates himself in me, and reveals himself to me, my answer may perhaps provoke your smiles or laughter, and even scandalize you. I believe in God as I believe in my friends, because I feel the breath of his affection, feel his invisible and intangible hand drawing me, leading me, grasping me."

1056. "The essence of religion is a belief in a relation to God involving duties superior to those arising out of any human relation," former Chief Justice Charles Evans Hughes wrote. "One cannot speak of religious liberty with a proper appreciation of its essential and historic significance without assuming the existence of a belief in a supreme allegiance to the will of God."

1057. "Oh, Doctor, do tell me. What do you think of God?" asked an enthusiastic lady of Benjamin Jowett of Balliol. "That, my dear young lady, is a very unimportant question; the only thing that signifies is what God thinks about me."

1058. "I still can't believe in God," says a young doctor, dying as a result of a Chinese epidemic in A. J. Cronin's *The Keys of the Kingdom.* The priest, attempting to comfort the doctor, says: "Does that matter now? He believes in you."

1059. One of the striking incidents in Lloyd Douglas' *Invitation to Live* is Sally Singley's visit with Dean Harcourt, whose words of counsel had given many people a new hold on life. Sally had failed as an actress. She had thrown away her great opportunity because of conceit, disregard for authority, and blindness to her own limitations. Defeated, discouraged and cynical, she said to the dean, "I'm not even sure that I believe in God." "That's not important just now," he replied. "I mean, it isn't quite so urgent, at present, whether you believe in God as whether he can believe in you. If you will conduct yourself in a manner that might encourage him to believe in you, the time may come when you feel that you should return the compliment."

1060. William Cowper was subject to moments of deep melancholy. One night in such a mood he called a cabby and directed him to drive to the banks of the Thames River. The city of London was blanketed with an impenetrable fog. For more than an hour the cab driver groped his way along the streets and yet did not find the river. His passenger grew more and more impatient until at last he leaped from the cab, determined to find his watery grave unassisted. Groping through the fog, he was astonished when he found himself at his own doorstep. Going to his room he penned the words of his beautiful hymn:

God moves in a mysterious way
His wonders to perform.
—JAMES A. SIMONS

1061. A little boy asked his father if anyone had ever seen God. The father quickly dismissed the question. Later the boy asked his minister the same question. The minister dismissed the question. Determined to get an answer the boy asked an old man whom others would think unable to comment reasonably on any question. But he did have an answer. "Sometimes," the old man said, "I thinks as I never sees anything else."

Companionship with God

1062. The husband of Alice Freeman Palmer, first president of Wellesley, wrote of her: "God was her steady companion, so naturally a part of her hourly thought that she attached little consequence to specific occasions of intercourse. . . . She had no fixed times of prayer."

1063. Charles H. Spurgeon, declaring the secret of his life, said, "I looked at God and he looked at me, and we were one forever."

Confidence in God

1064. A mother and her little four-year-old daughter were preparing to retire for the night. The child was afraid of the dark and the mother, alone with the child, felt fearful also. When the light was out, the child caught a glimpse of the moon outside the window. "Mother," she asked, "is the moon God's light?" "Yes," said the mother, "God's lights are always shining." The next question was, "Will God blow out his lights and go to sleep?" And the mother replied, "No, my child. God never goes to sleep." Then out of the simplicity of a child's faith she said that which gave reassurance to the fearful mother, "Well, so long as God is awake, I am not afraid."
—F. S. EITELGEORGE

1065. Kagawa, when he was once threatened with blindness and lay for months in the dark with scorching pain in his eyes, wrote: "Health is gone. Sight is gone. But as I lie forsaken in this dark room, God still gives light. At the center of things there is a Heart. On yonder side of darkness there is light. To me all things are vocal. O wonder words of love! . . . God and every inanimate thing speak to me! Thus, even in the darkness, I feel no sense of loneliness. . . . Prayer continues. . . . In the darkness I meet God face to face. . . . I am being born, born of God. . . . I am constantly praising God for the joy of the moments lived with him."
—WILLIAM AXLING, *Kagawa*

1066. Lord Ashley before the battle of Edge Hill prayed: "O Lord, thou knowest how busy I must be this day. If I forget thee, do not thou forget me."

1067. A minister called on an old Scottish lady who was dying. Wishing to test her faith, he said: "Janet, what would you say if, after all he had done for you, God should let you perish?" The lady thought a moment and then replied: "Even as he likes; if he does, he will lose more than I'll do; for I would lose my soul; but he would lose his honour, for his word would be broken."

Co-operation with God

1068. Zwingli said: "A Christian man's task is not to talk grandly of doctrines, but always to be doing hard and great things with God."

1069. When asked what was his father's definition of faith, the son of Dr. Howard Taylor, founder of the China Inland Mission, said: "Common sense in active co-operation with God."

1070. William James in *Varieties of Religious Experience* wrote: "We and God must have business one with the other, and in opening our hearts to him our highest destiny is fulfilled."

1071. Jacob Riis, who gave his life to combating the evils of the slums of lower New York's East Side, said: "We fight to win, for we fight with God for his children."

1072. Over the French College of Physicians may be seen these words cut in stone: "I dressed his wounds; God healed him."

1073. A man prayed earnestly that God might with his finger touch a certain man. Suddenly he stopped his prayer, explaining: "God said to me, 'You are my finger.' Now I must go and touch the man."

1074. Kepler, looking up from his mathematical computations, said: "I think thy thoughts after thee, O God."

1075. When a group of clergymen told Lincoln during the Civil War, "Let us have faith, Mr. President, that the Lord is on our side in this great struggle," the president answered quietly: "I am not at all concerned about that, for I know that the Lord is always on the side of the right; but it is my constant anxiety and prayer that I and this nation may be on the Lord's side."

1076. In his closing remarks to a group of new soldiers the commanding officer said: "In addition to all that I have said remember this—perhaps a time will come in your military experience when you will discover that only you, the enemy, and the Lord will be on the battlefield. Men, be sure the Lord is on your side!"

1077. In May, 1792, William Carey, the shoe cobbler who became the founder of modern missions, preached a sermon to the people of the Nottingham Association in England. As a result the people raised the funds to send Carey to India. That sermon today is particularly remembered for these words:

Expect great things from God.
Attempt great things for God.

1078. A farmer picked a wild rose which had grown on a vacant lot near his buildings and giving it to a friend said: "God made this rose." Later he selected a beautiful cultivated rose from his garden and said: "See what God and man have made together."

1079. Sir Wilfred Grenfell in *The Fisherman Saint* said: "My own faith is that so marvelous is this human life of ours that (I say it reverently) God himself cannot save the world without us. This is for me a definitely sufficient explanation of why we are here."

1080. Stradivarius, the great violinmaker, declared: " 'Tis God gives skill, but not without men's hands. He could not make Antonio Stradivarius' violins without Antonio."

God the Creator

1081. Charles Kingsley told of a heathen khan in Tartary who was visited by a pair of proselytizing Moolahs. The first Moolah said: "O Khan, worship my God. He is so wise that he made all things!" Moolah No. 2 said: "O Khan, worship my God! He is so wise that he makes things make themselves." No. 2 won the day.

1082. After hearing that God created the world in six days a little boy asked his teacher: "What business has God been in since?"

Dedication to God

1083. David Livingstone had every reason in the world to stay quietly at home in Scotland and worship his God in a cultured and dignified manner. But this is what he early said about himself: "I will place no value on anything I have or may possess except in its relation to the Kingdom of God. Anything I have will be given or kept according as giving or keeping it I shall most promote the Kingdom of my Saviour."
—FRANK FAGERBURG

1084. John Knox once remarked: "The world is still waiting to see what God can do with a man wholly consecrated to his service."

1085. Jonathan Edwards wrote the following resolution in his diary: "Resolved first, that every man should live, always and everywhere, at his highest and best for God. Resolved second, whether any other man in the world strives to do so or not, I will, so help me God!"

1086. When asked the secret of his success in the Salvation Army, General William Booth said: "I will tell you the secret. God has had all there was of me. There have been men with greater brains than I, men with greater oppor-

tunities. But from the day I got the poor of London on my heart and caught a vision of what Jesus Christ could do with them, on that day I made up my mind that God should have all of William Booth there was. And if there is anything of power in the Salvation Army today, it is because God has had all the adoration of my heart, all the power of my will, and all the influence of my life."

1087. Lord, make me a channel of thy peace
That where there is hatred I may bring love,
That where there is wrong I may bring the spirit of forgiveness,
That where there is discord I may bring harmony,
That where there is error I may bring truth,
That where there is doubt I may bring faith,
That where there is despair I may bring hope
That where there are shadows I may bring thy light,
That where there is sadness I may bring joy.

Lord, grant that I may seek rather
To comfort—than to be comforted;
To understand—than to be understood;
To love—than to be loved;
For it is by giving—that one receives;
It is by self-forgetting that one finds;
It is by forgiving that one is forgiven;
It is by dying that one awakens to eternal life.
—FRANCIS OF ASSISI

1088.
Lord, in the strength of grace,
    With a glad heart and free,
Myself, my residue of days,
    I consecrate to thee.

Thy ransomed servant, I
  Restore to thee thine own;
And from this moment live or die
  To serve my God alone.
          —CHARLES WESLEY

Denial of God

1089. "You are little children sitting on the curbstone hunting in the gutter for things," George MacDonald told men of his day. "Behind you is a King's palace, finer than Buckingham. In it your Father sits. But you won't listen. You won't even turn around to look. You just keep on hunting in the gutter for things, and it doesn't matter whether it's rotten vegetables or pennies or shillings you find there. They can't make you happy without your Father."

1090. "Vanessa is so good and so fine," says Benjie to his mother in Hugh Walpole's story *Vanessa*. "She believes in God, you know, Mother." "And don't you?" "You know that I don't," says Benjie. "Not as she does. I may be wrong. I dare say I am. But I *must* be honest. I don't *see* things that way. I'm ignorant. I don't know any more than the next fellow, and I want the next fellow to believe as he sees, but I must be allowed to see for myself. I can't *see* God anywhere. The things that people believe are fine for them but nonsense to me. To me as I am now. I've got all my life in front of me and everything to learn. God may be proved to me yet. I hope he will be." "Proved! God can't be proved, Benjie. He must be felt." "Yes," says Benjie, "I suppose so. That may come to me one day. Meanwhile—a heathen and a vagabond can't marry Vanessa."

Evidences of God

1091. A small daughter of a minister went home from church and exclaimed to her mother: "Daddy was preaching that God is bigger than we are. If God was bigger than we are and lived inside us, everybody could see him." The mother told her daughter that that was what her father really meant.—PAUL DE MEURERS

1092. A great Hindu said: "Why are you so anxious to see God with your eyes closed? See him with your eyes open—in the form of the poor, the starved, the illiterate, and the afflicted."

1093. On one of the battlefields of the World War, two men stood together. One of them looked out bitterly over the hideous sights of no man's land and said: "Look at that. Where is God now?" The other also looked, looked at the torn ground, the jagged, broken wire, the bodies of wounded men and dead men; but he looked also at something else. Out into the zone of fire two stretcher-bearers were going. "He is *there*," he said. "There is God."
—WALTER RUSSELL BOWIE, *Remembering Christ*

1094. After a city dweller had watched the hatching of chicks in an incubator, he turned to his friends and exclaimed: "Now that's a thing to have seen; after that there is no use in telling me that there is no God."

1095.
In wonder-workings, or some bush
  aflame,
  Men look for God and fancy Him
    concealed;
  But in earth's common things He
    stands revealed
While grass and flowers and stars spell
  out His name.
         —MINOT J. SAVAGE,
           "In Common Things"

1096. Robert Stuart MacArthur, a great preacher of an earlier generation, said:

"The mountains are God's majestic thoughts. The stars are God's brilliant thoughts. The flowers are God's beautiful thoughts."

1097. "How do you know there is a God?" a traveler asked an Arab. Pointing to a track in the sand the Arab answered: "How do I know that a camel and not a man made that track?" Then pointing to the golden rays of the setting sun he added simply: "That is the footprint of something greater than man."

1098. The favorite answer of E. I. Bosworth to the question, "How do you know there is a God?" was an anecdote about a small boy whom he once met flying a kite so high that it was out of sight. To the query, "How do you know there is any kite there at all?" the boy replied, "I feel the pull of it."

Finding God

1099. Michael Fairlee in his story "The Roadmaster," tells of a certain organ-grinder who one day had as his sole auditor a small girl. After listening to the music the little girl put up her little face to be kissed. The organ-grinder, who wanted pennies and not kisses, slapped the child ruthlessly and moved on. The memory of the little girl haunted the organ-grinder months later when he was in the hospital as the result of an accident. He determined that when he left the hospital, he would find the small girl whose face was continually before him. He never did find the girl. But the memory of the face made a profound change in the man. The author says: "That man saw a little child and looked on the face of God."

1100. "I find God," E. Stanley Jones has written, "in eight ways. There may

be others, but they are subsidiary. These are the outstanding ways: (1) Through the life and teaching of Jesus as contained in the Scriptures. (2) Through the accumulated wisdom of the centuries, mediated to us through the church. (3) Through disciplined group guidance. (4) Through individual counsel. (5) Through opening providences. (6) Through the discovery of natural law by scientific investigation. (7) Through our heightened moral intelligence. (8) Through the Inner Voice."
—*How Does God Guide Us?*

1101. In *God the Invisible King*, H. G. Wells wrote: "Religion is the first thing and the last thing, and until a man has found God he begins at no beginning; he works to no end. Life falls into place only with God, who fights through man against Blind Force and Might and Nonexistence; who fights with man against the confusion and evil within us and without and against death in any form; who loves us as a great captain loves his men and stands ready to use us in his immortal adventure against waste, disorder, cruelty, and vice; who is the end, who is the mean, who is the only King."

1102. Tolstoy has described a man sitting in a boat which has been pushed off from an unknown shore; he has been shown the opposite shore, and given a pair of oars, and left alone. Straight out into the stream he rows; but then the current gets hold of him and deflects him. Other boats are there; some have thrown their oars away, a few are struggling against the stream, most are gliding with it quite content. "Is this the way?" he asks some of them; and a chorus of voices replies: "Of course it is. What did you think? There can be no other way." And so he drifts on; but suddenly he grows conscious of a sound, menacing, terrible—the roar of rapids. The man comes to himself, remembers what he had forgotten—the oars, the course, the opposite shore—and madly he begins to row upstream against the current, crying: "Fool that I was to drift!" He rows on until safety is reached. "Now," says Tolstoy, "that current is the tradition of the world, the oars are free will, the opposite shore is God."

1103. Hoxie N. Fairchild in *Toward Belief* relates his discovery of faith: "I tried my best, with rather complete lack of success, to live up to the ethical precepts of Christ. I thought much of God and of my relationship to him. I prayed and meditated. I studied the Bible and followed a homemade course of readings in the history and philosophy of religion. I went to church, not as a mere spectator but as a reverent worshiper. I fear that as a result I have become one of those irritating persons who say they *know* that Christianity is true. I have no words in which to describe what has happened. No mystical illumination has fallen to my lot, nor am I aware of any radical inward rebirth. But I think I know the truth of the text in the Epistle of St. James: 'Draw nigh to God and he will draw nigh to you.' The world looks different to me, and I feel myself in some measure a different man. I have gained a peace and a happiness which I could never have created by my own unaided powers, and I believe that I have found God in my prayers. Anyone who reads this Book can have the same experience if he seeks it. Until he seeks it, nothing that I could say of it would have any meaning for him."

1104. A party of travelers on the fringe of the Sahara stopped at a mud-thatched village near a mission station. A boy with only a loincloth about his waist was sitting in the shade of a tree with a copy of one of the Gospels in his hand. The leader of the party told the guide to say to the boy that he would give him an orange if he would tell them where to find God. The boy stood up and said to the guide, "Tell the man I will give him two oranges if he will tell me where God is not to be found."

1105. An African youth from the Gold Coast, after listening to a discussion on the possibility of finding God in the sunset, exclaimed: "You can find God in nature, but you can find the nature of God only in the Bible."

1106. When he read the words of a French scientist who said, "I have swept the universe with my telescope, and I find no God," J. W. Hawley wrote: "Of course that is as unreasonable as for me to say, 'I have taken this violin apart. I have examined each piece with my microscope, and I find no music.'"— *These Prophetic Voices*

Friendship with God

1107. In George Bernard Shaw's play *Saint Joan,* Joan says, as she goes to the stake to be burned: "Well, my loneliness shall be my strength too: it is better to be alone with God: his friendship will not fail me, nor his counsel nor his love. In his strength I will dare and dare and dare until I die."

1108. Someone overhead the late Bishop Matthew Simpson in his evening devotions pray: "Father, we are in the same relations."

Glory of God

1109. It has been said that Bach wrote above each of his compositions, "Only for the glory of God," and at their close, "With the help of Jesus Christ."

1110. The epitaph of a certain shoemaker reads: "Here lies the body of John Smith, who for forty years cobbled shoes in this village to the glory of God."

1111. "If I only knew that God was as good as that woman, I should be content," says a character in George Macdonald's *Robert Falconer*. "Then you don't believe that God is good?" asks another. "I didn't say that, my boy. But to know that God was good and kind and fair—heartily, I mean, and not half-way with if's and but's. My boy, there would be nothing left to be miserable about."

Guidance of God

1112. On Easter, 1942, General MacArthur cabled his minister: "At the altar where I first joined the sanctuary of God, I ask that you seek divine guidance for me in the great struggle that looms ahead."

1113.
He that is down need fear no fall,
    He that is low, no pride:
He that is humble, ever shall
    Have God to be his guide.
        —BUNYAN, *Pilgrim's Progress*

Hand of God

1114.
Because the way was steep and long,
    And through a strange and lonely
        land,
God placed upon my lips a song,
    And put a lantern in my hand.[1]
—JOYCE KILMER, "Love's Lantern"

1115. Said one of Luther's enemies: "Tell me. When the whole world turns against you—Church, State, princes, people—where will you be then?" "Why, then as now," cried Luther, "in the hands of Almighty God!"

1116. In *Androcles and the Lion,* George Bernard Shaw represents a Roman officer as saying to a Christian maid who is about to be thrown to the lions that it is the height of folly to sacrifice herself for the sake of a silly Christian legend and the vague hope of some future reward. The maid, Lavinia, answers: "If there were no future, or if the future were one of torment, I should have to do just the same. The hand of God is upon me."

1117. Said Dr. Edward Wilson, who died with Scott in the Antarctic: "This I know is God's own truth, that pain and troubles and trials and sorrows and disappointments are either one thing or another. To all who love God they are love tokens from him. To all who do not love God and do not want to love him they are merely a nuisance. Every single pain that we feel is known to God because it is the most loving touch of his hand."

1118. In a broadcast during World War II, King George VI quoted the following lines from *The Gate of the Year* by M. Louise Haskins:

And I said to the man who stood at the gate to the year: "Give me a light that I may tread safely into the unknown."

And he replied:

"Go out into the darkness and put your hand into the Hand of God. That shall be to you better than light and safer than a known way." [2]

[1] From *Poems, Essays and Letters* by Joyce Kilmer. Copyright 1914, 1917, 1918 by Doubleday & Co., Inc. Used by permission.

[2] Used by permission of Christy & Moore, Ltd.

1119.
That in even savage bosoms
There are longings, yearnings, strivings
For the good they comprehend not,
And the feeble hands and helpless,
Groping blindly in the darkness,
Touch God's right hand in that darkness
And are lifted up and strengthened.
—LONGFELLOW, "Song of Hiawatha"

1120. Helen Keller says: "If the blind put their hand in God's, they find their way more surely than those who see but have not faith or purpose."

1121. A mother had two sons, one a gardener and the other a potter. Said the gardener: "O mother, pray God for rain to water my plants." Said the potter, "O mother, pray God for sunshine to dry my pots." Now the mother loved them equally well. Shall she pray for rain or sun? Nay, she would best leave it in the hands of God.—HARRY EMERSON FOSDICK, *The Meaning of Prayer*

1122. A man was twitting a humble old woman who was a devoted Christian. "Suppose," said he, "that Christ would let you slip out of his hand." "Ah," she replied confidently, "I am his hand." —JOHN C. COPENHAVER

1123. Pearl Buck has told the story of a monkey who wanted to get away from God, but though he had struggled, he had never succeeded. He was a fine jumper, and one day he decided that he would give a great leap that would certainly take him out of God's hand. He jumped as far as he could and landed on the top of a great mountain in a strange country. "Ah," he cried, "I have escaped him this time." Then he heard God's voice very near him: "Dear little monkey, you have jumped only to the base of my thumb. You are still in God's hand."

Help of God

1124. When Lincoln was about to leave Springfield for Washington to be inaugurated, he spoke to his fellow townsmen with these words: "I now leave, not knowing when or whether ever I may return, with a task before me greater than that which rested upon Washington. Without the assistance of that Divine Being who ever attended him, I cannot succeed. With that assistance, I cannot fail."

1125. When Napoleon threatened to invade England, a national day of humiliation and prayer was appointed in England, and the following note appeared in the *Christian Observer*: "His Majesty has been graciously pleased to appoint Friday the 25th of May next, to be observed throughout England and Ireland as a day of public humiliation and fasting. We earnestly hope it may be observed in a proper manner. We subjoin a hymn for the occasion, which has just reached us in time to obtain a place in this number." The hymn was "Dread Jehovah! God of nations!" by Thomas Cotterill. It has been a hymn of peoples facing danger and peril for many generations since that time.

1126. Benjamin Franklin at eighty-one addressed the members of the Constitutional Convention with these words: "I have lived a long time; and the longer I live, the more convincing proofs I see of this truth, that God governs in the affairs of men. And if a sparrow cannot fall to the ground without his notice, is it probable that an empire can rise without his aid? We have been assured in the Sacred Writings, that 'except the Lord build the house, they labor in vain that build it.' I firmly believe this; and I also believe that without his concurring aid we shall succeed in this political building no better than the builders of Babel."

1127. A boy in northern India was about to take his examinations. He was in a Christian school. He prayed for God's help, and this was his prayer: "Our Father, help me to pass my examinations. May my whole class pass. May the whole school pass. May the whole world pass."—DANIEL J. FLEMING, *The World at One in Prayer*

1128. After the death of his wife John Calvin, overwhelmed with grief, wrote to his friend William Farrell: "I went to a secret place to pray. . . . May the Lord . . . strengthen you by his spirit, and may he support me also under the heavy affliction which would certainly have overcome me had not he who raises up the prostrate, strengthens the weak, and refreshes the weary, stretched forth his hand from heaven to me."

1129. One of the tenderest stories coming from World War II is that of a small English girl who prayed, "O God, bless Mary and John, Joan and Michael, and, O God take care of yourself or we shall all be sunk."

1130.
Grant me, O God, thy merciful protection;
And in protection give me strength, I pray;
And in my strength, O grant me wise discretion;
And in discretion make me ever just;
And with my justice may I mingle love,
And with my love, O God, the love of thee;
And with the love of thee the love of all.
                    —AUTHOR UNKNOWN

Justice of God

1131. Anne of Austria said to Richelieu: "My Lord Cardinal, God does not pay at the *end of every week*, but *at the end* he pays."

1132. Victor Hugo in *Les Miserables* asks of Napoleon's struggle at Waterloo, "Was it possible for Napoleon to have won that battle?" "No," he answers. "Why? On account of Wellington, on account of Blücher? No. On account of God. It was high time that this monstrous man should fall. The excessive weight of this man on human destiny disturbed its equilibrium. This single individual was counting more than the whole of mankind. The hour had come for supreme incorruptible Justice to take notice. Napoleon had been denounced in the Infinite, and his downfall had been determined. He was obstructing God. Waterloo is no mere battle; it is a change of front on the part of the universe."

Kingdom of God

1133. "The kingdom of heaven is within you," says a message of Jesus from the Oxyrhynchus papyri, "and whosoever shall know himself shall find it." —LESLIE D. WEATHERHEAD, *In Quest of a Kingdom*

1134. Richard Roberts tells of a student of Tolstoy who was haled into court for refusing military service. When he defended himself by quoting from the Gospels, the judge impatiently said, "But that is the kingdom of Heaven; and it has not come yet." The student replied: "Sir, it may not have come for you, but it has come for me."

1135. "Above all things," said Henry Drummond to a group of Harvard students, "do not touch Christianity, unless you are willing to seek the kingdom of heaven first."

Knowing God

1136. Thomas Carlyle, welcoming a new minister to the parish of Craigenputtock, said: "What this country needs is a man who knows God other than by hearsay."

1137. A British weekly tells of the meeting of an aged minister and a distinguished actor at a social gathering. When the actor was asked to give a reading, he repeated at the minister's request the Twenty-third Psalm. Such was the beauty of his voice and the charm of manner that a murmur of praise ran around the room. Then he invited the minister to repeat the same psalm. When the old minister finished, all eyes were filled with tears, for he had spoken with deep tenderness and understanding. Said the actor: "I know that psalm, but you know the Shepherd."—WILBUR KEESEY

1138. In the second century when the storm of persecution broke over the little churches at Lyons and Vienne in southern Gaul, their chief pastor, an infirm man over ninety, was haled before the magistrate's tribunal, where a mob shouted for his death. Asked by the judge, "Who is the god of the Christians?" he replied: "If thou art worthy, thou shalt know."—HENRY SLOANE COFFIN, *What Men Are Asking*

1139. After Mark Twain had made his triumphant tour through Europe, where he was honored by great universities and kings, his daughter said: "Daddy, I guess pretty soon you will know everybody except God."

Laws of God

1140. "You cannot break the laws of God," writes Maude Royden Shaw, "but you can break yourself against them."

1141. Lyman Abbott in *What Christianity Means to Me,* written in his eighty-fifth year, said: "It was not until at about eighteen years of age when I came under the influence of Henry Ward Beecher's preaching that I began to understand that Jesus Christ is not a lawgiver but a lifegiver, and that one is not a Christian because he obeys the laws of God, but he obeys the laws of God because he is a Christian."

Love of God

1142. A thousand years ago Bernard of Clairvaux wrote: "Do you awake? Well, he too is awake. If you rise in the nighttime, if you anticipate to your utmost your earliest awaking, you will already find him waking—you will never anticipate his own awakeness. In such an intercourse you will always be rash if you attribute any priority and predominant share to yourself; for he loves both more than you, and before you love at all."

1143. John Donne, the seventeenth-century English preacher, said: "One of the most convenient hieroglyphics of God is a circle; and a circle is endless; whom God loves, he loves to the end; and not only to their own end, to their death, but to his end; and his end is that he might love them still."

1144.
A weathercock that once placed
    A farmer's barn above,
Bore on it by its owner's will
    The sentence, "God is love."

His neighbor passing questioned him,
    He deemed the legend strange—
"Now, dost thou think that, like the vane,
    God's love can lightly change?"

The farmer smiling shook his head.
"Nay, friend, 'tis meant to show
That 'God is love' whichever way
The wind may chance to blow.
—AUTHOR UNKNOWN

1145. Someone said of Dick Sheppard: "Were all other proofs to fail me, that man alone would compel me to believe that God exists, and that God is love."

1146. "I knew God experimentally," was the witness of George Fox, the founder of the Quakers. "I was as one who has the key that opens. I was taken up into the love of God. I saw that there was an ocean of darkness and death. But I saw that there was an infinite ocean of light and life and love which flows over the ocean of darkness, and in that I saw the infinite love of God."

1147. When a missionary had told a Chinese mother about the love of God, the mother exclaimed: "I've always thought there should be a God like that."

1148. Kagawa tells how a Christian missionary helped him to understand the love of God. While he was spending a sick period alone during his student days, a man knocked at the door. He requested the visitor *not* to enter. "Do not come in: I have a contagious disease." But the missionary went to Kagawa's side and said: "I have something more contagious than disease. I have come with the love of God."

1149. One of Wesley's helpers, John Nelson, was thrown into a dungeon underneath a slaughterhouse. He tells us "it stank worse than a hogsty by reason of the blood and filth that flowed into it from above." Then he adds: "My soul was so filled with the love of God that it was a paradise to me."—LESLIE D. WEATHERHEAD, *Jesus and Ourselves*

1150.
He paints the lily of the field,
Perfumes each lily bell:
If He so loves the little flowers,
I know He loves me well.
—MARIA STRAUS

Love Toward God

1151. An old woman was seen coming along the streets of Strasbourg a great number of years. She was carrying a pail of water in one hand and a torch in the other. When asked what she was about, she answered that with the pail of water she was going to put out the flames of hell and with the torch she was going to burn up heaven, so that in the future men could love the dear Lord God for himself alone and not out of fear of hell or out of craving for reward.
—DOUGLAS V. STEERE, *Prayer and Worship*

1152. A little girl, not yet fully prepared, got up to recite Psalm 23 in a church-school program. She didn't recite the psalm as most of us know it, but what she said is true: "The Lord is my Shepherd; that's all I want."

Mercy of God

1153. When a good farmer named Bob Pericord died, friends discovered an epitaph which he had written for his grave:

Have mercy, Lord, as I would
If I were Lord,
And you were old Bob Pericord.

1154.
I never cut my neighbor's throat,
My neighbor's purse I never stole;
I never spoiled his house and land,
But God have mercy on my soul!

For I am haunted night and day
  By all the deeds I have not done.
O unattempted loveliness!
  O costly valour, never won! [3]
—MARGUERITE WILKINSON, "Guilty"

Name of God

1155. "I have known God all my life,"
an Indian once told a missionary, "and
now you have told me his name."

1156. A genuine Moslem necklace contains ninety-nine beads, each bead re-
minding the devout follower of Islam of
"the ninety-nine beautiful names of
God." These names the Moslem recites
during his daily meditation.

Nearness of God

1157. It is said that when Augustine
and his mother, Monica, were at Ostia
resting for the voyage home, he expressed his fear that she might die far
from home. The old woman comforted
him with these words: "No one, my
son, is ever far from God."

1158. Dwight L Moody asked Andrew
Bonar of Scotland: "Dr. Bonar, these
people would like to know how you live
this victorious life about which you
have been preaching." Dr. Bonar replied: "I do not like to speak of myself,
but for fifty years I have had access to
the throne of grace."

1159. Thornton Wilder in *Our Town*
showed in a striking manner the relationship of the individual to God. Jane
Crofut's address on the envelope sent to
her by her minister when she was sick
read: "Jane Crofut; the Crofut Farm;
Grover's Corners; Sutton County; New
Hampshire; United States of America;
Continent of North America; Western

[3] Used by permission.

Hemisphere; the Earth; the Solar System; the Universe; the Mind of God."

Need of God

1160. "The greatest question of our
time," says Will Durant, the philosopher, "is not communism versus indi-
vidualism, not Europe versus America,
not even the East versus the West: it
is whether man can bear to live without God."

1161. A motto on the desk of a distinguished businessman reads: "How
great a God we need; and how much
greater is our God than our greatest
need."

1162. "If there wasn't a God," said the
skeptical Rousseau, "we would have to
invent one to keep people sane."

1163. A young man held hard by a
habit that was determining the entire
system of his living went to his minister, saying: "I do not believe in God,
but if you do, for God's sake pray for
me, for I need him."—HARRY EMERSON
FOSDICK, *On Being a Real Person*

1164. A Negro in the midst of the
earthquake in Charleston said: "Good
Lord, come and help us; oh, come now,
and come yo'self, Lord; 'taint no times
for boys."—FREDERICK K. STAMM, *In
the Shadow of the Cross*

1165. It has been reported that Rudyard
Kipling, when desperately sick and
burning with fever, tossed to and fro
on his bed and mumbled words which
no one could quite understand. One
morning a nurse bent over him and
asked, "Mr. Kipling, what is it you
want?" The poet ceased his rest-
lessness, opened his weary eyes, and
feebly whispered, "I want God."—S. A.
CAMPBELL, *Grit to Grapple with Life*

1166.

> Forgive me if too close I lean
> My human heart on thee.
> —John G. Whittier, "Faith"

1167. After her sister Emily had died of tuberculosis and while another sister, Anne, was slowly losing her strength, Charlotte Brontë wrote in a letter: "We saw Emily torn from the midst of us when our hearts clung to her with intense attachment and when loving each other as we did—well it seemed as if (might we but have been spared to each other) we could have found complete happiness in our mutual society and affection. She was sacrcely buried when Anne's health failed, and we were warned that consumption had found another victim in her. I have learned that we are not to find solace in our own strength: we must seek it in God's omnipotence. Fortitude is good, but fortitude itself must be shaken under us, to teach us how weak we are."

Plan of God

1168. A revealing bit of dialogue from John Galsworthy's *Maid in Waiting* contains a discussion between Dinny and her mother, Lady Cherwell. "I suppose there is an eternal plan," Dinny says, "but we're like gnats for all the care it has for us as individuals." "Don't encourage such feelings, Dinny," says her mother; "they affect one's character." "I don't see," replies the daughter, "the connection between beliefs and character. I'm not going to behave any worse because I cease to believe in Providence or an afterlife." "Surely, Dinny—" "No; I'm going to behave *better*; if I'm decent it's because decency's the decent thing, and not because I'm going to get anything by it." Then the mother asks: "But why is decency the decent thing, Dinny, if there's no God?"

1169. When William Braisted was a small boy, he prayed: "O God, plan our lives for us better than we can plan them for ourselves, and don't let us get in the way." Following God's plan Braisted secured college and medical training and became a missionary to China.

Praise to God

1170. "What else can I, a lame old man, do," exclaimed Epictetus, "than sing hymns to God? If I were a nightingale, I would play the part of a nightingale. But I am a rational creature; and I ought to praise God. This is my work. I do it; nor will I desert this post so long as I am allowed to keep it. And I exhort you to join in the same song."

1171.

> We often praise the evening clouds,
>   And tints so gay and bold,
> But seldom think upon our God,
>   Who tinged these clouds with gold.
>   —Sir Walter Scott,
>   "On the Setting Sun"

Presence of God

1172. "When you have shut the doors and made a darkness within," said Epictetus, "remember never to say that you are alone; for you are not alone, but God is within."

1173. Clement of Alexandria in the second century described with poetic insight the effect of religious vision upon the tasks of the common life: "Holding festival then, in our whole life, persuaded that God is altogether on every side present, we cultivate our fields, praising; we sail the sea, hymning; in all the rest of our conversation we conduct ourselves according to rule."
—Georgia Harkness, *Religious Living*

1174. John Baillie made it a practice to open his course on the "Doctrine of God" at Edinburgh University with these words: "Gentlemen, we must remember that in discussing God we cannot talk about him without his hearing every word we say. We may be able to talk some of our fellows, as it were, behind their backs, but God is everywhere, yes, even here in this classroom. Therefore, in all of our discussions we must be aware of his infinite presence and talk about him, as it were, before his face."

1175. Lord Moynihan of Leeds, a famous physician, was asked if he objected to many observers at an operation. "Well," he said, "it is like this: there are just three people in the theatre when I operate—the patient and myself." "But that is only two," a friend suggested. "Who is the other?" The physician said: "God."

1176. "When I am operating," said a famous surgeon, "I feel the presence of God so real that I cannot tell where his skill ends and mine begins."

1177. When Sir Ernest Shackleton returned to England to report on his Antarctic explorations, he told the king of his consciousness of the presence of God while he traveled lands never visited by man before: "Bending above the oars, struggling through the snow, battling across the ranges, *always* there was with us *Another. He* made the difference between triumph and disaster. *He* brought us through."

1178. Three men were treading over the inhospitable mountains and treacherous glaciers of South Georgia in the Antarctic, in an attempt to rescue the rest of the South Polar party. Later Sir Ernest Shackleton wrote in his diary: "When I look back at those days, I have no doubt that Providence guided us. . . . During that long and racing march of thirty-six hours over the unnamed mountains and glaciers of South Georgia it seemed to me that we were four, not three. I said nothing to my companions on this point, but afterwards Worsley said to me, 'Boss, I had a curious feeling on the march that there was another person with us.' Crean confessed the same idea. One feels the dearth of human words, the roughness of mortal speech, in trying to describe things intangible, but a record of our journeys would not be complete without a reference to a subject so very near to our hearts."

1179. An atheist went into a schoolroom and wrote on the blackboard: "God is nowhere." A little girl rose from her seat and said: "Oh, sir, that's wrong. It should be 'God is now here.'"

1180. "I came about like a well-handled ship," said Robert Louis Stevenson of a decisive period in his life. "There stood at the wheel that unknown steersman whom we call God."

1181. When Alfred Tennyson was near death, someone asked him if there was anything he wanted. "Yes," said the great poet, "a new vision of God."

1182. Edwin Booth is reported to have run his theater as though it was a church. When a minister, fearing the criticism of his parishioners, asked Booth if there was a back door in his theater by which he might attend a particular performance, Booth replied: "There is no door in my theater through which God cannot see."

1183.

> God be in my head,
> And in my understanding;
> God be in my eyes,
> And in my looking
> God be in my mouth,
> And in my speaking;
> God be in my heart,
> And in my thinking;
> God be at my end,
> And at my departing.
> —*Sarum Primer* (A.D. 1558)

1184. Jeremiah E. Rankin, writer of the hymn "God Be with You Till We Meet Again!" tells in these words the story of the hymn's origin: "Written in 1882 as a Christian good-by, it was called forth by no person or occasion, but was deliberately composed as a Christian hymn on the basis of the etymology of 'good-by,' which is 'God be with you.'"

Seeking God

1185. Some years ago a former president of the Argentine Republic was making an address in which he was giving the reasons for the difference between the relatively slow progress made by South America and the phenomenal progress made by North America in the same period of time. He said: "Herein lies the reason: Our forefathers came to South America seeking gold, whereas the early settlers of North America came to that continent seeking God."
—LUTHER WESLEY SMITH

1186. E. Stanley Jones reminds us that in 1852 two covered wagon caravans started out from Omaha across the wide expanses toward the Far West. For days they went in parallel lines, and then they diverged in more ways than one. The Mormons had written on their covered wagons: "God Seekers." The other group, who represented the gold rush, put on their wagons: "Gold Seekers." The former pioneers built a city; the latter found gold but left nothing.

1187. "If we seek God for our own good and profit," said Johannes Eckhart, "we are not seeking *God.*"

1188. Mary Kingsley tells of a medicine man in Africa who came to death's gate. He applied all his herbs and spells, and conducted all his well-worn rites before his idols without effect. At last wearied of it all, he took his idols and his charms down to the seashore and flung them into the surf and said: "Now I will be a man and meet my God alone."
—T. H. DAVIES, *The Inner Circle*

1189. "I would not seek thee," Blaise Pascal wrote, "unless thou hadst already found me."

Supremacy of God

1190. "From my undergraduate days at Cornell University," writes Georgia Harkness, "one of my deepest impressions is the inscription over the entrance to the main hall of the College of Arts and Sciences, 'Above all nations is humanity.' To this conviction, which an increasing number of thoughtful people now accept, must be added another, 'Above all humanity is God.'"—*Prayer and the Common Life*

1191. A great Christian shoe manufacturer had for his motto: "God first, others second, shoes third."

1192. The seal of one of the Waldensian churches pictures an anvil and a number of broken hammers with the motto:

> Hammer away ye hostile hands!
> Your hammers break;
> God's anvil stands!

Surrender to God

1193.

Laid on thine altar, O my Lord divine,
  Accept this gift today, for Jesus' sake:
I have no jewels to adorn thy shrine,
  No far-famed sacrifice to make;
But here within my trembling hand I
    bring
  This will of mine—a thing that seem-
    eth small
But thou alone, O Lord, canst under-
    stand
  How when I yield thee this, I yield
    mine all.

—AUTHOR UNKNOWN

1194. When E. Stanley Jones asked
Kagawa, the great Japanese Christian,
what was the first thing in prayer,
Kagawa answered: "Surrender."

1195. "It seems to me that science
teaches in most unmistakable terms the
Christian conception of the entire surrender to the will of God," Thomas
Huxley wrote Charles Kingsley. "Science
says to sit down before the facts as a
little child, be prepared to give up every
preconceived notion, be willing to be
led to whatever end Nature will lead
you, or you will know nothing."

Thanksgiving to God

1196. Working in his laboratory and
hospital at Bangalore in an effort to
discover the protozoan which causes
malaria, Sir Ronald Ross wrote:

I pace and pace, and think and think,
    and take
  The fever'd hands, and note down all
    I see,
That some dim distant light may haply
    break.

The painful faces ask, Can we not cure?
  We answer, No, not yet; we seek the
    laws.

O God, reveal through all this thing
    obscure
  The unseen, small, but million-mur-
    dering cause.[4]

Several years later he wrote in grateful
triumph:

This day relenting God
  Hath placed within my hand
A wondrous thing; and God
  Be praised. At His command,

Seeking His secret deeds
  With tears and toiling breath,
I find thy cunning seeds,
  O million-murdering death.

I know this little thing
  A myriad men will save.
O Death, where is thy sting?
  Thy victory, O Grave?[5]

1197. An English clergyman noticed a
small boy who entered his church frequently to pray. "Do you often come
here to pray?" the minister asked. "Four
times in the last five days," the lad said.
"Have you someone fighting at Dun-
kerque?" "Yes, my daddy," the lad
answered, adding, "but he got home today, so I came to thank God."

1198. The story is told of a Russian
girl who in her examination for a government position was asked: "What is
the inscription on the Sarmian wall?"
She guessed that it might be "Religion
is the opiate of the people," but not
being sure she walked seven miles from
Leningrad to the Sarmian wall to check
on her answer. Fearfully she looked

[4] From *Philosophies*. Used by permission
of John Murray, London.

[5] From *Philosophies*. Used by permission of
John Murray, London.

upon the wall, where she found just what she had written, "Religion is the opiate of the people." Relieved, she fell to her knees, crossed herself, and said, "Thank God!"

1199.
We thank thee, Lord, on this recurring
  day,
  For liberty to worship as we will;
We thank Thee for the hero souls of
  old,
  Who dared wild seas their mission to
  fulfill.
Oh, gird our hearts with stalwart faith
  in good,
  Give us new trust in Thy providing
  hand,
And may a spirit born of brotherhood
  Inspire our hearts and bless our native
  land.[6]
          —Thomas Curtis Clark,
            "Thanksgiving"

1200. "I think my imprisonment belongeth to the holy humor of God," Martin Niemoller wrote to his wife after six months spent in jail. "First the mocking jibe, 'Now we have got that fellow!' and then the imprisonment; and what are the consequences? Full churches, a praying community! To get bitter about such things would be shameful ingratitude."

Trust in God
1201.
Whoever plants a leaf beneath the sod,
And waits to see it push away the clod,
  He trusts in God.

Whoever says, when clouds are in the
  sky,
"Be patient, heart; light breaketh by and
  by,"
  He trusts in God.

[6] Used by permission of the author.

Whoever sees 'neath winter's field of
  snow
The silent harvest of the future grow,
  God's power must know.

Whoever lies down on his couch to
  sleep,
Content to lock each sense in slumber
  deep,
  Knows God will keep.
          —Author Unknown

1202. In the sixteenth century when King Philip of Spain was subduing Holland and robbing the people of their civil and religious liberties, Diedrich Sonoy, the lieutenant governor of North Holland, wrote to William, Prince of Orange, asking whether he had arranged some foreign alliance. The prince replied: "You ask if I have entered into a firm treaty with any great king or potentate; to which I answer that before I ever took up the cause of the oppressed Christians in these provinces, I had entered into a close alliance with the King of kings; and I am firmly convinced that all who put their trust in him shall be saved by his almighty hand. The God of armies will raise up armies for us to do battle with our enemies and his own."

1203. Hugh Mackail, the Covenanter preacher who was sent to the Edinburgh scaffold in December, 1666, called to his friends as he was led for the last time down to the Tolbooth, "Trust in God! Trust in God!" Then seeing a friend, he called: "Good news! I am within four days' journey of enjoying the sight of Jesus Christ."

1204. On the night before August 27, 1776, George Washington, fearful that attacks might be made by sea and land on the American forces stationed on

Long Island, found that sleep had escaped him until he realized that "the same Providence that rules today will rule tomorrow."

1205. A Negro threatened with return to slavery said as the funeral procession of Lincoln approached: "They needn't crow. God isn't dead."

1206. During the Civil War the Secretary of the Treasury wrote to the Director of the Mint at Philadelphia, saying: "No nation can be strong in the strength of God or safe except in his defense. We recommend that the trust of the people in God be declared on their coins." Accordingly orders were given to prepare a motto to express national recognition and trust in God. At first this read: "God, our trust." Later the inscription was changed to read: "In God we trust."—HERBERT W. HAHN

1207.
It fortifies my soul to know
That though I perish, truth is so;
That, wheresoe'er I stray and range,
Whate'er I do, Thou dost not change.
I steadier step when I recall
That, if I slip, Thou dost not fall.
—ARTHUR HUGH CLOUGH,
 "With Whom Is No Variableness,
 Neither Shadow of Turning"

1208. Sir Wilfred Grenfell told of a man seventy-three years old who came to him with twelve five-dollar bills for use for food for needy neighbors. When Sir Wilfred told the old man, "You are getting old, and you should not cut the last plant away yet," the old man replied: "God will take care; guess I can trust him. It wouldn't do not to have used that sixty dollars, and have sent folks away hungry, would it? It would look as if I didn't have much trust in him."

1209. There is a story which Principal Robert Rainy used to tell about a man in Edinburgh who was a bad character and a confirmed lawbreaker. He had only one redeeming feature in his life— his love for his little girl, who was an only child, the very image of her dead mother. He committed burglary and was put into prison. During the term of his sentence the child died. On the day when he came out he learned of her death. It was a shattering blow. He could not go back to the house. In his wild and bitter distraction he resolved that when night came he would fling himself over the Dean Bridge and end it all. At midnight he stood on the bridge. He was climbing the parapet when suddenly, for no reason that he could think of, there flashed into his mind the opening words of the Apostles' Creed—"I believe in God, the Father Almighty." And he stepped back. He knew nothing of God, but he did know something of fatherhood. "Why," he found himself saying, "if that is what God is, if God is like that, then I can trust him with my lassie—and with myself!" And from that moment death receded; life began anew.—JAMES S. STEWART, *The Gates of New Life*

1210. "I do not know how the loving father will bring out light at last, but he knows and he will do it," affirmed David Livingstone.

1211. A Negro is quoted as having prayed: "O God, help me to understand that you ain't gwine to let nothin' come my way that you and me together can't handle."

1212.
Whoever falls from God's right hand
Is caught into his left.[7]
    —EDWIN MARKHAM,
     "The Divine Strategy"

[7] Used by permission of Virgil Markham.

Victory of God

1213. "Do you expect to be able to do anything in a land that vast?" someone asked Robert Morrison when he began his pioneer work in Chinese missions. "No," Morrison answered, "but I expect *God will.*"

1214. Caesar said: "I came, I saw, I conquered." When John Sobieski appeared before the pope with the Mussulman standards captured before Vienna, he said: "I came, I saw, God conquered."

Voice of God

1215. In an interview with King Charles, Joan of Arc spoke of the strange voices she heard. Charles, irritated, said that the voices should come to him, the king, and not to a mere subject. Joan answered: "They do come to you; but you do not hear them. If you prayed from your heart and listened, you would hear the voices as well as I do."

1216. E. Stanley Jones tells of a Swedish literary woman who wanted God to tell her what the next step in her career was to be. At length she seemed to hear God say: "How could you expect me to speak when you have gagged me so long?"

1217. "How rare to find a soul still enough to hear God speak," said Fénelon.

1218. Bishop William A. Quayle, the story goes, went to bed one night, but sleep escaped him because of his distractions over problems he could not solve. Then he heard the voice of God speak: "Quayle, you go to bed. I'll sit up the rest of the night."

Will of God

1219. William James in *The Varieties of Religious Experience* wrote: "Whoever not only says but feels, 'God's will be done,' is mailed against every weakness; and the whole historic array of martyrs, missionaries, and religious reformers is there to prove the tranquil-mindedness, under naturally agitating or distressing circumstances, which self-surrender brings."

1220.
Back of the loaf is the snowy flour,
  And back of the flour the mill;
And back of the mill is the wheat and
    the shower,
  And the sun and the Father's will.[8]
    —MALTBIE D. BABCOCK,
    "Our Daily Bread"

1221. The motto in G. Campbell Morgan's study reads: "The Will of God—Nothing More, Nothing Less."

1222. "O Lord," prayed Augustine, "grant that I may do thy will as if it were my will; so that thou mayst do my will as if it were thy will."

1223. When Alan Cameron, the Covenanter, was in prison, soldiers entered bearing the head of his son Richard. The old man staggered as if struck in the face with a whip. But then he lifted his head. "It is the Lord," he said. "Good is the will of the Lord."

Work of God

1224. Hudson Taylor once said: "I used to ask God to help me. Then I asked if I might help him. I ended up by asking him to do his work through me."

[8] Reprinted from *Thoughts for Everyday Living* by Maltbie D. Babcock; copyright 1901 by Charles Scribner's Sons, 1929 by Katherine T. Babcock; used by permission of the publishers.

1225. A Salvationist visiting Nottingham chapel, where William Booth was converted, kneeled near the commemorative tablet and prayed: "O God, do it again! Do it again."

1226. One morning, following a terrific thunderstorm, a little child came downstairs and said: "Daddy what was God doing last night? Was he making the morning?" And the father replied: "Yes, dear, I guess God was making the morning."—Elmer LeRoy Hobbs

1227. Said Gladstone: "The task of statesmanship is to discover where God Almighty is going during the next fifty years."

GOOD

1228. James A. Froude, the great historian, declared that "in the long run it is well with the good, and in the long run it is ill with the evil."

1229. Said Phillips Brooks: "No man or woman of the humblest sort can really be strong, gentle, pure, and good without the world being better for it, without someone being helped and comforted by the very existence of that goodness."

1230. Writes Preston Bradley in *Mastering Fear:* "I have known what it is to go into the pulpit full of fear. Sometimes I have thought I could not go out. But do you know what saved me? I substituted for the fear the constructive thought that I am attempting to do good, that I am attempting to be helpful, that I am attempting to be encouraging, that there can be no penalty for the doing of good. When my mind was flooded with this thought, fear was crowded out."

1231. "I'm not always good," confided a little girl, "but when I'm not good, I'm miserable."

1232. When a church worker was urging a small boy to attend Sunday school, telling him that he would learn how to be a good boy, the lad said: "There's no use in my going. I already know how to be a better boy than I am."—Thomas F. Carroll

1233. One little girl prayed: "O Lord, make all the bad people good, and all the good people nice."

1234. When asked what was wrong with the world, an old Negro minister said: "The good ain't able and the able ain't good."

GOOD WILL

1235. Walter W. Van Kirk lists the following as "Ten Commandments of Good Will":

1. I will respect all men and women regardless of race and religion.

2. I will protect and defend my neighbor and my neighbor's children against the ravages of racial or religious bigotry.

3. I will exemplify in my own life the spirit of good will and understanding.

4. I will challenge the philosophy of racial superiority by whomsoever it may be proclaimed, whether they be kings, dictators, or demagogues.

5. I will not be misled by the lying propaganda of those who seek to set race against race or nation against nation.

6. I will refuse to support any organization that has for its purpose the spreading of anti-Semitism, anti-Catholicism, or anti-Protestantism.

7. I will establish comradeship with those who seek to exalt the spirit of love and reconciliation throughout the world.

8. I will attribute to those who differ from me the same degree of sincerity that I claim for myself.

9. I will uphold the civil rights and religious liberties of all citizens and groups whether I agree with them or not.

10. I will do more than live and let live—I will live and help live.

1236. A young American girl was teaching in a Chinese village that was about to be looted by a vicious bandit and his followers. That meant something worse than death to women in the town. This girl loaded some ponies with food and presents, and with a friend marched off to the bandit camp in the hills, walked untouched through the armed guard, befriended the chief, surprised him with kindness and fearless good will, and, like a good American, even persuaded him to pose for a photograph. She came away with a promise that her village would be unharmed, and the promise was kept.—ROBERT RUSSELL WICKS, *The Reason for Living*

1237. As Robert E. Lee ordered the withdrawal of his troops at Gettysburg, a wounded Union soldier, recognizing him, shouted tauntingly, "Hurrah for the Union!" Lee dismounted and approached the prostrate soldier with intent, as the latter thought, to kill him. But the sorely tried leader merely grasped the man by the hand and said: "My son, I hope you will soon be well."

GOSPEL

1238. "I reckon him a Christian indeed," wrote Matthew Henry, "that is neither ashamed of the gospel nor a shame to it."

1239. William E. Gladstone, British statesman and prime minister, said: "Talk about the questions of the day; there is but one question, and that is the gospel. It can and will correct everything needing correction."

1240. "We do believe it in a way," said Robert Rainy of the gospel, "but we are no longer startled by it in our own minds."

1241. William Lyon Phelps in his *Autobiography with Letters* wrote: "I remember an earnest Protestant pastor who conceived it his duty during an entire presidential campaign to preach against one of the candidates. The trouble with any minister who has only one idea is that his flock know what he is going to say; they lose interest and stay away. And this man kept it up; after the candidate whom he had opposed was elected, and he with other men at a club was listening to the election returns, he cried out in distress of mind, 'Oh, what shall I do now?' Professor Lounsbury remarked, 'There is only one thing for you to do now, Doctor; and that is to preach the gospel.' "

1242. When a shipload of slaves had been delivered to an American port during colonial times, a minister arose in the pulpit to thank God for "bringing these benighted blacks under the influence of the gospel."

GOSSIP

1243. George Meredith said a gossip is "a beast of prey who does not even wait for the death of the victim he devours."

1244. Augustine had a motto printed on the wall of his dining room: "He who speaks an evil word of an absent man or woman is not welcome at this table."

1245. Heywood Broun once related the story of a mother who told her children to divide all people into two classes—friends and strangers. Friends we love too well to gossip about; strangers we know too little.

1246. Sir Robert Peel, dining in a West End mansion one evening, heard a slanderous story told. He rose and took leave of his host. "Surely you are not going," said the latter in consternation. "Yes," said Sir Robert sternly. "I am still a gentleman, and I hope I am a Christian."

1247. There is a legend of a peasant with a troubled conscience who went to the village priest for advice. The peasant had repeated some slander about a friend and later he had found that his words were untrue. He asked the priest what he could do to make amends. The priest told the man: "If you want to make peace with your conscience, you must fill a bag with goose feathers and go to every door in the village and drop a feather on each porch." The peasant took a bag, filled it with goose feathers, and did as he was told. Then he went back to the priest and asked: "Is this all that I need to do?" "No, that is not all," was the answer. "There is one thing more, take your bag and gather up every feather." The peasant left. After a long period he returned, saying, "I could not find all the feathers, for the wind had blown them away." The priest said, "So it is with gossip. Unkind words are so easily dropped, but we can never take them back again."—R. C. FLEISHER

1248.
There is so much good in the worst of us,
And so much bad in the best of us,
That it ill behoves any of us
To find fault with the rest of us.
         —AUTHOR UNKNOWN,
           "Charity"

1249. When Talleyrand was told that a certain man was saying unkind and untrue things about him, he retorted: "That surprises me; I have never done him a favor."

1250. "So live," advised Will Rogers, "that you would not be ashamed to sell the family parrot to the town gossip."

GRACE

1251.
All treasures of wisdom and truth and holiness are in God.
Through constant fellowship with Christ true Christian character takes shape within the soul. Therefore, pray for:
The grace of a thankful and uncomplaining heart;
The grace of courage, whether in suffering or in danger;
The grace of boldness in standing for what is right;
The grace of bodily discipline;
The grace of strict truthfulness;
The grace of charity—refraining from hasty judgments;
The grace of silence—refraining from hasty speech;
The grace of forgiveness toward all who wrong us;
The grace of tenderness toward all who are weak;
The grace of steadfastness in continuing to desire and to pray.
         —JOHN BAILLIE

1252. "The grace of God is the good which God puts into each concrete situation over and above all that man can do or plan or even imagine," says Henry Nelson Wieman.

1253. Over the fireplace of a clubhouse belonging to a group of Alcoholics Anonymous is a plaque bearing this inscription: "But for the grace of God."

1254. Robert Louis Stevenson in *The Ebb Tide* says: "Why not the grace of your Maker and Redeemer? He who died for you, he who upholds you, he whom you daily crucify afresh? There is nothing but God's grace. We walk upon it; we breathe it; we live and die by it: it makes the nails and axles of the universe; and a puppy in pajamas prefers self-conceit."

1255. "A British Tommy gave me a synopsis of the sermon," recalls Joseph Fort Newton, "and I can still see his big blue eyes and hear his soft voice as he told me point by point, what the preacher had said. The subject was 'The Grace of God,' and the Tommy closed his account with exquisite courtesy in these words: 'The minister told us that the grace of God is plentiful, sufficient for all need, and near at hand, but he did not tell us what the grace of God is; perhaps you, sir, will be good enough to do that.'"—*The New Preaching*

GRATITUDE

1256.
Thou that hast given so much to me,
Give one thing more—a grateful heart;
Not thankful when it pleaseth me,
As if Thy blessings had spare days;
But such a heart, whose pulse may be
Thy praise.
—GEORGE HERBERT, "Our Prayer"

1257. André Maurois in his biography of Disraeli writes: "Society found Disraeli's marriage at thirty-three to an ignorant and frivolous widow of forty-five ridiculous. To him it was a paradise of adoration, a refuge of lasting tenderness. True, Mary Anne was ignorant, but what did that matter? She had good sense, gave sound political advice, and was a useful companion in campaigns. Her frivolous talk amused and relaxed Disraeli; he had too many brilliant friends in women to want to withstand assaults of wit in his own home. Frank to the point of tactlessness, of freakish and detestable taste in dress and furniture, Mrs. Disraeli was continually exposing herself and her husband to ridicule in the noble houses they visited. But though pride and sensibility made Disraeli alive to the situation, he never reproached her. A daring friend once remarked that he must be a man of extraordinary qualities if his wife's conversation never annoyed him. Disraeli replied: 'Not at all; I possess one quality in which most men are deficient—gratitude.'"

1258. When the parents of a young man killed in the war presented a gift to their church in their son's memory, the mother of another youth suggested to her husband that they do the same thing. "But our son came home," the father said. "That's just the point," the mother said. "Let us make a gift because he did come home."

1259. The inscription written by their children for the graves of David Livingstone's parents at Hamilton, Scotland, reads:

To show the resting place of
Neil Livingstone
And Agnes Hunter, his wife,
And to express their thankfulness to God
Of their children
For poor and pious parents.

1260. After spending more than ten years in a detailed study of the life of Robert E. Lee, Douglas Freeman said: "I have been fully repaid by being privileged to live . . . for more than a decade in the company of a great gentleman."

GROWTH

1261. Lyman Abbott told this "Parable of the Acorn": "I pluck an acorn from the greensward and hold it to my ear; and this is what it says to me: 'By and by the birds will come and nest in me. By and by I will furnish shade for the cattle. By and by I will provide warmth for the home in the pleasant fire. By and by I will be the shelter from the storm to those who have gone under the roof. By and by I will be the strong ribs of the great vessel, and the tempest will bear against me in vain while I carry men across the Atlantic.' 'O foolish little acorn, wilt thou be all this?' I ask. 'Yes, God and I.'"

1262. "Forget the past," says Myrtle Reed. "Whatever is past is over, and I'm thinking you have no more to do with it than a butterfly has with the empty chrysalis from which it came. The law of life is growth, and cannot linger —we must always be going on."

GUIDANCE

1263. Deep in the Mammoth Cave of Kentucky is a bronze tablet which reads: "Out of the lowest depths there is a path to the loftiest heights." A reader of the inscription is ever aware of a guide nearby who will show him the way out.

1264. When an American wrote to Granville Sharp saying that in respect for his great virtues he had named one of his sons after him, Sharp replied: "I must request you to teach him a favorite maxim of the family whose name you have given him—'Always endeavor to be really what you would wish to appear.'"

H

HANDICAPS

1265. Helen Keller has written: "I thank God for my handicaps, for through them I have found myself, my work, and my God."

1266. Roland Hayes, the Negro singer, was told by Sir George Henschel: "You don't sing *with* a cold, you sing *around* it." That counsel helped Hayes, who had been unable to give a good performance because of a bad cold.

1267. When three-year-old Louis Braille was boring holes with an awl in a heavy piece of leather in his father's harness shop in Coupvray, France, back in 1812, an accident with the awl caused blindness. Seventeen years later the totally blind youth invented the Braille system, a system now used all over the world, bringing incalculable blessing to thousands of blind persons. Not only did the invention bring "sight" to young Braille, but his tragedy was the means of helping many generations of blinded persons.

1268. The "Hallelujah Chorus" was written by Handel, who at the time was fifty-six years old, poor, and suffering from a paralyzed right side and right arm.

1269. Ludwig van Beethoven, the son of a poor drunken father, became deaf at the age of twenty-eight. When he conducted the first performance of his *Ninth Symphony*, he could not hear the thunder of applause, and only in his mind could he hear the music.

1270. Millet, the French painter, completed his famous "Angelus" under the most depressing conditions. "We have only enough fuel to last us for two or three days," he wrote, "and we don't know how we are going to get any more, for they won't let us have any without money." Yet from such circumstances came one of the most soul-satisfying pictures to be found.

1271. Wolfgang Mozart wrote some of his finest music while suffering poverty and want. Although posterity regards him as one of the greatest musicians, he died in poverty and was buried in a pauper's grave.

1272. A friend of Lord Byron, a cripple from his youth, said of the poet: "He brooded over that blemish as sensitive minds will brood until they magnify a wart into a wen. His lameness certainly helped to make him skeptical, cynical, and savage."

1273. Catherine Booth in the last year of her life said she could not remember one day free from pain. Robert Louis Stevenson wrote stories of heroism while tuberculosis had him by the throat. Helen Keller has been blind and deaf from infancy. Henry Martyn the Indian missionary fought consumption of the lungs while carrying on evangelistic work in incredibly difficult circumstances. Theresa endured unending headaches accompanied by fever and subsequently paralysis. Sir Walter Scott was incurably lame. George Matheson was incurably blind. Beethoven was incurably deaf. Ignatius Loyola who founded the Jesuit order was in lifelong pain. Pascal reported that he had been in pain from his eighteenth year to the year of his death. Cowper and Samuel Johnson suffered from what now would be called chronic anxiety neurosis. They were both in daily fear of insanity.— LESLIE D. WEATHERHEAD, *The Significance of Silence*

HANDS

1274. Leslie D. Weatherhead in *The Transforming Friendship* quotes the following passage from *My Lady of the Chimney Corner:* "God takes a han' wherever He can find it and jist diz what He likes wi' it. Sometimes He takes a bishop's and lays it on a child's head in benediction; then He takes the han' of a docther t' relieve pain, th' han' of a mother t' guide her chile, an' sometimes He take th' han' of an aul craither like me t' give a bit comfort to a neighbour. But they're all han's touch't be His Spirit, an' His Spirit is everywhere lukin' fur han's to use."

1275. "All my life I have been seeking to climb out of the pit of my besetting sins," wrote Seneca. "And I can't do it: and I never will, unless a hand is let down to me to draw me up."

1276. An old Alpine guide saw a man trembling on the brink of a crevasse, stretched out his hand to him, and said in a strong, clear voice: "Here, man, take this hand. It has never lost a man."

1277. When Heine stood before the great statue Venus de Milo he exclaimed: "But oh! what was it worth? For she has no arms, the goddess, no hands to reach out and help poor beaten souls like me!"

1278.
The touch of human hands—
Not vain, unthinking words,
Not that cold charity
Which shuns our misery;
We seek a loyal friend
Who understands,
And the warmth, the pulsing warmth
Of human hands.[1]
   —THOMAS CURTIS CLARK,
    "The Touch of Human Hands"

1279. "How will Jesus recognize me when I meet him?" a seriously sick woman who had devoted many years of her life to the care of her motherless brothers and sisters asked her minister. "Show him your hands," the minister said.

1280. In the city of Nuremberg lived two boys, Albrecht Dürer and Franz Kingstien. Both had artistic ability and longed to become famous as artists. To this end they studied and toiled. As time went on, it developed that Albrecht undoubtedly had genius, while his friend Franz had only a love for art. Each attempted an etching of the Passion of our Lord; but when Franz stood before Albrecht's beautiful production, he raised his hands in a gesture of despair. "Albrecht, it is useless," he said; "I can never become an artist. You will be famous, but I never." "Hold your hands just as they are; do not move them," said his friend. "You shall be famous, too." Whereupon he seized his brush and painted those imploring hands that have become universally known and admired.—WILLIAM S. ABERNETHY, *Left-handed Folks*

1281. Edwin Booth, the famous actor and brother of John Wilkes Booth, was visiting a friend who had made a collec-

[1] Used by permission of the author.

tion of plaster of Paris casts of the hands of famous people. As Booth went from one cast to another, he described the type of person according to the lines of the plaster hands. "Here is one," he said, "the hand of a person who tried to serve and help his fellow men. He was humble, yet his character was stalwart and true and strong." The friend tried to change the subject, for he knew, as did some of those around, that this was the hand of Lincoln.—JOSEPH BACCUS

HAPPINESS

1282. When asked to write a message on the flyleaf of a Bible, George V wrote: "The secret of happiness is not to do what you like to do, but to learn to like what you have to do."—JAMES GORDON GILKEY, *When Life Gets Hard*

1283. "I have found that most people are about as happy as they make up their minds to be," Lincoln said.

1284. Frank Crane used to say: "It takes so little to make people happy. Just a touch, if we know how to give it, just a word fitly spoken, a slight readjustment of some bolt or pin or bearing in the delicate machinery of a soul."

1285. "The happiness of life is made up of minute fractions—the little soon-forgotten charities of a kiss or smile, a kind look, a heartfelt compliment, and the countless infinitesimals of pleasurable and genial feeling," wrote Samuel Taylor Coleridge.

1286. It was said of Francis Xavier: "Sometimes it happened that if any of the brothers were sad, the way they took to become happy was to go and look at him."

1287. "If you ever find happiness by hunting for it," Josh Billings wrote, "you will find it as the old woman did her spectacles, safe on her nose all the time."

1288. "You seek happiness?" asks Maurice de Guerin. "It is the sweet, fine rain that penetrates the heart and later wells forth in tears."

1289. Fanny Crosby, the blind hymn writer, used to say: "Don't waste any sympathy on me. I am the happiest person living."

1290. "A happy man or woman," wrote Robert Louis Stevenson, "is a better thing to find than a five-pound note. He or she is a radiating focus of good will; and their entrance into a room is as though another candle had been lighted."

1291. "Everywhere there is speed, noise, confusion," said Chesterton, "but nowhere deep happiness and quiet hearts."

HARDSHIP

1292. Lafcadio Hearn, the European who became a naturalized Japanese, wrote this description of his native servant: "My Japanese cook always wears a smiling, healthy, pleasing face. He is decidedly a good-looking young man. But one day I happened to glance through the hole in the partition and saw him when he was sitting alone in the kitchen. The face was not the same at all. It was thin and drawn, and showed queer lines worn by old hardships. But when I went to speak to him, he suddenly changed, and became young and attractive once more. My cook wears a mask of happiness as part of his etiquette."

1293. Robert Stopford, one of Nelson's commanders, after telling of many hardships and trials, exclaimed: "We were half-starved, and otherwise inconvenienced by being so long out of port. But our reward was—we were with Nelson."

HATE

1294. Booker T. Washington, the Negro educator, said: "I will not permit any man to narrow and degrade my soul by making me hate him."

1295. A woman who was trying to whip up hatred toward our war enemies complained: "How can you hate with Jane Addams in the room?"—E. STANLEY JONES, *Abundant Living*

1296. Sidney Smith is said to have remarked: "No, I don't know that man, and I don't want to know him. If I knew him, I might not hate him, and I want to hate him."

1297. Cicero so hated Clodius, his enemy, and was so little ashamed of it, that two years after that enemy's death at the Battle of Bovillae, Cicero was dating his letters "The 560th day after Bovillae."—HARRY EMERSON FOSDICK, *Manhood of the Master*

HEART

1298. When Stephen of Colonna fell into the hands of his base assailants, and they asked him in derision, "Where is now your fortress?" Stephen replied, "Here," and placed his hand on his heart.

1299. "The best and most beautiful things in the world cannot be seen or touched," writes Helen Keller, "but are just felt in the heart."

1300.
We marvel at the silence that divides the
    living and the dead.
  Yet more apart

Are they who all life long live side by
    side
Yet never heart by heart.
         —AUTHOR UNKNOWN

1301. When Sir Walter Raleigh had laid his head upon the block, the executioner asked whether it lay aright. "It matters little, my friend," Sir Walter said, "how the head lies, provided the heart be right."

HEAVEN

1302.
Then let us learn the language of that
    home
    Whilst here on earth we be,
Lest our poor hearts for want of words
    be dumb,
    In that high company.
         —AUTHOR UNKNOWN

1303. A small girl one evening looked up wondering at the star-studded sky and exclaimed: "If the wrong side of heaven looks like this, what must the right side be like!"

HELL

1304. There is an apocryphal story of the man who, having spent some time in heaven, was relegated to the shades of Hades. Asked what he missed most from his heavenly raptures, he replied: "The sound of trumpets in the morning."

1305. "Hell," said A. J. Cronin in *The Keys of the Kingdom*, "is the place where one has ceased to hope."

HELPFULNESS

1306. Charles Kingsley said: "Make a rule, and pray to God to help you keep it, never, if possible, to lie down at night without being able to say: 'I have made one human being at least a little wiser, or a little happier, or at least a little better this day.' You will find it easier than you think and pleasanter."

1307. John Calvin's coat of arms was a flaming heart from which was stretched a helping hand. Beneath was this inscription: "My heart I give Thee, Lord, eagerly and sincerely."

1308. "Nothing," wrote George MacDonald, "makes one feel so strong as a call for help."

1309. Charles Brookfield, an actor, read a mistaken report of his death in the newspapers. The portion of the obituary notice which he most fancied read: "Never a great actor, he was invaluable in small parts."

1310. Said Olive Schreiner, author of *Woman and Labor:* "What matters it to me if I am not at the oar when the little boat is pulled into harbor. To know that I have pulled at the oar, that is enough for me."

1311. When Jacob Riis published *How the Other Half Lives,* his friend Theodore Roosevelt read it and at once went down to lower Manhattan and climbed the creaking stairs to congratulate the writer. As Riis was not at home, Roosevelt left a visiting card, after writing on it: "Have read your book and came to help."

1312. A Negro was walking along Forty-second Street in New York City. He was carrying two heavy suitcases. Suddenly a hand was laid on one of the suitcases. "Pretty heavy, brother; suppose you let me take one; I'm going your way." The two men walked along for several blocks, talking as though they were old friends. "And that," said Booker T. Washington long afterward,

"was the first time I ever saw Theodore Roosevelt."—GORDON L. WITHERS

1313. A gangster shot down his enemy one day upon the street. A passing automobile stopped, and a woman hurried to the side of the wounded man. The gunman with his smoking weapon came to the woman and shook her shoulders roughly as she knelt beside his victim. "See here, lady," he rasped. "This ain't none of your business. If you know what's healthy for you, you'll move on, and do it quick." The woman did not even look up. "Excuse me," she said, "this *is* my business. I am a nurse. I am bound to go to the help of anyone who is sick or wounded, no matter who. I'd do the same for you. Now run along and let me alone."—WALTER M. HORTON, *Our Christian Faith*

1314. Far upon the Alpine passes the Romans built their roads that travelers might pass from Italy to northern Europe. But in winter snow would cover the roads and travelers would be lost. A man by the name of Bernard devoted himself to dwelling at the highest pass to rescue those who were lost in the storm. They called him St. Bernard. People never forgot his service, and long years afterward when those friendly huge dogs were trained to rescue Alpine travelers, the only name that fitted them was the name of the man who had dedicated his life years before. —RUSSELL J. CLINCHY, *A Reasonable Faith*

1315. Lafcadio Hearn tells of a Chinese rice farmer who from his hilltop farm saw the ocean swiftly withdrawn and knew that as a result of an earthquake the withdrawal would be followed by a great tidal wave. Knowing too that his neighbors working in the low fields would be swept away if they were not warned, the farmer set his own fields on fire and furiously rang the temple bell. His neighbors, seeing the farm on fire, rushed to the hilltop. From that height they saw great waves sweeping the fields they had just left.

1316. A king placed a heavy stone in the middle of a road. People thronged by, stepped over the boulder, kicked it angrily, murmured, grumbled, but none removed the stone. Finally one man came along, saw the obstacle, picked it up to make the way easier for those who would come after him. Under the stone the king had placed a purse filled with gold.

1317. "Is your father at home?" a lad sitting on the village doctor's doorstep was asked. "No," he said, "he's away." "Where do you think I could find him?" "Well," the boy said with a thoughtful air, "you've got to look for him some place where people are sick and hurt, or something like that. I don't know where he is; but he's helping somewhere."— W. L. PHILLIPS

1318. A man went to a train to meet a missionary. "I hope I'll recognize him," he said. A friend replied: "Oh, you will. He'll be helping somebody off the train."

1319. William E. Gladstone stopped his preparation of a speech to be delivered in Parliament the next day to go to the bedside of a dying boy. It is reported that when the statesman returned to his study to continue his speech, he said: "That speech may fail or not; the empire may fail or not; but in helping that boy I have tasted exquisite joy."

1320. When Bishop Booth of Vermont died, a friend said: "I know where the bishop is tonight. His soul has gone to hell." Then the friend added: "That's the only place he can be happy; there's such work to do there."

1321. A small boy going home in the dark was whistling. When asked why, he said: "I thought if there was some other little boy out in the dark and he was scared, he'd like to hear me whistling."

1322. In the battle of Bannockburn, in which Scotland won its independence from England, there came a critical moment when the issues of the battle hung in the balance. Only a little thing was required to turn the tide either way. Then it was that the boys and old men and cripples, who had been left behind to attend to the Scottish camp took pikes and poles and what flags they could find and marched toward the battle to see how it was progressing. The British, seeing the dust on the horizon and the Scottish pennons waving in the breeze, mistook it for a new army and turned and fled.—GLENN CLARK, *The Lord's Prayer*

1323. Once when Mrs. Margaret Wilson, a blind comptometer operator, stood at the corner of a busy street in Berkeley, California, waiting for someone to help her across the street, a man stepped up and asked: "May I go across with you?" "I'd be very glad if you would," replied Mrs. Wilson. "You know," the man said when they had safely crossed the thoroughfare, "when one has been blind as many years as I have it's a mighty big favor to have someone help him across the street."

1324. Two brothers, wishing to perpetuate their memory, each undertook a task. The one built a monument to himself. His name and worthy inscriptions were carved on the granite. The other dug a well (for weary travelers)

beside a desert highway. There were no inscriptions, for the well needed none.

1325. In the year 1912 England sent her greatest steamship across the Atlantic Ocean. It was the "Titanic," the largest ship built up to that time. Half way across the ocean the ship hit a submerged iceberg and soon sank, carrying to death most of the passengers. At the moment of the tragedy the steamship "California" was only about thirty miles away. It was before the days of full and complete radio service, though the wireless was in existence. Wireless operators at that time were few, and there was only one of them on the "California." He closed his apparatus that night at 10:30 and went to bed. An hour later the "Titanic" operator was sending out frantic S O S signals, but the wireless set on the "California" was closed and deaf to the pleas for help. The "Titanic" went down while another ship which could have reached her side in less than an hour went sailing on her course totally unaware of the tragedy. —Russell J. Clinchy, *A Reasonable Faith*

HERITAGE

1326. "No Christian today has the right to poke fun at the narrowness of our forefathers," said John S. Bonnell. "Our boasted breadth has come to us at the expense of depth. We are broad and shallow; they were narrow and deep."

1327.
I am the owner of the sphere,
Of the seven stars and solar year,
Of Caesar's hand, and Plato's brain,
Of Lord Christ's heart, and Shakespeare's strain.
                —Emerson, *History*

1328. Francis G. Peabody tells us that the freshmen of a certain university at its three hundredth anniversary carried a banner with the inscription, "This university has waited three hundred years for us." One might also say, "Modern man is blessed because through long centuries men have striven to make the world a more perfect home for the body, mind, and soul of men."

HERO

1329. Guiseppe Garibaldi, the Italian patriot, said: "It is the big demand that makes the heroic spirit. It is the big demand that makes the big soul."

1330. Ralph Waldo Emerson defined the hero as the man who is immovably centered.

HESITATION

1331. "I never in my life felt more certain that I was doing right than I do in signing this paper," Lincoln said. "But I have been receiving calls and shaking hands since nine o'clock this morning, till my arm is stiff and numb. Now this signature is one that will be closely examined, and if they find my hand trembled they will say, 'He had some compunctions.' But anyway, it is going to be done." With these words Lincoln signed the Emancipation Proclamation.

1332. Before his conversion Augustine prayed: "O God, make me pure, but not now."

HISTORY

1333. Charles A. Beard, the historian, has said that the study of history has taught him: (1) When it gets dark enough, the stars come out. (2) The bee fertilizes the flower it steals from. (3) Whom the gods would destroy they first make mad. (4) The mills of God grind slowly, but they grind exceeding small.

1334. At a banquet given in New York City in the winter of 1932 Dwight Morrow was to have been the chief speaker. However, so many had spoken before he was called upon that it was almost midnight when he was presented. The year 1932 was at the very trough of the depression, and each address had been characterized by gloom and pessimism until there seemed to be no place whatever for hope or optimism. Morrow rose and very slowly and quietly spoke a single sentence: "Hope is greater than history."—BRUCE R. BAXTER

HOLINESS

1335. A jealous minister exclaimed, "Has Dwight L. Moody a monopoly of the Holy Spirit?" "No," someone remarked, "but the Holy Spirit has a monopoly of Moody."

1336. John Steinbeck relates in *The Grapes of Wrath* how Casey, the preacher, discovers the meaning of the word "holy": "I ain't sayin' I'm like Jesus. But I got tired like Him, an' I got mixed up like Him, an' I went into the wilderness like Him, without no campin' stuff. Nighttime I'd lay on my back an' look up at the stars; morning I'd set an' watch the sun come up; midday I'd look out from a hill at the rollin' dry country; evenin' I'd foller the sun down. Sometimes I'd pray like I always done. On'y I couldn' figure what I was prayin' to or for. There was the hills, an' there was me, an' we wasn't separate no more. We was one thing. An' that one thing was holy. . . . An' I got thinkin', on'y it wasn't thinkin', it was deeper down than thinkin'. I got thinkin' how we was holy when we was one thing, an' mankin' was holy when it was one thing. An' it on'y got unholy when one mis'able little fella got the bit in his teeth an' run off his own way, kickin' an' draggin' an' fightin'. Fella like that bust the holiness. But when they're all workin' together, not one fella for another fella, but one fella kind of harnessed to the whole shebang—that's right, that's holy."

HOME

1337. One day when Robert Rainy, the great churchman, was facing much criticism and general misunderstanding, a friend said that he could not understand how Rainy could bear it all. "Ah, but then, you see," said Rainy, "I'm very happy at home!"

1338. The great Madame Ernestine Schumann-Heink wrote the following in answer to the question, "What is home?": "A roof to keep out the rain? Four walls to keep out the wind? Floors to keep out the cold? Yes, but home is more than that. It is the laugh of a baby, the song of a mother, the strength of a father, warmth of loving hearts, light from happy eyes, kindness, loyalty, comradeship. Home is first school and first church for young ones, where they learn what is right, what is good, and what is kind; where they go for comfort when they are hurt or sick; where joy is shared and sorrow eased; where fathers and mothers are respected and loved. Where children are wanted; where the simplest food is good enough for kings because it is earned; where money is not so important as lovingkindness; where even the teakettle sings from happiness. That is home. God bless it!"

1339.

A house is built of logs and stone,
  Of tiles and posts and piers;
A home is built of loving deeds
  That stand a thousand years.
          —VICTOR HUGO

1340. A fireplace motto reads:

The beauty of the house is order;
The blessing of the house is content-
    ment;
The glory of the house is hospitality;
The crown of the house is godliness.

1341.
So long as there are homes where fires
    burn
    And there is bread,
So long as there are homes where lamps
    are lit
    And prayers are said;
Although people falter through the
    dark—
    And nations grope—
With God himself back of these little
    homes—
    We have sure hope.[2]
          —GRACE NOLL CROWELL,
    "So Long As There Are Homes"

1342. "Unless religion can be at home
in the home," writes E. Stanley Jones
in *The Christ of Every Road*, "no
amount of religion in the Temple can
save us."

1343. Charles L. Slattery relates the
story of a woman who told her husband one evening that the new pastor
had called during the day. "What
did he say?" the husband asked. The
wife replied: "He asked a very strange
question. He asked: 'Does Christ live
here?'" "Did you tell him that we are
respectable people who read the Bible
and pray every day and go to church
every Sunday?" asked the husband. "He
didn't ask that," the wife said. "He only
asked: 'Does Christ live here?'"

1344. Robert E. Speer used to tell of
the father who wanted to have a talk
with his son before the boy left the
farm. No words were spoken, but they
went around the home and around the
place, where associations of the boy's
life and play and family ties would be
recalled. The father then said to his
son: "I have only one thing to say to
you—allus do as you have a mind to."
—C. L. SEASHOLES

1345.
Home is the place where, when you
    have to go there,
They have to take you in.[3]
          —ROBERT FROST,
          "Death of the Hired Man"

1346. "Why do I need a home?" a
modern young woman said to a real
estate agent. "I was born in a hospital,
educated in a college, courted in an automobile, and married in a church. I live
out of the delicatessen and paper bags.
I spend my mornings on the golf course,
my afternoons at the bridge table, and
my evenings at the movies. And when
I die, I am going to be buried at the
undertaker's. All I need is a garage."

1347. It is said that when Andrew
Carnegie was building a new house,
he gave orders to the architect to have
inscribed on the living-room fireplace
this motto: "The hearth our altar; its
flame our sacred fire." After the fireplace was built, the architect said, "You
will have to choose another motto; that
one is too long." "No," said Carnegie,
"I want that motto. Tear down the fireplace and build a bigger one." The
architect informed him, "You cannot
have a bigger fireplace without having

[2] From *The Light of the Years*. Copyright
1936 by Harper & Bros.; renewed 1964 by
Grace Noll Crowell. Reprinted by permission
of Harper & Row, Publishers.

[3] From *Complete Poems of Robert Frost*,
1949. Copyright 1930, 1949 by Henry Holt
& Co., Inc. Used by permission.

a bigger room." "All right," was the reply, "tear out the walls and build a bigger room." "But a bigger room will throw the whole house out of proportion," remonstrated the architect. "Tear the house down, then," said Carnegie, "and build a bigger one. I must have that motto."—C. A. PEPPER

HONESTY

1348. When a knave said to Colonel Charteris, a man distinguished for his honesty, "I would give a thousand pounds for your good name," the colonel asked why. The knave retorted, "Because I could make ten thousand by it."

1349. Years ago the Viceroy of Naples, the Duke of Osuna, made a visit to Barcelona, Spain. There in the harbor lay a convict galley ship. The duke went aboard and, calling each prisoner, he asked what had brought him there. One after another of the prisoners excused himself, assuring the duke that it was through no fault of his own. One said a judge had accepted a bribe to convict him; another proclaimed that his enemies had sworn falsely; while still another claimed that he had been betrayed by his friends. Finally one prisoner spoke, "My lord, I am justly here. I wanted money, so I stole a purse. I deserve what I now suffer." The duke was so surprised by this honest confession that he said to the man for the benefit of the other convicts: "You are entirely too bad to be among so many innocent men." And he pardoned the honest confessor.—R. C. FLEISHER

HONOR

1350. Mark Twain, realizing that the publishing house he owned faced bankruptcy, knew that the law would permit him to escape an enormous debt. As an honorable man he determined not to escape but to face the responsibility. At the age of sixty he embarked on a lecture tour with these words: "I am confident that if I live I can pay off the last debt within four years, after which, at the age of sixty-four, I can make a fresh and unincumbered start in life," adding, "Honor is a harder master than the law."

1351. "We do not honor the fathers," Justin Wroe Nixon has written, "by going back to the place where they stopped but by going on toward the things their vision foresaw."

HOPE

1352. A discouraged man in London was on his way to drown himself when he saw a copy of Watts's painting "Hope." He looked carefully at the picture of the blindfolded woman sitting upon the top of the world and playing upon the one string left on her lyre. "Well, I have one string—I have a little boy at home," the man exclaimed as he retraced the steps he had taken.

1353. After seeing Watts's painting titled "Hope," Harold Begbie wrote:

One star, one string, and all the rest
   Darkness and everlasting space,
Save that she carries in her breast
   The travail of the race.

Born thro' the cold and soundless deep
   Of ruin riding in the air,
She bows, too heavenly to weep,
   Too human to despair.

And ever on her lonely string
   Expects some music from above,
Some faint, confirming whispering
   Of Fatherhood and love.

One star, one string, and through the
   drift

Of aeons, and with human cries,
She waits the hand of God to lift
The bandage from her eyes.

1354.
Hope, like the taper's gleaming light,
Adorns the wretches' way;
And still, as darker grows the night,
Emits a brighter ray.
—OLIVER GOLDSMITH, *The Captivity*

1355. "Man is based on hope," wrote Thomas Carlyle. "He has no other possession but hope."

1356. When Alfred Tennyson learned of the death of his closest friend, Arthur Hallam, the poet felt great despair. Triumphantly, however, he conquered his doubts and fears through his faith in God and the future. This hope he immortalized in the elegy "In Memoriam," honoring his friend. One of the memorable lines from this poem speaks of "the mighty hopes that make us men."

HUMILITY

1357. Phillips Brooks said: "The true way to be humble is not to stoop until you are smaller than yourself, but to stand at your real height against some higher nature that will show you what the real smallness of your greatness is."

1358. An old adage reads: "A mountain shames a molehill until they are both humbled by the stars."

1359. When an American college student visited the home of Beethoven at Bonn, she asked permission to play on the piano. After playing a few bars of the "Moonlight Sonata," she turned to the guard and said: "I suppose all of the great pianists have played during visits here." "No, miss," the guard said.

"Paderewski was here two years ago but said he was not worthy to touch it."

1360. "I sought out my favorite armchair and enjoyed myself for a couple of hours," said Mendelssohn speaking of the Uffizi Gallery in Florence. "This is a spot where a man feels his own insignificance and may well learn to be humble."

1361. Rabbi Joshua was once taunted by an emperor's daughter on his mean appearance. He pointed to the earthen jars which contained her father's wines. Whereupon she placed the wine in silver vessels; but it turned sour. The rabbi then ventured to remind her that the humblest vessels sometimes contain the highest wisdom.—A. T. ROBERTSON, *The Glory of the Ministry*

HUMOR

1362. In a recent biography of Lincoln this significant incident is recorded. "One day during the most crucial period of the Civil War, Lincoln called a cabinet meeting and announced that business of the utmost importance would be considered. When his advisers gathered, he entered the room and glanced swiftly at the circle of anxious faces. Then he quietly picked up a book by Artemus Ward and began to read aloud one of its most uproarious chapters. By the time he had finished the chapter the indignation of the cabinet members was painfully apparent. What did Lincoln mean by bringing busy men there to hear a funny story? Finally Lincoln laid the book down and sighed deeply. 'Gentlemen,' he said, 'why don't you laugh? With the fearful strain that is on me night and day I should die if I did not laugh occasionally. You need this medicine as much as I.' Then he turned to his tall hat on the table and drew from it what Secretary Stanton later described as 'a little white paper.' It was the first draft of the Emancipation Proclamation."

1363. After having been subjected by their officers to one foul joke after another, a private turned to another private and said: "What do they think we are? Pigs?"

1364. Harold Lloyd at one time refused a million-dollar movie contract because he did not think the humor in a certain scenario was wholesome. "If I can't be funny and clean, then I'll just be clean," he stated.

HUSBAND AND WIFE

1365. Just after she celebrated her twentieth wedding anniversary Mrs. Dwight Morrow sat at a dinner next to Paderewski and was reminded of a time when she heard the great pianist from a gallery seat in Northampton Academy of Music. Paderewski asked if she often went back to her alma mater. "Yes, I like to go back and sit in my old chapel seat, thinking how much happier I am now than I ever thought I should be," Mrs. Morrow answered. Becoming interested, Paderewski stopped eating. "You don't mean to tell me you are happier now than you thought at eighteen you would be?" "Yes, indeed!" Mrs. Morrow answered. Paderewski made her a deep bow. "Mrs. Morrow," said he, "I want to meet your husband."—MARY MARGARET McBRIDE

1366. Gilbert Frankau in his story "Peter Jackson" describes the experiences of a man who fell in love with his own wife.

1367. When a woman was severely sick, her husband told her the great love he had always felt toward her. The wife, smiling to hear words she had longed for, said: "Why did you wait so long to tell me this?"

1368. After his wife's death, Carlyle wrote in his diary: "Oh, if I could see her once more to let her know that I always loved her. . . . She never did know it."

1369. When Baron Bunson lay dying, he looked up at his wife and said: "In thy face I have seen the eternal."

1370. Robert E. Lee not long before he died referred to the oak in the yard of the Fitzhugh mansion at Chatham overlooking Fredericksburg: "It was under that oak that I courted my wife; and standing yonder on Marye's Height, at the fiercest moment of the battle of Fredericksburg, I yearned to get a sight of that tree. When the smoke cleared a bit, I caught a glimpse of its upper branches—and it strengthened me for the day's work."

1371. Leslie Stephens, feeling the full force of the difficulties to faith, parted with Christianity. When his wife died, he began a sentence in a letter to Lowell: "I thank—" then recollecting that he had none to whom he could think himself indebted for the dear companion of his heart, and for his affection for her, he wrote: "I thank—something—that I loved her as heartily as I know how to love."—HENRY SLOANE COFFIN, *What Men Are Asking*

1372. When someone said to Mrs. Albert Einstein, "I imagine that you understand all about Mr. Einstein's theory of relativity," Mrs. Einstein answered: "No, I don't know much about that, but I do know Mr. Einstein."

1373. In a beautiful tribute to his wife Ramsay MacDonald, three times British prime minister, said: "To turn to her in stress and storm was like going into a sheltered haven where waters are at rest. When I was weary and worn, buffeted and discouraged, thinking only of giving up the thankless strife, . . . my lady would heal and soothe me with her cheery faith and conviction, and send me forth to smite and be smitten."

1374. When the "Titanic" went down in 1912, Mrs. Isadore Strauss was one of the few women who were not rescued. Safety was offered to her, but because her husband could find no room in the lifeboats, she said: "We have been long together through a great many years. We are old now. Where he goes, I will go."

1375. "What do people say when they get married, mother?" asked a small boy. "Why, they promise to love and be kind to each other," his mother answered. "You're not always married, are you, mother?" the boy protested.

1376. When Thomas Chalmers in the course of his pastoral visitations stopped at the home of a venerated old man who exclaimed that his wife and he hadn't had a quarrel in thirty years, the minister struck his cane on the floor and said: "Terribly monotonous, man! Terribly monotonous!"

1377. One day, Lytton Strachey tells us in his *Queen Victoria*, Prince Albert in wrath locked himself in his room. Victoria, no less furious, knocked on the door to be admitted. "Who is there?" he asked. "The Queen of England" was the answer. He did not move, and again there was the hail of knocks. The question and the answer were repeated many times; but at last there was a pause, and then a gentle knocking. "Who is there?" came once more the relentless question. But this time the reply was different. "Your wife, Albert." And the door was immediately opened.

1378. A wife described her husband, who was an actor, with these words: "He is a comedian on the stage, but a tragedian at home."

1379. As the ambulance took his wife away to a mental hospital, her thoughtless husband remarked: "I can't for the life of me understand what's wrong. Why, she ain't been out of the kitchen in twenty years."

HYMN

1380. The rules which John Wesley suggested for the singing of hymns in church are: (1) Learn the tune. (2) Sing the hymns as they are printed. (3) Sing all. "If it is a cross to you, take it up and you will find a blessing." (4) Sing lustily and with a good courage. (5) Sing modestly. Do not bawl. (6) Sing in time. Do not run before or stay behind. (7) Above all, sing spiritually. Have an eye to God in every word you sing. Aim at pleasing him more than yourself or any other creature. In order to do this attend strictly to the sense of what you sing, and see that your heart is not carried away with the sound, but offered to God continually.

1381. Charles Wesley, brother of John Wesley, wrote more than six thousand hymns. Both he and his brother declared that they made more converts through their hymns than through their preaching.

1382. Long before Christian peoples became enthusiastic about church unity, the Christian hymnal represented the sharing of faith. Side by side are hymns written by members of all denominations. Baptist writers include Lydia Baxter, who wrote "Take the Name of Jesus with You," and Joseph Gilmore, who wrote "He Leadeth Me, O Blessed Thought"; Quaker writers include Bernard Barton, "Lamp of Our Feet, Whereby We Trace," and John Greenleaf Whittier, "Dear Lord and Father of Mankind"; Episcopal hymnists, Joseph Addison, "The Spacious Firmament on High," and William C. Doane, "Ancient of Days"; Congregational, Washington Gladden, "O Master, Let Me Walk with Thee," and Ray Palmer, "Jesus, Thou Joy of Loving Hearts"; Methodist, Charles Wesley, "Jesus, Lover of My Soul," and Mary Lathbury, "Break Thou the Bread of Life"; Unitarian, John S. Dwight, "God Bless Our Native Land," and Oliver Wendell Holmes, "Lord of All Being, Throned Afar"; Presbyterian, Maltbie D. Babcock, "Be Strong, We Are Not Here to Play," and James W. Alexander, "O Sacred Head, Now Wounded"; Dutch Reformed, George Washington Bethune, "It Is Not Death to Die"; and Roman Catholic, Joseph Mohr, "Silent Night, Holy Night" and John Henry Newman, "Lead, Kindly Light."

I

IDEAS

1383. Old Bill Tate said of the Wright brothers: "I knew as soon as I saw those boys that they were different from the folks down here. They had an idea. It possessed them. I used to listen as they argued by the hour. I didn't understand what they were driving at, but I understood them. I knew that they would get there."

1384. When a neighbor of Emerson returned a copy of Plato, the sage of Concord asked if the book was enjoyable. "It was that," replied the neighbor. "This Plato has a lot of my ideas."

1385. "Ideas are poor ghosts until they become incarnate," George Eliot wrote.

1386. Two Chinese coolies were arguing heatedly in the midst of a crowd. An onlooker who witnessed the worldly altercation was told the coolies were "fighting." When he expressed surprise that no blows were struck, his Chinese friend informed him: "The man who strikes first admits that his ideas have given out."

1387. John Erskine, noted educator and author, has said: "Very few college students will ever sit down and in cold blood have an idea; it is just too much for them."

IMAGINATION

1388. "It is the imagination," said Sherwood Anderson, the short-story writer, "that drives us on, that can destroy us, that sometimes makes a man do heroic deeds, that produces all of our art and poetry, that has produced all inventions that make modern life so strangely different from life a few generations ago." —T. V. SMITH, *Discipline for Democracy*

1389. "Fancy plays like a squirrel in its circular prison and is happy," wrote John Ruskin, "but imagination is a pilgrim on the earth—and her home is in heaven."

1390. Robert de Baudricourt in *Saint Joan* by George Bernard Shaw says of the voices Joan hears, "That's all imagination." "Of course," Joan replies. "That is how the messages of God come to us."

1391. One of the men who send Joan to the stake in George Bernard Shaw's play *Saint Joan* afterward confesses that he has done a very cruel thing because he did not know what cruelty was like until he saw a young girl burning to death. Whereupon the Bishop of Beauvais asks: "Must then a Christ perish in torment in every age to save those who have no imagination?"

IMMORTALITY

1392. The symbol of immortality has ever been the butterfly, which, lying seemingly dead within the cocoon, breaks forth into an unrealized beauty when its moment of glory comes.

1393. On a brass plate in the floor of the old church which stands in the Middle Temple Court in London and dates back to the days of the crusaders in the twelfth century are these words: "He died the only kind of death it is worth to die—a death for God, for the Right, for Liberty. Such a death is immortality."

1394. Longfellow wrote about Charles Sumner:

Were a star quenched on high,
For ages would its light,
Still travelling downward from the sky,
Shine on our mortal sight.

So when a great man dies,
For years beyond our ken,
The light he leaves behind him lies
Upon the paths of men.

1395. Buried at Alton, Illinois, is Elijah Parish Lovejoy, a stanch advocate of the abolition of slavery. His enemies took from him his printing press and eventually killed him. After his death Wendell Phillips spoke of him in this way: "Lovejoy, people called you imprudent because you jeopardized your life for a great cause. But I have noticed how prudently most people creep into nameless graves, while now and then some forget themselves into immortality."

1396. Robert Lowry speaks in this manner of the writing of his hymn "Shall We Gather at the River?": "One afternoon in July, 1864, when I was pastor at Hanson Place Baptist Church, Brooklyn, the weather was oppressively hot, and I was lying on a lounge in a state of physical exhaustion. I was almost incapable of bodily exertion, and my imagination began to take to itself wings. Visions of the future passed before me with startling vividness. The imagery of the Apocalypse took the form of a tableau. Brightest of all were the throne, the heavenly river, and the gathering of the saints. My soul seemed to take new life from that celestial outlook. I began to wonder why the hymn writers had said so much about the 'river of death' and so little about the 'pure river of water of life, clear as crystal, proceeding out of the throne of God and of the Lamb.' As I mused, the words began to construct themselves. They came first as a question of Christian inquiry, 'Shall we gather?' Then they broke out in chorus as an answer of Christian faith, 'Yes, we'll gather.' On this question and answer the hymn developed itself. The music came with the hymn."

1397. Aristides, writing about A. D. 125, explained to the pagans the new confidence concerning the dead in Christ with these words: "And if any righteous man among them passes from the world, they rejoice and offer thanks to God; and they escort his body as if he were setting out from one place to another near."

1398. "God fills the world with turbulence," said Martin Luther, "in order that we may hope for another life."

Assurance of Immortality

1399. "Some morning you will read in the papers," Moody told a group of friends, "that D. L. Moody is dead. Don't believe a word of it! At that moment I shall be more alive than I am now. I was born of the flesh in 1837— I was born of the Spirit in 1856. That which is born of the flesh may die; that which is born of the Spirit shall live forever."

1400. With these words William Jennings Bryan stated eloquently his faith in immortality: "In Cairo, I secured a few grains of wheat that had slumbered for more than thirty centuries in an Egyptian tomb. As I looked at them this thought came to my mind: If one of those grains had been planted on the banks of the Nile the year after it grew, and all its lineal descendants had been planted and replanted from that time until now, its progeny would today be sufficiently numerous to feed the teeming millions of the world. An unbroken chain of life connects the earliest grains of wheat with the grains we sow and reap. There is in the grain of wheat an invisible something which has power to discard the body that we see, and from earth and air fashion a new body so much like the old one that we cannot tell the one from the other.

"If this invisible germ of life in the grain of wheat can thus pass unimpaired through three thousand resurrections, I shall not doubt that my soul has power to clothe itself with a new body suited to its new existence, when this earthly frame has crumbled into dust."
—*In His Image*

1401. After the death of Quentin Roosevelt in the First World War, his father, Theodore Roosevelt, dictated the following inscription for his cross: "He has outsoared the shadows of our night."

1402. After a soldier had seen one of his companions blown to pieces by a shell, he said thoughtfully, "It will take more than that to stop you."

1403. When a preacher in a funeral sermon for a fellow minister said, "Our dear brother has departed, and we shall never look upon him again," an aged saint exclaimed, "Thank God, that's a lie!"

1404. On his eightieth birthday Alfred Tennyson said: "I do not know what I have done that so many people should feel grateful to me, except that I have always kept my faith in immortality."

Belief in Immortality

1405. "I believe in the immortality of the soul, not in the sense in which I accept the demonstrable truths of science, but as a supreme act of faith in the reasonableness of God's work," said John Fiske.

1406. "The blazing evidence of immortality is our dissatisfaction with any other conclusion," said Ralph Waldo Emerson.

1407. Cicero, after the death of his daughter, expressed his belief in immortality: "If I am wrong in this, that I believe the souls of men to be immortal, I willingly delude myself; nor do I desire that this mistake in which I take pleasure should be wrested from me as long as I live; but if I, when dead, shall have no consciousness, as some narrow-minded philosophers imagine, I do not fear lest dead philosophers should ridicule this my delusion."

1408. When a friend asked Theodore T. Munger concerning his faith in immortality, he said: "I believe with all my heart in God, the infinite Lover of men, and I rest my destiny in his hands."

1409. "I feel in myself the future life," Victor Hugo said. "I am like a forest cut down; the new shoots are stronger and livelier than ever. I am rising, I know, toward the sky. The sunshine is on my head. The earth gives me its generous sap, but heaven lights me with the reflection of unknown worlds. For half a century I have been writing my thoughts in prose and in verses. History, philosophy, drama, romance, tradition, satire, ode, and song—I have tried all. But I feel I have not said the thousandth part of what is in me. When I go down to the grave, I can say, like many others, 'I have finished my day's work.' Life is a thoroughfare. It closes on the twilight; it opens on the dawn."

1410. Just before his death Alfred Tennyson said: "The life after death is the cardinal point of Christianity. I believe that God reveals himself to every individual soul; and my idea of heaven is the perpetual ministry of one soul to another."

1411. "I have never seen what to me seemed an atom of proof that there is a future life," wrote Mark Twain. "And yet—I am strongly inclined to expect one."

1412. Writes Carl Knudson: "While serving as a naval chaplain in the South Pacific it was my duty to take the body of a sailor, killed in action, to a military cemetery on an island in the New Hebrides. The brother of the deceased, who had been a shipmate on our cruiser, was the only mourner present. As the benediction was being pronounced, the brother broke down and sobbed. To my utter astonishment a native gravedigger, dressed only in a loincloth, came up to him, put his toil-hardened hands on the sailor's shoulder and said in fairly good pidgin English: 'Don't you cry for your brudder; he don't have to fight no mo' wars. He's safe in the arms of Jesus.'"

1413. William R. Harper, onetime president of the University of Chicago, on his deathbed prayed: "May there be for me a life beyond this life; and in that life may there be work to do, tasks to accomplish. If in any way a soul has been injured or a friend hurt, may the harm be overcome if it is possible."

IMPOSSIBILITY

1414. When Artur Rubenstein, in New York City one week end, was invited to attend church, he said: "Yes, if you will take me to hear a preacher who will tempt me to do the impossible." —RALPH A. SOCKMAN, *The Highway of God*

1415. A distinguished engineering firm announced as its motto: "We specialize in the impossible." That should be the slogan of the Christian Church.

1416. When told that the Alps stood in the way of his armies, Napoleon, who believed that "impossible is a word only to be found in the dictionary of fools," said with determination: "There shall be no Alps." Thereupon a road was constructed across the Simplon, a district previously considered inaccessible.

1417. When an old reformer had his projects rejected on the ground that they were impossible, he retorted, "Impossible! If that is all there is against them, let us go ahead."

1418. "The only difference between the difficult and the impossible," said an old-time reformer, "is that the impossible takes a little longer time."

1419. Once there was an emperor who would call in his counselors to ask their advice about some project that he was contemplating. We are told that this ruler liked to be advised that the thing he proposed to do was utterly impossible. Then he set out to do it, and he rarely failed to accomplish the seemingly impossible.—CAREY S. OSBORNE

1420. On the wall of one of the offices of "the fighting Seabees" during World War II was this motto: "The difficult we do immediately; the impossible takes a little longer."

1421. "Put forth thy hand in God's name" was the challenge of Thomas Carlyle. "Know that the word 'impossible' where truth and mercy and the everlasting voices of nature order, has no place in the brave man's dictionary."

INDIFFERENCE

1422. "The penalty good men pay for indifference to public affairs," said Plato, "is to be ruled by evil men."

1423. At the close of World War I a story, perhaps apocryphal, was told of a certain mountaineer who wandered into town on Armistice Day, and from the bells and whistles learned for the first time a war had been going on.—GEORGIA HARKNESS, *The Faith by Which the Church Lives*

1424. A man who was listlessly hacking on a log was asked what he was making. "Dun'no," he answered. "Maybe a house, maybe a god."

INDIVIDUAL

1425. A college professor, expressing to his students the significance of the individual in a world of millions of people, took a glass of water from one side of his desk and carefully moving it to the other side said, "Gentlemen, I have changed the order of the universe."—JOSEPH BACCUS

1426. "What is in the world today that wasn't here fifteen years ago?" the teacher asked her class. "Me!" exclaimed a small boy in the first row. Of course he was right and just as correct as if the teacher had asked what is in the world today that wasn't here a thousand or a million years ago.

1427. Channing Pollock, it is said, was sitting in a restaurant with Basil King when they heard a woman at the next table say to her companion: "It's a disgraceful state of affairs, but what can one man do?" King leaned over to his friend to remark: "Shall we tell her that everything of importance in the world was begun by one man or one woman?"—G. MERRILL LENOX

INFIDELITY

1428. Said Thomas Paine: "It is necessary to the happiness of man that he be mentally faithful to himself. Infidelity does not consist in believing or disbelieving; it consists in professing to believe what he does not believe. It is impossible mental lying has produced in society."

1429. Once when Robert Ingersoll was lecturing, he took out his watch and said: "I will give God five minutes to strike me dead for the things I have said." When Theodore Parker heard that nothing happened during that five-minute period, he remarked: "And did the gentleman think he could exhaust the patience of the Eternal God in five minutes?"

INFLUENCE

1430. When Stopford Brook was gathering material for his life of Robertson of Brighton, he visited a bookstore in Brighton where he saw a picture of Robertson on the wall. "Yes," said the bookseller, "whenever I am tempted to do anything mean, I look at that face, and it recalls me to my better self."—HARRY EMERSON FOSDICK, *The Meaning of Prayer*

1431. "He made me a Christian, and he never knew that he was doing it," said Stanley about Livingstone.

1432. After visiting Tolstoy, William Dean Howells wrote to a friend: "I can never again see life in the way I saw it before I knew him."

1433. A pupil of Mary Lyon of Mount Holyoke said of her: "One could not go wrong in her presence."

1434. Of one man it was said: "This is a thing to be written on a man's tomb, 'His presence made bad men good.'"

1435. "Before she came," said a Crimean soldier about Florence Nightingale, "there was cussin' and swearin', but after that it was as 'oly as a church."

1436. Having spent an afternoon with Horace Bushnell, who was then at the point of death, Joseph Twitchell wrote in his diary: "As I left the house, I felt a lively sense of things eternal and a desire to live in them."

1437. Newell Dwight Hillis witnessed a mob, fearless in the face of the cannon fire on all sides, rush through a Paris street. They had gone only a few blocks when their leader stopped them, saying, "Citizens it is de la Eure. Sixty years of pure life is about to address you." Hillis offered this comment when he related the experience: "A true man's presence transformed a mob that cannon could not conquer."

1438. A perplexed student once went with his questions to the office of Phillips Brooks. After the interview the young man realized that he had not asked his questions. "Never mind," he thought, "what I needed was not the solution of a special problem but the contagion of a triumphant spirit."

1439. A London boy many years ago ran away from home and became a sea-man. One day, passing a church while on leave, he entered and gave his heart to Christ. Later he became a preacher, and his message inspired Thomas Scott to enter the ministry. Scott in turn inspired Cowper, who wrote many of our hymns. Cowper inspired Wilberforce in his fight to free the slaves in England.

1440.

Every soul that touches yours—
Be it the slightest contact—
Get therefrom some good;
Some little grace; one kindly thought;
One aspiration yet unfelt;
One bit of courage
For the darkening sky;
One gleam of faith
To brave the thickening ills of life;
One glimpse of brighter skies—
To make this life worth while
And heaven a surer heritage.
                    —GEORGE ELIOT,
          "Making Life Worth While"

INGRATITUDE

1441. When asked what lesson he had learned from civilization, an old Indian replied: "Ingratitude."

1442. Says Aunt Het: "I don't mind sacrificin' myself for my family. What aggravates me is havin' 'em act like it was just my duty and nothin' to take any special notice of."

1443. When the ministry of Robert Walpole fell and a hostile vote was being taken in the House of Commons, Walpole, watching those who voted against him, said to one who sat near him: "Young man, I will tell you the history of all these men as they come in: That fellow I saved from the gallows. And that one from starvation. This other one's son I promoted."—CLARENCE E. MACARTNEY

INSPIRATION

1444. A secret of the success of Tchaikovsky may be found in his comment: "Work, work, work, and on top of the work comes the inspiration."

1445. Trevelyan in his life of Garibaldi, the Italian patriot, tells of a young volunteer who, having come from a home of luxury, was asked why he stayed on the battlefield when he could return to a home of ease. "You may well ask," the young man said. "A fortnight ago I was in despair myself and thought of giving up the whole thing. I was sitting on a hillock. . . . Garibaldi came by. He stopped. . . . I had never spoken to him. . . . Perhaps I looked very dejected, and indeed I was. Well, he laid his hand on my shoulder and simply said, with that . . . voice that seemed almost like a spirit speaking inside me, 'Courage! Courage!' Do you think I could ever turn back after that?"

1446. Dorothy Whitney Straight, after the death of her husband, Willard Straight, wrote to Herbert Croly: "But just because he taught me to see life with new eyes, just because he liberated my spirit and brought me life and the abundance of it, now that he is gone I cannot feel that the meaning and joy of existence have gone, too. Had he given me less, I should find myself less equipped to meet life without him now. But having given me everything, I can still feel that life is the adventure that he revealed, the quest for reality that he enjoyed, the great enterprise in which he so vigorously and gallantly participated."—H. D. CROLY, *Willard Straight*

INSULT

1447. Nanak, a medieval Indian saint, once said to a disciple: "Farid, if a man insult thee, stoop and touch his feet.

Thus enterest thou the temple of the Lord."

1448. When Alice Freeman Palmer was asked by an undergraduate if she did not become disgusted when insulted, the former president of Wellesley said: "I am too big to be insulted."

INTEGRITY

1449. Charles H. Spurgeon said of Gladstone: "We believe in no man's infallibility, but it is restful to feel sure of one man's integrity."

1450. John Bennett in *Social Christianity* defines integrity as the harmony between a man's inner purposes and his outer actions.

1451. During World War I, *Punch* published a cartoon which related the story of Belgium's refusal to let the German army use that small country as a corridor for an invasion of France. In the cartoon the Kaiser taunts Albert, King of the Belgians: "So you see you have lost all!" Albert replies: "But not my soul!"

INTERDEPENDENCE

1452. "Many times a day I realize how much my own outer and inner life is built upon the labors of my fellow men, both living and dead, and how earnestly I must exert myself in order to give in return as much as I have received," writes Albert Einstein.

1453. While a famous organist played to an approving audience, a small boy behind the screen was hard at work pumping the organ. During the intermission the small boy said proudly to the famous man, "Aren't we wonderful?" "Who's we?" said the organist abruptly. A few minutes later the organist returned to the console and went through all the motions of playing, but no music came forth. Again and again he began, but no music was heard. Finally a voice came from behind the screen: "Now who's we?"

INTERFAITH

1454. When four chaplains—a Roman Catholic priest, a Jewish rabbi, and two Protestant ministers—gave their life belts to four soldiers after the American cargo-transport "Dorchester" was torpedoed in February, 1943, the Postmaster General heard the story that the four men of God went down with their ship, their heads together in a common prayer, and designed a commemorative stamp bearing the inscription, "Interfaith in Action."

1455. Barney Ross, the former prize fighter, after a terrible night on Guadalcanal wrote: "Suddenly I heard all our voices and realized we were all praying. I was praying to a Jewish God. Atkins, my pal in the nearest foxhole, was praying to a Baptist God. The kid with a hole in his body and the middle finger of his right hand stuck in it to try to stop the blood was praying to a Catholic God. The guy with his shoulder almost torn off, who was something else, was praying. . . . It suddenly struck me that there was no real difference between us at all, . . . and I couldn't help but wonder if people have to come that close to death to realize that we are all on the same side and all trying to get to the same place."

1456. The father of Albert Schweitzer was a Lutheran pastor whose congregation worshiped in the same church which was used at a different hour by Roman Catholics. "One thing more I have taken with me into life from this little church that was Catholic and Protestant at the same time—I mean religious tolerance," Albert Schweitzer has said.

1457. A woman in Labrador had tuberculosis of the ankle, and Dr. Wilfred Grenfell amputated her leg. On his next visit to the United States, when speaking in a Congregational church, he asked if anyone knew of a person who could donate an artificial limb to the needy woman. After the address a Methodist woman went up to him and said that her husband, a Presbyterian, had died and left behind him a good wooden leg. Said Grenfell: "When I, an Episcopalian, took that Presbyterian leg, given to me by a Methodist in a Congregational church, back to Labrador, it fitted my Roman Catholic friend and she could walk."—WALTER DUDLEY CAVERT, *Remember Now . . .*

1458. George Hodges used to say that he scarcely believed that the devil is terrified when he sees a Presbyterian forefinger, or a Baptist middle finger, or an Episcopalian thumb, or a Methodist third finger, or some other denominational little finger pointed at him. But when those fingers and that thumb are all doubled up in one compelling fist, then the devil begins to take notice.

1459. John Frederic Oberlin, a Protestant pastor of a French village church, one morning rescued a Jewish peddler from a threatening mob. Taking him home, the minister placed him at the table with the rest of the family. That evening the Catholic priest came in for a chat, and the three of them—the Protestant minister, the Catholic priest, and the Jewish peddler—sat down before the fire. The mood of the evening was mellow, and the priest turned to the minister and said, "How I wish, my friend, that you and I were of the same religion!" The minister was silent a moment, and then, putting one arm around the Catholic and the other around the Jew, he said, "Those who love are of the same religion."—RUSSELL J. CLINCHY, *A Reasonable Faith*

1460. "Oh, what are the things we seek to differ about compared with the deep things of God?" Archbishop Robert Leighton once exclaimed.

INTERNATIONALISM

1461. On Commonwealth Avenue in Boston is a monument to William Lloyd Garrison. On it are carved the words which Garrison put in his paper, *The Liberator:* "My Country is the World— My Countrymen are all Mankind."

1462. On the wall of the room in which Victor Hugo died were found the following prophetic lines in Hugo's writing:

I represent a party which does not yet exist:
   the party of revolution, civilization.
This party will make the twentieth century.
There will issue from it first
   the United States of Europe, then
   the United States of the World.

1463. S. H. Prince, a Canadian professor, while visiting in America said: "We need more statesmen like Cecil Rhodes, who could think in world terms; more poets like Shakespeare, poets of the human race; more writers like Kipling, who could sing of the Five Nations and the Seven Seas; more preachers like John Wesley, who saw the world as his parish. We must cultivate the international mind; we must pray for the international heart; we must develop the international conscience."

1464. Several years ago the Rockefeller Foundation told the story of Asibi, a West African, who supplied the blood from which the vaccine for yellow fever has been derived. After Asibi became ill with yellow fever and recovered, some of his blood became the source of all the yellow fever vaccine manufactured since 1937. The original strain of virus obtained from this humble Negro has since gone from laboratory to laboratory, offering immunity to millions of people in many countries. The Foundation report closes with these words: "Through the creative imagination of science the blood of one man in West Africa has been made to serve the whole human race."—MURRAY A. FIGG

1465. During World War II a cartoonist drew a large globe representing the world, but instead of being divided into countries there were no boundary lines. The caption read: "Draw your own boundaries." The cartoonist was thinking of advancing armies which made boundaries meaningless, but a Christian would think of the brotherhood of faith which rendered boundaries meaningless also.

1466. G. Bromley Oxnam has said: "The covered wagons have become wings; the pony express is the radio; the world is physically one; it must be united spiritually. Those who realize this fact are the builders of tomorrow."

INTOLERANCE

1467. An eminent Roman Catholic ecclesiastic declared at a meeting of Catholics, Jews, and Protestants some time ago: "We propose a campaign of intolerance—against intolerance."

1468.
And when religious sects ran mad,
   He held, in spite of all his learning,

That if a man's belief is bad,
  It will not be improved by burning.
    —W. M. PRAED, "The Vicar"

1469. "He who does not believe my doctrine," said Martin Luther in a moment of passion, "is sure to be damned."

1470. "History is made up very largely of the record of man's intolerance to man," writes Winfred E. Garrison in his volume *Intolerance*. "Part of that record is red with the blood of its victims and vibrant with their groans. Part of it also is warm with the glow of the faith and zeal of those who have sought, at their own peril, to turn others from the error of their ways or to break down some system which they deemed hostile to the welfare of men. But the story of intolerance is also the story of all the world's prophets and saviors, its moral leaders and social reformers, as well as its tyrants and inquisitors."

INVENTION

1471. Many years ago a bill was introduced into Congress to close the government patent office. "Every conceivable invention," explained the sponsor of the measure, "has already been made."

1472. At the age of twenty-six Alexander Graham Bell, working on his first experiments with the telephone, asked his friend, Joseph Henry, "What would you advise me to do: publish it and let others work it out, or attempt to solve the problem myself?" "You have the germ of a great invention," said Henry. "Work at it."

J

JUDAS

1473. Toyohiko Kagawa in *Behold the Man* describes Judas as looking into the eyes of Jesus and seeing himself reflected. "He found himself reflected therein during the eternal span of a single moment, the lifetime of the world. There he beheld himself stripped to his inner core; neither a cloak for his thoughts nor a cover for his desires. But it was he, not Jesus, who could see the reflection so mirrored."

1474. Frank S. Mead has called Judas "the man who might have been."

JUDGMENT

1475. Dwight Morrow, when asked the reason for his success in dealing with the people of Mexico, said: "I never judge a person until I discover what he would like to be as well as what he really is."

1476. Sioux Indians used to make the following prayer: "Great Spirit, help me never to judge another until I have walked two weeks in his moccasins."

1477. Judgment ripens with age, or so Benjamin Franklin thought when he wrote in *Poor Richard's Almanac,* "At twenty years of age the will reigns; at thirty the wit; at forty the judgment."

JUSTICE

1478. Justice is symbolized on courthouses and elsewhere by the figure of a blindfolded woman with scales in her hand, the implication being that the essence of justice is the weighing of the facts in hand with an impartiality which might be lost if we could see the parties involved. But such a portrayal is hardly adequate. To put it graphically though crudely, the blindfold should be removed and spectacles should be substituted. If we would weigh a situation justly, we must see not only the persons involved but also their backgrounds.—RALPH W. SOCKMAN, *The Highway of God*

1479. The statue "Christ of the Andes" atop the Andes Mountains between Chile and Argentina marks the averting of a war between the countries through the pleas of Bishop Benavente of Argenina, who said: "My country may be wrong in this matter; let us find out where the real answer lies; let us see who is wrong. Let us not think of our own nation but of justice."

K

KAGAWA

1480. When Kagawa was living in the slums of Kobe, he once invited a distinguished preacher to speak at a public meeting. Wearing the garments of the poor with whom he lived, Kagawa met his guest at the train; but the guest, mistaking him for a porter, ordered, "Here, fellow, carry my bags. I am looking for Kagawa."—CHARLES H. HEIMSATH, *Sermons on the Inner Life*

1481. When Kagawa became conscious of the fact that he would probably go blind, he declared: "The darkness is a holy of holies of which no one can rob me. In the darkness I meet God face to face."

KINDNESS

1482. Kosciusko, the famous Polish patriot and general, was very benevolent. Sending a messenger on a hurried errand, he bade him ride his own horse. But the man was long gone, and on returning said that next time he must take another horse, for that one insisted on stopping at every poor hovel and with every beggar by the way as if he had stopped to give alms at every wayside call.

1483.
I have no need of any creeds,
  They but confuse the mind.
For all the creed this old world needs
  Is that of being kind.
          —AUTHOR UNKNOWN

1484.
"What is real Good?"
I asked in musing mood.

Order, said the law court;
Knowledge, said the school;
Truth, said the wise man;
Pleasure, said the fool;
Love, said a maiden;
Beauty, said the page;
Freedom, said the dreamer;
Home, said the sage;
Fame, said the soldier;
Equity, the seer;—

Spake my heart full sadly,
"The answer is not here."
Then within my bosom
Softly this I heard:
"Each heart holds the secret;
Kindness is the word."
          —JOHN BOYLE O'REILLY,
          "What Is Good?"

1485. Phillips Brooks said: "If there is any good that I can do or any kindness that I can show, let me do it quickly, for I shall not pass this way again."

1486. When Eugene Debs was imprisoned as a conscientious objector, he became interested in a Negro prisoner who was said to be incorrigible, devoid of a spark of goodness. Since the Negro would not speak to anyone, Debs started a campaign of kindness by leaving an orange on the Negro's bed and going off without a word. In spite of many rebuffs he gradually penetrated the hard exterior of the man, and the two became fast friends. Years later at the news of Debs's death the Negro, now a useful citizen, made the discerning comment: "He was the only Jesus Christ I ever knew."

1487. One evening two vagrant players, a man and his wife, appeared at the inn, ragged, hungry, forlorn, business having fallen to zero. Touched by their plight Robert Louis Stevenson exerted himself, and a liberal purse was made up for them. In return they related their experiences and misfortunes on the road, recitals which Stevenson afterward worked into the short story, "Providence and Guitar." When two years later the story was printed and paid for, Stevenson sent the couple the whole amount received that they might thereby be assisted in the education of their little hunchbacked daughter in Paris.

1488. An old church in London has a window called "The Peddler's Window." Long ago a peddler was treated kindly by church members and in remembrance left his savings to the church.

1489. Madame Chiang Kai-shek closed a commencement address at Wesleyan College, Macon, Georgia, several years ago with these words:

Life is mostly froth and bubbles;
  Only two things stand like stone:
Kindness in another's troubles,
  Courage in your own.

1490. During World War II an English newspaper carried the following story: A German pilot sat down to dinner in an officers' mess of the R.A.F. His plane had been shot down by one of the Hurricane fighters, but because of the courage and bravery he had shown he was invited to dine with the men against whom he had fought. He shook hands with all his hosts. They toasted him, and he toasted them. Then he buried his face in his hands and sobbed aloud. After an embarrassing moment he said: "Please forgive me. Your kindness has overwhelmed me. For most of my life I have been taught to dislike the English. For these last five years I have been made to hate them. I was told that if the English captured me, they would starve and torture me. Instead, you have broken me with your kindness. Gentlemen, I salute you." The officers all rose and saluted him.—F. S. EITELGEORGE

1491. A legend tells us that many years ago an innkeeper threw stones and drove away many swallows, but a padre at the Mission of San Juan de Capistrano fed them and gave them shelter. For more than a century the swallows have arrived at the mission on March 19 each year and have been sheltered until they fly away again on October 23 for the winter.

1492. It was said of Henry Ward Beecher that no one ever felt the full force of his kindness until he did Beecher an injury.—HARRY EMERSON FOSDICK, *Manhood of the Master*

1493. Jane Addams of Hull House fame was told of a foreigner who was in a prison. She visited the man and afterward said: "I found a bitter, hardened man. He came to this country with hope in his heart, but he found indifference, misunderstanding, hatred, poverty, and despair. I believe if one single person had spoken kindly to him he would not have become a murderer. Now we are too late."

1494.
That best portion of a good man's life,
His little, nameless, unremembered acts
Of kindness and of love.
    —WORDSWORTH, "Tintern Abbey"

L

LABOR

1495. Richard Clarke Cabot suggests in *What Men Live By* that there are three kinds of labor. One is toil that is tedious and tiresome without any hope of reward; this is drudgery. Another is activity that is unpleasant and tedious but carries with it the hope of reward; this is work. Then there is the kind of activity that is so enjoyable that one is eager to do it regardless of the reward or compensations; this is play.

1496.
This is the gospel of labor—
  Ring it, ye bells of the kirk—
The Lord of Love came down from
    above
  To live with the men who work.
This is the rose that he planted,
  Here in the thorn-cursed soil—
Heaven is blest with perfect rest;
  But the blessing of earth is toil.[1]
      —HENRY VAN DYKE,
          "The Gospel of Labor"

1497. A hundred years or so ago in Scotland the Paisley weavers sent a petition to Parliament asking for some relief of the intolerable strain of life. The hours of labor were long and the work difficult. They said in effect: "Take our leisure time if you must have it. But you are robbing us of things even more precious. For when we kneel in prayer, we are so exhausted that we fall asleep; and when we go to church, our minds, drugged with toil, are too weary to follow the service. Take our rights; take our lives; but leave us God. For him, too, you are filching from us."

LAUGHTER

1498. Rubens, the famous artist, used to say that he could with one stroke of his brush change a weeping child into a laughing one.

1499. A character in S. N. Behrman's play *No Time for Comedy* says: "It's all right to laugh under fire—that's courage—but not sitting on the side lines—that's callousness."

1500. "Outside I laugh; inside I never laugh," said Oliver Wendell Holmes; "the world is too sad."

1501. A celebrated Glasgow doctor examined a patient having a desolate spirit, and said: "There is nothing wrong with you. Go hear Grumaldi, the clown, and laugh and you will be well." "But," the patient answered, "I am Grumaldi."

LAZINESS

1502. Professor George H. Palmer of Harvard used to tell of a boy lying in bed very late in the morning and being called by his mother. "Aren't you ashamed to be lying here so late?" said the mother, and the boy answered, "Yes, mother, I am ashamed, but I had rather be ashamed than get up!"

1503. A lazy student was looking through a microscope watching minute

---

[1] Used by permission of the publishers, Charles Scribner's Sons.

animal life pass through one generation after another. Suddenly the boy stood up, saying: "I see it now. I am a single link between the generations before me and those who may come after. I will not be a rotten link in that chain!"

LEADERSHIP

1504. Vassar College wrote to the father of an applicant, asking if his daughter was a leader. The father replied: "I am not sure about this, but I know she is an excellent follower." The president of the college answered the father by writing: "As our freshman group next fall is to contain several hundred leaders, we congratulate ourselves that your daughter will also be a member of the class. We shall thus be assured of one good follower."

1505. In a flag-draped showcase in the State House at Hartford, Connecticut, is an old, weatherworn stone slab upon which is engraved a memorial tribute to Israel Putnam, an officer in the American Revolution. Part of the inscription is no longer legible, but the following words stand out clearly: "He dared to lead where others dared to follow."
—Delaine E. Story

1506. When a group of Sheridan's men during a dark moment in the Civil War found themselves cornered they broke rank and galloped away for their lives. Just then Sheridan himself arrived. Waving his sword above his head, he shouted: "Men, we are going the other way!" Inspired by the presence of their leader, the men formed ranks again and marched forward to victory.

1507. It is reported that Colonel Theodore Roosevelt at San Juan Hill never said "Go!" to his Rough Riders. Always his command was, "Come on, boys!"

1508. Lawrence of Arabia, one of the most colorful characters in World War I, wrote of the Arabs: "No man could be their leader except he ate the ranks' food and wore their clothes, lived on a level with them, and yet appeared better in himself."

1509. A high-school girl came into the kitchen one morning wearing a gray stocking on one foot and a brilliant red stocking on the other foot. Her father, rather surprised, asked if that was the way the girls at school were dressing. "Well," the daughter said, "they weren't yesterday, but they will be tomorrow."

1510. Chester Rowell relates the old story of the man who was running as quickly as possible after a crowd of people. While trying to catch up with them, he was asked the reason for his hurry. His answer was: "I've got to catch up with them. I'm their leader."

1511. "No man is good enough to govern another man without that man's consent," Lincoln declared in one of his debates with Douglas.

1512. A shrewd politician, when asked how he had been so successful in politics, said: "I always wait to see which way the wind is blowing and then make my plans accordingly."

1513. When a party of Arctic explorers went to search, years ago, for Sir John Franklin among the snows and icebergs, they encountered cold so intense that the thermometer sank to seventy degrees below zero, and the strongest men, overcome with cold, lay down to sleep. But the leader knew that half an hour of that treacherous sleep would leave every one of them stiff with death. He roused them up. They said, "We are not cold. We only want a little rest." So the leader struck them, boxed them, bruised them, and did everything to drive off the fatal slumber. And the arm that aroused them was the arm that saved them.

LIBERTY

1514. When a staff officer said to George Washington during one of the dark periods of the Revolutionary War, "General, we are lost; everything is lost," Washington replied, "Sir, you do not know the resources and genius of liberty."

1515. "A work of God, or a work worthy of God, must necessarily be a work of liberty," said Alexandre Vinet.

1516. When asked if she would remain in America if she could, a foreign student commented: "You meet when and where you please, and speak as freely as you like, either in criticism or praise of persons and ideas. You have morning newspapers that give you full accounts of world happenings. You enjoy the benefits of countless inventions to make life interesting and comfortable. You have plenty of light. America is, indeed, a wonderful land in which to live." Then, considering the question, she added: "I should like the advantages of your way of living, but I am afraid I am not a big enough person to live in such liberty."—MINNIE SANDBERG SEARS

1517. "The love of liberty is the love of others," said William Hazlitt. "The love of power is the love of ourselves."

LIFE

1518. Bede in his *Ecclesiastical History* records the words with which one man persuaded an Anglo-Saxon king to adopt Christianity for his people: "The present life of man, O King, seems to me . . . like the fight of a sparrow through the room wherein you sit at supper in winter with your ministers, a good fire burning in the midst while storms rage everywhere abroad; the sparrow, I say, flying in at one door and immediately out at another, whilst he is within is safe from the wintry storm; but he immediately vanishes out of your sight into the dark winter from which he had emerged. So this little of man appears for a brief space, but of what went before or what is to follow, we are utterly ignorant. If, therefore, this new doctrine contains something more certain, it seems justly to deserve to be followed."

1519. Studdert-Kennedy, chaplain to George V, said that when he stood before God, one question would be asked by the Almighty: "Well, what did you make of it?"

1520. A woman now distinguished in public life complained to her mother of the many hardships which she had to face in her early years. "See here," the mother said, "I have given you life; that is about all I will ever be able to give you—life. Now you stop complaining and do something with it."—HARRY EMERSON FOSDICK, *On Being a Real Person*

1521. Iago says of Cassio: "He hath a daily beauty in his life that makes me ugly."—SHAKESPEARE, *Othello*

The Empty Life

1522. Ben Robertson in *Red Hills and Cotton* tells of this inscription on a tombstone near his boyhood home: "Born 1810. Died 1890. Lived 50 years."

1523. George Bernard Shaw has suggested the epitaph most appropriate for many men might read: "Died at thirty, buried at sixty."

1524. When a man was asked to explain the meaning of an epitaph he had written for his tomb ("Born —— a human being; died —— a wholesale grocer"), he said: "I was so busy selling groceries that I did not have time to get married and have a family. There was a whole area of life crowded out by the grocery business. I was so busy selling groceries that I didn't have time to travel, even though I had the money. I was so busy selling groceries I did not have time for the drama, for lectures, for concerts, or for reading. I was so busy selling groceries I did not have time for community service—religious, social, or political. All of these areas of life were pushed out by the grocery business. I was successful. I became a wholesaler. But I was so busy making a living I never had time to live."—CLYDE E. WILDMER

1525. When a certain religious group took as a motto some years ago these words, "Millions now living will never die," someone commented: "Yes, but the tragedy is that millions now living are already dead and don't know it."

1526. H. G. Wells said: "There was a time when my little soul shone and was uplifted at the starry enigma of the sky. That has gone absolutely. Now I can go out and look at the stars as I look at the pattern of the wallpaper on a railway station waiting room."

1527. Near the body of a young man who had taken his life this note was found: "I leave to society a bad example. I leave to my friends the memory of a misspent life. I leave to my father and mother all the sorrow they can bear in their old age. I leave to my wife a broken heart, and to my children the name of a drunkard and a suicide. I leave to God a lost soul who has insulted his mercy."—HARRY EMERSON FOSDICK, *A Great Time to Be Alive*

1528. When Ralph Barton, one of the most popular of American cartoonists, took his own life, he left this message: "I have run from wife to wife, from house to house, and from country to country in a ridiculous effort to escape from myself. In doing so I am very much afraid that I have caused a great deal of unhappiness to those who have loved me. . . . No one thing is responsible for this, and no one person—except myself. . . . I've done it because I am fed up with inventing devices for getting through twenty-four hours every day."

1529. A sophomore student of average ability was talking over his troubles with his counselor. His college courses were not going well. He had made no future plans. "What school areas do you like best?" asked the counselor. After a few moments of thought the young man replied, "I don't know." "What do you like to do in your spare time then?" the counselor continued. "Oh, uh—nothing, I guess," was the reply. "Well, what are you interested in?" Again the same reply, "Nothing."

The Full Life

1530. "I'm going to live till I die," said an old Quaker of eighty-two years, "and then I'm going to live forever."

1531. "O God," prayed an old man, "help me to live while I am alive."

1532. A small boy, just learning to write, ended a letter to his uncle in this way: "I send you my love. I hope you live all your life."—LESTER A. WELLIVER

1533.
Whatever crazy sorrow saith,
No life that breathes with human breath
Has ever truly long'd for death.

'Tis life, whereof our nerves are scant,
Oh, life, not death, for which we pant;
More life, and fuller, that I want.
　　　　　　—ALFRED TENNYSON,
　　　　　　　　"The Two Voices"

1534. The love of life common to men of all generations is vividly expressed by Achilles to Odysseus: "I would rather be on earth as the hired servant of another, in the house of a landless man with little to live upon, than be king over all the dead."

1535. When asked how long it took to paint a certain picture, Joshua Reynolds said: "All my life."

Goal of Life

1536. After a teacher had told his students how they should play the game of life, one puzzled student asked: "But how can we play the game when we don't know where the goal posts are?"

1537. At the age of ten Henry Ashurst wrote in his speller in a childish but firm hand: "Henry Fontaine Ashurst, U. S. Senator from Arizona." Thus he announced the great ambition of his life.

1538. Sir Isaac Newton, goaded by someone for his painstaking preparation for life, said: "I care not how late I come into life, provided I only come fit."

1539. Frank Horne, the great Negro track star, once gave the following advice about living and running a race: "Live as I have taught you, boy. It's a short dash. Dig your starting holes deep and firm; lurch out of them into the straightaway with all the power that is in you; look straight ahead to the finish line; think only of the goal. Run straight, run high, run hard. Save nothing and finish with an ecstatic burst that carries you hurtling through the tapes to victory."—JACKSON WILCOX

Meaning of Life

1540. Said William James: "For my own part, I do not know what the sweat and blood and tragedy of this life mean, if they mean anything short of this. If this life be not a real fight, in which something is eternally gained for the universe by success, it is no better than a game of private theatricals from which one may withdraw at will. But it *feels* like a real fight."

1541. "Over half a century ago," writes Archer Wallace in *Leaves of Healing,* "two statesmen in turn delivered addresses at a great British university. Both men were well known to the students and were held in high esteem, but their messages differed widely. Benjamin Disraeli said: 'If you would succeed, know the temper and spirit of the times in which you live and act accordingly.' Nothing could have been more characteristic than the advice from William Gladstone: 'Do not drift with the age. Have fixed principles and stand by them.' In this latter statement one senses the emphatic conviction of a man who was determined to stand by his convictions, whatever the cost."

1542. Dr. Carl Jung, the Swiss psychiatrist, has quoted one of his patients as saying: "If only I knew that my life had some meaning and purpose, then there would be no silly story about my nerves."

1543. "The world is disintegrating before our eyes," writes Harris Franklin Rall, "for lack of authority that shall be something more than force, for lack of spirit that shall be stronger than fear, hate, and selfishness, and lack of faith that will give meaning to life and courage to live."

1544. Unseen influences which make life meaningful are illustrated in Jules Breton's famous painting, "The Song of the Lark," in which no lark is seen.

1545. "There is no reason to suppose," writes Joseph Wood Krutch, a modern agnostic, "that man's own life has any more meaning than the life of the humblest insect that crawls from one annihilation to another."

1546. After the suicide of a young man his father, a university professor, said: "The reason my son committed suicide is that he could see no reason in life." Then he added: "If you quit kidding yourself, you have to admit that there is no reason in living."

Purpose of Life

1547. Asked Horace Traubel: "What can I do? I can talk out when others are silent. I can say *man* when others say *money*. I can stay up when others are asleep. I can keep working when others have stopped to play. I can give life big meanings when others give life little meanings. I can say love when others say hate. I can say every man when others say one man. What can I do? I can give myself to life when other men refuse themselves to life."

1548. George Bernard Shaw has said: "I am convinced that my life belongs to the whole community; and as long as I live, it is my privilege to do for it whatever I can, for the harder I work the more I live. I rejoice in life for its own sake. Life is no brief candle for me. It is a sort of splendid torch which I got hold of for a moment, and I want to make it burn as brightly as possible before turning it over to future generations."

1549.
Whether we climb, whether we plod,
  Space for one task the scant years lend,
To choose some path that leads to God,
  And keep it to the end.[2]
    —LIZETTE WOODWORTH REESE,
     "Heroism"

1550. An anxious parent was speaking with a friend about his unappreciative children. "Maybe," the friend suggested, "you have tried to give them too much to live with and not enough to live for."

1551. "What did God ever make such a world for anyway?" one young person complained, adding, "I could make a better world than this myself." "That," a friend suggested, "is just the reason God put you into this world—to make it a better world. Now go ahead and do your part."

1552. Some time ago a young Chinese girl was executed for being a communist. Before her death she spoke to her relatives, many of them Christian: "You are weeping for me. You should weep for yourselves. I am dying for a cause. You will go on living—for what?"

1553. George Eliot has described her memorable character Silas Marner as a man who had no ultimate purpose in life: "His life had reduced itself to the mere functions of weaving and hoarding, without a contemplation of an end towards which the functions tended. . . . So year after year Silas Marner

[2] From *The Selected Poems of Lizette Woodworth Reese.* Copyright 1926 by Holt, Rinehart and Winston, Inc. Copyright 1954 by C. Reese Dietrich. Reprinted by permission of Holt, Rinehart and Winston, Inc.

had lived in this solitude, his guineas rising in the iron pot, and his life narrowing and hardening itself more and more into a mere pulsation of desire and satisfaction which had no relation to any other being."

1554. When a small child lost her birth certificate, she cried to the teacher: "I've lost my excuse for being born."

Rules for Life

1555. "The rule that governs my life is this: Anything that dims my vision of Christ, or takes away my taste for Bible study, or cramps my prayer life, or makes Christian work difficult, is wrong for me, and I must, as a Christian, turn away from it." So wrote Wilbur Chapman.

1556. When a friend wrote to Turgenev, the great Russian novelist of an earlier day, "It seems to me that to put oneself in the second place is the whole significance of life," the writer replied, "It seems to me to discover what to put before oneself, in the first place, is the whole problem of life."

1557.
Man cannot live by bread alone,
   This has been proven o'er and o'er—
Yet still men try to satisfy
   The inner life with earthly store.
          —AUTHOR UNKNOWN

1558. "The great use of life is to spend it for something that outlasts it," said William James.

1559. "The lesson of life," wrote Emerson, "is to believe what the years and centuries say against the hours."

The Short Life

1560. Disraeli said: "Life is too short to be little."

1561.
Life is too short to waste
   In critic peep or cynic bark,
Quarrel or reprimand:
   'Twill soon be dark;
Up! mind thine own aim, and
   God speed the mark.
          —EMERSON, "T. J. W."

1562. After her death Emily is given an opportunity to go back to a scene of her childhood in Thornton Wilder's drama *Our Town*. Thinking of the life she has lived and of her failure to appreciate its significance, she exclaims: "It goes so fast. We don't have time to look at one another. . . . I didn't realize. So all that was going on and we never noticed. . . . One more look. Good-by. Good-by, world. Good-by, Grover's Corners . . . Mama and Papa. Good-by to clocks ticking . . . and Mama's sunflowers. And food and coffee. And new-ironed dresses and hot baths . . . and sleeping and waking up. Oh, earth, you're too wonderful for anybody to realize you. Do any human beings ever realize life while they live it?—every, every minute?"

1563.
Forenoon and afternoon and night—
   And day is gone—
So short a span of time there is
   'Twixt dawn and evensong.

Youth—middle life—old age—
   And life is past—
So live each day that God shall say,
   "Well done!" at last.
          —EDWARD ROWLAND SILL, "Life"

1564. How many persons, thrilled with the possibilities of life and yet aware of the brevity of life, have sympathized with the sentiment expressed on the grave of a youth in an old New England cemetery: "This is what I expected, but not so soon."

1565. "The men whom I have seen succeed best in life," wrote Charles Kingsley, "have always been cheerful and hopeful men who went about their business with a smile on their faces and took the changes and chances of this mortal life like men, facing rough and smooth alike as it came."

LIGHT

1566. On the Eddystone lighthouse on the English coast are these words: "To give Light is to save Life."

1567. John Henry Jowett used to tell of the farmer who gave him a lantern when he had to meet a train on a stormy night, saying: "Just to help you to see where you are going, and to keep you out of the ditch." Then the farmer added: "Do you see that glimmer of light yonder? That is Saddleworth station. Make for that." The lantern gave him a light for each step, Jowett later recalled, and the glimmer in the distance appointed the course of his journey.

1568. Under the picture of Peter Milne in the church he founded on the little New Hebrides island of Nguna are these words:

When he came there was no light;
When he died there was no darkness.

1569. A motto adopted some time ago by The American Friends Service Committee is: "It is better to light a candle than to curse the darkness."

1570. One mother relieved a child's fear of darkness by explaining: "There's nothing to be afraid of. Darkness isn't anything. It's only the absence of light."

1571. In a severe storm at night on Lake Erie a passenger vessel was trying to make the harbor at Cleveland. The lighthouse had been struck by lightning, and the ship could not get its direction in the storm. But in the distance the captain could see the little lights at intervals along the breakwater. Although the great beacon light was out, the captain, watching these little lights closely, was able to bring his ship safely into the harbor. The lower lights had saved his vessel. One of the passengers on this vessel, so the story goes, wrote the evangelistic song "Brightly Beams Our Father's Mercy" shortly after reaching Cleveland.

1572. "Where there is fire," Woodrow Wilson said, "thither will men carry their lamps to be lighted."

1573. Harry Lauder said: "I could tell where the lamplighter was by the trail of light left behind him."

1574. The story is told of two men who went out one night to explore the world. One took a torch with him, but the other said he'd find his way without a light. The latter, upon his return, said, "I found nothing but darkness." The former said: "Everywhere I went I found light."

1575. There was once a cave which lived under the ground, as caves have the habit of doing. It had spent its life in darkness. It heard a voice calling to it: "Come up into the light; come and see the sunshine." The cave retorted: "I don't know what you mean; there isn't anything but darkness." Finally the cave ventured forth and was surprised to see light everywhere. Looking up to the sun the cave said: "Come with me and see the darkness." The sun asked: "What is darkness?" The cave replied: "Come and see." One day the sun accepted the invitation. As it entered the cave it said: "Now show me your darkness." But there was no darkness!

LINCOLN

1576. Someone has said of Lincoln: "He plucked a thistle and planted a rose wherever a rose would grow."

1577. "I see they got a new baby today over to Tom and Nancy Lincoln's cabin," observed a neighbor when Abraham Lincoln was born. "He's the homeliest critter I ever laid eyes on."

1578. Charles A. Beard, the historian, has written of Lincoln: "He was uncouth in manner, coarse sometimes in speech, tall, lanky, homely, awkward. Yet the severest of his critics was arrested by something compelling about the personality of Lincoln—something transcending the roughness of the frontier."

1579. A mother one evening was walking with her young daughter past the old Lincoln home in Springfield. The small girl, not realizing the truth of her words, exclaimed: "Oh, Mother, Mr. Lincoln forgot to put out his light when he went away."

1580. Secretary of War Stanton, when told of the death of Lincoln, with whom he often found himself in vigorous disagreement, said, "Now he belongs to the ages."

1581. Long ago Edmund Burke said that a nation is a contract in which three parties are involved: the dead, the living, and those yet unborn. It is thus a legacy, a trust, and a prophecy. Lincoln was true to his trust and kept his contract with Washington, at what cost we know and with what result history records. Nay, more; he kept his contract with us, foreseeing a time when a hundred millions of people would live under one flag. Looking forward, he saw that our task is to show that the great common people, for whom the nation was established, working together through institutions devised to discover and make effective their collective will, can create and uphold a social order that is just and wise and free, demonstrating that no man by reason of birth or station is unfit to have a share in that vision and labor. By as much as we keep faith with Lincoln, we shall bequeath to our sons no tumbled house.
—Joseph Fort Newton, *The Angel in the Soul*

1582. "I don't know who my grandfather was," Lincoln once said when asked about his ancestry, "but I am much more concerned to know what his grandson will be."

LISTENING

1583. An excited little boy was telling his father a story. "Slow up, Sonny, you are talking too fast," the father said. "Oh, no, Daddy, I don't talk too fast. You just listen too slow."

1584. When Napoleon was making plans to invade England, he was told that an American wanted to see him. "I can give him two minutes," Napoleon said. But two minutes was not long enough to grasp the significance of so revolutionary an idea as a ship propelled by steam. Had Napoleon listened longer to Robert Fulton, the history of the world might have been altered.

LONELINESS

1585. One day when Rupert Brooke was sailing from Liverpool for New

York he noticed that everyone had friends who were there to wave farewell. But the poet had no friends there and felt very lonely. Then he saw a little urchin on the quay. Brooke rushed back on the quay and got hold of the urchin. "What is your name?" he asked. "William." "Do you want to earn sixpence, William?" William did! "Then wave to me when the boat goes." Brooke never forgot the figure of this little urchin who, with a dirty handkerchief, took from him his loneliness.—LESLIE D. WEATHERHEAD, *The Eternal Voice*

1586. When asked if his life was not a lonely one, the keeper of a lighthouse said: "No, we do not think it unpleasant or even lonely here. We know that we are perfectly safe. Our business is to keep our lamps burning brightly all the time and to see that the reflectors are clear so that those who are in danger may be guided to safety."

LOVE

1587. "Love," says Henry W. Shaw, "looks through a telescope; envy, through a microscope."

1588. A definition of love which won a nationwide newspaper contest reads: "Love is the doorway through which the human soul passes from selfishness to service and from solitude to kinship with all mankind."

1589. "Not where I breathe," Robert Southwell said, "but where I love, I live."

1590. William Jennings Bryan told of a farmer boy who, after months of bashfulness, finally said to the girl he loved: "Mary, I've been lovin' you for a long time. I can't talk much, but will you be my wife?" Mary replied: "Yes, John, I've been loving you, too. I'll be happy

to be your wife." Late that night when John was alone, he looked up at the stars and was heard to say: "O Lord, I ain't got nothin' 'gin nobody now."

1591. "I love you when you're good," a father told his small daughter. The little girl answered quickly: "I love you all the time, Daddy."

1592. The grave of Charles Kingsley in Eversley churchyard is marked by a white marble cross on which are his chosen words: *Amavimus. Amamus. Amabimus.* (We have loved. We love. We shall love.)

1593. In Hermann Sudermann's drama *John the Baptist,* Herodias says that John, who has lived in the wilderness, does not understand the ways of men. "You seem to me to be so distant that the very beat of the human heart appears to you to be folly," she cries. "The hot wind has taught you to hate—but what do you know of those who live and die for the sake of love? Having stolen into the desert, you creep forth to charge others with guilt." "You speak of love— even you?" says John. "Do you know in what form sin likes best to appear? Say Pride, say Hate, say what you will, and I will laugh at you. Sin likes best to call itself Love!"

1594. Wishing to receive the affections of his subjects, Frederick the Great struck a subject with a whip one day and exclaimed: "Confound you! I want you to love me."

Christian Love

1595. Celsus, critic of early Christians, said: "These Christians love each other even before they are acquainted."

1596. One of Jimmy Doolittle's flyers, after spending many months in a

Japanese prison, said: "They were ignorant and mean, but we thought there was some good in them. The only way to develop that goodness would be by understanding and education—not by brutally mistreating them as they were doing us. You can smile if you want to, but it made sense to me in that prison camp, and it still does. So I'm going to a missionary school for training, and then I'm going to return to Japan and spend the rest of my life there, teaching the importance of love among men."

1597.

The man is happy, Lord, who love like
  this doth owe:
Loves thee, his friend in thee, and for
  thy sake, his foe.
        —RICHARD C. TRENCH

Love and Hate

1598. One of the earliest written documents, dating to 3000 or 3500 B.C., reads: "Life is given to the peaceful, and death is given to the guilty, the peaceful being 'he who does what is loved,' and the guilty, 'he who does what is hated.'"

1599. "Hate cannot destroy hate, but love can and does," is the opinion of Daniel A. Poling. "Not the soft and negative thing that has carried the name and misrepresented the emotion, but love that suffers all things and is kind, love that accepts responsibility, love that marches, love that suffers, love that bleeds and dies for a great cause—but to rise again."

1600.

I do not love thee, Dr. Fell:
The reason why I cannot tell;
But this I know, and know full well:
I do not love thee, Dr. Fell.
        —THOMAS BROWN

Influence of Love

1601. "Love," said Francis of Assisi, "sets my heart ablaze."

1602. "What we love we shall grow to resemble," wrote Bernard of Clairvaux.

1603. When Gandhi was nearly slain by a fanatical Moslem in 1908, he turned to his adherents and said: "This man did not know what he was doing. I will love him and win his love." A year later the Moslem, against whom Gandhi refused to witness, wrote offering his apologies and admiration.

1604.

I hold it true, whate'er befall,
  I feel it, when I sorrow most;
'Tis better to have loved and lost
Than never to have loved at all.
    —TENNYSON, "In Memoriam"

1605. "I have committed myself to love," said one college professor when a friend asked the secret of his happy life. "I have put self out of the picture, and consequently I do not fear anything."

Need of Love

1606. A man and his wife were at an orphanage where they hoped to adopt a child. One boy appealed to them in particular. After they explained to the small child the many things they would give him and how much he would be grateful for, he said: "If you have nothing to offer except a good home, clothes, toys, and the other things most kids have—why, then, I would just as soon stay here." "What on earth do you want besides those things that you mention?" the woman asked. The little boy replied: "I want someone to love me."
    —WILLARD M. HEWLETT

1607. One young woman wrote in explanation of her suicide: "I am killing myself because I have never sincerely loved any human being in all my life." —HARRY EMERSON FOSDICK, *On Being a Real Person*

1608.
In all the crowded universe
There is but one stupendous word:
  Love.
There is no tree that rears its crest,
No fern or flower that cleaves the sod
Nor bird that sings above its nest,
But tries to speak this word of God.
            —JOSIAH GILBERT HOLLAND

LOYALTY

1609. In the days of feudalism a serf, deciding to remain with his lord, said: "Dear my lord, I am liege man of thine for life and limb and earthly reward, and I will keep faith and loyalty to thee for life and death, so help me God."

1610. Alfred Tennyson in a tribute to Queen Victoria wrote: "Oh, loyal to the royal in thyself."

1611. Reinhold Niebuhr in his *Leaves from the Notebook of a Tamed Cynic* wrote: "Narrow loyalties may become more dangerous than selfishness."

1612. "The tragedy of the world is that men have given first-class loyalty to second-class causes, and these causes have betrayed them," Lynn Harold Hough says.

1613. A loyal son of old Kentucky, just on the eve of the Civil War, was faced with the grave problem of which side he should support. This is the way he solved the problem: If the country should split, he would side with the South against the North. If the South should split, he would side with Kentucky against the other southern states.

If Kentucky split, he would side with his county against the rest of the state. And if his county split, he would side with his town against the rest of the county.

LUTHER

1614. Thomas Carlyle said of Martin Luther: "I call this Luther a truly great man. He is great in intellect, great in courage, great in affection and integrity; one of our most lovable and gracious men. He is great, not as a hewn obelisk is great, but as an Alpine mountain is great; so simple, honest, spontaneous; not setting himself up to be great, but there for quite another purpose than the purpose of being great. . . . What were all emperors, popes, and potentates in comparison? His light was to flame as a beacon over long centuries and epochs of the world; the whole world and its history was waiting for this man."

1615. Thomas Carlyle in his *Heroes and Hero-Worship* credits Martin Luther with releasing those Christian forces which eventuated in the salutary effects of the French Revolution, parliamentary government in England and other European nations, and the American democracies.

1616. Heinrich Heine, the German poet and critic, called Luther's hymn "A Mighty Fortress Is Our God" the "Marseillaise of the Reformation," adding: "A battle hymn was this defiant song with which he and his comrades entered Worms. The old cathedral trembled at these new notes, and the ravens were startled in their hidden nests in the towers. This hymn, the Marseillaise of the Reformation, has preserved its potent spell even to our days, and we may yet use again the old mailed words."

1617. When someone once said, "What the world needs is another Martin Luther," a friend replied: "No, what the world needs is several little Luthers."

LYING

1618. After a small child had been caught telling a lie, the child said, "I wish I could get over this lying business." To this a wise parent said, "Yes, people won't like you if you lie." "I don't even like myself," the child added.
—FRANK B. FAGERBURG

1619. A small boy, when asked for a definition of a lie, said: "It is an abomination to the Lord but an ever-present help in time of trouble."

M

MAN

1620. An old proverb reads: "God sleeps in the tree, dreams in the animal, and wakes in the man."

1621. A Chinese proverb says: "If you are planning for a year, plant grain. If you are planting for a decade, plant trees. If you are planning for a century, plant men."

Belief in Man

1622. John Wesley's belief in the honesty of his fellow men led his brother Charles to say that anybody could deceive him. To this John replied: "I believed in everybody. Charles did not, and Charles was more often deceived than I."

1623. "Astronomically speaking, man is negligible," Harry Elmer Barnes said. "Astronomically speaking," replied George A. Coe, "man is the astronomer."

1624. Rufus Jones once related a legend concerning Moses which suggested that Moses on his way up Mount Pisgah, the Mountain of Death, prayed to the Lord that he might go for a little into the Promised Land which he could see before his dying eyes. But the Lord said to him: "Moses, you lost faith in me, and I forgave you that. You lost faith in yourself, in the powers of your own leadership, and I could forgive you that. But then you lost faith in these people and in their divine possibilities.

That I cannot forgive. For without that faith it is impossible for you to enter the Promised Land."

Frustrations of Man

1625. A cynic has compared the life of man with the flight of a bird, starting nowhere, arriving nowhere, but in flight superb.

1626. H. L. Mencken's estimate of man was suggested by these words: "Man is a sick fly taking a dizzy ride on a gigantic flywheel."

Greatness of Man

1627.
Though his beginnings be but poor and low,
Thank God, a man can grow! [1]
　　　—Florence Earle Coates,
　　　　"Per Aspera"

1628. The Greek word for man is *anthropos*, which means literally "the upward-looking one."

1629. After the tragic sinking of the "Titanic" an American newspaper carried two pictures. One showed the ship's side torn open and about to sink—the symbol of fragility—and underneath the picture were these words, "The weakness of man; the supremacy of nature." The other illustration showed the passengers stepping back to give the one place in the lifeboat to a woman with her baby in her arms. Under this picture

[1] Used by permission of the Pennsylvania Co.

were the words, "The weakness of nature; the supremacy of man."— LUTHER WESLEY SMITH, *And So I Preached This*

1630. "I realize," said Henri Amiel, "with intensity that man in all he does that is great and noble is only the organ of something or someone higher than himself."

1631. William Shakespeare makes a striking tribute in *Julius Caesar:*

His life was gentle, and the elements
So mixed in him that Nature might
     stand up,
And say to all the world, "This was a
     man!"

1632. Commenting on the Civil War, one historian wrote: "Lee's army was defeated at Gettysburg, but not Lee."

Nature of Man

1633. In the tombs of the ancient Orphics, recently unearthed, were found little tablets which bore the following inscription: "I am a child of earth and of starry heaven."—HAROLD COOKE PHILLIPS, *Seeing the Invisible*

1634. Discussing the question of whether human beings and the universe have meaning, Aldous Huxley in his book *Ends and Means* wrote: "This is a question which a few years ago I should not even have posed. For, like so many of my contemporaries, I took it for granted that there was no meaning. . . . I had motives for not wanting the world to have a meaning, consequently assumed that it had none, and was able without any difficulty to find satisfying reasons for this assumption. Most ignorance is vincible ignorance. We don't know because we don't want to know. It is our will that decides how and upon what subjects we shall use our intelligence. Those who detect no meaning in the world generally do so because, for one reason or another, it suits their books that the world should be meaningless."

1635. In a letter to a young man Charles Kingsley, the English cleric, wrote: "The human race may, for practical purposes, be divided into three parts —honest men, who mean to do right and do it; knaves, who mean to do wrong and do it; fools, who mean to do which ever of the two is pleasanter. And these last may be divided into black fools and white fools—black fools, who would rather do wrong than right, but dare not unless it is the fashion; white fools, who would rather do right than wrong, but dare not unless it is the fashion."

1636. A legend tells us that once the gods became displeased with man's desire to equal the supernatural, and so they took away that spark of their life which was in man. Not knowing where they might hide it from him, they finally resolved: "We will hide the spark safely in a place where man will never look for it. We will hide it securely in his own heart."

1637. Father Taylor of Boston once chided a legislator for voting against his principles. The legislator said: "But the pressure was terrific." Said Father Taylor: "Man, where are your inner braces?"

1638. Roger Babson tells of visiting a farmer who took great pride in his stock. The pedigree was hanging in front of every cow on his farm. Blueprints were kept in the office with the record of each animal. Babson said to the farmer, "What about your laborers?" and he replied, "Oh, they are all alike to me."

Paradox of Man

1639. A modern Frenchman has said: "Do you know what makes man the most suffering of all creatures? It is that he has one foot in the finite and the other in the infinite, and that he is torn between two worlds."

1640. Lin Yutang says: "A Chinese may be poor, ragged, unwashed, unkempt, and illiterate, yet have poise, dignity, courtesy, and an intuitive feeling for carrying off a situation with ease and naturalness."

1641. One man, on looking at the title of Dr. George A. Dorsey's book, *Why We Behave Like Human Beings,* exclaimed: "The answer is clear—most of us don't."

1642. George Lansbury of England said to E. Stanley Jones: "As I near eighty and look back across my life, I see that I have not been unsuccessful, but if I had it to do over again, I think I would give my whole life to the changing of men, for without that change nothing can be changed."

MARRIAGE

1643.
A love that lasts forever:
A friendship naught can sever;
A courage never failing,
Though evil seems prevailing;
And joyous, radiant living,
Made glorious by its giving;
A faith strong and enduring,
Unworthy thoughts obscuring;
And eyes for seeing beauty
In work, in play, in duty;
Life ever onward flowing
And more abundant growing;
Love, courage, faith, and sweetness
To make up life's completeness.
　　　　—S. G. FISHER,
　　　　　"For Newly-weds"

1644. At the wedding of Great Britain's Princess Elizabeth, the Archbishop of Canterbury said: "The ever-living Christ is here to bless you. The nearer you keep to him, the nearer you will be to one another."

1645. Katherine Mansfield, writing to another novelist, Sylvia Lynd, said: "What is happening to 'modern pairs'? They are almost extinct. I confess, for my part, I believe in marriage. It seems to me the only possible relation that really is satisfying. And how else is one to have peace of mind and do one's work? To know *one other* seems to me a far greater adventure than to be on kissing acquaintance with dear knows how many. It certainly takes a lifetime, and it's far more 'wonderful' as time goes on. . . . People nowadays seem to live in such confusion. . . . I wish you'd write a novel about married happiness. It is time for one."

1646.
Going my way of old,
　　Contented more or less,
I dreamt not life could hold
　　Such happiness.

I dreamt not that love's way
　　Could keep the golden height,
Day after happy day,
　　Night after night.[2]
　　　　—WILFRED WILSON GIBSON,
　　　　　"Marriage"

1647.
The kindest and the happiest pair
Will find occasion to forbear;
And something, every day they live,
To pity, and perhaps forgive.
—WILLIAM COWPER,
　"Mutual Forbearance Necessary to
　the Happiness of the Married State"

[1] From *Collected Poems.* Used by permission of The Macmillan Co.

1648. One wonders, when he hears that so-and-so have been married for thirty years and never had the least difference, if perhaps there has not been a good deal of indifference.

MARTYRDOM

1649. Hugh Latimer, the English martyr, turned to his fellow sufferer as the fires were being kindled at their stakes and said: "Be of good comfort, Master Ridley, and play the man; we shall this day light such a candle by God's grace in England as I trust shall never be put out!"—H. N. HART, *Living Religion*

1650. In *The Mortal Storm* by Phyllis Bottome the story is told of a Jewish scientist confined in a concentration camp. The son asks the scientist: "But could they, Father, could they kill you?" To this the father replies: "If they kill me, it would not help to spread their creed. It is those who kill who are weakened and what ideas they have are discredited by their acts. The ideas we stand for cannot be killed. All persecution is a sign of fear."

MASTER

1651. "As I would not be a slave," Abraham Lincoln, "so I would not be a master."

1652. The story is told that Diogenes, the Greek philosopher, was captured by pirates and later put up for sale on the slave block. Looking around, Diogenes saw a vacant-looking young man, very richly dressed, who stood by. "Sell me to that man," he said. "He looks as if he needed a master."

MEDITATION

1653. Anker-Larsen, a well-known Danish writer, tells of an old Danish peasant who on his deathbed asked of his son only one promise: that he should sit *alone* for a half-hour each day in the best room of the house. "The son did this and became a model for the whole district. This father's command had taken thought for everything: for eternity, soul-deepening, refinement, history."—DOUGLAS V. STEERE, *Prayer and Worship*

1654. "A holy life does not live in the closet," wrote E. M. Bounds, "but it cannot live without the closet."

1655. When Borglum began his famous statue of Lincoln, which is in Newark, he took as his inspiration the reported practice of Lincoln during the dark third year of the Civil War of going out alone on the balcony at night to pray to God under the stars. The statute shows the brokenhearted president seated, his head uncovered and bowed in reverent meditation.

MINISTRY

1656. When a woman asked a man if he was a minister, the man, who was a minister, asked the woman how she knew. "Because, sir, you have a Bible face."

1657. Late one night the wife of a dying man knocked at the door of Henry Drummond's home. She begged him to come to see her husband at once. "He is not able to speak to you or to see you," she said, "and he may not be able to hear you, but I would like him to have a breath of you about him before he dies."—HARRY O. RITTER

1658. "I might have been a minister myself," Oliver Wendell Holmes once said, "for aught I know, if a certain clergyman had not looked and talked like an undertaker."

1659. A little boy, after passing the minister at the door of the church, began to cry. When his mother asked the reason for his tears, the little boy said: "I smiled up at God, but he didn't smile back at me!"—ALBERT W. BEAVEN

1660. When great crowds of people had gathered into the piazza in front of the old palace to watch the execution of Savonarola, someone snatched the reformer's robe from his back. "O sacred habit," Savonarola said, "how much I desire thee! By the grace of God thou wast granted to me; and I have preserved them unstained to this moment. Now I do not abandon thee, but thou art taken from me."

Achievements of Ministers

1661. Richard Baxter, when he went to Kidderminster as pastor, said: "In some streets there was only one family which worshiped God." When he completed his ministry there, he said: "When I came away, there were some streets in which there was not a single family where they did not have family prayer every day."

1662. A contemporary described the secret of Dwight L. Moody's ministry in this manner: "I saw at once. Moody was simply bubbling over with the glory of his message. He reveled in it. His joy was contagious. Men leaped out of darkness into light and lived the Christian life from that hour."

1663. When a minister at Ipswich, Massachusetts, was presented to George Washington, the minister removed his hat. "Put on your hat, parson," Washington said, "and I will shake hands with you." "I cannot wear my hat in your presence, general," the minister protested. "Oh, yes," Washington said.

"You did what you could, and I have done no more."

1664. John Wesley crowded into his life the work of any five ordinary men. On his seventy-second birthday he noted in his *Journal*: "I considered how it is that I find just the same strength as I did thirty years ago. The grand cause is the good pleasure of God. The chief means are (1) my constantly rising at four o'clock in the morning for about fifty years, (2) my generally preaching at five o'clock, (3) my never traveling less by sea and land than 4,500 miles in a year."

Call of the Minister

1665. Paul Scherer has said: "There is such a thing as a call to the Christian ministry. It comes from the world—a world committing suicide."

1666. "Lord," an old Negro preacher prayed, "I'm clumsy-footed in this praying business. But you're to blame, Lord. I've always been clumsy-footed. You took me from behind the plow."

1667. Harry Emerson Fosdick describes his call to the ministry with these words: "Once a boy went with his family to church on Sunday morning. He was not trying hard. He did not even dream that anything important was about to happen. But as the sermon proceeded, something happened. Doors began to open in that young boy's mind. Visions came that he had never seen before, and a sense of direction he had not known. I was that boy. That happened over fifty years ago. I never have escaped the influence of that hour. Strange what a few moments of released power, when one is not trying, can do for all the years afterward when one is trying!"

1668. Booker T. Washington used to tell of an Alabama Negro who declared:

"De cotton am so grassy, de work am so hard, and de sun am so hot, dat I believe dis darky am called to preach."

1669. When Leslie D. Weatherhead asked a theological student about his call to the ministry, the student told of a preacher who had challenged him. "Who was the preacher?" Weatherhead asked. "I can't remember," said the student. "You can't remember?" Weatherhead exclaimed. "I only know," said the youth thoughtfully, "that God spoke to me that night."—*The Eternal Voice*

Minister and Congregation

1670. Dr. Andrew Bonar, with his little daughter, went into his church one weekday, seating her in a rear pew. After a long wait she stood up to look for her father. He was in a pew, his head bent forward. Soon he moved to another, then another, and another. Sometimes she would see him carefully examine the name plates to find the pews he desired. She did not understand it at the time, but as she grew in stature and the pewholders grew in grace, she learned the significance. The shepherd was praying for the sheep in the very spot where each worshiped.—CHESTER E. TULGA

1671. The firm bond that existed between John Fredric Oberlin and his parish was laid each morning in the hour that he devoted to prayer for his individual parishioners. We are told that as they went past his house at this hour in the morning, they did so in quiet, for they knew what was happening there.—DOUGLAS V. STEERE, *Prayer and Worship*

1672. "Doctor," a friend said to Woodrow Wilson's father, a Presbyterian minister, "your horse looks better groomed than yourself." "Yes," replied Dr. Wilson, "I take care of my horse. My congregation takes care of me."

1673. "What sort of minister have you?" a man asked a friend. "Well, I really don't know," said the friend. "On Sunday he is incomprehensible; then for the rest of the week he is invisible."

Task of the Minister

1674. The ministry of letters is told with these words inscribed upon the portals of the Post Office building in Washington, D.C.:

The messenger of sympathy and love,
Servant of parted friends,
Consoler of the lonely,
Bond of the scattered family,
Enlarger of common life,
Instrument of trade and industry,
Promoter of mutual acquaintance of peace and of good will among men and nations.

1675. John Wesley commissioned George Shadford with these words: "I let you loose, George, on the great continent of America. Publish your message in the open face of the sun, and do all the good you can."

1676. An editor of John Wesley's *Journal* has written: "The great purpose of his life was doing good. For this he relinquished all honor and preferment; to this he dedicated all his powers of body and mind; at all times and in all places, in season and out of season, by gentleness, by terror, by argument, by persuasion, by reason, by interest, by every motive and every inducement, he strove, with unwearied assiduity, to turn men from the error of their ways and awaken them to virtue and religion. To the bed of sickness or the couch of prosperity; to the prison or to the hospital; to the house of mourning or the house of feasting; wherever there was a friend to serve or a soul to save, he readily repaired. He thought no office too humiliating, no condescension too low, no undertaking too arduous to reclaim the meanest of God's offspring. The souls of all men were equally precious in his sight, and the value of an immortal creature beyond all estimation."

1677. Wallace Petty wrote discerningly: "We are not confronted with the task of convincing skeptical minds that the religion of Jesus is reasonable; we are up against the more stupendous enterprise of convincing pagan hearts that it is desirable."

1678. William Lyon Phelps in his *Autobiography with Letters* recalls hearing Henry Drummond say at Yale in 1887: "We come not to save your souls but to save your lives. We want you to be Christians, not because you might die tonight but because you are going to live tomorrow."

1679. When a lyceum head offered Charles H. Spurgeon a contract for fifty nights at a thousand dollars a night to come to America and lecture, he answered: "I can do better than that. I can stay in London and save fifty souls."

1680. "I am old-fashioned enough to think that a minister should be at least as much concerned about the unconverted as he is about the unemployed," said Dr. Christie of Winnipeg.

1681. "Forget about yourself," an older minister suggests to a self-conscious young minister in Le Grand Cannon's novel *A Mighty Fortress*. "What you want to do is to think about those people. Then maybe you can make them forget about themselves. That's what

they've come for. When you can give it to 'em, you'll be a preacher."

MIRACLE

1682. "Every moment of this strange and lovely life from dawn to dusk," wrote Beverley Nichols, "is a miracle. Somewhere, always, a rose is opening its petals to the dawn. Somewhere, always, a flower is fading in the dusk. The incense that rises with the sun, and the scents that die in the dark, are all gathered, sooner or later, into the solitary fragrance that is God. Faintly, elusively, that fragrance lingers over all of us."

1683. "Miracles take place," said Martin Luther, "not because they are performed, but because they are believed."

MISERY

1684. Henry Drummond's "Receipt for Misery" was: "Be a halfhearted Christian."

1685. Pascal said: "All men's miseries derive from not being able to sit quiet in a room alone."

MISFORTUNE

1686. A physician commenting upon a certain individual's tendency to brood over some misfortune said: "She is making a career of her misfortune."

1687. In his *Sketch Book*, Washington Irving wrote: "Little minds are tamed and subdued by misfortune; but great minds rise above it."

MISSIONS

1688. Four hundred years ago Francis Xavier said: "You may be very sure of one thing—the devil will be tremendously sorry to see the Society of Jesus enter China."

1689. William Carey said that he went to India as a missionary *in order to save England*. He was right when he believed that the missionary activities of the English churches would kindle a new flame of enthusiasm in the English parishes.

Achievements of Missions

1690. On the grave of George Dana Boardman, pioneer missionary in Burma, are these words: "His epitaph is written in the adjoining forests. Ask in the Christian villages of yonder mountains—Who taught you to abandon the worship of demons? Who raised you from vice to morality? Who brought you your Bibles, your Sabbaths, and your words of prayers? Let the reply be his eulogy—*A Cruce Corona*."

1691. When Charles Darwin, the great scientist, in his famous voyage in the "Beagle" visited Tierra del Fuego and saw the utter savagery and beastliness of the natives, he deliberately, in the exercise of his trained scientific judgment, pronounced them beyond hope. Years afterward he stopped there on another voyage. In the meantime missionaries had carried the gospel to these hopeless creatures. Upon seeing the change, Darwin could hardly believe the evidence of his senses. In his *Journal of Researches,* speaking of his fondness for placing side by side a heathen and a Christian Fuegian, he writes: "It was without exception the most curious and interesting spectacle I ever beheld. I could not have believed how wide was the difference between savage and civilized man. . . . The success of the mission is most wonderful, and charms me, as I always prophesied utter failure. I could not have believed that all the missionaries in the world could have made the Fuegians honest. The mission is a grand success. . . . The march of

improvement consequent on the introduction of Christianity throughout the South Seas probably stands by itself in the record of history." After this Darwin became a contributor to foreign missions.

1692. Said James Chalmers, martyred missionary of New Guinea: "I have had twenty-one years' experience among the South Sea Islanders, and for at least nine years of my life I have lived with the savages of New Guinea. I have seen the semicivilized and the uncivilized; I have lived with the Christian native, and I have lived, dined, and slept with the cannibal. But I have never yet met a single man or woman, or a single people, that your civilization without Christianity has civilized. Wherever there has been the slightest spark of civilized life in the Southern Seas, it has been because the gospel has been preached there; and wherever you find in the island of New Guinea a friendly people, or a people that will welcome you, there the missionaries of the cross have been preaching Christ."

1693. When Allen Gardiner attempted to preach the gospel to the natives of Tierra del Fuego, he was driven back by the unfriendly inhabitants. He returned to his home and pleaded with his people to outfit him once more. When he landed a second time, the superstitious natives killed his companions and drove Gardiner to the shelter of his little boat. Later rescuers found words he had written shortly before his death: "My little boat is a Bethel to my soul. Asleep or awake, I am happier than tongue can tell. I am starving, yet I feel neither hunger nor thirst. I feed on hidden manna and drink at the King's well. I am not disappointed, for I remember that one soweth and another reapeth." Today thousands of natives, now devoted Christians, water Gardiner's grave with their tears.—WILLIAM E. PHIFER, JR., *The Cross and Great Living*

1694. Mission work in China appeared to be hopeless when Robert Morrison landed in Canton in 1807. Many years later when a leader in the new Republic of China was asked when the Chinese Revolution began, he replied: "On the day that Robert Morrison, the missionary, landed in Canton."

1695. Robert Louis Stevenson, when in the South Seas attempting to regain his health, met the missionary, James Chalmers. He later said that Chalmers was one of the great men of that day. "If I had known you when I was a boy," he told the missionary on one occasion, "how different my life would have been!"

Criticism of Missions

1696. In 1789 when William Carey announced his plan to go as a missionary to India, he was bitterly opposed by the East India Company. The directors assembled and issued the following proclamation: "The sending out of missionaries into our Eastern possessions is the maddest, most extravagant, most costly, most indefensible project which has ever been suffered by a moon-struck fanatic. Such a scheme is pernicious, imprudent, useless, harmful, dangerous, profitless, fantastic. It strikes against all reason and sound policy. It brings the peace and safety of our possessions in peril."—STANLEY HIGH, *The Church in Politics*

1697. In 1812 when the Massachusetts Senate was asked to incorporate a new mission board, opposition arose when the legislators said that "the country had no religion to spare."

Hardships of Missions

1698. James Chalmers near the close of his long career as a missionary said: "Recall the twenty-one years, give me back all my experiences, give me its shipwrecks, give me its standing in the face of death, give it me surrounded with spears and clubs, give it me back again with spears flying about me, with the club knocking me to the ground, give it me back—and I will still be your missionary."

1699. "Exposed to robbers by night and invaders by day," wrote Ann Judson, wife of the missionary pioneer, in her journal at Rangoon, Burma, "we both unite in saying that we were never happier."

1700. In his autobiography, *A Labrador Doctor*, Sir Wilfred Grenfell tells a story which has characterized the courageous Christian missionary. One day he was summoned to a village on the Labrador coast to perform an emergency operation. Wishing to reach the stricken patient as quickly as possible, he drove his dog team across a river which seemed to be frozen. The ice, however, gave way, and the doctor and his dogs were thrown into the freezing water. After considerable effort he succeeded in pulling himself and his dogs onto a huge cake of drifting ice which immediately began to carry them toward the Atlantic Ocean. Realizing that the river banks had few inhabitants, Grenfell's only hope was that fishermen near the mouth of the river might rescue him. In his own words the missionary has described this harrowing experience: "Night found me ten miles on my seaward voyage. I had killed three of my dogs, stripped off their skins, and wrapped their fur about me as a coat. Their bodies I piled up to make a windbreak on the ice. At intervals I took off my clothes, wrung them out, swung them in the wind, and then put them on again, hoping that the heat of my body would dry them. Forcing my biggest dog to lie down I cuddled close to him, drew the improvised dog-skin rug over me, and eventually dropped to sleep. The hand that was against the dog stayed warm, but the other was soon frozen. About midnight I awoke shivering. The moon was just rising, and the wind and current were sweeping me steadily toward the open sea. But somehow my faith was unshaken. After all, it seemed the natural thing for a Labrador doctor to be drifting toward the portal of death on a half-frozen stream. And quite unbidden the words of a hymn I had learned in boyhood began running through my mind:

"My God and Father, while I stray
Far from my home on life's rough way
O teach me from my heart to say,
    Thy will be done!"

Medical Missions

1701. A Chinese son, leading his blind father, walked sixty miles to Christ's Hospital on a mission compound. A nurse met him at the door, and he asked: "Is this Christ's Hospital?" "Yes, it is," the nurse replied. "Is Christ here? I came to see him that he might heal my blind father." The nurse hesitated a moment, then said: "Yes, he is here. Come right in." Presently the missionary doctor, a true interpreter of Christ, came in.—ALMA J. NOBLE

1702. Ira Gillett, missionary in Portuguese East Africa, tells the story of a group of natives who made a long journey and walked past a government hospital to come to the mission hospital for treatment. When asked why they had walked the extra distance to reach the mission hospital when the same medicines were available at the government

institution, they replied: "The medicines may be the same, but the hands are different."—BRUCE R. BAXTER

Need of Missions

1703. Imagine a professor of philosophy sitting down at his desk to work on his lecture for the following day. Like some other people, he cannot work at an untidy desk. So he proceeds to clear away the papers strewn upon it, papers which have been put there probably by a lady who acts on the principle, "When you don't know what to do with pamphlets, magazines, handbills, and the rest of the clutter that gets pushed into the mailbox, put it on father's desk." The professor picks up a magazine published by the Paris Missionary Society. He is about to throw it into the wastebasket, when, on mechanically opening it, he catches the title of an article, "The Needs of the Congo Missions." The professor reads it through and puts it down. In his diary that night he writes the words: "My search is over." The professor was Dr. Albert Schweitzer, and the "chance" reading of a missionary report took one of the most scholarly and gifted men in Europe to study medicine at the university in which he was a professor and then spend his life in Equatorial Africa. Though he has doctor's degrees in philosophy, theology, medicine, and music, his best years have been given to a mission station, Lambaréné, in French Equatorial Africa.—LESLIE D. WEATHERHEAD, *The Significance of Silence*

1704. A huge black stone in Westminster Abbey marks the final resting place of David Livingstone. Around the side of the stone is this inscription in gold letters: "Other sheep I have, which are not of this fold."

1705. A missionary told an American businessman that thirty million Chinese beyond his station had no Christian teaching. Just then a wagonload of lamps and cans of oil passed them and moved on toward the interior of the country. Noticing the label on one of the boxes, "Made in Connecticut, U.S.A.," the businessman said: "We send them lights for their homes, but we do not send them light for their hearts."

Praise of Missions

1706. An American Embassy member who had never had much use for Christian missions saw something of the work being done in Chengtu by missionaries and Chinese Christians. Suddenly one day while in the midst of an earnest discussion he said: "You know, I believe you have something after all. My contacts in recent months with all sorts of people, particularly in government circles, have convinced me that, more than any economic development, what China needs is character—simple honesty and moral and ethical standards. I don't see it being developed anywhere the way it is in your Christian universities. Yes, I believe you have something there."

1707. Henry Morgenthau, when American ambassador to Turkey, wrote: "The missionaries have the right idea. They go straight to the foundations and provide those intellectual, physical, moral, and religious benefits upon which alone any true civilization can be built."

1708. Robert Louis Stevenson said: "I had conceived a great prejudice against missions in the South Seas, and I had no sooner come there than that prejudice was at first reduced, and then at last annihilated. Those who deblaterate against missions have only one thing to do, to come and see them on the spot."

Support of Missions

1709. Someone asked Phillips Brooks what he would do first if he were called to be the pastor of a broken-down church —a church that had lost its building, was not able to support a pastor, and was torn by internal dissension. He hesitated a moment and then replied: "I should get all the people together, preach the greatest sermon I could on world-wide missions, and take the best offering I could get for work in heathen lands." —WILLIAM M. ELLIOTT, JR., *Coming to Terms With Life*

1710. When an artist was asked to paint a picture of a dying church, he did not depict a small congregation in a ruined building. Rather he showed a stately edifice, with a rich pulpit, organ, and beautiful windows. But in the porch there was hung a small box, with the words above it, "Collection for Foreign Missions." And just where the contributions should have gone, the slit was blocked by a cobweb.

Work of Missions

1711. Pearl Buck in *The Fighting Angel* wrote: "The early missionaries were born warriors. To them religion was a banner under which to fight. No weak or timid soul could sail the seas to foreign lands and defy dangers and death unless he carried his religion as a banner under which even death would be a glorious end. . . . To go forth, to cry out, to warn, to save others—these were frightful urgencies of the soul already saved."

1712. Concerning the work of missionaries in the Hawaiian Islands, Mark Twain wrote: "The benefit conferred upon this people by the missionaries is so prominent, so palpable, and so unquestioned, that the frankest compliment I can pay them, and the best, is simply to point to the condition of the Sandwich Islands in Captain Cook's time, and their condition today. The work speaks for itself."

1713. E. Stanley Jones quotes the experience of a Hindu principal of a college: "I once saw Christ, and I have never forgotten the vision. The plague was raging in the city, and everybody had fled in terror, except the sick and dying. Whole sections were deserted. I drove down through the plague-stricken section, and to my surprise I saw a missionary lady, Mrs. D——, coming out of one of the houses where there was plague. She came with her hands extended before her and said: 'I am sorry, Mr. S——, that I cannot shake hands with you, my hands are plague-stained.' As I looked at her with her plague-stained hands, I saw Christ."

1714. When Stanley went to Africa to find Livingstone he carried with him letters from England. When he gave them to him, Livingstone looked through the bundle quickly, sorting out those messages from his family. "Listen to what my daughter, Agnes, writes me," he said to Stanley. "'Much as I wish you would come home, father, I had rather that you finished your work to your own satisfaction than return merely to gratify me.'"

1715. "I was once traveling in an Oriental country," Francis G. Peabody told his students at Harvard, "where life was squalid, women despised, and houses built of mud; and of a sudden I came upon a village where all seemed changed. The houses had gardens before them and curtains in their windows; the children did not beg of the passer-by but called out a friendly greeting. What had happened? I was fifty miles from a Christian mission-station, and this mission had been there for precisely fifty

years. Slowly and patiently the influence had radiated at the rate of a mile a year, so that one could now for a space of fifty miles across that barren land perceive the salt of the Christian spirit and could see the light of the Christian life shining as from a lighthouse fifty miles away."—*Mornings in the College Chapel*

MISTAKE

1716. Someone has said: "There are always two reasons for a mistake, the reason *given* and the *real* reason."

1717. "When I was in Persia," writes Leslie D. Weatherhead, "I said to a student, watching with me the weaving of a carpet, 'What happens when the boys make a mistake?' 'Well,' he said, 'quite often the artist does not make the boy take out the wrong color. If the artist is a great enough artist, he weaves the mistake into a pattern.'"

1718. "Life is like war," wrote F. W. Robertson of Brighton. "It is a series of mistakes, and he is not the best Christian or the best general who makes the fewest false steps. He is best who wins the most splendid victories by the retrieval of mistakes."

MONEY

1719.
Dug from the mountainside, washed
     from the glen,
Servant am I or master of men.
Steal me, I curse you;
Earn me, I bless you;
Grasp me and hoard me, a fiend shall
     possess you;
Live for me, die for me,
Covet me, take me,
Angel or devil, I am what you make me.
            —AUTHOR UNKNOWN

1720. When H. V. Morton asked a rustic peasant, who was carving wooden bowls on his doorstep in a far corner of England, how much money he made at his business, the wood carver replied: "I am not making money. I am making bowls."

1721. An old man named Candelario found a seven-hundred-dollar nugget in the gulches of Sandia Peak, near Albuquerque. "As soon as my luck was known," he said, "I became Don Candelario; within a week I was Don Juan Candelario; then Don Juan de Candelario, Caballero. My name grew for three weeks, till my gold was gone. Then I became simply Old Candelario again." —*National Georgraphic Magazine*

1722. When a Negro was asked the cause of the depression, he said: "I guess the white folks just bought more than they could pay for."

1723. Said Louis Agassiz, the scientist: "I have no time to make money. I am searching for truth."

1724. Someone has said: "Mammon holds the one outpost Christianity has not been able to conquer."

1725. It has been said: "Money is a purchaser of anything except happiness and a passport to any place except heaven."

Love of Money

1726. One day a rich but miserly Chassid came to a rabbi. The rabbi led him to the window. "Look out there," he said, "and tell me what you see." "People," answered the rich man. Then the rabbi led him to a mirror. "What do you see now?" he asked. "I see myself," answered the Chassid. Then the rabbi said: "Behold, in the window there is glass, and in the mirror there is glass. But the glass of the mirror is covered with a little silver, and no sooner is a little silver added than you cease to see others and see only yourself."— S. ANSKY, *The Dybbuk*

1727. One morning this note was handed to a preacher in his pulpit: "Please offer special prayers for a member of this congregation who is growing wealthy."

1728. "As a rule the 'almighty dollar' bequeathed to sons or daughters by millions proves an almighty curse," cautioned Andrew Carnegie.

1729. One of the tragedies in the life of Mark Twain is explained by a biographer with these words: "He tried to play the businessman in place of being a great artist. The reason was primarily that he became more or less intoxicated with money."

Use of Money

1730. "When I have any money, I get rid of it as quickly as possible, lest it should find a way into my heart," John Welsey said.

1731. A small boy who had been given two nickels—one for Sunday school and the other for himself—was running down the street one Sunday morning. Suddenly he dropped one of his nickels. He watched the nickel roll along the sidewalk and then out of sight. "Well," he muttered, "there goes God's nickel."

Value of Money

1732. Rudyard Kipling, English poet, speaking to a graduating class at McGill University, advised the graduates not to care too much for money or power or fame; for, he said in effect, "Someday you will meet a man who cares for none of these things . . . and then you will know how poor you are."—GEORGE A. BUTTRICK, *Christ and Man's Dilemma*

1733. Abe Martin, the cartoonist, said some years ago: "I notice that the people of America have plenty of money for everything—except necessities."

MORALITY

1734. "Nothing that is morally wrong," said Gladstone, "can be politically right."

1735. Theodore Roosevelt was right when he said: "To educate a man in mind and not in morals is to educate a menace to society."

MOTHER

1736. An old Jewish proverb says: "God could not be everywhere, so he made mothers."

1737. William Makepeace Thackeray in *Vanity Fair* wrote: "Mother is the name for God in the lips and hearts of little children."

1738. A beggar once asked Edward VII, then Prince of Wales, for money. Realizing that the beggar did not know his identity, the prince reached into his pocket, saying: "I will give you a picture of my mother." The beggar was surprised to find that the gold coin which he was given had an image of Queen Victoria on it.

Mother's Example

1739. Four clergymen were discussing the merits of the various translations of the Bible. One liked the King James Version because of its beautiful English; another, the Revised Version of 1881 because of its literal and accurate translation of the original Hebrew and Greek; the third, James Moffatt's translation for its up-to-date vocabulary. The fourth was silent. When asked to express his opinion, he replied, "I like my mother's translation best." The others were surprised. "I didn't know your mother translated the Bible," one said. "Oh, yes," came the reply. "She translated it into life, and it was the most convincing translation I ever saw."— J. C. MITCHELL

1740. Thomas Carlyle, recalling his mother's praying, wrote: "The highest whom I knew on earth, I saw bowed down to a Higher in heaven. Such things, especially in infancy, reach inward to the very core of your being."

1741. In Foochow there are three graves side by side. Two of them are the graves of the daughters of a widow in Australia. Those two girls went out as missionaries to China, and they were both murdered. When the news came to the widow in Australia that her daughters had been killed, she was sixty-two years of age. She sold all that she had. She went to the place where her two girls had been murdered. She learned the Chinese language, set up a school, and gave twenty years of service to China. She died at the age of eighty-two and was buried near her daughters.—LESLIE D. WEATHERHEAD, *The Eternal Voice*

Indebtedness to Mother

1742. "If I am thy child, O God," said Augustine at the time of his conversion, "it is because thou didst give me such a mother."

1743. John Quincy Adams said: "All that I am my mother made me."

1744. Albert E. Bailey tells the story about two bills, Harry's bill to his mother and Mother's bill to Harry. The first bill itemized the various jobs Harry had done about the house, and ended: "Total that Mother owes Harry, $.12." The bill was promptly paid. The other bill, which Harry found under his pillow the next morning, read something like this:

For food for Harry, 10 years $0.00
For clothing and home, 10 years.. 0.00
For toys and skates and a bicycle.. 0.00
For taking care of Harry during
　　pneumonia 0.00
_____
Total that Harry owes Mother.... $0.00

1745. A boy had obtained a job—his first—and was boasting of the amount of work he did. "I get up at half past five and have my breakfast," he said. "Anyone else get up too?" he was asked. "Oh, yes, Mother gets my breakfast, and then she gets Dad's at half past six." "And your dinner?" "Oh, Mother gets that, too, and then she gets Father's." "Has she the afternoon to herself?" "Oh, no, she cleans up, looks after the children, and gets tea for Dad and me when we come home. Then we read the newspapers and go to bed." "And your Mother?" "Well, she does a bit of sewing then, when all is cleaned up after tea." "What wages do you get?" "Oh, I get ten shillings, and Dad gets four pounds." "Mother? Oh, she don't get wages. She don't do no work."—*The London Times*

Mother's Influence

1746. When James Harper, who later became an eminent publisher, left his old-fashioned home to go to New York City, his mother kissed him good-by, saying: "James Harper, you are going to a strange city. Remember your mother's blood is in your veins, and don't disgrace it."

1747. Following the death of his wife J. Sterling Morton, President Cleveland's Secretary of Agriculture, took his three children to their mother's grave. The epitaph read: "Caroline French, wife of J. Sterling Morton, and mother of Joy, Paul, and Mark Morton." After reading aloud the inscription the father said: "If any of you ever does anything that would cause your mother grief or shame if she were alive, I will chisel your name off that stone." The names are still there.

Mother's Love

1748. After a mother had spent most of her time and strength caring for her child whose mind and body were retarded, a friend offered sympathy for the suffering and sacrifice she was making. "Oh, you don't understand," said the woman, "if you think I am to be pitied. I would do it a hundred times, if only once he would look into my face and say, 'Mother.'"

1749. In *Forty Years for Labrador,* Sir Grenfell, the famous Labrador doctor, recalled a memory from his youth when he attended Marlborough College in England: "My dear mother used to post me a little box of flowers each week. The picture of my mother, with the thousand demands and worries of a large school for small boys on her hands, finding time to gather, pack, address, and post each week with her own hands so fleeting and inessential a token of her love, has a thousand times arisen in my memory and led me to consider some apparently quite unnecessary little token of my love as being well worth the time and trouble."

1750. A little girl was told by her mother to play with her dolls, for Mother was busy. The girl complained: "I just love them and love them, and they never love me back."

Love Toward Mother

1751. John Galsworthy in *Forsyte Saga* gives the conversation between a mother who has been away for a few days and her son who wants to know where she has been and what she has seen. "Nothing but beauty," the mother says of her visit to the seashore. "What exactly is beauty?" the boy asks, adding, "can I see it?" "Yes," the mother replies, "you see it every day. The sky is beautiful, the stars and moonlight nights, and then the birds, the flowers, the trees—they're all beautiful. Look out of the window—" After looking out of the window the boy turns back to his mother and says: "I know! You are it, and all the rest is make-believe."

1752. When the squadron under Dewey arrived at Manila Bay just before the battle with the Spanish ships, a sailor asked permission to jump overboard for his coat, which somehow had fallen into the water. He was refused, jumped anyhow, climbed aboard again with the coat, and was promptly arrested. Dewey summoned the man and inquired why he had disobeyed orders. The sailor broke down. "In the pocket," he explained, "was my mother's picture, and I didn't want to lose it." Dewey had him released.

1753. Caruso is reported to have said that the most perfect singing he ever heard was his mother's when he was a boy.

MUSIC

1754. "Shepherd of Tender Youth," the oldest hymn in the Christian hymnal, was written by Clement of Alexandria, who for many years was head of the first known Christian school, the catechetical school of Alexandria. It dates back to about A. D. 200.

1755. Servant and master am I; servant of those dead and master of those living. Through me spirits immortal speak the message that makes the world weep, and laugh, and wonder, and worship. I tell the story of love, the story of hate, the story that saves, and the story that damns. I am the incense upon which prayers float to heaven. I am the smoke which palls over the field of battle where men lie dying with me on their lips. I am close to the marriage altar, and when the graves open I stand near by. I call the wanderer home, I rescue the soul from the depths, I open the lips of lovers, and through me the dead whisper to the living. One I serve as I serve all; and the king I make my slave as easily as I subject his slave. I speak through the birds of the air, the insects of the field, the crash of waters on rock-ribbed shores, the sighing of wind in the trees, and I am even heard by the soul that knows me in the clatter of wheels on city streets. I know no brother, yet all men are my brothers; I am the father of the best that is in them, and they are fathers of the best that is in me; I am of them, and they are of me. For I am the instrument of God.—AUTHOR UNKNOWN, "I Am Music"

1756. Fritz Kreisler has written: "I have not the slightest consciousness of what my fingers are doing when I play. I concentrate on the ideal of the music that I hear in my head, and I try to come as near to that as I can. I do not think of the mechanics at all. You might say that a musician who does have to think of the mechanics is not ready for public performance."

1757. Asked the secret of his musical ability, Ole Bornemann Bull, the Norwegian violinist, told a group of Princeton students: "It is not so much the bow, and not altogether the quality of the instrument, but I never play until my own soul is thrilled; and then the music is the expression of my soul life."

1758. "Give me a laundry list," said Rossini, the composer, "and I will set it to music."

N

NAME

1759. Alexander the Great once met a slovenly, poorly poised soldier of his command and asked: "What is your name?" The soldier replied: "Alexander, sir." The king then said: "Change your name or change your ways."

1760. Hans Christian Andersen told of two small girls at a children's party in Denmark who were quarreling over the comparative power and wealth of their respective fathers. The youngster who asserted that her father was a Groom of the Chambers seemed to be winning the verbal battle. "And Groom of the Chambers is a very high office," she declared. "Those whose names end with 'sen' can never be anything at all. We must put our arms akimbo and make the elbows quite pointed so as to keep these 'sen' people at a great distance."

"Oh, if I could be one of them!" thought a little boy peeping through the crack of the door of the kitchen, where he was occupied in turning the spit for the cook. And strangely enough his wish was to be gratified even though his name ended with "sen," for many years later the same boastful children, now grown to mature men and women, visited a great house filled with magnificent art objects and owned by that very wistful boy who looked longingly in on their party, now the great sculptor Thorwald-*sen.*

1761.

Who steals my purse steals trash; 'tis something, nothing;
'Twas mine, 'tis his, and has been slave to thousands;
But he that filches from me my good name
Robs me of that which not enriches him,
And makes me poor indeed.
　　　　—SHAKESPEARE, *Othello*

1762. A census man was going his rounds, and he knocked at one door to learn who lived behind it. He asked the woman who opened it how many children she had. She said: "Well, there's Willie and 'Orace and Ethel—" He interrupted: "Never mind names. I just want numbers." Then she grew indignant: "They haven't got numbers; every one of them's got names."—LESLIE D. WEATHERHEAD, *The Transforming Friendship*

NATION

1763. Over the doorway of the Nordiska Museum in Stockholm are words which explain the greatness of Sweden: "We are a small nation, but we should think great things."

1764. When, after devastating bombardments, the Nazis moved into Narvik, Norway, the mayor said to a group of newspapermen: "The mountains are still ours."

NATURE

1765.

If chance could fashion but a little,
  With perfume for each tiny leaf,
And furnish it with sunshine and with
    shower,
  Then chance would be creator, with
    power
To build a world for unbelief.
            —FRED EMERSON,
                "The Grave Digger"

1766.

I need not shout my faith. Thrice elo-
    quent
  Are quiet trees and the green listening
    sod;
Hushed are the stars, whose power is
    never spent;
  The hills are mute; yet how they
    speak of God! [1]
            —CHARLES HANSON TOWNE,
                "Silence"

1767.

These are the things I prize
And hold of deepest worth:
Light of the sapphire skies
Peace of the silent hills
Shelter of the forest
Comfort of the grass
Shadows of the clouds that quickly pass,
And, after showers, the smell of flowers
And the deep brown earth;
But best of all, along the way,
Friendship and mirth. [2]
            —HENRY VAN DYKE,
                "The Things I Prize"

1768.

There is beauty in the forest
  When the trees are green and fair,
There is beauty in the meadow
  When wild flowers scent the air.

[1] Used by permission of the author's niece,
Miss Ora Searle.
[2] Used by permission of Charles Scribner's
Sons.

There is beauty in the sunlight
  And the soft blue beams above.
Oh, the world is full of beauty
  When the heart is full of love.
            —AUTHOR UNKNOWN

1769. "I gladly pay the rent of my house because I therewith get the horizons and the woods which I pay no rent for," Ralph Waldo Emerson once remarked. "For daybreak and evening and night, I pay no tax. I think it is a glorious bargain which I drive with the town."

NEED

1770. One of the most astonishing figures in American history is George Rogers Clark, who during the Revolution led a Virginia force into the Northwest Territory and won that vast region for the United States. But his reward was enmity and neglect, and in his old days he was impoverished. His native state, contrite, made him a present of a magnificent sword. In wrath he snapped the blade. "When Virginia needed a sword," he said bitterly, "I gave her one. Now I want bread."

1771. In his story "What Shall It Profit?" Leo Tolstoy tells of a land-hungry man who went to a distant country where the headman of a tribe offered to give him for a thousand rubles all the land he could walk around in a day. The man was told to put his money down on a certain spot and then walk till sunset. When he returned to his money, all lands enclosed by the path of his steps were to be his. So the man started, hurrying as fast as possible and returning after great exertion to the point of departure. But the task had been too great for him, and he fell dead where he had begun. In the end six feet of ground was all he claimed, for the rest was of no use to him.

NEW YEAR

1772. January is named for the Roman god Janus. An ancient Roman coin, now in the British Museum, pictures the god as having two heads: one looks back toward yesterday, and the other looks forward to tomorrow.

1773.
And now I have my New Yeark book to
    fill;

No word yet penned in it, nor any blot
Upon the clean white sheets, the pages
    still
Uncut, though dated day by day. Just
    what
They will record, God only can fore-
    tell—
And, after all, perhaps it is as well.[3]
        —Ethel Romig Fuller

[3] Used by permission of the author.

O

OBEDIENCE

1774. When Mr. Cobb, the clerk of the peace in the town of Bedford, went to see John Bunyan in prison, he said: "What benefit will it be to your friends if you should be sent away across the seas?" "Sir," Bunyan replied, "the law hath provided two ways of obeying. The one to do that which I in my conscience do believe that I am bound to do actively; and where I cannot obey it actively, there I am willing to lie down and to suffer what they shall do unto me."

1775. Archibald Rutledge told the story of meeting a Negro turpentine worker whose faithful dog had died a few moments earlier in a great forest fire because he would not desert his master's dinner pail which he had been told to watch. With tears on his face the old Negro said: "I always had to be careful what I tole him to do, 'cause I knowed he'd do it."

1776. A little girl, when asked if she always came when her mother called, said: "Yes, but sometimes I go so far away I can't hear her call."

OBSTACLES

1777. A certain pastor was asked to tell the secret of his power to overcome great obstacles. He said: "When the house is dark, I do not try to sweep away darkness with a broom; I light a candle."

1778. When asked what helped him over the great obstacles, a successful businessman replied, "The other obstacles."

1779. In his *Journal,* Emerson wrote the following about his neighbor Thoreau: "Henry Thoreau made, last night, the fine remark that, as long as a man stands in his own way, everything seems to be in his way."

OPPORTUNITY

1780. A mother took her small son to a distinguished man, saying: "I would like to have my boy shake hands with you." Noting that the boy offered him his left hand, the minister asked him for his right hand. The boy shook his head and replied: "I can't because I have marbles in it."

1781. Mark Twain, after losing money several times on impractical inventions, was one day approached by a stranger. "I'm not asking you to invest a fortune," the stranger said, showing his invention. "You can have as large a share as you want for $5.00." But Mark Twain said no. The invention didn't seem profitable. So Alexander Graham Bell left the novelist's home.

1782. When Michelangelo, the great sculptor who was converted through the martyrdom of Savonarola, became a Christian, a jealous man induced the pope to order him to paint the ceiling of the Sistine Chapel, believing that he could never learn to use the brush as he did the chisel and that failure and disgrace would follow. For four years Michelangelo painted while lying on his back. When he had finished, there was no faliure but the "mightiest series of paintings the world had ever seen."

—J. P. BERRY

OPTIMISM

1783. A Moslem monarch was thus advised by his chief astrologer: "Black days are ahead, O Mighty One. Your friends will fall on every side. You will be left alone." The prophecy was displeasing, and he ordered the astrologer decapitated. A new chief astrologer came with his prediction: "You are a most favored one, O Mighty Ruler. Allah grants thee long life. Honor will adorn thy shoulders after all thy contemporaries have passed away." This wise man was rewarded with great wealth.

1784. An optimist has been defined as "one who makes the best of it when he gets the worst of it."

1785. "Optimism," someone has said, "is the consciousness of hidden reserves."

1786. A small shrub growing next to a tall pine looked at the ground and said: "See how tall I am." But the pine, looking at the sky, said: "See how short I am."

1787. A dear old lady with more unconscious insight than learning once said: "My eyes are getting troublesome. I shall have to go to an optimist." —WILLARD BREWING, *Faith for These Times*

OWNERSHIP

1788. A rabbi was asked to settle a dispute between two men over the ownership of a certain piece of land. "I shall ask the land to which of you it belongs," said the rabbi. He put his ear to the ground and then said: "The land says it belongs to neither of you, but that both belong to it. Dust thou art, to dust returnest!"

1789. A tramp, so the story goes, being ordered out of a nobleman's yard, questioned the owner's title. The latter explained that the title to the land had come down to him in unbroken line from father to son through a period of seven hundred years, beginning with an ancestor who fought for it. "Let's fight for it again," suggested the tramp. —WILLIAM JENNINGS BRYAN

1790. A New Zealand cannibal once supported his claim to a piece of land on the ground that the title passed to him when he ate the former owner.

P

PATIENCE

1791. John Wesley's father once asked his wife: "How could you have the patience to tell that blockhead the same thing twenty times over?" "Why," she replied, "if I had told him but nineteen times, I should have lost all my labor."

1792. A little girl gave her idea of the true greatness of patience with this story: "Once there was a woman who did a big washing and hung it on a line to dry. The line broke and let it fall in the mud, but she didn't say a word. She did the washing all over again, and the second time she spread it on the ground. That night a dog walked over it with his muddy feet. When she saw it, she didn't cry a bit. All she said was, 'Ain't it funny, he didn't miss a piece.' That was true patience, but it is only people who have done washing that know it."—Nora Lesher

1793. When Da Vinci was painting his "Last Supper," he was chided for standing hours before the canvas without making a stroke. He replied: "When I pause the longest, I make the most telling strokes with my brush."

PATRIOTISM

1794. When stricken with paralysis at the age of forty-six, Louis Pasteur said: "I am sorry to die; I wanted to do much more for my country."

1795. Mazzini, the nineteenth-century Italian patriot, spoke judiciously when he said: "The honor of a country depends much more on removing its faults than on boasting of its qualities."

1796. The enthusiastic, one hundred per cent American ought to be reminded occasionally that to love one's country it is not necessary to hate other countries.

1797. Ralph Waldo Emerson said: "Your American eagle is very well. Protect it here and abroad. But beware of the American peacock."

1798. "There is no better example of the definition of pride than the definition of patriotism," G. K. Chesterton wrote. "It is the noblest of all natural affections exactly so long as it consists of saying, 'May I be worthy of England!' It is the beginning of one of the blindest forms of Pharisaism when the patriot is content to say, 'I am an Englishman!' "

1799. Nurse Edith Cavell, just before she was tragically shot by the Germans as a spy, said: "I see that patriotism is not enough. I must die without hatred or bitterness toward anyone."—Frank Fagerburg

PEACE

1800. The night before Franklin D. Roosevelt died, he wrote: "We seek peace—enduring peace. More than an end to war, we want an end to the beginnings of all wars—yes, an end to this brutal, inhuman, and thoroughly impractical method of settling differences between governments. The mere conquest of our enemies is not enough. We must go on to do all in our power to conquer the doubts and the fears, the ignorance and the greed which made this horror possible. Today we are faced with the pre-eminent fact that, if civilization is to survive, we must cultivate the science of human relationships—the ability of all peoples, of all kinds, to live together and work together, in the same world, at peace. Today as we move against the terrible scourge of war —as we go forward toward the greatest contribution that any generation of human beings can make in this world —the contribution of lasting peace, I ask you to keep up your faith. . . . The only limit to our realization of tomorrow will be our doubts of today. Let us move forward with strong and active faith."

1801. When Basil Mathews asked Sir Alfred Zimmern, "What, in your opinion, is the great obstacle between us and the building of enduring world peace," Sir Alfred answered, "The small-scale individual."

1802. A Christian approach to international understanding was suggested by the cartoonist who after World War I pictured world leaders seated at a peace council. Each had his portfolio. At the table sat also Christ—with his portfolio.

1803. Toward the close of World War II, J. N. Darling drew a cartoon showing an American soldier about to chop down a large, terrifying tree labeled "World War II." A group of civilians and diplomats with portfolios of postwar peace plans stood near by. The soldier was saying, "I'll cut down the tree; but God help us if you don't prevent its sprouting again."

1804. When Japan surrendered, General MacArthur said: "We have had our last chance. If we do not now devise some greater and more equitable system, Armageddon will be at our door. The problem basically is theological and involves a spiritual recrudescence and improvement of human character. . . . It must be of the spirit if we are to save the flesh."

Inner Peace

1805. Over the high and massive gate of a monastery are carved in the stone arch these words: *Pax Intrantibus* (Peace to all who enter).

1806. An English psychiatrist has written: "With peace in his soul a man can face the most terrifying experiences. But without peace in his soul he cannot manage even as simple a task as writing a letter."

1807. In the midst of World War II a European Christian remarked: "On the surface there is storm, but twenty fathoms down it is quite calm."

PEOPLE

1808. "I think the greatest thing in the world," said John Galsworthy, "is to believe in people."

1809. Alice Freeman Palmer once said: "It is people that count. You must put yourself into people; they touch others; these, others, and so you go on working for others forever."

1810. When someone objected that there were no completely praiseworthy characters in her book *South Riding*, Winifred Holtby explained: "I intended to make them good, but they would not be."

1811. A man sat down next to Will Rogers at a wayside lunchroom and engaged in conversation. "What's wrong with the world?" the man asked. "I dunno," Rogers replied. "I guess it's people."

1812. When Father Taylor of Boston was dying, a friend said: "Never mind, Father, you will soon be among the angels." "I don't want to be among the angels," Father Taylor replied. "I want to be among folk."—WILSON O. WELDON

PERFECTION

1813. Once there lived a Greek sculptor whose unfinished arm of a woman is one of the art treasures of the world. It was found in the Parthenon at Athens, and there lay beside it a tablet inscribed with these words: "I cannot carve my dream in marble. I am very ill. I am alone. I can no longer hold my tools. Good-by." All that is left is the unfinished arm, but it is perfect.

1814. "I cannot see where you have made any progress since the last time I was here," a visitor to the studio of Michelangelo said. "I have retouched this part," the master said, "polished that, softened this feature, brought out that muscle, given more expression to the lip and more energy to the limb." "But those things are all trifles!" exclaimed the visitor. "That may be," said Michelangelo, "but trifles make perfection, and perfection is no trifle." —WALTER DUDLEY CAVERT, *Remember Now . . .*

1815. One day Michelangelo was giving every effort to the making of a flower box. A duke watched the craftsman for some time and then commented that he, so great an artist, should not give so much time to such an endeavor,

for, after all, who would notice its perfection. "My spirit does," Michelangelo said. "Do you suppose that the Carpenter of Nazareth ever made anything less well than he could? that he was ever satisfied with anything less perfect than it could be made?"

1816. When a friend was looking at the work of William W. Story, the famous sculptor, he asked: "For which of these things you have done do you care the most?" To this the sculptor replied: "I care most for the statue I'm going to carve next."

PERSECUTION

1817. When the Roman emperor threatened to banish Chrysostom, the early Christian preacher, he answered: "Thou canst not, for the world is my Father's house. Thou canst not banish me." When the emperor threatened to kill him, he said: "Thou canst not, for my life is hid with Christ in God." When he threatened to take away his treasure, Chrysostom said: "My treasure is in heaven, and my heart is there." Finally the emperor said he would take away his friends. To this the Christian said: "That thou canst not, for I have a Friend in heaven from whom thou canst not separate me. I defy thee; there is nothing thou canst do to hurt me." —HOWARD WAYNE SMITH

1818. During the Diocletian persecutions when the temples, sacred books, and homes of the Christians were burned and Christians were deprived of all civil rights, and honors were denied, the emperor, as an evidence of the severity of this persecution, struck a coin with the inscription, "The Christian name extinguished."

1819. When Andrew Melville, an early Scotch reformer, was threatened by the

Earl of Morton, he said: "Tush, sir, threaten your courtiers after that manner. It is the same to me whether I rot in the air or in the ground. It will not be in your power to hang or exile truth."

PERSISTENCE

1820. "The hero," Emerson said, "is no braver than an ordinary man, but he is brave five minutes longer."

1821. One of the secrets in the great life of Jacob Riis, American social worker and writer, is suggested by him in this thought: "When nothing seems to help, I go and look at a stonecutter hammering away at his rock perhaps a hundred times without as much as a crack showing in it. Yet at the hundred and first blow it will split in two, and I know it was not that blow that did it—but all that had gone before."

1822. A young boy was watching a stonecutter. "Why do you use so many chisels?" he asked, seeing one chisel after another thrown in a heap near by. "Well, the stone is hard and chisels get dull," the stonecutter said. "It takes many chisels to carve a record into granite."

1823. A fisherman in the Adirondack forest once saw a large tree growing six feet off the ground on top of a huge rock. The seedling of that tree began growing in the earth that had gathered in a crack. The roots reached out where more nourishment lay and followed several dirt-filled cracks down to the earth, where they continued their search for satisfaction until the full-size tree stood there holding the rock in a cage of roots. But on the side of the rock where no cracks offered satisfaction no roots went forth.—ROBERT RUSSELL WICKS, *The Reason for Living*

1824. When asked how he had discovered the law of gravity, Sir Isaac Newton replied: "By thinking about it continuously. I keep the object of my research constantly before me, waiting until the first light begins to dawn, little by little; finally this changes, and at last the light is complete."

1825. Some years ago a Midwestern university unveiled a tablet to one of its alumni who was an undistinguished man. In his undergraduate years he had entered into many college activities, but he never had been president of anything. For four years he had gone out for football, but he had never played on the first team or been allowed in any important game. His scholastic average was in the B's. When World War I came, he served in a minor capacity in a medical unit, and one day met his death trying to help a wounded man under fire. The French Government posthumously conferred on him the *Croix de Guerre*. So his alma mater unveiled a tablet in his honor, and on it the inscription is written: "He played four years on the scrubs—he never quit."—HARRY EMERSON FOSDICK

1826. An old McGuffey reader told the story of a small boy who undertook the task of shoveling through a great drift of snow. When asked how such a small boy with a small shovel expected to clear away so much, the lad replied: "By keeping at it, sir."

1827. There is a famous statue in Mexico by Jesus Garcia, entitled "In Spite Of." The sculptor lost his right hand in the midst of his work on the statue. He determined that he would finish it. He learned how to carve with his left hand and finished it—and better, perhaps, than he would have done with his right hand. For a quality of life had gone into the statue. So they called the statue "In Spite Of."— E. STANLEY JONES

PERSPECTIVE

1828. "Let us keep our silent sanctuaries," wrote Étienne Sénancour, a French writer, "for in them the eternal perspectives are preserved."

1829. "You call the chessboard black," says Browning's Bishop Blougram in effect, "but try looking at it from another point, and see if you don't have to call it white!"

1830. In the house on top of Mt. Tom, in Massachusetts, a fine old gentleman used to show the western horizon of the Berkshire foothills through a window that had four panes of different-colored glass. You got an impression of the same landscape through each pane, but through the blue you had the look of winter, through the brown a touch of autumn, through the green a hint of early spring, and through the red a reminder of a summer sunset.—ROBERT RUSSELL WICKS, *The Reason for Living*

1831. When Lincoln Steffens was a boy, he watched an artist at work painting a picture of a muddy river. He criticized the picture because there was so much mud in it, to which the artist replied: "You see the mud in the picture, my boy. All right, there is mud, and lots of it. But I see the beautiful colors and contrasts, the beautiful harmonies, and the light against the dark." "Mud or beauty—which do we look for as we journey through life?" Steffens later wrote. "If we look for the mud and ugliness, we find them—they are there. If we look for beauty, character, nobility, we find them, too. Just as the artist found beauty in the muddy river, because that is what he was looking for, we will find in the stream of life those things which we desire to see. To look for the best and see the beautiful is the way to get the best out of life."

1832. One day John Ruskin saw some mud beside a little stream, and, scooping up a handful, he took it to his laboratory to analyze it. He found in the mud four things—sand, clay, carbon, and water—and in these he discovered four potentialities: in the sand the potential sapphire; in the clay, the opal; in the carbon, the diamond; and in the water, the potential snowflake.—HOWARD D. BARE

1833. The doctor in Florence Barclay's *The Rosary* says to his patient: "See a few big things. Go in for big things. You will like to remember when you are bothering about pouring water in and out of teacups that Niagara is still flowing."

1834. The English critic G. K. Chesterton said: "One sun is splendid; six suns would be only vulgar. One tower of Giotto is sublime; a row of towers of Giotto would be only like a row of white posts. The poetry of art is in beholding a single tower; the poetry of nature in seeing the single tree; the poetry of love in following the single woman; the poetry of religion in following the single star."

PERSUASION

1835. William Jennings Bryan told of a man in a town in Nebraska who said to a friend, "Well, I never heard Bryan, and I thought I would come and see what he has to say," and then added quickly, "But he will not convince me."

1836. In speaking the important thing is not how eloquently you speak, but the effect of your words on your audience. When Cicero had finished speaking, the people said, "How well he spoke." When Demosthenes had finished speaking, the people said, "Let us march against Phillip."—A. N. Fox, *Modern Debating*

1837. The *Quo Vadis* Chapel on the Appian Way leading out of Rome perpetuates an ancient tradition that when Peter had come to the conclusion that he had failed in his atempt to convert the Romans he determined to leave the city. As the Prince of Apostles left what was later to be called the Eternal City, Christ appeared to him. *"Quo vadis?"* Christ asked. "Whither goest thou?" The Master's question made Peter realize that no one else could do the work which he had been called to. He returned to Rome, where he died at last a martyr's death.

PIONEERS

1838. A character in Louis Bromfield's *Possession*, a modern young man of the Middle West, says, "My grandfather set out into a wilderness to conquer and subdue it. It was a land filled with savages and adventure. I, too, must have my chance. I am of a race of pioneers, but I no longer have any frontier."

1839. Rufus Jones used to tell of a little shrine he found high in the mountains of Switzerland. The shrine was marked "Das Enderwelt," a contraction for the German phrase, "The end of the world." Beyond the bushes Jones found a small trail and concluded that someone had refused to believe that it was "the end of the world" and had made a trail that led beyond.

POSSESSIONS

1840. "Remember, what you possess in the world will be found at the day of your death to belong to someone else," Henry van Dyke said, "but what you are will be yours forever."

1841. Stephen Vincent Benét in *James Shore's Daughter* described a still too-common attitude of certain men of great possessions: "He had another thing already, that enormous arrogance of the rich—an arrogance so vast and unconscious that it seems like a natural force. It lies underneath the good manners, and you don't often touch it. But when you do, it has none of the warmth and gayety of vanity. It is cold as the front-hall marbles; cold as steel and stone."

1842.
To get his wealth he spent his health
 And then with might and main
He turned around and spent his wealth
 To get his health again.
—Author Unknown

1843. An epitaph proposed for Hitler's grave read: "This is positively my last territorial demand."

PRACTICE

1844. "If I miss a day's practice," a distinguished musician said, "I notice the difference in performance; if I miss two days' practice, my best friends notice it; and if I miss three days, the loss is evident to all."

1845. A teen-age girl said to Marian Anderson, "I would give anything in the world if I could sing like that." The singer smiled and replied. "Would you give eight hours of practice a day?"

1846. To an admiring person who asked him to tell her how she might learn to draw freehand circles as perfect as his, Holman Hunt is said to have replied: "All that you need to do, madame, is to practice eight hours a day for forty years."

1847. "I often think it would be an eye opener to students to hear the way Rachmaninoff practices," writes Arthur Hirst. "I have heard him going through passages he has played for years, at a snail's pace, with loving care for every note, every metrical accent, every shade of tone. I have seen him sit down to his piano, immediately after getting home from a recital, to practice some bar which had not given him satisfaction. That artistic conscience may perhaps be taken as the symbol of his greatness, for it is really a matter of true service to the ideal he has in mind."

1848. A piano teacher took her young students to see Paderewski. When teacher and student arrived, the master pianist was practicing. When the teacher asked the maestro for some message of encouragement for the student, Paderewski pointed to the music on the rack and said: "Do you see this composition? I—I—'the great Paderewski'—eighty-five times I practice this page."

1849. Amiel confessed in his *Journal*: "I am always practicing, but never performing."

PRAISE

1850. Hans Christian Andersen, recalling the way in which he had been severely criticized when young, said: "Blame stumps me. Praise encourages me and makes me cling to God."

1851. "The praise that comes of love," James M. Barrie remarked, "does not make us vain, but humble rather."

PRAYER

1852. Shortly before his death in 1940, Peter Wust, a European philosopher, told some of his students who had asked for a final reflection upon life: "The magic key is not reflection, as you might expect from a philosopher, but it is prayer. Prayer as the most complete act of devotion makes us quiet, makes us objective. A man grows in true humility in prayer. Prayer is the final humility of the spirit. The greatest things in existence will only be given to those who pray. In suffering one learns to pray best of all."—HAROLD A. BOSLEY, *On Final Ground*

1853. "Prayer," said Robert Hall, "serves as an edge and border to preserve the web of life from unraveling."

1854. "I pray on the principle that the wine knocks the cork out of a bottle," said Henry Ward Beecher. "There is an inward fermentation, and there must be a vent."

1855. Shortly before his death Oliver Cromwell prayed: "Lord, though I am a miserable and wretched creature, I am in covenant with thee through grace, and I may, I will come to thee for thy people. Thou has made me, though very unworthy, a mean instrument to do them some good, and thee service; and many of them have set too high a value upon me, though others wish and would be glad of my death. Lord, however thou do dispose of me, continue to do good for them. Give them consistency of judgment, one heart, and mutual love; and go on to deliver them, and with the work of reformation; and make the name of Christ glorious in the world. Teach those who look too much on thy instruments to depend more upon thyself. Pardon such a desire to trample upon the dust of a poor worm, for they are thy people too. And pardon the folly of this short prayer;—even for Jesus

Christ's sake, and give us a good night, if it be thy pleasure. Amen."

Achievement Through Prayer

1856. "Twelve years ago I undertook to practice prayer in earnest," wrote Winifred Kirkland in *As Far As I Can See,* "something very different from my previous sleepy petitions as I snuggled into bed, and also different from the terror-stricken appeals I had sent to God when some loved one was in peril, or I myself was threatened with despair. Twelve years ago I found it hard enough to hold my attention on my praying for ten minutes a day, now an hour is not enough for the direction and the communion that have become as indispensable as my food and drink."

1857. James Stalker in his *Imago Christi* wrote: "A wise man once said to me that he was too busy to be in a hurry; he meant that if he allowed himself to become hurried, he could not do all that he had to do. There is nothing like prayer for producing this calm self-possession."

1858. Dostoevski, the great Russian novelist, once said: "Be not forgetful of prayer. Every time you pray if your prayer is sincere, there will be new feeling and new meaning in it which will give fresh courage."

1859. Glenn Clark has said: "Prayer is governed by the same laws that govern the growth of the flower in the crannied wall. It is controlled by the same laws that control the flow of a stream, for, as God is in all things, so are his laws prevailing in all things. As prayer is life raised to the highest degree, so the laws of prayer are the laws of life raised to their highest expression. The man who learns and practices the laws of prayer should be able to play better, to work better, to love better, to serve better, for to learn how to pray is to learn how to live."

1860.

More things are wrought by prayer
Than this world dreams of. Wherefore, let thy voice
Rise like a fountain for me night and day.
For what are men better than sheep or goats
That nourish a blind life within the brain,
If, knowing God, they lift not hands of prayer
Both for themselves and those who call them friend?
For so the whole round earth is every way
Bound by gold chains about the feet of God.

—ALFRED TENNYSON,
"Morte D'Arthur"

Answered Prayer

1861. "Who riseth from prayer a better man," said George Meredith, "his prayer is answered."

1862. The story is told that a Methodist minister in Stroudsburg, Pennsylvania, prayed that God would destroy the liquor traffic, and that he would begin the good work by striking the local brewery with lightning. The next day the requested thunderstorm appeared, and the brewery was destroyed. The brewer heard about the prayer the minister had made, and sued him for damages. The county court dismissed the case. The brewer was among the faithful, the county court among the skeptics.—WILLIAM E. PHIFER, JR., *The Cross and Great Living*

1863. During World War I, President Wilson appointed a day of prayer. After that day the German armies were not able to make a single advance. The retreat that ended in disaster began shortly after the American people had called upon God for victory.

Aspects of Prayer

1864. Said Phillips Brooks: "Prayer is not the overcoming of God's reluctance; it is the taking hold of God's willingness."

1865. A Chinese scholar says: "Prayer is that exercise by which I bring myself into such communion with God that I become possessed of God's plan, God's thought, and God's passion for the world."

1866. When a native Christian asked a missionary to teach him geography, the missionary asked the reason. "I wish to study georgraphy," the native said earnestly, "so that I may know more about which to pray."

1867. "All his thoughts of people gradually turned to prayers" was the remark made concerning the missionary John Forman.

1868. When a student one day entered the laboratory of Pasteur, he found the scientist bent over his microscope. Not wishing to disturb him the student started to leave. When Pasteur looked up, the student said: "I thought you were praying." "I was," Pasteur said as he turned again to his microscope.

Belief in Prayer

1869. "The privilege of prayer to me is one of the most cherished possessions," wrote Sir Wilfred Grenfell, "because faith and experience alike convince me that God himself sees and answers, and

his answers I never venture to criticize. It is only my part to ask. It is entirely his to give or withhold, as he knows is best. If it were otherwise, I would not dare to pray at all. In the quiet of home, in the heat of life and strife, in the face of death, the privilege of speech with God is inestimable. I value it more because it calls for nothing that the wayfaring man, though a fool, cannot give —that is, the simplest expression to his simplest desire. When I can neither see, nor hear, nor speak, still I can pray so that God can hear. When I finally pass through the valley of the shadow of death, I expect to pass through it in conversation with him."

1870. When asked for the strongest argument for prayer, Samuel Johnson, a devout churchman, said: "Sir, there is no argument for prayer."

1871. When the Federal Constitutional Convention opened its session in Philadelphia, June 28, 1787, Benjamin Franklin arose and said: "Mr. President, in the beginning of the contest with Great Britain, when we were sensible of danger, we had daily prayer in this room for divine protection. Our prayers were heard and answered. I have lived long sir, a long time, and the longer I live the more convincing proofs I see of the truth that God governs in the affairs of men. I therefore beg leave to move that henceforth prayers, imploring the assistance of heaven and blessings upon our deliberations, be held in this assembly every morning." The motion was carried.

1872. Boyd Barrett in *The Magnificent Illusion* relates that as boys in Ireland his brothers called the place in the home where his mother knelt regularly to pray the "Amen Corner." Years later he returned and asked the occupants if he might go once more into his childhood home. He paused at the "Amen Corner" and looked carefully at the marks made by hairpins when his mother leaned against the wall as she knelt in prayer.

1873. "You have, as I verily believe and am persuaded," Oliver Cromwell wrote to his admirals at sea, "a plentiful stock of prayers going for you daily, sent up by the soberest and most approved ministers and Christians in this nation; and, notwithstanding some discouragements, very much wrestling of faith for you; which is to us, and I trust will be to you, a matter of great encouragement."

1874. George Whitefield, the eighteenth-century evangelist, always took with him on his preaching missions a little crippled man who utterly believed in prayer. Very rarely did the crippled man attend the meetings. He often did not leave his hotel room. But his prayers, even more than Whitefield's preaching, were the cause of the wonderful results.—GLENN CLARK, *The Lord's Prayer*

1875. During a particularly hot summer a group of farmers met in their church to pray for rain. After the meeting a little girl asked her father if the people truly expected that it would rain. "Yes, of course," the father said. "Otherwise we wouldn't be here." "But, Daddy," the girl protested, "I didn't see any umbrellas in the congregation."

1876. Monica, the mother of Augustine, prayed constantly that her son might turn from his wayward life to Christ. Once when she was particularly discouraged, she was consoled by a certain bishop: "The child of so many prayers can never be lost."

Futile Prayers

1877. Centuries ago in mountainous Tibet in central Asia, a Buddhist inventor provided the followers of Gautama Buddha with a prayer machine. A large hollow wheel forming a drumlike container was set beside a mountain path. The empty interior was filled with a thousand prayers printed on red slips of paper. A handle permitted the passersby to give the wheel a turn, and each revolution of the wheel gave the Buddhist credit for having prayed a thousand prayers. Years later the wheel was changed to a water wheel so that no human effort was needed to turn it. Each revolution of the wheel counted for a thousand prayers to some worshiper's account.—JOHN J. BUCHANAN

1878. When the murderer, Macbeth, tried to pray, the prayer stuck in his throat.

1879. The king in Shakespeare's *Hamlet,* being plagued by the murder of his brother, goes to the chapel to pray. Realizing that there is an inconsistency between the manner of his actions and the words of his prayer, he exclaims:

"My words fly up; my thoughts remain below;
Words without thoughts never to heaven go."

1880.
Two went to pray? Oh, rather say
One went to brag, the other to pray;
One stands up close and treads on high
Where the other dares not send his eye;
One nearer to God's altar trod,
The other to the altar's God.
> —RICHARD CRASHAW,
> "In the Temple"

1881. A small boy, when asked if he ever prayed, answered: "Sometimes I pray, but sometimes I just say my prayers."

1882. A little boy reported to his mother: "Mommie, I don't have to say my prayers any more. *I know them now.*"

Learning to Pray

1883. A farmer once heard a little orphan boy who had never had much opportunity in life repeating the letters of the alphabet over and over again as he knelt on the hard, stony ground of a field near the farmer's house. "What are you doing, lad?" asked the farmer. "Please, sir, I'm praying," returned the child. "But, boy, that's not praying," said the man. "Yes, sir, I know it's not," said the boy. "But, you see, I don't know how to pray, and I heard the minister say that if a person talked to God he would know what that person needed most. I thought I would just say the alphabet and let God put the letters together into the kind of prayer that I would like to say."—WILLIAM E. PHIFER, JR., *The Cross and Great Living*

1884. Deane Edwards offers the following suggestions on how to pray: *Pray* where you are. God is present everywhere and ready to listen. *Pray* when possible in a quiet spot where you can be alone. It is well to fix your mind deliberately on God, apart from confusing distractions. *Pray* to God simply and naturally as to a friend. Tell him what is on your mind. Get help from the prayers of others. *Pray* remembering the good things God has done for you. Reckon up your blessings from time to time and give thanks for them. *Pray* for God's forgiveness for the unworthy things that you may have done. He is near to a humble and contrite heart. *Pray* for the things that you need, especially those that will make your life

finer and more Christlike. *Pray* for others, remembering the situations they confront and the help they need. *Pray* for the world in its need, asking God to bring better things and offering your help to him. *Pray* above everything else that God's will may be done in you and in the world. His purposes are deeper and wiser than anything we can imagine. *Pray* and then start answering your prayer.

Listening to God

1885. When a little girl had finished her evening prayers, she remained at her bedside for some time. Finally her mother told her to get into bed. "I was just waiting," the girl protested, "to see if God had anything to say to me."

1886. "Prayer at its highest is a two-way conversation," writes Frank Laubach, "and for me the most important part is listening—to God's replies."

1887. Savonarola said ironically that the saints of his day were so busy talking to God that they could not listen to him.

The Lord's Prayer

1888. Robert Browning had a rare, microscopic power in one of his eyes. It is said that he often amused friends by writing the Lord's Prayer on a small piece of paper and then covering it with a shilling. When one person was relating this story, he said: "And with how many other things do the rest of us cover the Lord's Prayer!"

1889. A small boy, repeating the Lord's Prayer one evening, prayed: "And forgive us our debts as we forgive those who are dead against us."

1890. When speaking with a friend about the Lord's Prayer, Samuel Taylor Coleridge said: "Oh, dear friend, to pray, to pray as God would have us; to pray with all the heart and strength; with the reason and will, to believe vividly that God will listen to your voice through Christ, and verily do the thing he pleaseth thereupon—this is the last, the greatest achievement of the Christian's warfare on earth. Teach us to pray, O Lord!"

Need of Prayer

1891. A non-Christian after visiting in the Orient related that a native woman threw herself upon the steps of a pagan temple and prayed that her sick child would be cured. When she had finished, the visitor asked the woman to whom she prayed. "I do not know," she said, "but surely somewhere there must be someone to hear a mother's cry and keep a mother's heart from breaking."

1892. "We hear in these days of scientific enlightenment a great deal of discussion about the efficacy of prayer," wrote William James, "and many reasons are given us why we should not pray, whilst others are given why we should. But in all this very little is said of the reason why we do pray. . . . The reason why we do pray is simply that we cannot help praying."

1893. "I have been driven many times to my knees by the overwhelming conviction that I had nowhere else to go," wrote Lincoln.

1894. "I allus say ma prayers 'cause dey is jes' some things I doan know what else to do about," said an old Negro deaconess.

1895. "There are times in a man's life," Victor Hugo said, "when, regardless of the attitude of the body, the soul is on its knees in prayer."

1896. In the records of Francis Asbury it is stated that when his work increased and the burdens became heavier, he "henceforth resolved to pray seven times each day instead of five as formerly."

1897. The need for prayer at the beginning of the day was once illustrated by a comparison to watch winding. "When do you wind your watch?" a jeweler asked a man who complained that his watch was not keeping accurate time. "At night, of course, as everyone else does." "No," said the jeweler, "most people may wind their watches at night, but not jewelers; for one who knows the mechanism of a watch knows that it is best to begin the day on a full spring."—JAMES D. MORRISON

1898. A soldier wounded at Fort Wagner during the Civil War was asked if he prayed. "I prayed last Saturday night," was the response, "when we were in that fight at Wagner. I guess everbody prayed *there*."

1899. "What is the use of praying?" asked Andrew Carnegie. "I already have everything I want. What more could I ask for?"

Requirements for Prayer

1900. "Our prayers must mean something to us," Maltbie Babcock wrote, "if they are to mean anything to God."

1901. One of Jane Austen's prayers begins: "Grant us grace, Almighty Father, so to pray as to deserve to be heard."

1902. G. Campbell Morgan says: "A man may offer a prayer, beautiful in diction and perfect in the number of its petitions, but if it gives him gratification afterward, that prayer cannot have been truly prayed."

1903.

He prayeth well who loveth well
Both man and bird and beast.
He prayeth best who loveth best
All things, both great and small;
For the dear God who loveth us
He made and loveth all.
—SAMUEL TAYLOR COLERIDGE,
"The Rime of the Ancient Mariner"

1904. During the war with the Japanese, Madame Chiang Kai-shek said to her mother, a woman of strong Christian faith: "Mother, you're so powerful in prayer, why don't you pray that God will annihilate Japan—by an earthquake or something?" The mother answered: "When you pray, or expect me to pray, don't insult God's intelligence by asking him to do something which would be unworthy even of you, a mortal."

Time of Prayer

1905. Brother Lawrence, a humble layman who served in the kitchen of a monastery in Paris, said: "For me the time of action does not differ from the time of prayer; and in the noise and clatter of my kitchen, while several persons are together calling for as many different things, I possess God in as great tranquillity as when upon my knees at the Blessed Sacrament. Sometimes, indeed, my faith becomes so clear that I almost fancy that I have lost it—the shadows which veil our vision usually seem to be fleeing away, and there begins to dawn that day which is to be without cloud and without end, the glorious day of the life to come."

1906. Madame Chiang Kai-shek several years ago wrote: "My mother was not a sentimental parent. In many ways she was a Spartan. But one of my strongest childhood experiences is of Mother going to a room she kept for the purpose on the third floor to pray. She spent hours in prayer, often beginning before dawn. When we asked her advice about anything, she would say, 'I must ask God first.'"

1907. Faith Baldwin, the novelist, describes the experience of a young girl whose pilot fiancé was killed in the war. "I went to church every day and prayed," the girl said. "I prayed every night almost every waking hour. But he was killed. I shall never pray again nor enter a church."

PREACHER

1908. Bernard of Clairvaux, speaking to his brother Cistercian preachers, said: "If then you are wise, you will show yourself rather as a reservoir than as a canal. For a canal spreads abroad water as it receives it, but a reservoir waits until it is filled before overflowing, and thus communicates, without loss to itself, its superabundant water."

1909. On one occasion Phillips Brooks was coming down the aisle after preaching, and one plain man nudged another and said: "I say, Bill, it makes you feel good just to look at him."

1910. "A good preacher should have these qualities and virtues: first, he should teach systematically; second, he should have a ready wit; third, he should be eloquent; fourth, he should have a good voice; fifth, a good memory; sixth, he should know when to make an end; seventh, he should be sure of his doctrine; eighth, he should venture and engage body and blood, wealth and honor, in the world; ninth, he should suffer himself to be mocked and jeered of everyone," suggested Martin Luther in 1569.

1911. "The preacher for this day must have the heart of a lion, the skin of a hippopotamus, the agility of a greyhound, the patience of a donkey, the wisdom of an elephant, the industry of an ant, and as many lives as a cat," said Edgar deWitt Jones.

Criticism of Preachers

1912. "How one longs on one side for the clear spirit of Fénelon," wrote Sheila Kaye-Smith in a commentary on modern preaching, "for the piercing grace of Francis de Sales, for the light and sanity of Pascal; on the other for the fire of Savonarola, for the enthusiasm of the Wesleys, or even of George Fox shouting, 'Woe! Woe to the bloody city of Litchfield!' I know that there are preachers today who shout, 'Woe!' but it is always from a safe distance. They will not shout woe to Litchfield or any bloody city from its own market place."

1913. Swinburne described a particular religious preacher with this pointed sentence: "For their tender minds he served up half a Christ."

1914. Samuel Taylor Coleridge, who for some time had been a Unitarian minister, asked his friend Charles Lamb, "Have you ever heard me preach?" "Yes," Lamb replied, "I've never heard you do anything else."

Responsibility of Preachers

1915. In Ian Maclaren's *Bonnie Brier Bush* a young preacher is beautifully counseled by his old mother: "Jamie, speak a gude word for Jesus Christ!"

1916. Bishop Charles Gore used to give his final charge to candidates on the eve of their ordination in these impressive words: "Tomorrow I shall say to you, wilt thou, wilt thou, wilt thou? But there will come a day to you when

Another will say to you, hast thou, hast thou, hast thou?"—JAMES S. STEWART, *Heralds of God*

1917. "Don't go out for popularity," Charles H. Spurgeon warned divinity students. "Preach nothing down but the devil, and nothing up but Christ!"

1918. "The test of a preacher," wrote Francis of Sales, "is that his congregation goes away saying, not, 'what a lovely sermon,' but, 'I will do something!' "

Sincerity of Preachers

1919. In a letter which Dr. John Brown wrote to Dr. John Cairns, the former said: "It is related of David Hume that having heard my great-grandfather preach, he said: 'That's the man for me. He means what he says. He speaks as if Jesus Christ were at his elbow.' "— LESLIE D. WEATHERHEAD, *The Eternal Voice*

1920. George Whitefield's preaching continued to the time of his death. He preached two hours in the morning with no other visible girding than his passion, for he was almost too weak to stand; and the crowd assembled that evening before the door of the house where he was staying, and thronged the hallway, impatient to hear the man they loved. "I am tired," said Whitefield, "and must go to bed." He took a candle and was going to his bedroom when the sight of the people moved him. He paused on the staircase and began to preach. The crowd looked up—and he preached. There was something— nay, Someone—whom he must give; some veritable power and mercy for them through him; he *must* speak. He preached until the candle went out in its socket. That night he burned out the candle also of his own life—which shineth always.—GEORGE A. BUTTRICK, *Jesus Came Preaching*

1921. Thomas Ken, writer of "Praise God, From Whom All Blessings Flow," was chaplain to Mary, sister of Charles II. It is said that the king once said concerning Ken's courageous preaching: "I must go and hear Ken tell me my faults."

PREACHING

1922. Robert Wodrow in *Analecta* tells of an English merchant who three hundred years ago went on a business trip to Scotland and during his visit heard distinguished preachers. At St. Andrews he listened to Robert Blair. "That man," he said, "showed me the majesty of God." Afterward he heard "a little fair man" preach—this was Samuel Rutherford: "And that man showed me the loveliness of Christ." Then at Irvine he heard a discourse by "a well-favored, proper old man"—David Dickson: "And that man showed me all my heart."—JAMES S. STEWART, *Heralds of God*

1923. One day Lyman Beecher agreed to exchange pulpits with a neighboring minister who believed strongly in predestination. As the ministers passed each other on the designated Sunday, Beecher's friend said, "Dr. Beecher, I wish to call to your attention that before the creation of the world God arranged that you were to preach in my pulpit and I in yours on this particular Sabbath." "Is that so?" Beecher exclaimed. "Then I won't do it." And forthwith he turned his horse and started back for his own parish.

1924. "The best way to revive a church," said Dwight L. Moody, "is to build a fire in the pulpit."

1925. Dean Willard L. Sperry tells of a boy who wrote across his examination paper this explanation: "It is very difficult to express on paper to another ideas which one does not have in his head." So also for the preacher who does not have an experience of God in his heart.

Manner of Preaching

1926. "The Christian Church does not need more *popular* preaching," challenges Walter Russell Bowie, "but more *unpopular* preaching."

1927. During the early days of the American Revolution a minister entered his pulpit, preached upon the justice of the claims made against England, proclaimed the obligation of all good men to fight for their liberties, and then, flinging aside his robe, showed that he was wearing the uniform of an officer in the Continental Army.

1928. A distinguished minister questioned an equally distinguished actor concerning the difference in their appeal to people. "Why is it," asked the minister, "that you appear night after night before great crowds, and I am getting no crowd at all? Your words are sheer fiction, and mine are essential and unchangeable truth." The actor's answer was, "It is all quite simple. I present my fiction as though it were truth. You present your truth as though it were fiction."

PREJUDICE

1929. A man sat before the fireplace in his club, seemingly wrapped in thought. Two friends looked at him, and one said: "Jones is thinking very deeply tonight." The other man, who knew Jones more intimately, replied: "Jones thinks he is thinking, but he is merely rearranging his prejudices."—WALTER DUDLEY CAVERT, *Remember Now . . .*

1930. When President Davis of the Confederacy asked Robert E. Lee for his opinion of General Whiting, Lee said that Whiting was an exceptionally qualified man. A friend protested to Lee, saying, "Don't you know what unkind things Whiting has been saying about you?" "I understand," Lee said, "but the president desired to know my opinion of Whiting, not Whiting's opinion of me."

PREPAREDNESS

1931. In one of the best-known Lincoln stories we are told that a man, seeing young Lincoln intently reading a book, said, "Hello, Abe, studying law? Do you expect to be president some day?" "Don't know," Lincoln answered, "but I am going to be ready for anything God may have for me to do."

1932. When men were first drafted in World War II, a young Negro boy, unable to cope with the questionnaire, turned the sheet over and wrote, "I'm ready when you are," and mailed it to his draft board.

PRIDE

1933.
An apology
Is a friendship preserver,
Is often a debt of honor,
Is never a sign of weakness,
Is an antidote for hatred,
Costs nothing but one's pride,
Always saves more than it costs,
Is a device needed in every home.
—AUTHOR UNKNOWN

1934. When a man boasted in the presence of Joseph Parker that he was a self-made man, Parker commented: "Well, sir, that relieves the Lord of a great responsibility."

1935. Two men approached the gates of the Heavenly City. One, proud and arrogant, hurried ahead that he might enter first. He pulled himself up to his full height only to find that the gate was not high enough for him. In his despair he exclaimed: "I have read that the gateway to the Kingdom was narrow, but who could have been foolish enough to build it so low?"—JAMES R. WEBB, JR.

1936. A workman standing on the banks of the Clyde River in Scotland as the *Aquitania* made its first trip said: "I tell you, it is something to have put rivets into a boat like that!"

1937. Although Charles V was haughty and proud, he stooped one day to pick up a fallen brush for Titian and said that he was pleased to wait upon so great a genius.

1938. "You make pretty good hammers here," a visitor said to a workman in a factory. "No, sir," was the answer, "we make the best hammers that can be made."

1939. When Albert Schweitzer one day began the building of a hospital, a native was asked to help. The native, however, refused, saying that he was an intellectual. "I thought I was an intellectual once," Schweitzer said as he returned to his work.

PROFANITY

1940. In 1776 George Washington issued a general order which stated in part: "The General is sorry to be informed that the foolish and wicked practice of profane cursing and swearing, a vice heretofore little known in an American army, is growing into fashion. He hopes the officers will, by example as well as influence, endeavor to check it, and that both they and the men will reflect that we can have little hope of the blessing of Heaven on our arms if we insult it by our impiety and folly. Added to this, it is a vice so mean and low, without any temptation, that every man of sense and character detests and despises it."

1941. With justifiable pride an Indian boasted of his old culture. "We Indians," he said, "never had words for swearing until we met the white man."

1942. Woodrow Wilson once told the story of a time when a man of profane language cursed in the presence of the president's father, a clergyman. "I beg your pardon," the man said to the clergyman. "Oh, sir, you have not offended me," Wilson reported his father as having said. "All profane language is an offense toward him whose name is profaned."

PROSPERITY

1943. "There is," writes Washington Irving in his *Sketch Book,* "in every true woman's heart a spark of heavenly fire, which lies dormant in the broad daylight of prosperity; but which kindles up, and beams and blazes in the dark hour of adversity." What he says about women applies equally to men.

1944. C. S. Lewis in *The Screwtape Letters* says that years of prosperity are "excellent campaigning weather" for the Devil. "Prosperity knits a man to the World. He feels that he is 'finding his place in it,' while really it is finding its place in him."

PURPOSE

1945. Said one college graduate: "College gave us spokes but no hub. We came away with knowledge but no purpose, and therein is our dilemma."

1946.
This life were brutish did we not sometimes

Have intimations clear of wider scope,
Hints of occasion infinite, to keep
The soul alert with noble discontent
And onward yearnings of unstilled desire;
Fruitless, except we now and then divined
A mystery of Purpose, gleaming through
The secular confusions of the world,
Whose will we darkly accomplish, doing ours.
> —JAMES RUSSELL LOWELL,
> "The Cathedral"

1947. A Japanese proverb reads:

The pine hath a thousand years,
The rose but a day—
But the pine with its thousand years
Glories not o'er the rose with its day,
If each but serves its purpose
Ere it passes away.

1948. When young Henry Fawcett was hunting with his father, an accidental firing of a gun blinded the boy. "I made up my mind within ten minutes after the accident," he later wrote, "to stick to my main purpose so far as in me lay." He earned his way through Cambridge University, became professor of political economy in that school, and later was made postmaster general of England.

1949. When the other soldiers laughed at an Athenian soldier who was crippled, he silenced them by saying: "I am here to fight, not to run."

1950. When a man complimented Handel for the fine entertainment he offered in "He Was Despised and Rejected," Handel said: "My lord, I should be sorry if I only entertained you. I wish to make you better."

1951. Blucher riding through London said, "What a city to loot." Booth walking through the same city said, "What a city to save."

1952. When John Wanamaker, great Christian merchant of Philadelphia, was asked what is the greatest lack in the young men of today, he replied: "Purpose."

1953. Lincoln once attended a camp meeting of a famous evangelist. During the progress of the meeting the preacher said: "All who want to go to heaven stand up." When Lincoln didn't stand up, the preacher said: "Do you want to go to hell, Mr. Lincoln?" "No," smiled the youthful Lincoln, "I want to go to Congress."

Q

QUESTION

1954. Rosalind in *As You Like It* fires question after question: "What did he do? What said he? How looked he? Wherein went he? Did he ask for me? Where remains he? How parted he with thee? And when shalt thou see him again?" Then she adds breathlessly: "Answer me in one word."

1955. Will Rogers once said that he believed in college "because it takes children away from home just when they begin to ask questions."—GLENN RANDALL PHILLIPS

R

RACE PREJUDICE

1956. H. G. Wells wrote: "There is no more evil thing in this present world than race prejudice, none at all! I write deliberately—it is the worst single thing in life now. It justifies and holds together more obscene cruelty and abomination than any other sort of error in the world."

1957. A group of Negro boys are reported to have concluded the pledge of allegiance to the flag with these words: "With liberty and justice for all—but me."

1958. A young Negro student said: "If you discriminate against me because I am uncouth, I can become mannerly. If you ostracize me because I am unclean, I can cleanse myself. If you segregate me because I am ignorant, I can become educated. But if you discriminate against me because of my color, I can do nothing. God gave me my color. I have no possible protection against race prejudice but to take refuge in cynicism, bitterness, hatred, and despair."—HARRY EMERSON FOSDICK, *A Great Time to Be Alive*

1959. "Why don't you admit your inferiority?" a man once asked a Negro. "I am a child of God, and out of loyalty to my Father I cannot accept that I am inferior," he replied.

1960. After a visit with President Lincoln in the White House, Frederick Douglass, the Negro leader, said: "Lincoln is the first white man I ever spent an hour with who did not remind me that I am a Negro."

1961. One woman showed her intolerance by saying: "We love the Negro—*as a Negro.*"

1962. A Negro lady, when asked to move into the Jim Crow coach on a train, muttered as she left her place: "God is getting mighty tired of all this." —E. STANLEY JONES, *The Way*

1963. "Do you believe in racial equality?" a young man was asked. "Yes—but I don't practice it," he replied.

1964. When a white soldier refused to salute a Negro paymaster, the latter took off his coat, hung it over the back of a chair, and then told the private to salute the uniform. When the white soldier did this, he was paid.

1965. A Frenchman who had held strong anti-Semitic prejudices before World War II met a Jew in the days following the Nazi occupation. In a friendly manner which he had not known before this Frenchman said to the Jew: "Friend, these Nazis have taken everything away from me, even my anti-Semitism."

1966. When Marian Anderson sang in Washington, there was a blind girl present who insisted on shaking the hand of the great Negro contralto. Her companion arranged for the meeting. Thereupon the sightless one said: "Oh, that God had opened my eyes for that one instant that I might have seen her face." Her companion thoughtlessly said: "She is only black." "No," said the blind girl. "She could never have been *only* anything. I know her face was as beautiful as her trembling fingers."

1967. The Rockefeller Foundation Report for 1942, written at the height of World War II, spells out man's interdependence with man: "An American soldier wounded on a battlefield in the Far East owes his life to the Japanese scientist Kitasato, who isolated the bacillus of tetanus. A Russian soldier saved by a blood transfusion is indebted to Landsteiner, an Austrian. A German is shielded from typhoid fever with the help of a Russian, Metchnikoff. A Dutch marine in the East Indies is protected from malaria because of the experiments of an Italian, Grassi; while a British aviator in North Africa escapes death from surgical infection because a Frenchman, Pasteur, and a German, Koch, elaborated a new technique." That is one way of illustrating what we mean when we say we are brothers one of another, and that this is one of the incontrovertible facts upon which we build our Christian faith and seek to build a Christian world.—HAROLD A. BOSLEY, *A Firm Faith for Today*

1968. A company of Negro soldiers were in the camp at Fort Dodge, Iowa, during World War II. A group of them were selected for officers' school and sent to Arkansas to receive that training. Upon arrival they were met with a rather cool reception, and the first time they were lined up for instruction the white officer assigned to them spoke in bitter tones: "This thing has been forced upon me. I didn't join the army to train a gang of Negroes. So long as I am your commanding officer you will work fifteen hours a day, and if you get commissions it will be in spite of me." When the men were dismissed, they were ripe for a race riot. Some wanted to waylay the officer and beat him up. Finally a quiet little man secured the attention of the group and spoke to them: "Listen, fellows, we are Negroes, but we are also American soldiers. We represent the best that our race affords, or we wouldn't have been selected for this special training. Our honor is at stake, and the eyes of America are upon us. Let's play the game, and be as square as we can about it, and trust in God." His counsel prevailed, and the men agreed to do as he suggested. No group of soldiers ever worked harder than this company of Negroes. Their rifles were never clean enough; their clothes were never neat enough; their marching was never done. Toward the end of the course the white officer in charge seemed to relent a little, and when the examinations were over 55 per cent had passed and received their commissions as lieutenants in the army—a very creditable percentage of the whole. A near-by city found its Negro population giving a farewell dance for the successful contestants on the night the school closed. Oddly enough the white officer was present, and he asked to make a statement. He explained that his attitude toward the Negro race was occasioned by the fact that his father, who had been a sheriff in Oklahoma, had been killed by Negro bandits. From the day of his father's death he had vowed that he would avenge that murder in every way possible upon the whole race of Negro people. He had become known far and wide for the intensity of his feeling against them, and when he had been assigned the duty of training a company of Negro soldiers he had welcomed it as an opportunity to wreak further displeasure upon a group over which he had complete authority. But they had beaten him at his game. They had seen, through the leadership of one man of insight, that the only way to gain life was to lose it. So they had submitted to the punishment; and now, on the night of the graduation, here was the white officer with tears in his eyes saying: "I'm proud of this company. I love every man in it. And I'm your friend until I die."—WILLIAM E. PHIFER, JR., *The Cross and Great Living*

1969. When a distinguished Negro man had traveled to Europe on a crowded ship, he considered the manner in which he had been given a cabin by himself and had been served his meals there alone. Then to a ship official he said: "The joke is on my side. You are packed in like sardines in a tin; I have a cabin to myself, a table to myself, a whole steward to myself!"

1970. The prize-winning suggestion in a contest held to determine what punishment should be meted out to Hitler read: "I suggest that Hitler be wrapped in a black skin and be made to live out the balance of his days in the American democracy."

1971. When a small child came to her mother and expressed her first feeling of race prejudice, the mother said: "Why, don't you know that Jesus was a Jew?" To this the child said: "Well—anyway—God was an American."—RALPH W. SOCKMAN, *The Unemployed Carpenter*

1972. One Negro leader has said that for American harmony the black and white races must work together—like the black and white keys of a piano.

1973. Frank P. Graham, a southerner, in a decision on the question of equal pay for Negro and white workers for the War Labor Board, said: "Slavery gave the Negro his Christianity. Christianity must give the Negro his freedom. This freedom must give the Negro equal rights to home and health, education and citizenship, and an equal opportunity to work and fight for our common country."

1974. Alexander Pope aptly described the prejudiced person not only of his day but also of our own when he wrote: "It is with narrow-minded people as with narrow-necked bottles, the less they have in them, the more noise they make in pouring it out."

RAINBOW

1975. An unidentified writer exclaimed: "The soul would have no rainbow had the eyes no tears."

1976. A pilot who had looked for the pot of gold at the end of the rainbow when a child related that high in the heavens the rainbow has no end; it is a complete circle.

1977. When leaving a movie, a small boy said to his father: "I have been laughing and crying for the last two hours. Is there a rainbow in my face?"

RECIPROCITY

1978. When Tsze-kung, a disciple of Confucius, asked his master, "Is there one word which may serve as a rule for all one's life?" Confucius answered: "Is not 'reciprocity' such a word? What you do not want done to yourself, do not do to others."

1979. When a father, reading aloud to his family one morning, came to the words, "Children, obey your parents in the Lord," he reread the words, emphasizing the reading for the benefit of his children. Reading further he came to the words, "Ye fathers, provoke not your children to wrath." "That's a good text, Dad. Read it again," one of the sons exclaimed.

1980. "Dad, you and me are partners, ain't we?" a small boy asked. "Yes, we are partners," was the father's answer. "That means," continued this thoughtful youngster, "that you can go into my pockets any time you please and get what I have." "Fine," said the father. "But it also means that I can go into your pockets any time I want to and get what I please, doesn't it?" The father demurred; he was a little afraid of that.—CLOVIS G. CHAPPELL, *These Prophetic Voices*

1981. "How is it," asked a miller of a farmer, "that when I came to measure those ten barrels of apples I bought from you I found them nearly two barrels short?" "Singular, very singular, for I sent them to you in ten of your own flour barrels," the farmer said.

RECOMPENSE

1982. Two boys were working their way through Leland Stanford University. Their funds got desperately low, and the idea came to one of them to engage Paderewski for a piano recital. The great pianist's manager asked for a guarantee of $2,000. The boys went ahead and staged the concert. They worked hard, only to find that the concert had totaled them only $1,600. So the boys sought the pianist, told him of their effort and result, and handed him the entire $1,600, accompanying it with a promissory note of $400. "No, boys," returned Paderewski, "that won't do." Then tearing up the note and returning the $1,600, he said to them: "Now take out

of this your expenses, give yourselves each 10 per cent of the balance for your work, and let me have the rest."

The years rolled by, the Great War came and went, and Paderewski was striving with might and main to feed the starving thousands of his beloved Poland. There was only one man in the world who could help Paderewski and his people. Before he could stretch forth the hand for help, thousands of tons of food began to come into Poland for distribution by the Polish premier. After the starving were fed, Paderewski journeyed to Paris to thank Herbert Hoover for the relief sent him.

"That's all right, Mr. Paderewski," was Hoover's reply. "I knew the need was great. Besides, you don't remember it, but you helped me once when I was a student at college, and I was in a hole."—EDWARD W. BOK, *Perhaps I Am*

1983. A rich woman died and was received by the angel Gabriel at the gate of Heaven. He took her to see where she was to live, and on the way she admired a splendid house built of gold and precious stones. On asking who lived there she was told the name of a man she had known on earth, and she exclaimed vehemently because he had been so poor and unimportant. "Yes," agreed Gabriel, "but he was able to send these materials up to us." They passed a house built of ivory and lovely-colored marble, and the lady was disgusted to hear it was that of a woman who had been a slum dweller on earth. She had, however, sent up the materials so that her handsome house could be built. Presently a wretched little mud hovel was reached, and the angel intimated that it was the new arrival's house. She exclaimed in horror. "We are very, very sorry," said her guide, "but we did our best with the materials you sent up."

REFORM

1984. T. R. Glover told the story of an agnostic friend who claimed that he could reform a drunkard without the aid of religion. So to work he went, but as soon as he considered some progress to be noticeable the drunkard wandered back into one of his familiar haunts. "What about your drunkard friend?" Glover asked one day. "I was getting on fairly well," the agnostic said, "when a lot of rough people in red jerseys arrived with an atrocious brass band. Somehow these repulsive fellows got hold of him. I don't know exactly what happened, but they seem to have made him kneel down and pray. Anyhow he can walk past a pub by himself now."— LESLIE D. WEATHERHEAD, *How May We Find Him?*

1985. Robert Louis Stevenson told of four reformers who met under a bramble bush. They were all agreed the world must be changed. "We must abolish property," said one. "We must abolish marriage," said the second. "We must abolish God," said the third. "I wish we could abolish work," said the fourth. "Do not let us get beyond practical politics," said the first, adding, "The first thing is to reduce men to a common level." "The first thing," said the second, "is to give freedom to the sexes." "The first thing," said the third, "is to find out how to do it." "The first step," said the first, "is to abolish the Bible." "The first thing," said the second, "is to abolish the laws." "The first thing," said the third, "is to abolish mankind."

REGRET

1986. Robert Robinson, the author of "Come, Thou Fount of Every Blessing," was converted through the preaching of George Whitefield. At the age of twenty the preaching of John Wesley led him into the ministry. Two years later, in 1757, while pastor in Norwich, he wrote this great hymn of praise. When many years later he had turned from his faith, a woman reproved him for his waywardness and read to him the words of his own hymn. "Madam," he is reported to have replied, "I am the poor, unhappy man who composed it; and I would give a thousand worlds, if I had them, to enjoy the feelings I had then."

1987. "You don't know," cries the chaplain in Shaw's *Saint Joan*, breaking in wildly after he has consented to the saint's death and has stood and watched her die, "you haven't seen: it is so easy to talk when you don't know. But when it is brought home to you; when you see the thing you have done; when it is blinding your eyes, stifling your nostrils, tearing your heart, then—then—O God, take away this sight from me! O Christ, deliver me from this fire that is consuming me! She cried to Thee in the midst of it: Jesus! Jesus! She is in Thy bosom; and I am in hell forevermore."

RELIGION

1988. J. R. Miller said: "To me religion means just one thing: Jesus and I are friends."

1989. Donald Hankey wrote from the trenches: "Religion is betting one's life there is a God."

1990. "Your religion is good if it is vital and active," wrote Charles Wagner, "if it nourishes in you confidence, hope, love, and a sentiment of the infinite value of existence; if it is allied with what is best in you against what is worst, and holds forever before you the necessity of becoming a new man; if it makes you understand that pain is a deliverer; if it increases your respect for the conscience of others; if it renders forgiveness more easy, fortune less arrogant, duty dear, the beyond less visionary. If it does these things, it is good, little matter its name; however rudimentary it may be when it fills this office, it comes from the true source, it binds you to man and to God."

1991. When asked for a definition of his religion, Abraham Lincoln quoted a faithful old man he had known in Indiana: "When I do good, I feel good; when I do bad, I feel bad; and that 's my religion."

1992. "Religion is the appreciation of life's spiritual values and the interpretation of life, its origin, its purpose, and its destiny, in terms of them," writes Harry Emerson Fosdick.

1993. Someone has written wisely: "Nobody is anything except as he joins himself to something. You cannot be a whole unless you join a whole. This, I believe, is religion."

1994. William James once said that religion is always a dull habit or an acute fever.

1995. "Some people have just enough religion to make them uncomfortable," said John Wesley.

1996. A man visiting in the South called a Negro on the station platform to the train window and said, "Uncle, is there anybody in this town enjoying religion?" To which the old Negro replied: "Them's that's got it, is."— E. Stanley Jones, *Abundant Living*

1997. The Soviet Commissar of Education is reported to have said: "I find that religion is like a nail: the harder you hit it, the deeper you drive it."

1998. Walter Rauschenbusch said: "Religion in the past has always spent a large proportion of its farce on doings that were apart from the real business of life, on sacrificing, on endless prayers, on traveling to Mecca, Jerusalem, or Rome, on kissing sacred stones, bathing in sacred rivers, climbing sacred stairs, and a thousand things that had at best only an indirect bearing on the practical social relations between men and their fellows."

Empty Religion

1999. "I used to be concerned about religion," said a foreign professor to Henry Drummond, "but religion is a great subject, and I was busy, and there was little time to settle it for myself: so I became a Catholic, and instead of dabbling any longer in religion myself, just left it to the church to do everything for me. Once a year I go to mass."

2000. A Japanese Christian has written:

> A religion
>   That does nothing
>   That gives nothing
>   That costs nothing
>   That suffers nothing
>   Is worth nothing.

2001. A Hindu made the following confession: "I get up at four and go through my religious exercises anud ceremonies until nine, and then I go to my business till five, and between those hours God knows what I do! But I become religious again after returning from my business until time to go to bed."

2002. "Nowhere in the world at any time has religion been so thoroughly respectable as with us," writes John Dewey, "and so nearly totally disconnected with life."

2003. "Don't get too religious-minded," suggests a character in Hugh Walpole's *The Inquisitor*. "What do you mean?" is the reply. "Religion drives out friendship," says the first character, "and as a matter of fact, I need a friend just this moment. I had the shock of my life once. I had a friend for five years—the best I ever had, kind, humorous, intelligent, understanding, unselfish. Then this good man met God and became such friends with him that he was always talking to him. God is love, he said morning, noon, and night. We must love everybody all the time. He was so snobbish about his new splendid divine friendship that he soon came to love nobody. When I told him this one day, he was deeply hurt, and he never spoke to me again. I've missed him ever since and thought ill of religion." "I expect that it wasn't God he met," said the second character, "but his own glorified idea of himself."

2004. Far too many Christians exhibit the spirit of the Buddhists of Burma, who have a saying: "Life is divided into three parts. The first part is for pleasure; the second is for accumulation of money and goods; the third is for religion."

2005. Carl Jung, the Swiss psychologist, in his book *Modern Man in Search of a Soul* wrote: "Among all my patients in the second half of life—that is to say, over thirty-five—there has not been one whose problem in the last resort was not that of finding a religious outlook on life. It is safe to say that every one of them fell ill because he had lost that which the living religions of every age have given to their followers, and none of them has been really healed who did not regain his religious outlook."

Personal Religion

2006. "The heart of religion," said Martin Luther, "lies in its personal pronouns."

2007. After Dr. Wilfred Grenfell heard Dwight L. Moody's plea for Christian leadership, a friend said to Grenfell: "Will, did I hear right that you got religion?" "No," Grenfell answered, "something more important has happened—religion got me."

2008. An aged Scotsman gave this advice to David Livingstone: "Now, lad, make religion the everyday business of your life, and not a thing of fits and starts."

2009. John Watson, the great Scotch preacher and teacher, said: "No doctrine of the Christian religion is worth preserving which cannot be verified in daily life."

2010. The strongest argument which Daniel Webster knew for religion was an old aunt who lived up in the New Hampshire hills.

2011. Lord Melbourne, so the story says, left hurriedly from a church where a revival was being held, exclaiming: "This has come to a pretty pass when religion is made to invade the sphere of private life."

2012. Robert A. Millikan, Nobel prize winner in physics, has described the responsibilities of science and religion: "The purpose of science is to develop, without prejudice or preconception of any kind, a knowledge of the facts, the laws, and the processes of nature. The even more important task of religion, on the other hand, is to develop the conscience, the ideals, and the aspirations of mankind."

RELIGIOUS EDUCATION

2013. A teacher was asked by a school inspector, "Where in your curriculum do you teach religion?" The teacher replied: "We teach it all day long. We teach it in the arithmetic class by accuracy. We teach it in language by learning to say what we mean. We teach it in history by honesty. We teach it in geography by breadth of mind. We teach it in handicraft by thoroughness. We teach it in astronomy by reverence. We teach it on the playground by fair play. We teach it by kindness to animals, by courtesy, by good manners to one another, and by helpfulness in all things. We teach it by showing the young that we, their elders, are anxious to stand by all the time without patronage."
—THOMAS B. MATHER

2014. "If we work upon marble, it will perish," said Daniel Webster. "If we work upon brass, time will efface it. If we rear temples, they will crumble to dust. But if we work upon men's immortal minds, if we imbue them with high principles, with the just fear of God and love of their fellow men, we engrave on those tablets something which no time can efface, and which will brighten and brighten to all eternity."

2015. Of the 109 colleges established in colonial America 106 were begun by religious denominations.

2016. The first president of Columbia University declared: "The chief thing that is aimed at in this college is to teach and engage the children to know God in Jesus Christ and to love and serve him in all sobriety, godliness, and righteousness of life."

2017. Anna Jameson, nineteenth-century English art critic, said that "the true purpose of education is to cherish and unfold the seed of immortality already sown within us; to develop, to their fullest extent, the capacities of every kind with which the God who made us has endowed us."

2018. "Religion is not taught," said Dean W. R. Inge. "It is caught."

REPUTATION

2019. Said Louis Pasteur: "A man of science should think of what will be said of him in the following century, not of the insults or the compliments of one day."

2020. Frederick the Great toward the end of his career said: "I hope that posterity will distinguish the philosopher from the monarch in me and the decent man from the politician."

2021.
What I am, what I am not, in the eye
Of the world, is what I never cared for
  much.
                    —ROBERT BROWNING,
                     "The Inn Album"

RESPONSIBILITY

2022. When a parishioner of John Henry Jowett, the great preacher of Carr's Lane, Birmingham, and Buckingham Gate, Westminster, exclaimed that he heard the preacher every Sunday, a friend said: "What a terrible responsibility!"

2023. A responsibility which Ralph Waldo Emerson thought every man should face was: "Open doors for the coming generation to pass through."

2024.
"To you the torch we fling"—
  The challenge yet is heard,

Bequest of fullest sacrifice,
    A life-demanding word.
Yet this thought with it comes,
    A question tinged with doubt—
Shall we the torch to others pass
    Whose light we've let go out? [1]
—ARTHUR B. DALE, "The Torch"

2025. "Every Christian truth," Harry Emerson Fosdick says, "gracious and comfortable, has a corresponding obligation, searching and sacrificial."

2026. It is much easier to say, "It is your affair, not *ours*," than it is to say, "It is your affair, not *mine*."—HAROLD COOKE PHILLIPS

2027. A Chinese emperor, so Mencius writes, after building the first dykes for Chinese rivers, said, "I feel personally responsible for every man who drowns in China."

2028. Florence Nightingale said to the trained nurses who were with her in the Crimea: "Young women, the strongest will be wanted at the washtub."

2029. A group of friends in England sent a motorboat to Labrador, knowing that Sir Wilfred Grenfell needed a faster means of communicating with sick people in that cold and isolated outpost. When the motorboat was delivered, the Laborador doctor put it to immediate use. A plea came for help from one of the islands. Although the night was dark and foggy, Grenfell did not hesitate to leave. He knew that the motorboat was equipped with a compass which would direct him through the fog and storm. After traveling for many hours through the storm-tossed seas, Grenfell realized that he was lost. Consequently the sick woman died, and the doctor

himself almost lost his life. Investigation later showed that the reason for this Labrador tragedy rested with an irresponsible workman in Liverpool. When fastening the compass to the boat, this workman made the mistake of using a steel rather than a brass screw. This shiftlessness meant that the steel screw deflected the compass needle and took Grenfell far from the destination he had determined to reach.

RETRIBUTION

2030. A man living in Kansas told that when he was a young man, a neighbor living on a farm adjoining his father's once offended him. In order to get revenge he went several miles away and got some Johnson grass, a very obnoxious grass that when once started on a farm is almost impossible to get rid of, and one night sowed this neighbor's field with this grass. In a short time the grass came up and greatly damaged the farm. A few years later this man fell in love with one of the daughters of this farmer and married her. When the farmer died, he willed this farm to this daughter. For thirty years this man said he had been fighting that Johnson grass, reaping what he had sown.—R. T. WILLIAMS

2031. "The dice of God are always loaded," warned Ralph Waldo Emerson. "Every secret is told, every crime is punished, every virtue rewarded, every wrong redressed, in silence and certainty. The thief steals from himself. The swindler swindles himself."

REVERENCE

2032. Among the gods of sixteenth-century China are some that seem ugly and grotesque. But those artisans of the Ming dynasty created at least one image that has a lesson for today—a woman's figure finely molded with twenty-four

[1] Used by permission of the author.

outstretched hands and open arms—the many-handed goddess of mercy.

2033. A teacher in a mission school in Scotland asked her class, "What is a prophet?" There was a long silence. Then a small lad said timidly: "It's a man who gets to know what God's thinking."

2034. S. Parkes Cadman writes of the occasion when a Scottish university conferred an honorary degree upon David Livingstone. "There is a custom in the Scottish universities that the recipient of an honory degree is fair sport for the students and must run the gantlet of their raucous remarks. The students sit in the balcony, calling out what they please. Is the candidate for honors a soapmaker who is become a doctor of law? No gift to the university will silence the greeting, 'Hi, Old Soapmaker.' Many wondered what the students would do when David Livingstone rose to receive his degree." Dr. Cadman described him: "He stood, one arm hanging at his side; his shoulder had been torn by a lion in the forests of Africa. His skin was like leather." What did the students do? "They rose and stood in absolute silence."

2035. Oliver Wendell Holmes said: "I have in my heart a small, shy plant called reverence; I cultivate that on Sunday mornings."

2036. "A man who bows down to nothing," said Dostoevski, "can never bear the burden of himself."—*A Raw Youth*

RIGHT

2037. When asked if he had difficulty reconciling his private morality with his public acts, Lord Grey, onetime prime minister of Great Britain, said: "No, for the right thing is always the right thing to do."

2038. Someone has described our age in these words: "We are at one of those cynical junctures of history where men have discovered the almost rightness of a great deal that is wrong, and the almost wrongness of a great deal that is right."

2039. Fulton J. Sheen of Catholic University, Washington, has said: "Right is right if nobody is right, and wrong is wrong if everybody is wrong."

2040. Ovid, the Latin poet who was a contemporary of Jesus, wrote:

I see the right, and I approve it, too;
Condemn the wrong, and yet the wrong
　pursue.

2041. Mark Twain's Huckleberry Finn said: "Well then, what's the use you learning to do right when it's troublesome to do right and ain't no trouble to do wrong?"

2042.
They are slaves who fear to speak
For the fallen and the weak,
They are slaves who will not choose
Hatred, scoffing, and abuse,
Rather than in silence shrink
From the truth they needs must think;
They are slaves who dare not be
In the right with two or three.
　　　—James Russell Lowell,
　　　　"Stanzas of Freedom"

2043. These words of William Jennings Bryan are indicative of his strong Christian leadership and statesmanship: "Never be afraid to stand with the minority when the minority is right, for the minority which is right will one day be the majority; always be afraid to stand with the majority which is wrong, for the majority which is wrong will one day be the minority."

2044. When the work of the League of Nations seemed futile, Henry Sloane Coffin asked the aged William Howard Taft, long enthusiastic for the success of the league, "What do you think of the League now?" Taft answered, "You ought to know that in our world the best things get crucified; *but they rise again.*"—God Confronts Man in History

ROADS

2045. In one of George Moore's novels there is a description of Irish peasants who have been set to work, just to keep them busy, at building roads that run out and end in dreary bogs. George Moore writes: "The road which leads nowhere is difficult to make; for a man to work well there must be an end in view."

2046.
Great roads the Romans built that men
    might meet,
    And walls to keep strong men apart—
    secure.
Now centuries are gone, and in defeat
    The walls are fallen, but the roads
    endure.
      —ETHELYN MILLER HARTWICH,
      "What Shall Endure?"

S

SACRIFICE

2047. "People talk of the sacrifice I have made in spending so much of my life in Africa," David Livingstone wrote. "Can that be called a sacrifice which is simply paid back as a small part of a great debt owing to our God, which we can never repay? Is that a sacrifice which brings its own best reward in healthful activity, the consciousness of doing good, peace of mind, and a bright hope of a glorious destiny hereafter? Away with the word in such a view, and with such a thought! It was emphatically no sacrifice. Say rather it is a privilege. Anxiety, sickness, suffering, or danger, now and then, with a foregoing of the common conveniences and charities of this life, may make us pause, and cause the spirit to waver and the soul to sink, but let this only be for a moment. All these are nothing when compared with the glory which shall hereafter be revealed in and for us. I never made a sacrifice. Of this we ought not to talk when we remember the great sacrifice which he made who left his Father's throne on high to give himself for us."

2048. In old Russia when a commander wished to inspire a recruit with a challenge for service, he told of the sacrifice of Turkestan. The Russian army was small. The Asiatic foe came swooping down in overwhelming numbers. The guns had been halted a mile in the rear. Between the little army and the artillery lay a deep ditch which it could not cross. It was guns now or annihilation. Immediately a whole company of infantry threw itself into the ditch and filled it to the brim with living bodies. The guns went over at a gallop, and the sacrifice of a company in the ditch saved not only an army but a nation.— J. W. HAWLEY, *These Prophetic Voices*

2049. Father Brebeuf was killed by the Iroquois many years ago when the French were settling Ontario. After his death a brother priest said: "No, it is not for me to grieve. Rather it is for all of us to be worthy of such a splendid sacrifice. This country has been sanctified by the blood of a man holy and courageous, even as the world was sanctified by the blood of him who died upon the cross."

2050. After the terrific bombardment of Coventry during World War II search parties found the body of a nurse in the hallway of a heavily bombed hospital. The nurse was dead, but underneath her prostrate form was a small baby who was still breathing. Friends of the nurse recalled the valorous manner in which the nurse had fought her way through the flames that had swept the halls, and her urgings: "We must save the children. They are the hope of the empire."

2051. When the body of Abraham Lincoln lay in state at Cleveland on the sad journey to Springfield, a poor Negro woman held her little child up to see his face, saying: "Take a long, long look, honey. Dat man died for you."

2052. After Hoover Dam was completed, a fitting tribute was paid to those who had sacrificed for its construction with the inscription: "For those who died that the desert might bloom."

2053. When Quintin Hogg, a philanthropist, was asked what it cost him to build the Polytechnic Institute in London, he said: "Not very much. Only one man's lifeblood."

SAFETY

2054. When asked if it is safe to work among lepers, Sam Higginbottom, missionary in India, said: "Yes, it is safer to work among lepers, if it is my job, than to work anywhere else."

2055. In Willa Cather's *Death Comes for the Archbishop* there is an account of why the Acoma Indians in Colorado chose to live on mesas. The rock gave safety. The plains, with Apaches on the south and Navajos on the north, were the scene of a periodic man hunt; but the mesa was accessible only by a narrow rock staircase which a few men could defend against a host. Thus "these Indians, born in fear and dying by violence for generations, had at last taken this leap away from the earth, and on that rock had found the hope of all suffering and tormented creatures— safety."—GEORGE A. BUTTRICK, *Prayer*

SAINT

2056. One of the most satisfying definitions of saints is that of Nathan Söderblom: "Saints are persons who make it easier for others to believe in God."

2057. "A saint," suggested Lawrence Housman, "is one who makes goodness attractive."

2058. G. K. Chesterton described a saint as one who exaggerates what the world neglects but needs.

2059. A little French boy was asked to define a saint. All he could think of were the figures he had seen in the stained-glass windows of the church. So he answered, "A saint is a man the light shines through."—JOHN G. KOEHLER

2060. "A saint is a man of conviction," said H. L. Wayland, "who was cannonaded while he was alive and is canonized after he is dead."

2061. "What do you want?" a friend asked William A. Quayle shortly before his death. "I want the fellowship of the saints," was the bishop's reply.

2062. Two sheep thieves were caught, and the authorities branded on their foreheads the letters "S T" for "Sheep Thief." One man, wishing to escape the censure of the townsmen, moved to another village. The second thief remained in the community of his crime. Through the years he attempted to make up for his sin. When old age came, the letters were still on his forehead, but when children asked what the "S T" meant, the parents would say that they meant "Saint."

2063. Among documents found in an old New England church were these resolutions: "Be it resolved: The earth is the Lord's and the fullness thereof. Be it resolved: That the fullness thereof belongs to the saints. Be it resolved: That we are the saints!"

SALVATION

2064. William Tyndale in the earliest English version of the New Testament uniformly translated the Greek word *soteria,* "salvation," as "health."

2065. An old Negro woman at a Virginia camp meeting said: "De Lawd done saved me through and through and foh keeps."

2066. "A man with a hard and dirty face went to an altar of prayer," writes E. Stanley Jones in *The Way,* "and prayed in desperation, 'O God, if you can save a sinner like me, why in hell don't you do it quicker?' Then his face melted into tenderness, and upon it came the smile of heaven, and the happy man said, 'Boys, he's done it.' And he had!"

2067. Hugh Vernon White contrasts Christianity and Buddhism in these words: "Buddhism is salvation from suffering; Christianity is salvation from sin."

SATISFACTION

2068. An old farmer listed his property for sale. When the real estate agent had written up the advertisement, he read it to the farmer for his approval. After the reading was completed, the farmer thought for a moment and then said: "I don't believe I want to sell. That's the kind of place I've been looking for all my life, and I didn't know I had it until you described it for me."

2069. When his brother wrote that he planned to leave Illinois and move to Missouri, Lincoln wrote: "Dear Brother: When I came into Charleston day before yesterday, I learned that you are anxious to sell the land where you live and move to Missouri. I have been thinking of this ever since and cannot but think such a notion is utterly foolish. What can you do in Missouri better than here? Is the land any richer? Can you there, any more than here, raise corn and wheat and oats without work? Will anybody there, any more than here, do your work for you? If you intend to go to work, there is no better place than right where you are; if you do not intend to go to work, you cannot get along anywhere. Squirming and crawling about from place to place can do no good."

2070. "I am richer than you are," a poor man told a rich man. "How can that be?" asked the rich man. "I have as much money as I want," said the poor man, "and you haven't."

2071. "If there is anything," exclaimed Rabbi Duncan, "in which I would be inclined to contradict my Lord, it would be if I heard him say, 'Well done, good and faithful servant.'"

SELF

2072. "If a man is interested in himself only, he is very small; if he is interested in his family, he is larger; if he is interested in his community, he is larger still," was Aristotle's suggestion for self-measurement.

2073. "You sweat too much blood for the world," Leo Tolstoy told an enthusiastic young reformer. "Sweat some for yourself first. . . . If you want to make the world better, you have to be the best you can. . . . You cannot bring the Kingdom of God into the world until you bring it into your own heart first."

2074. Joseph Fort Newton in a commentary on modern times wrote: "When a man loses faith in God, he worships humanity; when faith in humanity fails, he worships science, as so many are trying to do today. When faith in science fails, man worships himself, and at the altar of his own idolatry he receives a benediction of vanity. Hence the tedious egotism of our day, when men are self-centered and self-obsessed, unable to get themselves off their hands."

2075. Woodrow Wilson suggested: "I take leave to believe that he who sets out to develop his own character will develop only that which will make him intolerable to other men."

Self-Centered

2076. Everyone has heard of the old man who made the prayer:

Lord, bless me and my wife,
My son John and his wife,
Us four and no more.

Farther down the same street was a childless couple who prayed:

Lord, bless us two,
And that will do.

Around the corner lived an old bachelor whose prayer was:

Lord, bless only me,
That's as far as I can see.

—Walter Dudley Calvert, *Remember Now . . .*

2077.
I gave a little tea party
This afternoon at three.
'Twas very small, three guests in all—
I, myself, and me.
Myself ate up the sandwiches
While I drink all the tea,
'Twas also I who ate the pie
And passed the cake for me.
—Author Unknown

2078. "One of the smallest packages we ever saw was a man wrapped up wholly in himself," suggests an unknown writer.

2079. "Nothing is so dull as to be encased in self, nothing so exhilarating as

to have attention and energy directed outward," says Bertrand Russell in *The Conquest of Happiness*.

2080. "Most men," said Thomas Erskine of Linlathen, "are so possessed by themselves that they have no vacuum into which God's deep water may rise."

2081. "He who will live for himself shall have small troubles," Dean W. R. Inge has said, "but they will seem to him great. He who will live for others shall have great troubles, but they will seem to him small."

2082. After visiting with his close friend John Sterling, Thomas Carlyle wrote: "Spent nearly the whole day with Sterling, and in everything except opinions we agreed perfectly."

2083. A patient in a mental hospital thought that he was surrounded by an invisible circle over which he could not cross. Try as he would he could not cross the circle. An attending physician noted: "If this man could get beyond that imaginary circle, which is actually a circle of self-interest, he would be cured." After many months the patient's mind grasped the meaning of love for other people, and bit by bit through the denial of self-love and the expression of love for others he was satisfactorily cured.

2084. Ibsen describes the tragedy of self-centeredness in his drama *Peer Gynt*. The superintendent of an asylum for the mentally sick says: "It's here that men are most themselves—themselves and nothing but themselves—sailing with outspread sails of self. Each shuts himself in a cask of self, the cask stopped with a bung of self and seasoned in a well of self. None has a tear for others' woes or cares what any other thinks.

. . . Now surely you'll say that he's himself! He's full of himself and nothing else; himself in every word he says —himself when he's beside himself. . . . Long live the Emperor of Self!"

2085. Persons with expanded selves, who live objectively in other persons and in wide-flung interests, Harry Emerson Fosdick suggests, can possibly have the prayer answered:

O wad some pow'r the giftie gie us
To see oursels as others see us!

The egocentric's petition is habitually otherwise:

O wad some pow'r to others gie,
To see myself as I see me.

2086. The creed of Mammon reads: "Self-interest is the only sufficient motive to drive men to real achievement. Moral right must bow to economic necessity. The unrestricted play of self-interest makes for social well-being. Enlightened self-interest is but the common sense expression of Christian faith. Mammon loveth a cheerful taker. He who would be greatest among you must become the exploiter of all."—G. BROMLEY OXNAM, *Preaching in a Revolutionary Age*

Self-Control

2087. When Stephen H. Tyne was rebuked by a young minister for losing his temper, he replied: "Young man, I control more temper every fifteen minutes than you will in a lifetime."

2088. The statue of "The Belt Wrestlers" in Stockholm depicts two men fastened together by a belt. Each wrestler has a knife in his hand. Unable to separate themselves, the men must fight until one wins. The statue is an allegory of human life, for the two men represent the better self and the worse self struggling for supremacy.

2089.
I do not ask for any crown
   But that which all may win;
Nor try to conquer any world
   Except the one within.
Be thou my guide until I find,
   Led by a tender hand,
The happy kingdom in myself
   And dare to take command.
         —LOUISA MAY ALCOTT,
            "My Kingdom"

Self-Criticism

2090. Dwight L. Moody said, "I've had more trouble with D. L. Moody than with any other man I know."

2091. "There is one person whom it is my duty to make good," said Robert Louis Stevenson, "and that is myself."

2092. "Always there is a black spot in our sunshine—the shadow of ourselves," says Thomas Carlyle in *Sartor Resartus*.

2093. "Be not angry that you cannot make others as you wish them to be," wrote Thomas à Kempis, "since you cannot make yourself as you wish to be."

2094.
I like, mislike, lament for what I could
   not;
I do, undo, yet still do what I should not;
And, at the selfsame instant, will the
   thing I would not.
         —AUTHOR UNKNOWN

2095.
   If my religion's not all
      That it ought to be,
   The trouble's not with God,
      The trouble's with me.
         —AUTHOR UNKNOWN

2096. In the play *Green Pastures,* Noah says to the Lord, "I ain't very much, but I'se all I got."

Self-Love

2097. The world, Augustine said in *The City of God,* has been controlled by two parties: those who have governed by "love of self to the point of contempt of God" and those who have governed by "love of God to the point of contempt of self."

2098. When General Robert E. Lee found an officer under his command gazing with satisfaction in the mirror, the general said, "Sir, you must be the happiest man in the world." "Why?" questioned the officer. "Because," said Lee, "you are in love with yourself, and you haven't a rival in the whole world."

Self-Respect

2099. Prayed an old Edinburgh weaver: "O God, help me to hold a high opinion of myself."

2100. A great Russian writer tells the story of a brilliant musician who one day sat down at the piano and played with such feeling and power that all his associates in the room were hushed into reverence. When he had finished, there was silence until he spoke breaking the stillness he had produced by telling some ribald story. One of his companions, speaking for all, said indignantly: "Be quiet, man. You are not worthy to be yourself."—TREVOR H. DAVIS, *To Live in Christ*

Self-Sacrifice

2101. "All along the Christian course," Alexander Maclaren noted, "there must be set up altars to God on which you sacrifice yourself, or you will never advance a step."

2102. John Coleridge Patteson, the first missionary to the Melanesian Islands, was slain by the natives of the island of Nukapu in 1871. The children of those who slew him put a cross on his grave bearing the truthful inscription: "Whose life was taken by men for whom he would gladly have given it."

2103. In his book *Man, the Unknown,* Alexis Carrel wrote: "While surrounded by comfort, beauty, and mechanical marvels, man fails to realize that he is degenerating." Then he adds, "Deny yourself, for there is no more beautiful adventure than the renovation and remaking of mankind."

SELFISHNESS

2104. "Selfishness does not consist of wanting something for ourselves," Oscar Wilde wrote ironically, "but in wanting others to do something for us that we are not willing to do for ourselves."

2105. Maggie Tulliver, the heroine in *The Mill on the Floss* by George Eliot, when looking for an answer to her frustrated life, comes upon a marked passage in an old copy of *Imitation of Christ* by Thomas à Kempis which particularly catches her attention: "If thou goest here and there seeking thine own will, thou shalt never be happy or free from care."

2106. "I was called to the door one day by the cries of children in the street," wrote Roland Diller, one of Lincoln's Springfield neighbors, "and there was Mr. Lincoln, striding by with two of his boys, both of whom were wailing aloud. 'Why, Mr. Lincoln, what's the matter with the boys?' I asked. 'Just what's the matter with the whole world,' Lincoln replied. 'I've got three walnuts, and each wants two.'"

2107. The story is told of a monarch of old who one time invited his subjects to the palace for a celebration. Each subject was asked to bring a bottle of his finest wine. Now it happened that one subject, wishing to save his finest wine, thought that no one would know that he took water with him. When all the people were gathered together, the king told them to pour their wine into a huge cask which stood in the courtyard. After this had been done, the king invited the people to drink. To the startled king came the realization that each of his subjects had brought water!

2108. There is an Oriental story which relates the experience of a man who cried out of the depths of hell, making a plea to the gods for release. The gods asked him what good he had done in his life. All the man could remember was that, while walking in the woods one day, he saw a spider and did not kill it. At once the thin, silvery thread of a spider web was let down to him in hell. Seizing it eagerly, he was slowly being lifted out of his misery. Whereupon, his fellow sufferers, seeing him about to escape, clutched his garment and his feet, and all were lifted up together. But the man, fearing the web might break, cried, "Let go! Let go!" Alas, when they did let go, the thread broke, and all fell back together. In short, the thread was strong enough to lift all together, but it could not bear the heavy burden of a selfish soul.—FREDERICK KELLER STAMM, *The Conversations of Jesus*

2109. A certain gentleman was being conducted on a tour of the other world. On reaching the nether regions he was greatly surprised to find the people all seated at a banquet table loaded with appetizing food. On the wall was the one law of the place—strictly enforced.

Everyone must use the knives and forks provided by the management. But the tools of service had such long handles that no one could get a morsel of food near his mouth. They were all starving to death. And that was hell! In the celestial city our visiting friend also found the people seated at banquet tables loaded with the same food and holding the same long-handled forks. But they were having a delightful time. They were feeding each other. And that was heaven!—LEWIS L. DUNNINGHAM

2110. A Sunday-school teacher, after reading the story of the good Samaritan, asked her class what they learned from it. One little boy responded, "I have learned that when I get into trouble someone should help me out."

2111. Epictetus said: "See children thrusting their hands into a narrow-necked jar and striving to pull out the nuts and figs it contains; if they fill the hand, they cannot pull it out again, and then they fall to tears."

SELFLESSNESS

2112. Someone has said: "There is no end to the good that a man can do if he doesn't care who gets the credit."

2113. Eve Curie in the biography of her mother, *Madame Curie,* tells of her parents' decision to make their greatest discovery available to mankind. "When the therapeutic effects of radium became known, plans for exploitation of radioactive ores were made in several countries, particularly in Belgium and in America. But engineers could produce the 'fabulous metal' only if they knew the secret of the delicate operations involved. Pierre Curie explained these things to his wife Marie one Sunday morning. He had just finished reading a letter from some technicians in the United States who wanted to exploit radium in America, and asked for information. 'We have two choices,' Pierre told her. 'We can describe the results of our research without reserve, including the process of purification. . . .' Marie made a mechanical gesture of approval and murmured: 'Yes, naturally.' 'Or else,' Pierre went on, 'we can consider ourselves to be the proprietors, the "inventors" of radium, patent the technique of treating pitchblende, and assure ourselves of rights over the manufacture of radium throughout the world.' Marie reflected a few seconds. Then she said: 'It is impossible. It would be contrary to the scientific spirit.' Pierre's serious face lightened. To settle his conscience, he dwelt upon it, mentioning, with a little laugh, the only thing which it was cruel for him to give up: 'We could have a fine laboratory too.' Marie's gaze grew fixed. She steadily considered this idea of gain. Almost at once she rejected it. 'Physicists always publish their researches completely. If our discovery has a commercial future, that is an accident by which we must not profit. And radium is going to be of use in treating disease. . . . It is impossible to take advantage of that.' "

2114. "Meekness does not assert itself because it has something better to assert," writes a contemporary. "A man comes into his own not by slaying rivals but by slaying himself."

SERENITY

2115. "Serenity comes to the man who lives with an unfaltering faith in an unfailing God," says Joseph R. Sizoo. "The person who lives with eternity in his heart will find a strange calm in his spirit."

2116. "Remorse ruins serenity; our infidelities, which we so eagerly anticipate and which pass from expectation through enjoyment into memory, haunt us evermore," Harry Emerson Fosdick has written. "Ill will spoils serenity, as does the cherished grudge, the mean vindictiveness. Jealousy wrecks serenity, as in the old story where, from the day he began enviously eyeing David, Saul never had a peaceful moment more. Engrossing ambition, where a man's ego becomes the clamorous center of the universe— that exiles serenity."—*The Power to See It Through*

SERMON

2117. John Shepherd, who became distinguished for his outstanding success in the pulpit, made the following statement to young ministers toward the close of his eventful career. He said: "My secret is in three things: (a) the studying of my sermons very frequently cost me tears; (b) before I preach a sermon to others I derive good from it myself; and (c) I have always gone into the pulpit as if I were immediately after to render an account to my Master."

2118. Henry Ward Beecher claimed: "A sermon is not like a Chinese firecracker to be fired off for the noise which it makes. It is the hunter's gun, and at every discharge he should look to see his game fall."

2119. A sermon worth preaching once is worth repeating. This Thomas Chalmers learned when one day, grown weary of the great crowds that flocked into his services, he announced that the morning sermon would be repeated in the evening. Of course he expected thereby to have a smaller attendance in the evening. Just the reverse proved true, however, for when word was spread that a good sermon was to be repeated many did not wish to miss the opportunity.

2120. When Longfellow returned to his home after church one morning, he wrote in his diary: "John Ware of Cambridge preached a good sermon." Then he added: "I applied it to myself."

2121. A man, satisfied with the sermon of the morning, commented to his minister as he left the church: "That was a good sermon. I couldn't find myself pointed out once."

2122. "I got a five-dollar, a two-dollar, and a one-dollar sermon here," said a Negro clergyman. "Now ah wants to see by the collection which one you want."

Criticism of Sermons

2123. Henry Sloane Coffin once said that "the recipe for compounding many a current sermon might be written: 'Take a teaspoonful of weak thought, add water, and serve.' The fact that it is frequently served hot may enable the concoction to warm the hearers; but it cannot be called nourishing."

2124. "The sermon, it seems to me," wrote Sheila Kaye-Smith, "has a double function—to instruct the mind and to stir the emotions; but the modern sermon is a mere tickling of the ears."

2125. A preacher in a certain Pennsylvania city once preached a sermon describing the squalors and privations among the mill and factory laborers and their families at the other end of the town. After the service a good lady of his congregation came up to him reproachfully. "Why do you preach such sermons?" she asked. "You have harrowed me all up; I come to church to be spiritually uplifted and soothed."—WALTER PRICHARD EATON

2126. At the close of a highly intellectual sermon an aged Scotch woman is said to have cried out: "Aye, aye, but yon rope o' yours is nae lang enough tae reach the likes o' me."

2127. An admirer of a distinguished clergyman remarked: "President Holley was an excellent preacher—he never put any religion or politics in his sermon."

Delivery of Sermons

2128. A copy of the Methodist *Discipline* dated 1836 gives wise advice for the modern clergyman: "Always suit your object to your audience. . . . Choose the plainest text you can. . . . Take care not to ramble, but keep to your text, and make out what you take in hand. . . . Take care of anything affected, either in gesture, phrase, or pronunciation. . . . Do not usually pray, extempore, above eight or ten minutes (at most) without intermission."

2129. "Brethren," cried Father Taylor, the sailor-preacher, finding himself entangled in a sentence from whose labyrinthine subordinate clauses there seemed to be no exit, "I have lost the nominative of this sentence, and things are generally mixed up, but I am bound for the Kingdom anyhow!"

2130. "The sermon," says Charles R. Brown, "has dimensions—height, depth, and breadth. The people who do the listening are sometimes painfully aware of a fourth dimension—length."

2131. Bernard Iddings Bell writes that before a service of worship he prepares himself in this manner: "I shall get down on my knees; beat my breast—

inconspicuously—three times in token of my sinfulness; make the sign of the cross in token of my Master's love; and say a prayer which always goes about like this: 'God, this sermon is not much good, but I have worked honestly at it and it is the best I can do right now. If it is to do any good at all, it is you who will do that good and not I. Please use me in my sermon as best you can. I love you and I love these people. That's that. Amen.' "

SERMON ON THE MOUNT

2132. G. K. Chesterton said that at first thought the Sermon on the Mount seems to turn everything upside down, but on second thought it turns everything right side up.

2133. Drew Pearson has said: "Maybe we will wake up to the futility of old-fashioned diplomacy and the hopelessness of big armies and put our faith in friendship. In other words, everything else having failed, we might finally come around to practicing the Sermon on the Mount."

2134. During a debate on foreign policy in the British Parliament one member exclaimed that the policy was based on the Sermon on the Mount. A cynic called back: "If the British Empire is to be run on the principles of the Sermon on the Mount, all I can say is, 'God help us.' " The first member answered: "And he will."

2135. When word came that Mahatma Gandhi would pass through a certain Indian community, thousands of persons gathered to honor him. When the train stopped, they cried for a word of counsel. From beneath his garment he took a copy of the New Testament, and after reading a few verses from the Sermon on the Mount he turned to the people and said, "Now go to your homes and put these teachings into practice in all their rugged simplicity."

SERVICE

2136. When Charles R. Brown of Yale was addressing students on a western campus, he said: "I come from a larger university than this: it is larger than Columbia, or Yale, or all the American universities combined. It is the University of Life. Our colors are black and blue, for we learn our lessons by hard knocks. In this university there is only one examination day, and in that examination there is but one question. It is that question that I have come to ask you. What is life?" Then he continued: "Let us ask the Great Teacher of all the ages, and hear his answer by word and deed: life is service: 'Even as the Son of man came not to be ministered unto, but to minister.' "

2137. Albert Schweitzer in *Out of My Life and Thought* tells of the time in his life when he determined he would find something beyond himself to give his life to: "I settled with myself that I would consider myself justified in living till I was thirty for science and art, in order to devote myself from that time forward to the direct service of humanity. . . . What would be the character of the activities thus planned for the future was not yet clear to me. I left it to circumstances to guide me. One thing only was certain, that it must be directly human service, however inconspicuous the sphere of it."

2138. The friends of Louis Pasteur reported the scientist as often saying: "In what way can I be of service to humanity? My time and energy belong to mankind."

2139. A missionary agricultural school in India once closed its doors to all except Christian students. The director explained that with his meager funds he wished to admit only those who would use the instruction for others. "A Christian graduate will teach others," he said, "and he is worth a hundred times as much as a non-Christian."

2140. Louis Pasteur told Napoleon III: "All my ambition is to arrive at the knowledge of the causes of putrid and contagious diseases."

2141. Adam Clarke, the great biblical scholar of two hundred years ago, lies in Westminster Abbey. On his tomb is a candle, burned to the near socket, and around it these words: "In burning for others, I myself, also, have been consumed."

2142. "There is only one religion," wrote Sir Edward Burne-Jones. " 'Make the most of your best for the sake of others' is the catholic faith, which except a man believe faithfully he cannot be saved."

2143. When a friend asked Wilberforce, the great emancipator, if he was sure his soul was saved, the statesman, who gave his life to freeing the slave and helping the poor, replied: "I've been so busy I've forgotten I ever had a soul."

2144. Archbishop Nathan Söderblom used to say, "Doctrine divides but service unites."

2145. A business block in a western city bears this motto: "Service is the rent we pay for the space we occupy."

2146. A man hurried to the church door one Sunday noon and said: "Is the service over?" An usher who had grasped the implications of the minister's words that day said: "The worship is over, but the service is only beginning."

2147. When the wife of the late Bishop Frederick Bohn Fisher took an Indian child up in her arms, she did not know that the burning body of the child was tortured with typhus; but three days later she was dead. Her heartbroken husband wrote the tribute for the stone that marks her resting place: "She died serving." — G. BROMLEY OXNAM, *Preaching in a Revolutionary Age*

SHADOW

2148. It is the shadow of the metal rod on a sundial which tells an observer the time. One sundial had this inscription: "Without the shadow—nothing."

2149. It is said that Raphael wore a candle in his cap to keep his own shadow from his picture.

SHARING

2150. Says communism: "What's yours is mine; I'll take it." Says capitalism: "What's mine is my own; I'll keep it." Says Christianity: "What's mine is ours; I'll share it."

2151. One businessman, when asked the secret of his success, pointed to his motto: "Something in it for both of us!"

2152. One day a mountaineer invited a friend to climb with him to the top of a high peak. There they beheld a gorgeous sunset. The friend turned to the mountaineer and said: "Why are you crying?" The reply was: "All these years I have come here alone and filled my soul with this cup of God. Today I am happier than I have ever been, for this is the first time I have shared the glory with someone else."

2153. Father Damien, after working for eleven years among the lepers of Molokai, was writing one of his pleading letters to friends outside and used the phrase, "the lepers." Suddenly he stopped as if paralyzed. He had seen the fatal white spot on his own hand. Then he crossed out "the" and wrote *"we."*

SICKNESS

2154. A testimony of the way one man rose above sickness and despair is recorded by Edward Livingston Trudeau in *An Autobiography*: "As I look back on my life tuberculosis looms up as an ever-present and relentless foe. It robbed me of my dear ones and brought me my first great sorrows. It shattered my health when I was young and strong, and relegated me to this remote region [in the Adirondacks] where ever since I have seen its withering blight laid on those about me. And yet the struggle with tuberculosis has brought me experiences and left me recollections which I would not exchange for the wealth of the Indies."

2155. In a letter Robert Louis Stevenson wrote: "I am made of the stuff soldiers are made from, but God willed it that my battle should be one with medicine bottles and pill boxes."

SIGHT

2156. "The greatest thing a human soul ever does in this world is to *see* something, and tell what he *saw* in a plain way," said John Ruskin in *Modern Painters*. "Hundreds of people can talk for one who can think, but thousands can think for one who can see. To see clearly is poetry, prophecy, and religion —all in one."

2157. Helen Keller has said: "I have walked with people whose eyes are full of light, but who see nothing in wood, sea, or sky, nothing in city streets, nothing in books. Their souls voyage through this enchanted world with a barren stare."

2158. When asked to describe the Taj Mahal, a visitor from the Orient said: "I cannot. It is too vast, too beautiful, too great. But I have seen it; I have seen it."

2159. When a poor student took his canvas to Whistler, the artist, the student said: "I cannot paint what I see." Said Whistler: "Your trouble, my son, is to begin when you see what you paint."

2160. In *Locusts and Wild Honey*, John Burroughs says that the secret of observations lies in the habit of decisive gazing. "Not by a first casual glance, but by a steady deliberate aim of the eye, are the rarest things discovered. You must look intently and hold your eye firmly to the spot if you are to see more than do the rank and file of mankind."

SIN

2161. Early lists of the cardinal sins totaled *eight* sins. As late as John Damascene the compilation included the sin of "sadness." The seven sins we now know as the cardinal sins include: gluttony, impurity, avarice, anger, sloth, pride, envy. But in the earlier ages the church paid special attention also to sadness.

2162. Sin, said Thomas à Kempis, is first a simple suggestion, then a strong imagination, then delight, and then assent.

2163.
Manlike is it to fall into sin,
Fiendlike is it to dwell therein,

Christlike is it for sin to grieve,
Godlike is it all sin to leave.
                —Friedrich von Logau

2164. A definition of sin which comes from an old musical comedy is worth considering: "Sin ain't what you do; it's the way you feel after doing it."

2165. Carlyle once remarked that "the greatest security against sin is to be shocked at its presence."

2166. "My soul is like a mirror in which the glory of God is reflected," said Teresa, the great Spanish mystic, "but sin, however insignificant, covers the mirror with smoke."

2167. Goethe said: "If I were God, this world of sin and suffering would break my heart." It did break God's heart—on the cross.

2168. Says a senior devil in *The Screwtape Letters*: "We work under a cruel handicap. Nothing is naturally on our side. Everything has to be twisted before it is of any use to us."

2169. After a minister had spoken strongly against sin, one of his members said: "We don't want you to talk as plainly as you do about sin because if our boys and girls hear you talking so much about sin they will more easily become sinners. Call it a mistake, if you will, but do not speak so plainly about sin." The minister went to the medicine shelf and brought back a small bottle of strychnine marked "Poison." He said: "I see what you want me to do. You want me to change the label. Suppose I take off this label 'Poison' and put on some mild label, such as 'Essence of Peppermint.' Can't you see what would happen? The milder you make the label, the more dangerous you make the poison."—J. Wilbur Chapman

2170. Someone said: "Being a Presbyterian may not save you from sinning, but it will take the joy out of it."

2171. When Will Rogers chided a druggist for working too hard and suggested that the man take time off to have a good time, the druggist said: "I may not have a good time, but I sell a lot of headache medicine to some folks who do."

2172. A prominent novelist of skeptical persuasion visited out of curiosity a revival meeting. When the altar call was issued, a member of the revival team approached him. "Are you saved?" the novelist was asked. "No," the novelist replied. "Do you want God to forgive your sins?" "No," the novelist said smugly, "I like my sins."

2173.
This is the debt I pay
Just for one riotous day,
Years of regret and grief,
Sorrow without relief.

Slight was the thing I bought,
Small was the debt I thought,
Poor was the loan at best—
God! but the interest! [1]
            —Paul Laurence Dunbar,
            "The Debt"

2174. In one of Sidney Smith's cartoons Andy Gump told Chester that he had been disobeying too much. In order to bring it home to him the father drove a nail in a post in the back yard every time the son failed to obey. When the post was pretty well filled with nails,

[1] Reprinted by permission of Dodd, Mead & Co., from *The Complete Poems of Paul Laurence Dunbar*.

Chester turned over a new leaf, and Andy promised for each obedience to pull a nail out of the post. When the last nail was drawn, he called Chester to see that the record was clear. To his surprise Chester began to cry: "The scars are still there," he said.—ELBERT RUSSELL, *More Chapel Talks*

2175. "My sin is not a burden someone else can bear or a debt someone else can pay," writes Leslie D. Weatherhead in *A Plain Man Looks at the Cross*. "My sins have become myself. The habit tracks of my mind, even the molecules of my brain, are affected. 'I won't count time,' says the sinner after each new fall. Says William James, the psychologist, 'He may not count it, and a kind heaven may not count it, but it is being counted, just the same. Down among his nerve cells and fibres the molecules are counting it, registering, storing it up to be used against him when the next temptation comes.' "

SKEPTICISM

2176. A young skeptic wishing to test the wisdom of a seer held his closed fist before the venerated man. "What have I in my hand?" the youth asked. "A bird," was the answer. "Is it alive or dead?" queried the youth. The old man knew that the youth was sporting with him. If he replied dead, the youth would open his hand and let the bird fly away. If he replied alive, the youth would close his fist and crush the bird. So the seer said: "As you will, my son, as you will."

2177. Charles Henry Parkhurst once defined skepticism as "the friction caused by a small brain trying to absorb a great idea."

2178. When William Jennings Bryan wrote to Colonel Robert Ingersoll asking his views on God and immortality, Ingersoll answered: "I do not say that there is no God: I simply say I do not know. I do not say that there is no life beyond the grave: I simply say I do not know."

2179. "The age of *Amen* has given way to the age of *Oh, yeah?*" writes Gaius Glenn Atkins.

2180. Henry van Dyke said that the coat of arms of his generation was a question mark.

2181. To be on the safe side one skeptic is reported to have prayed, "O God, if there is a God, save my soul, if I have a soul."

SLANDER

2182. "A man that flattereth his neighbor spreadeth a net for his feet," William Cowper said. "He that slanders me paints me blacker than I am, and he that flatters me, whiter. They both daub me, and when I look in the glass of conscience, I see myself disguised by both."

2183. When a newspaper had published false and misleading accounts concerning a certain man, the man went to Dr. Edward Everett to inquire what action Everett would recommend. After listening patiently to the man's complaints, Everett said: "My dear sir, do nothing. Half the people who buy that paper never saw the article about you. Half the people who did see it failed to read it. Half of those who read it failed to understand it. Half of those who understood it knew you and refused to believe it. Half of those who believed it were people of no consequence anyway."

SMILE

2184.

A smile on your lips:
  Cheers your heart,
  Keeps you in good humor,
  Preserves peace in your soul,
  Promotes your health,
  Beautifies your face,
  Induces kindly thoughts,
  Inspires kindly deeds.
                        —AUTHOR UNKNOWN

2185. "Nothing on earth can smile but man!" said Henry Ward Beecher. "Gems may flash reflected light, but what is a diamond-flash compared to an eye-flash and a mirth-flash? Flowers cannot smile; this is a charm that even they cannot claim. It is the prerogative of man; it is the color which love wears, and cheerfulness, and joy—these three. It is a light in the windows of the face by which the heart signifies it is at home and waiting. A face that cannot smile is like a bud that cannot blossom, and dries up on the stalk. Laughter is day, and sobriety is night, and a smile is the twilight that hovers gently between both—more bewitching than either."

2186. When asked what in America most impressed him, Alexander Kerensky, a Russian, said: "That is easy. In America the people smile."

2187. When the frail Mary Bacheler of Hasseltine House was told, "You do well to smile," she responded: "I believe if I furnish the smile on the face, God will provide the mood in the heart."

2188.

They might not need me, yet they might.
I'll let my head be just in sight;
A smile as small as mine might be

Precisely their necessity.
                        —EMILY DICKINSON,
                          "A Smile as Small as Mine"

2189. An American officer in World War I wrote home: "You can truly think of me as being cheerful all the time. Why otherwise? I have thirty-eight men; and if I duck when a shell comes, all thirty-eight duck, and if I smile, the smiles goes down the line."

2190. Frowning is hard work. It takes sixty-four muscles of the face to make a frown and only thirteen to make a smile.

2191. Mrs. Wiggs of the Cabbage Patch spoke wisely when she said: "I have made it a practice to put all my worries in the bottom of my heart and sit on the lid and smile."

SORROW

2192.

I walked a mile with Pleasure;
  She chattered all the way,
But left me none the wiser
  For all she had to say.

I walked a mile with Sorrow,
  And ne'er a word said she;
But, oh, the things I learned from her
  When Sorrow walked with me!
                        —ROBERT BROWNING HAMILTON,
                          "Along the Road"

2193.

My life is but the weaving
  Between my God and me.
I only choose the colors
  He weaveth steadily.
Sometimes he weaveth sorrow
  And I in foolish pride,
Forget he sees the upper
  And I the under side.
                        —AUTHOR UNKNOWN

2194.
Only the soul that knows the mighty grief
Can know the mighty rapture. Sorrows come
To stretch out spaces in the heart for joy.[3]

—EDWIN MARKHAM,
"Victory in Defeat"

2195. E. Stanley Jones gives the following prescription for meeting trouble: "Don't think your case unique; it can be matched many times over. Don't give yourself to pity; the temptation will be to feel sorry for yourself; a self-pitying self is a pitiable self; don't allow yourself to slip on that. Don't give yourself to excessive grief. Many do it, thinking they thereby show their love. Don't retail your sorrows; doing so will cause them to grow. Don't resign yourself to sorrow and feel it will continue. Don't complain; the more you complain about things the more things you will have to complain about."

2196. "Who taught thee to sing?" one character asks another in a play by Ibsen. The answer is: "God sent me sorrow."

2197. Madame Schumann-Heink once said when criticizing a young artist: "She has a remarkable voice and the promise of a wonderful career, but she will not attain her full power until she has experienced more of the joys and sorrows of life."

SOUL

2198. Toyohiko Kagawa once said: "As the sculptor devotes himself to wood and stone, I would devote myself to my soul."

2199. "O! wait more and more," wrote Isaac Penington, the Quaker mystic, "to

[3] Used by permission of Virgil Markham.

know how to keep that silence, which is of the power; that in every one of you, what the power would have silent, may be silent. . . . Wait and labor, then, to know, understand, and be guided by the motives, leadings, drawings, teachings, quickenings, etc., of the thing itself within."

2200. A savage tribe in the Amazon valley is said to follow the strange practice of stopping now and then when on a long journey through the valley to let their souls catch up with their bodies.—JOHN MADISON YOUNGINER

2201. "I was just a kid," writes R. Lee Sharpe. "One spring day, father called me to go with him to old man Trussel's blacksmith shop. He had left a rake and a hoe to be repaired. And there they were ready, fixed like new. Father handed over a silver dollar for the repairing. But Mr. Trussell refused to take it. 'No,' he said, 'there's no charge for that little job.' But father insisted that he take the pay, still extending to him the dollar. 'Ed,' the blacksmith said, 'can't you let a man do something now and then—just to stretch his soul?'"

SPIRIT

2202. A girl who had been under the influence of Alice Freeman Palmer in college said: "Mrs. Palmer had a strange effect on me. When I saw her, I felt as if I could do things that I never dreamed of before. Even now whenever I think of her, I have a sense of dignity in my life. I do not know what it is. It seems as if her appreciation of the world of things puts a new spirit into me that carries me along until the next time I think of her. I should not care to go on in a world in which she hadn't been."

2203. Arrius, a Roman, spoke to Ben Hur in Lew Wallace's novel: "The hortator tells me thou art his best rower." "The hortator is very kind," Ben Hur said. "Hast thou seen much service?" "About three years." "At the oars?" "I cannot recall a day of rest from them," Ben Hur replied. "The labor is hard; few men bear it a year without breaking, and thou—thou art but a boy." Ben Hur answered: "The noble Arrius forgets that the spirit hath much to do with endurance. By its help the weak sometimes thrive when the strong perish."

2204. "There are only two forces in the world," Napoleon is reported to have said. "They are the spirit and the sword. And the spirit always conquers the sword."

2205. A young artist, dissatisfied with his work, borrowed the brush of a great painter. But the brush didn't make the young man work any better. "It is not the master's brush you need," a friend said, "but the master's spirit."

SPIRITUALITY

2206. When William James was asked to define what he meant by "spirituality," he thought for several moments and then said: "Phillips Brooks."

2207. "Two verbs have built two empires," wrote Augustine, "the verb 'to have' and the verb 'to be.' The first is an empire of things—material possessions and power. The second is an empire of the spirit—things that last.

2208. Nikolai Berdyaev, a Russian philosopher, said: "In the very act of affirming himself man has lost himself. He has conquered the earth, he has created the marvels, but his assurance in himself has gone. Dwarfed and insignificant he is left to contemplate the vast space he has discovered. When man broke away from the spiritual moorings of his life, he tore himself from the deeps and went to the shallows."— *Freedom and the Spirit*

2209. When Roger Babson asked Charles Steinmetz what line of research would see the greatest development during the next fifty years, the famous electrical engineer and physicist replied: "Mr. Babson, I think the greatest discovery will be made along spiritual lines. Here is a force which history clearly teaches has been the greatest power in the development of men and history. Yet we have merely been playing with it, and have never seriously studied it as we have the physical forces. Some day people will learn that material things do not bring happiness and are of little use in making men and women creative and powerful. Then the scientists of the world will turn their laboratories over to the study of God and prayer and the spiritual forces which as yet have hardly been scratched."

STARS

2210. Jeanbon St.-Andre, one of the leaders in the French Revolution, said to a peasant: "I will have all your steeples pulled down, that you may no longer have any object by which you may be reminded of your old superstitions." The peasant replied: "But you cannot help leaving us the stars."

2211. A small boy whose life had been spent in the heart of one of the great European cities rejoiced when the blackout war measure was taken. A darkened city offered him the first opportunity in his life to see the stars.

STEADFASTNESS

2212. Marcus Aurelius tells the story of the pilot who for many years steered his galley. On a stormy night in great danger the emperor came on deck to encourage the crew. The old pilot, who had lashed himself to the tiller, was praying to Neptune, and the emperor heard him say, "Father Neptune, you may sink me if you will, but whether you sink me or save me I will hold my tiller true."

2213. A man's ambition may never be realized, but the goal is worth struggling toward. Philip Sidney, courtier to Queen Elizabeth, put it in this manner: "Who shoots at the midday sun, though he be sure he shall never hit the mark, yet as sure he is he shall shoot higher than who aims but at a bush."

STEWARDSHIP

2214. John Wesley gave his estimate of Christian stewardship when he said: "The Christian must make all he can; he must save all he can; he must give all he can."

2215. Drs. William and Charles Mayo used much less than half of their income on themselves and their families. They counted their money a trust and used it for the service of others. William put it this way: "That holy money, as we call it, must go back into the service of that humanity which paid it to us. If we can train five hundred pairs of hands, we have helped hand on the torch."

2216. Fritz Kreisler said: "I was born with music in my system. It was a gift of God. I did not acquire it. So I do not even deserve thanks for the music. Music is too sacred to be sold, and the outrageous prices charged by musical celebrities today are truly a crime against society. I never look upon the money I earn as my own. It is 'public money.' It is only a fund entrusted to me for proper disbursement. I am constantly endeavoring to reduce my needs to the minimum. I feel morally guilty in ordering a costly meal, for it deprives someone else of a slice of bread, some child perhaps of a bottle of milk. My beloved wife feels exactly as I do about these things. In all these years of my so-called success in music we have not built a home for ourselves. Between it and us stand all the homeless in the world."

2217. "Not what you possess but what you do with what you have, determines your true worth," said Thomas Carlyle.

2218. A man who earned fifty dollars a week pledged two dollars weekly to his church. "I earn God's portion from eight to ten Monday mornings," he explained, adding, "and it is the best earned money of the week."

2219. The Lord is my partner: I shall not be troubled about temporal prosperity. He maketh me to live upon the fat of the land; he leadeth me away from bad investments; he restoreth my confidence in him; he leadeth me to know the blessings of scriptural giving. Yea, though I pass through a season of business depression, I will not fear for the outcome, for thou, O Lord, wilt not permit our enterprise to fail. Thou preparest a way and a will to enjoy spiritual blessings more than ever I have known before in all my Christian experience. Thou causeth thy fund to contain enough money and still some for every work of thine. Surely real prosperity —of the heart as well as the purse— shall continue with me as long as I confidently do my part and let him prove what he can do; and together we build up his kingdom unto everlasting day.—E. A. STANISTREET, *The Tither's Psalm*

2220. One day Heinrich Heine, a Jew, was being entertained by a wealthy Christian lady. Though he was known as one of the most brilliant conversationalists of his day, on this occasion he had nothing to say. Finally the irritated hostess berated him, saying: "Why are you so dumb?" Heine replied: "I am studying a problem which I cannot solve. I have been looking at these gold dishes, this fine linen, these splendid waiters, your great diamonds, and wondering what you Christians are going to do with the camel question."

2221. A man stepped into a drugstore one Sunday morning shortly before eleven, put a dime on the counter, and asked for two nickles. "Here they are," said the druggist, "and I hope you enjoy the sermon."

2222. John Wesley one day exclaimed: "Some of you Methodists are twice as rich as you were before you were Methodists; some of you are fourfold as rich; some of you are tenfold as rich; now, if, whilst you get all you can and save all you can, you do not give all you can, then you are tenfold more the child of hell than you were before."

2223. The Vicar of St. John's Church in Waterloo, England, contrived an original way of dispensing with annual church bazaars. To all the members of his congregation he sent the following bill: "Bus fare, admission, wear and tear on clothes and tempers, tea, useless articles—total . . . Please remit." The sums received were in excess of any previously raised.

STRUGGLE

2224. Alfred Russell Wallace, a famous scientist, once tried to help an emperor moth to free itself from the cocoon. With a knife the scientist split the cocoon, and the moth, once freed, crept moodily about, drooped perceptibly, and died. The furious struggle with the cocoon was nature's way of developing the splendid wings and of sending the vital fluids pulsing through the frame until every particle blushed with their beauty.

2225. Once when a British destroyer was lying in a harbor in the West Indies a violent storm arose. The captain ordered his ship out to sea into the very teeth of the storm. Two days later when his ship returned, the other ships in the harbor—those which had refused to face the tempest—were all wrecked.

2226. In *Brave New World*, Aldous Huxley creates an imaginary land where pain, trouble, and struggle are unknown. 'It is Christianity without tears." declares the Controller. "But," someone says, "the tears are necessary. You get rid of them. You just abolish the slings and arrows. It's too easy. I don't want comfort. I want God. I want poetry. I want real danger. I want freedom." "But you'll be very unhappy," says the Controller. "I claim," replies the other, "the right to be unhappy."

SUCCESS

2227. Elbert Hubbard described a successful man as one who has tried, not cried; who has worked, not dodged; who has shouldered responsibility, not evaded it; who has got under the burden, instead of standing off, looking on, and giving advice.

2228. The Ladder of Success

100%—I did.
90%—I will.
80%—I can.
70%—I think I can.
60%—I might.
50%—I think I might.
40%—What is it?
30%—I wish I could.
20%—I don't know how.
10%—I can't.
0%—I won't.

SUFFERING

2229. "It is by those who have suffered that the world has been advanced," said Leo Tolstoy.

2230. "I have known more of God since I came to this bed," said Ralph Erskine while his body was racked with pain, "than through all my life."

2231. In the bombardment of World War I, Cardinal Mercier saw his home torn by shells, his cathedral made a heap of debris, his priceless books burned, and his students killed. After that devastating experience Mercier said: "Suffering accepted and vanquished . . . will give you a serenity which may well prove the most exquisite fruit of your life."—WILLIAM M. ELLIOTT, JR., *Coming to Terms with Life*

2232. Oberlin, an illustrious French pastor, in comforting an afflicted lady used the following illustration: "Dear madam, I have before me two stones, alike in color, of the same water, clear, pure, and clean. Yet there is a marked difference—one has a dazzling brilliance; the other is quite dull. Why? Because one has received eighty cuts and the other only eight. The stone that has suffered much is brilliant; the one that has suffered little is dim and lusterless."—FRED R. CHENAULT

2233. Dr. Edward Judson, in speaking of the life of his father, Adoniram Judson, at the dedication of the Judson Memorial Church in New York City said: "Suffering and success go together. If you are succeeding without suffering, it is because others before you have suffered; if you are suffering without succeeding, it is that others after you may succeed."

Fellowship of Suffering

2234. In one of his three-minute plays Thornton Wilder tells of an infirm doctor who stood one day by the pool of Bethesda waiting for the water to be troubled that he might be made whole again. The angel who troubled the water came to him and said: "Stand back. Healing is not for you. Without your wound where would your power be that sends your low voice trembling into the hearts of men? We ourselves, the very angels of God in heaven, cannot persuade the wretched and blundering children of earth as can one human being broken on the wheels of living. In love's service only wounded soldiers will do."—*The Angel That Troubled the Waters*

2235. "It was in those who had recovered from the plague," wrote Thucydides, "that the sick and the dying found most compassion."

2236. David Hume, who had distinguished himself for his writings against the Christian faith, said in the days of grief following his mother's death: "I throw out my speculations to entertain the learned and metaphysical world, yet I do not think so differently from the rest of the world as one might imagine."

2237. "I have not suffered *by* the South," Lincoln told a friend, "but I have suffered *with* the South."

2238. At the moment of their calamity the survivors of the "Titanic" were not stunned, but "lifted into an atmosphere of vision where self-centered suffering merges into some mystic meaning. . . . We were all one, not only with one another, but with the cosmic Being that

for a time had seemed so cruel."—
GEORGE A. COE, *The Psychology of Religion*

SUN

2239. Phillips Brooks once told of a missionary in Africa who on a furlough bought a sundial that it might help his folk in the African village to tell the time of day. So he set it up in the midst of the village, but his people were so filled with admiration and wonder that straightway they built a roof over it to protect it from the sun and rain.— HARRY EMERSON FOSDICK, *Successful Christian Living*

2240. Asked to explain the charm of an old violin, the violinist said: "Ah, a great deal of sunshine must have gone into this wood, and what has gone in comes out."

SUNDAY

2241. A Chinese Christian tells of a man who went to market with a string of seven coins. Seeing a beggar whose need was greater than his own, the man gave six of the coins to the poor one. The beggar, instead of being grateful, followed the man until he found an opportunity to steal the seventh coin. This incident was used by the Chinese Christian to illustrate the fact that after God has given man six days, man has stolen the one day which God kept for himself.

2242. A famous physician, Sir James Crichton Browne, said: "We doctors, in the treatment of nervous diseases, are now constantly compelled to prescribe periods of rest. Some periods are, I think, only Sundays in arrears."

2243.
They're praising God on Sunday.
They'll be all right on Monday.
It's just a little habit they've acquired.[4]
          —BLISS CARMAN

SYMPATHY

2244. "I am sorry for the man who can't feel the whip when it is laid on the other man's back," Lincoln once characteristically said.

2245. William James told of a Russian noblewoman who sat in her luxurious box in the theater weeping over the make-believe hardships of the characters upon the stage. She wished that she might help those imaginary ills, about which she could do nothing, and all the while her coachman, whom she might have helped, slowly froze to death in the bitter cold of the night outside.

2246.
And a thousand million lives are his
Who carries the world in his sympathies.
      —JAMES RUSSELL LOWELL

[4] Reprinted by permission of Dodd, Mead & Co., and The Ryerson Press, from *Bliss Carman's Poems*.

T

TACT

2247. Roy L. Smith tells of a small boy who wrote to his pastor at the time of the pastor's retirement: "I have prayed God that he will keep you alive now that you have retired."

2248. An old Adirondack guide used to answer a newcomer's query concerning fishing with these words: "Well, the fishing is fine, but the catching is a little poor."

2249. After a day's hunting in India a young Englishman who was a poor shot said to his Indian attendant, "I didn't do so well today." "Ah, the young sahib shot very well," said the diplomatic Hindu, "but God was very merciful to the birds."

TEACHER

2250.
An Arabian proverb suggests:

He who knows not and knows not he
  knows not:
He is a fool—shun him;
He who knows not and knows he knows
  not:
He is simple—teach him;
He who knows and knows not he
  knows:
He is asleep—wake him;
He who knows and knows he knows:
He is wise—follow him.

2251.
Greeting his pupils, the master asked:
  What would you learn of me?

And the reply came:
  How shall we care for our bodies?
  How shall we rear our children?
  How shall we work together?
  How shall we live with our fellow
    men?
  How shall we play?
  For what ends shall we live? . . .
And the master pondered these words,
And sorrow was in his heart, for his own
Learning touched not these things.
—J. C. CHAPMAN AND C. S. COUNTS,
Principles of Education

2252. Fitzgerald Flournoy in his poem "To a College Professor" paid the following tribute to a teacher:

I cannot count the things you did for
  me.
You wakened me, and led me forth to
  find
Immortal company, and made me see
My path in the republic of the mind.[1]

2253. Harry Emerson Fosdick tells of a poor German schoolmaster who lived in a humble house in a small village. Carved over his doorway was this proud inscription: "Dante, Molière, and Goethe live here."

2254.
Mark Hopkins sat on one end of a log
  And a farm boy sat on the other.
Mark Hopkins came as a pedagogue
  And taught as an elder brother.
I don't care what Mark Hopkins taught,

[1] Used by permission of the author.

271

If his Latin was small and his Greek was
    naught,
For the farm boy he thought, thought
    he,
    All through lecture time and quiz,
    "The kind of man I mean to be
    Is the kind of man Mark Hopkins
    is." [2]
—ARTHUR GUITERMAN, "Education"

2255.

Lord, as thy word opens yon door, in-
    viting
Teacher and taught to feast this hour
    with thee;
Opens a book where God in human
    writing
Thinks his deep thoughts, and dead
    tongues live for me.

Too dread the task, too great the duty
    calling,
    Too heavy far the weight is laid on
    me!
Oh, if mine own thought should on thy
    words falling
    Mar the great message, and men hear
    not thee!

Give me thy voice to speak, thine ear
    to listen,
    Give me thy mind to grasp thy mys-
    tery;
So shall my heart throb and my glad
    eyes glisten,
    Rapt with the wonders thou dost show
    to me.
      —JAMES H. MOULTON,
      "At the Classroom Door"

2256. Josiah Royce wrote: "Harvard
University pays me for doing what I
would gladly pay for the privilege of
doing if I could only afford it."

[2] From *Death and General Putnam, and
101 Other Poems* by Arthur Guiterman, copyright 1939 by E. P. Dutton & Co., Inc. Renewal © 1967 by Mrs. Vida Lindo Guiterman. Reprinted by permission of the publishers.

2257. One day at the reunion of a class
which had graduated from college
twenty years before, a stockbroker who
had accumulated an immense fortune
approached a classmate who had spent
the years since graduation teaching in
a preparatory school. The stockbroker,
who had a fine scorn of nonfinancial
achievements, said with half-concealed
sarcasm, "So you teach Greek!" There
was a moment of embarrassed silence,
and then the teacher answered quietly,
"No, you're wrong. I teach boys. Greek
is what I start with."—JAMES GORDON
GILKEY, *Managing One's Self*

2258. Alexander the Great said: "My
father gave me life. My teacher taught
me how to live."

TEMPERANCE

2259. There is a Japanese proverb:

First the man—takes the drink,
Next the drink—takes the drink,
Then the drink—takes the man.

2260. There are only two stages in the
life of a drunk: (1) when he could
stop if he would and (2) when he would
stop if he could.

2261. Benjamin Franklin, a man of sage
counsels, wrote in 1780: "Temperance
puts wood on the fire, meat in the
barrel, flour in the tub, money in the
purse, credit in the country, clothes on
the bairns, intelligence in the brain, and
spirit in the constitution."

2262. In a speech on Washington's
birthday in 1842 Lincoln, speaking on
prohibition, said: "In it we shall find a
stronger bondage broken, a viler slavery
manumitted, a great tyrant deposed; in
it more of want supplied, more of
disease healed, more of sorrow assuaged.

By it, no orphans starving, no widows weeping. By it, none wounded in feeling, none injured in interest. If the grandeur of revolutions shall be estimated by the great amount of human misery they alleviate and the small amount they inflict, then indeed will this be the grandest the world shall ever have seen."

2263. When John Wesley was at Oxford University, he was astounded by the amount of drinking done by undergraduates. After writing to his mother for her counsel, he received the following word: "My dear Son: Remember that anything which increases the authority of the body over the mind is an evil thing."

2264. "I promised my mother a few days before her death that I would never drink intoxicating liquor," said Abraham Lincoln. "This promise, made when a boy, I have faithfully kept."

2265. Thomas Edison said: "To put alcohol in the human system is like putting sand in the bearings of an engine."

2266. William Jennings Bryan listed his reasons for prohibition: (1) God never made a human being who in a normal state need alcohol. (2) God never made a human being strong enough to begin the use of alcohol and be sure that he would not become its victim. (3) God never fixed a day in a human life after which it is safe to begin the use of intoxicating liquors.—*In His Image*

2267. Saul Kane, the man of hardened character in John Masefield's poem *The Everlasting Mercy*, is upbraided by a Quaker rescue worker in a saloon in an English village with these words:

"Saul Kane," she said, "when next you drink,
Do me the gentleness to think
That every drop of drink accursed
Makes Christ within you die of thirst,
That every dirty word you say
Is one more flint upon His way, . . .
Another nail, another cross.
All that you are is that Christ's loss."

2268. E. Stanley Jones in *The Way* writes: "When a young man, I preached in a Kentucky town on court day in the public square. A drunk stood near the box on which I stood and kept commenting to the crowd about my preaching. 'That young fellow makes me feel like crying.' He had a long stick upon which he leaned. At the close of the address I asked those who wanted to be converted to come to the mission. Among others, he came. I asked him if he wanted to be converted, and he replied, 'I'm drunk.' 'I know you are drunk,' I replied, 'but God can change you.' 'If you say so, it must be so,' he replied, and we bowed in prayer. As I was praying, he opened his eyes with a surprised look in them and said, 'Why He has saved me! And I am drunk too!' He arose and handed me his whisky bottle, saying, 'I don't want that.' I threw it out the window. He handed me his stick, upon which he leaned for support, and said, 'I don't need that either.' And he walked out of there perfectly straight. God had not only saved him; He had sobered him as well."

2269. Robert Louis Stevenson wrote: "Everybody soon or late sits down to a banquet of consequences."

2270. On the day in 1874 that David Livingstone was buried in Westminster Abbey, the streets of London were lined with thousands seeking to pay respect to the memory of the pioneer missionary.

In the crowd was noticed a poor old man, unkempt, poorly clad, weeping bitterly. Someone went up and asked him why he was weeping when all were seeking to honor the illustrious dead. "I'll tell you why," the sad old man replied. "Davie and I were born in the same village, brought up in the day school and Sunday school, worked together at the same loom. But Davie went *that* way and I went *this*; now he is honored by the nation, and I am neglected, unknown, and dishonored. I have nothing to look forward to but a drunkard's grave."

2271. A man past middle life went to Dante Gabriel Rossetti, taking with him some sketches and drawings. The fumes of liquor were on his breath; his eyes were bloodshot, his hands unsteady. Rossetti saw at a glance that the drawings were hopeless, and told him so. For a moment the visitor hesitated. Then he drew from an inside pocket another portfolio of drawings, saying they were the work of a young student. Rossetti was delighted and asked that the youth be sent to him. "Ah, sir," said the man, "I am, or rather I was, that youth. Your words, sir, have only confirmed my own suspicions. I have thrown away my best talents."

2272. A man promised a pastor that he would not drink again. After the pledge had been taken, the man appeared in the late evening and said he must be allowed to drink or he would die. The pastor told him to go home and die, and went on with his work. The next day the man appeared with a new confidence in his face and said, "I died last night."

2273. A man who had been a pitiful victim of drink said to W. S. Abernethy: "I have at last conquered the habit. It will never bother me again. I don't even pray about it any more."

2274. When asked why he put the words rags and bottles together in his call, "Any rags and bottles?" a ragman said: "Wherever you find bottles, you find rags."

2275. The shoemaker was a strict teetotaler, but this did not prevent him from being very good friends with the landlord of the local pub. One night he passed the inn doors just as the landlord emerged struggling with a hefty customer. "Give me a hand to get Bill here home!" he shouted. The shoemaker laughed and shook his head. "Not I, Jim," he replied. "You do as I do when I've done a really good job—just stick him up in the window for an advertisement."

2276. "Do you drink?" one man asked another. "That is my business, sir." "Have you any other business?" asked the first, by which he wished to discover whether a man who drinks much has any other business.

2277. When William Jennings Bryan attended a banquet honoring a Japanese admiral in Japan, he toasted the naval leader with water. When someone near by told him that such a toast would be regarded as an insult, Bryan said: "You have won victories on water, and I drink your health in water; whenever you win on champagne, I will drink health in champagne."

TEMPTATION

2278. Temple Gairdner said about a certain temptation: "Take it out into the desert with Christ and throttle it."

2279. "My temptations," said Martin Luther, "have been my masters in divinity."

2280. An old sea captain in a novel by Conan Doyle, *Micah Clarke,* explains his personal precaution against temptation by saying: "God is a pilot in course; when I had a pilot aboard o' my ship, however, it was always my way to keep my own weather eye open, d'ye see? The Pilot don't think none the worse of ye for it."

2281. Thomas A. Edison, when asked how he resisted temptations, said: "Never have any. I don't have time."

TEN COMMANDMENTS

2282.

In vain we call old notions fudge,
  And bend our conscience to our dealing;
The Ten Commandments will not budge,
  And stealing *will* continue stealing.
      —JAMES RUSSELL LOWELL,
      "International Copyright"

2283. When a boy was asked if he had learned the Ten Commandments, he replied: "I was going to learn them, but I heard talk that they were going to do away with them."

TENDERNESS

2284. On one occasion Andrew Bonar and Robert McCheyne, who were Scottish divines, were discussing their work. McCheyne asked Bonar what his theme had been the preceding Sunday. Bonar replied: "The wicked shall be turned into hell." Quickly McCheyne came back with the question: "Were you able to preach it with tenderness?"—RALPH W. SOCKMAN, *The Highway of God*

2285. Leonardo da Vinci is reported to have made the face of Judas in his famous painting "The Last Supper" similar to the appearance of a personal enemy. Tradition says that the painter found considerable trouble in painting the face of Jesus and succeeded only after he had painted out the face of Judas, reconciled himself with his enemy. You cannot paint the face of Jesus for an evil world, either actually or in a poetic sense, unless you have his spirit.

TEXT

2286. What converted Charles H. Spurgeon was not the Methodist lay preacher's sermon in the chapel at Colchester; it was the text—"Look unto me, and be ye saved, all the ends of the earth." "He had not much to say, thank God," declared Spurgeon afterward, "for that compelled him to keep on repeating his text, and there was nothing needed— by me, at any rate—except his text."

2287. The text from which John Bunyan preached to the multitudes—John 6:37. The text that saved William Cowper from suicide—Rom. 3:24, 25. The text that made Martin Luther the hero of the Reformation—Rom. 1:17. The text that comforted the troubled soul of John Wesley—Mark 12:34. The text that made David Livingstone a missionary—Matt. 28:19-20. The text to which John Knox anchored his soul —John 17:3. The text that gave William Carey a world vision—Isa. 54:2. The text that made William Penn a conqueror—I John 5:4. The text on which Michael Faraday staked everything— II Tim. 1:12.

THANKFULNESS

2288. George Washington in his first Thanksgiving Day proclamation said in part: "We unite in most humbly offering our prayers and supplications to the Great Lord and Ruler of nations and beseech him to pardon our national and other transgressions; to enable us all, whether in public or in private station, to perform our several and relative duties properly and punctually; to protect and guide all sovereigns and nations, and to bless them with good government, peace. and concord; to promote the knowledge and practice of true religion and virtue; and generally to grant unto all mankind such a degree of temporal prosperity as he alone knows to be best. Amen."

2289. There is a legend about two angels who were sent to earth to gather up the prayers of men. One was to fill his basket with the petitions of mankind. The other was to gather their prayers of thanksgiving. Some time later they went back to their Father's house. One had a basket heaped high and running over with the innumerable petitions of men. The other returned with a sad and heavy heart, for his basket was almost empty.

2290. An arresting sentence in *Ben Hur* by Lew Wallace reads: "In thankfulness for present mercies nothing so becomes us as losing sight of past ills."

2291. "Were there no God," Christina Rossetti exclaimed, "we would be in this glorious world with grateful hearts: and no one to thank."

2292. In St. Mary's Church at Cambridge, England, there is a hassock with these words embroidered on it: "Think —Thank." If we stopped to think more, we would stop to thank more.

2293. Long years ago, the historian tells us, our Pilgrim ancestors had the custom of putting five grains of corn upon each empty plate before the Thanksgiving dinner was served. In answer to the questions of their children the parents explained that their forefathers had come to such dire straits that there was an allowance per person of five grains of corn to eat each day.

2294. An old Scotch woman, when first she saw the sea, exclaimed: "I thank God for one thing of which there is enough."

THEFT

2295. When a woman dismissed her maid, she explained: "I had to dismiss her. I found that she was stealing those lovely Waldorf-Astoria towels I had." —E. STANLEY JONES, *Abundant Living*

2296. A father took his small son with him when he went to a neighbor's field to steal potatoes. Cautiously the father looked one way and then another before he climbed the fence. "Daddy," the son said, "you forgot something—you didn't look up."

THINKING

2297. "No one can think deeply," said Samuel Johnson, "without thinking religiously."

2298. "I study Portuguese while shaving," Shelley said by way of explanation of his time schedule. "I translate Spanish for an hour before breakfast. I read all the forenoon and write all the afternoon; every minute of the day is filled with something." An old Quaker who was listening to this report broke in to ask: "Friend, when doth thee do thy thinking?"

2299. "Learn to think," wrote an ancient. "It will profit you well, for there is so little competition."

2300. An unknown writer has said: "Five per cent of the people think; ten per cent think they think; and the rest would rather die than think."

2301. Someone has said: "You can lead a student to college, but you can't make him think."

2302. When Francis Bacon was asked what he thought was the outlook for the next generation, he declared: "Tell me what the young people are thinking, and I'll tell you."

2303.
I hold it true that thoughts are things
Endowed with body, breath, and wings.
And that we send them forth to fill
The world with good results or ill.

That what we call our secret thought
Flies to the earth's remotest spot,
Leaving its blessings or its woes
Like tracks behind it as it goes.
—Author Unknown

THOUGHTFULNESS

2304. An old blind man always carried a lantern. When someone asked him why he, a blind man, carried a lantern, he replied: "I carry a lantern to keep people who can see from bumping into me."

2305. When Rudyard Kipling and his wife lived in a farmhouse on the slope of a mountain in Vermont, they were asked by a woman who lived in a small house across the valley: "Be you the windows across the valley?" She told them the comfort that the lights from Kipling's house had always given her. "Be you going to stay and keep your lights burning or maybe be you not?" she asked. After that the Kiplings took down the curtains and shades on the back windows of their home that the light might shine the more brightly through the night.—Jessie Crawford

2306. Every time a fast transcontinental train passed a rather desolate homestead in the Midwest, a porter threw from the train a bundle of magazines and newspapers. When an interested passenger asked the porter why he did this, he replied: "Well, I thought they were lonely 'way out here and perhaps they'd like some reading matter. So I've been supplying them with reading matter for months now."

TIME

2307. Arnold Bennett wrote: "The supply of time is a daily miracle. . . . You wake up in the morning, and lo! your purse is magically filled with twenty-four hours of the unmanufactured tissue of the universe of life. It is yours! the most precious of your possessions."

2308.
    What time is it?
    Time to do well,
    Time to live better,
    Give up that grudge,
    Answer that letter,
Speak the kind word to sweeten a
        sorrow,
Do that kind deed you would leave till
        tomorrow.
            —Author Unknown,
            "What Time Is It?"

2309. "You cannot kill time without injuring eternity," cautioned Henry Thoreau.

2310. A change came in the preaching of Thomas Chalmers in the manse of Kilmany when he affirmed: "Mathematician that I was, I had forgotten two magnitudes—the shortness of time and the vastness of eternity."

2311. A prominent surgeon advised his interns: "Gentlemen, let us not hurry; we have no time to lose."

2312. "Where does the time go!" exclaimed a weary mother. "Why, Mother," her small daughter replied, "the time goes into all the things you do."

TODAY

2313. The following inscription on the back of an old bronze ox that stands on the beach at Kun Ming Lake in Japan was written eight centuries before Christ:

This little strip of light 'twixt night and
    night
Let me keep bright today,
And let no shadow of tomorrow
In sorrow from the dead yesterday
Gainsay my happiness today.
And if tomorrow shall be sad
Or never come at all,
I've had, at least, today.

2314.
Happy the man, and happy he alone,
He who can call today his own;
He who, secure within, can say,
"Tomorrow, do thy worst, for I have
    lived today.
Be fair or foul, or rain or shine,
The joys I have possessed, in spite of
    fate, are mine.
Not heaven itself upon the past has
    power,
But what has been, has been, and I
    have had my hour.
         —HORACE, "To Maecenas"

2315. "The flowers of all the tomorrows are in the seeds of today," says a Chinese proverb.

2316. Dr. William Osler, the surgeon, wrote: "The load of tomorrow, added to that of yesterday, carried today, makes the strongest falter. We must learn to shut off the future as tightly as the past."

2317.
I have no Yesterdays,
    Time took them away;
Tomorrow may not be—
    But I have Today.
       —PEARL YEADON McGINNIS

TOMORROW

2318. During World War II a cartoon appeared on the editorial page of a Washington, D. C., newspaper. Instead of showing animated figures, this cartoon was a complete black square. The title read: "The World of Tomorrow."

2319. The Chinese word for "tomorrow" is composed of two words, "bright day."

TREE

2320. On Long's Peak in the American Rockies there grew a huge tree which fell to earth not long ago. Experts said it was a mere sapling when Columbus discovered America, and it was two hundred years old when the Pilgrim Fathers landed on the eastern coast. Lightning had struck it fourteen times in vain, and it had survived hurricanes and avalanches for more than four hundred years. But it fell at last when countless tiny beetles penetrated its trunk and reduced its great heart to dust.—W. S. DANIELS

2321. The noblest tree in America may be the redwood named "General Sherman," which stands 285 feet high, 36 feet in diameter, and is 5,000 years old. It is still growing. When Moses was cradled in the Nile, this tree was then 1,000 years old. "These giant redwoods," said a keeper, "never acknowledge death." When asked the reason, he replied that it is because their roots reach out so far in every direction and are intertwined with the roots of other trees. —RAYMOND L. CORTNER

TROUBLE

2322. Dean W. R. Inge has said: "Worry is interest paid on trouble before it comes due."

2323. In one of Robert Louis Stevenson's letters he refers to days of depression when he saved himself by saying: "I must get out my wings."

2324. On an old dilapidated mantel these words were carved: "I am an old man and have had many troubles, but most of them never happened."

2325. The worst evil which man must endure, Disraeli thought, is the anticipation of the calamities that never happen.

2326.
Some of your hurts you have cured,
　And the sharpest you still have survived,
But what torments of grief you endured
　From evils that never arrived!
　　—RALPH WALDO EMERSON,
　　"Borrowing"

2327. A double bassoon player went to Toscanini a few moments before a symphony was to commence. He complained that his instrument was out of order and that it could not reach the note of E-flat. Toscanini bent his head in thought for a moment. Then he smiled at the musician and said: "That's all right. The note of E-flat does not appear in your music tonight."

2328. Wallace Irwin tells the following story: "Suppose that this here vessel," said the skipper with a groan, "should lose 'er bearings, run away, and jump upon a stone? Suppose she'd shiver and go down, when save ourselves we couldn't?" The mate replied: "Oh, blow me eyes! Suppose again she shouldn't?"

2329.
Count each affliction, whether light or
　grave,
God's messenger sent down to thee; do
　thou
With courtesy receive him; rise and
　bow;
And, ere his shadow pass thy threshold,
　crave
Permission first his heavenly feet to
　lave;
Then lay before him all thou hast.
　　—AUBREY DE VERE, "Sorrow"

2330. "How do you manage to keep fit under all this work and worry?" a friend asked Lloyd George during World War I. "Oh," said the prime minister, "with me a change of trouble is as good as a vacation."

2331. Two men rested at the top of a high mountain. The first man turned to the second climber and said: "What brings you 'way up here? That's a tough climb." "Well, it's like this," the second man said. "All my troubles and heartaches are down in that little valley, and when I'm down there, they seem pretty big. But up here they seem pretty small, especially when I see what a little bit of these big mountains my little valley is."—DON IAN SMITH

2332. An old German legend tells of a baron who built his castle on the Rhine. From crag to crag and from turret to turret he hung wires, hoping that the winds as they blew upon this great aeolian harp might make sweet music. Long and patiently he waited, and round his castle winds from the four corners of heaven blew, and still no music came. But one night there arose a hurricane, tossing the Rhine to fury; the black sky was stabbed with lightning, and the thunder rolled, the earth trembled, and the winds were mad and shrieking. The baron went to his great castle door to view the terrifying scene— and hark! the sound of music like angels singing through the storm. And suddenly he realized what had happened. His harp, strung from crag to crag, had come to life at last. The tempest had given it a soul. That oft-told tale goes down to the heart of life's deep mystery. How often it is that only when trouble comes does a man's true quality stand revealed. — JAMES S. STEWART

2333. William H. Ridgeway of Coatsville, Pennsylvania, tells of a Negro minister friend who asked him what he regarded as the most comforting verse in the Bible. After thinking a moment Ridgeway asked, "What is it?" " 'And it came to pass,' " the friend answered. "But that is not a Bible verse. It is only the beginning of one." "No," said the Negro minister, "those are the most comfortingest words in the Bible to me. It didn't come to stay — 'it came to pass.' "

2334.
What secret trouble stirs thy heart?
    Why all this fret and flurry?
Dost thou not know that what is best
In this too restless world is rest
    From overwork and hurry?
—HENRY WADSWORTH LONGFELLOW

TRUTH

2335. When workers in marble in ancient Rome accidentally chipped their statues, they would fill in the chipped places with wax of the same color as the marble and then sell their work as perfectly wrought. Other statue makers, wishing to sell honest products, stamped their product *sine cera* (without wax). From this custom has come the modern word "sincere."

2336. "When once I had seen the truth," said Euripides, "there was no drug that I could take to unsee it and lose again what I had seen."

2337. A short time before his death Sir Isaac Newton wrote: "I do not know what I may appear to the world, but to myself I seem to have been only like a boy playing on the seashore, and diverting myself in now and then finding a smoother pebble or a prettier shell than ordinary, whilst the great ocean of truth lay all undiscovered before me."

2338. The night before Woodrow Wilson made his address to Congress taking us into World War I, he, in conference with Frank Cobb, editor of the New York *World,* said: "From now on we shall not be able to tell the truth."— EDGAR DEWITT JONES, *Blundering into Paradise*

U

UNAWARE

2339. Several years ago a man in South Africa who was especially frugal refused to pay delivery charges for a box which had been shipped from England. The box stayed in the express office for several years, used upon occasion as a footstool. After the man's death the box was sold at an auction, and the purchaser opened the unclaimed box to find that it contained several thousand pounds sterling in English bank notes.

2340. Gold was discovered in South Africa when a traveler saw native boys casually playing games with nuggets.

2341. When the talented organist of Freiburg Cathedral became too old to play, they made him the custodian of the organ with full charge of the keys. A visitor one day asked for permission to play the famous old organ, but the custodian explained that no one but the organist and he were ever permitted to touch the keyboard. But the visitor was so insistent that after a time the old man reluctantly gave his consent. Soon the old cathedral was filled with glorious music. The old musician-custodian was surprised and thrilled. When the organist had finished, the old man asked his name, and the visitor replied: "I am Felix Mendelssohn." It is said that to the end of his days the old custodian often exclaimed: "Felix Mendelssohn—and I almost refused to let him play!"—Frank B. Fagerburg

UNDERSTANDING

2342. In one of Mrs. Humphrey Ward's novels one character says to another, "I thought, Elizabeth, you would understand me." Her friend answers, "That, Lucy, is something only your Maker could do. And sometimes God himself must be puzzled on account of you."

2343.
Flower in the crannied wall,
I pluck you out of the crannies,
I hold you here, root and all, in my hand,
Little flower—but if I could understand
What you are, root and all, and all in all,
I should know what God and man is.
—Tennyson,
"Flower in the Crannied Wall"

UNIVERSE

2344. When asked what question above all others he would wish an answer for, Ernst Haeckel, a German scientist and philosopher, replied: "The question I would most like to see answered is this, *Is the universe friendly?*"

2345. A contemporary atheist has shown the frustration of those who think as he does when he says: "Man is left more and more alone in a universe to which he is completely alien."

2346. James Russell Lowell said that "the universe is fireproof, and it is quite safe to strike a match."

2347. G. K. Chesterton has been quoted as saying: "When I go to engage lodgings, I do not inquire of the landlady, 'Where is the room located, how many windows has it, or what will be the charge?' But rather I say, 'Madam, what is your view of the universe?' If she is right there, she will be right in everything, and if she is wrong there, it does not matter what she says about other things."

USE

2348. A national broadcasting company some time ago received this letter from an old sheepherder in the hills of Idaho: "I enjoy your programs every week, and I want to ask a favor of you. It is rather lonely up here in the hills, and I have not much to amuse me except my radio. I used to play my old violin, but now it is badly out of tune. I wonder if you would be kind enough to pause on your next program to strike 'A' so that I might tune my violin and enjoy its music again." On the next program the announcer repeated the sheepherder's request to a nation-wide audience, and then 'A' was sounded that the violinist might get the right pitch.

2349. An interested spectator watched an artist sketching a landscape. When the artist skillfully interpreted the broad sweeping horizon, the spectator asked what was the secret of his success. "You must eliminate the unessential," the artist said.

2350. When Fritz Kreisler found a violin in a private collection, he asked the owner if he might play it. Finally, although reluctantly, he consented. "I played that day as though to ransom a captive," Kreisler said. When the master finished, the collector realized that such an instrument should not remain mute in a case but should be used.

2351. When Michael Faraday showed his first toy dynamo to a lady, she asked: "What use is it?" The inventor asked in reply: "What use is a newborn baby?"

2352. One of the finest pearl specimens is the famous "Thiers Necklace," which contains 145 finely graded, rose-pink pearls. Madam Thiers willed this necklace to the French government, and it was placed in a museum and never worn. In time the pearls lost their color and luster. A "pearl mother" was found who fondled them and wore them publicly under guard, and their beauty returned.—Clarence M. Gallup

2353. When George Washington Carver first set out to do something with certain abandoned farm lands, his friends said that the soil was unproductive. "It is the only soil I have," Carver said, "and it's not unproductive; it's just not used."

USELESSNESS

2354. The King of Siam, in other days, when he wished to ruin some courtier who had lost his favor, would present the courtier with a white elephant. It was only a king who could afford to keep such a monstrous pet, and the attempt to keep the elephant presented by the king would soon bring the new owner to bankruptcy.

2355. Charles Dickens has told the story about a man who was digging in his backyard and suddenly broke through the crust of the earth and fell into the world inside. There he found a very strange state of affairs. Every person was born physically perfect, but when he reached a certain age he lost all those parts of his body which he had not used. There was a hack driver with only a huge pair of hands and a distended stomach. There was a lawyer who had lost everything but his massive jaw. Two society girls were just bundles of nerves and blazing eyes. The old schoolmaster had nothing left but his heart.— J. W. HAWLEY, *These Prophetic Voices*

2356. When the artist Donatello would not accept a certain block of marble from the quarry in Florence because it was imperfect, Michelangelo took the rejected stone and carved from it his famous statue of David.

2357. One day Michelangelo found a piece of rough marble cast aside as useless. When told that no good thing could be wrought from it, Michelangelo said: "It certainly is not useless. Send it around to my studio. There is an angel imprisoned within it, and I must set it free."

2358. An old dictionary defines "uranium" as "a rare, heavy, white metallic element, . . . has no important uses."

V

VALUE

2359. H. C. Hony, an Englishman, some time ago took an old family heirloom from the wall of his home and sent it to be cleaned of dust and grime. When the cleaners removed the dirt, they were amazed to find the painting was by Thomas Gainsborough, whose "Blue Boy" brought the highest price ever paid for a painting. Hony was told that his painting, long considered no more than a family heirloom, was worth perhaps as much as half a million dollars.

2360. The story is told of a poor woman who applied to the Sultan of Turkey and asked for compensation for the loss of her property. "How did you lose it?" he inquired. "I fell asleep and robbers came and stole it." "But why did you fall asleep?" he queried. "I fell asleep because I believed that you were awake," was the astonishing reply. The sultan was pleased with her trust, it is said, and returned her goods.

2361. One of the many stories told concerning the sinking of the "Titanic" relates that a woman was given three minutes to return to her room for her valuables. She came back, not with money and jewels, but with three oranges. An hour before she would not have given anything for a crate of oranges, but death had boarded the ship, and suddenly oranges became more valuable than gold or jewels.

VICTORY

2362. When Nelson sent home to England his dispatches following the battle of the Nile, he wrote: "Victory is not a name strong enough for such a scene as this."

2363. Returning from battle Henry IV sighted a French nobleman named Crillon standing by the road. "Go hang yourself, Crillon!" the king exclaimed. "We had a great victory at Arques, and you were not there."

2364. A biographer tells how Ralph Waldo Emerson bore the tragic death of his young wife and two brothers, and the resignation from his church: "A doom seemed to hover over his family. Under the surface of his life, dark as it was at the moment, a purpose was taking form in his mind; he knew that he was born for victory."

VISION

2365. "A task without a vision is drudgery; a vision without a task is a dream; a task with a vision is victory," says an unknown writer.

2366. H. G. Wells in *The Research Magnificent* tells of a young man who saw life "as a succession of days . . . that became steadily more crowded with ignoble and trivial occupations. . . . Then suddenly he reached out his arms in the darkness and prayed aloud: 'O God, give me back my visions!' "

2367.
> The wicked and the weak, by some
>   dark law,
> Have a strange power to shut and rivet
>   down
> Their own horizons round us, to un-
>   wing
> Our heaven-aspiring visions.
>   —JAMES RUSSELL LOWELL

2368. John Henry Jowett in his Yale lectures on preaching tells of visiting a cobbler in Wales and asking if he did not feel cramped in his very small quarters. "No," said the man. Then he bade the preacher follow him to a window that opened toward the sea. "When I feel tired and cramped, I look through that window and it steadies me." His little room suggested world horizons.—ALEXANDER L. FRASER

2369. When someone asked the great Italian painter Raphael how he painted such wonderful pictures, he answered: "I simply dream dreams and see visions, and then I paint around those dreams and visions."

2370. "Who keeps one end in view makes all things serve," wrote Robert Browning.

2371. "A fanatic," George Santayana has said, "is one who, having lost sight of his aim, redoubles his effort."

W

WAR

2372. Sir Edward Grey, watching a lamplighter at work on a London street, just as World War I was beginning, said: "The lamps are going out all over Europe, and we shall not see them lit again in our lifetime."

2373. Napoleon used to say of his favorite general, Marshal Saxe: "I like him; he loses battles but wins wars."

Futility of War

2374. Once upon a time in the Middle Ages a Belgian peasant set out from his village for the fair at near-by Ciney. There he stole a cow which he took to another town. The owner of the animal followed him and was fortunate enough to meet his feudal lord, to whom he complained about the robbery. This mighty and righteous man told the thief that if he returned the cow, he would be forgiven. The peasant obeyed, but no sooner had he set foot on the territory of Ciney than he was arrested and hanged. The feudal lord to whom the peasant had paid allegiance took this unfair procedure as a personal offense and immediately attacked Ciney in force. At once the people of Huy, the Duke of Brabant, the counts of Flanders, Namur, and Luxemburg joined the fight. The War of the Cow of Ciney was waged for three years, during which twenty thousand people were killed.

2375. Ernest Hemingway, a distinguished American novelist, came back from the war to say: "I had seen nothing sacred, and the things that were glorious had no glory, and the sacrifices were like the stockyards at Chicago if nothing was done with the meat except to bury it."

2376.
Peace upon earth was said; we sing it
And pay a million priests to bring it.
After two thousand years of mass,
We've got as far as poison gas.[1]
—THOMAS HARDY, *Christmas, 1924*

Opposition to War

2377. One of the strongest satires against war is that which Mark Twain wrote in the form of a prayer: "O Lord our God, help us to tear their soldiers to bloody shreds with our shells; help us to cover their smiling fields with the pale forms of their patriot dead; help us to drown the thunder of the guns with the wounded, writhing in pain; help us to lay waste their humble homes with a hurricane of fire; help us to wring the hearts of their unoffending widows with unavailing grief; help us to turn them out rootless with their little children to wander unfriended through wastes of their desolated land . . . —for our sakes, who adore thee, Lord, blast their hopes, blight their lives, protract their bitter pilgrimage, make heavy their steps, water their way with their tears, stain the white snow with the blood of their wounded feet! We ask of one

[1] From *Winter Words.* Copyright 1928 by Florence E. Hardy and S. E. Cockrell. Used by permission of the Hardy Estate, The Macmillan Co., and Macmillan & Co., Ltd., London.

who is the Spirit of love and who is the ever faithful refuge and friend of all that are sore beset, and seek his aid with humble and contrite hearts. Grant our prayer, O Lord, and thine shall be the praise and honor and glory now and ever. Amen."

2378. Croesus, King of Lydia, is reported by Herodotus in 409 B.C. to have said to Cyrus the Persian: "No man is so foolish as to desire war more than peace; for in peace sons bury their fathers, but in war fathers bury their sons."

2379. When George Fox was offered a captaincy with the Puritans in their Parliamentary struggle, he refused to participate in warfare, saying that he "lived in virtue of that life and power which took away the occasion of all war."

2380. "I once talked to an old cannibal who, hearing of the Great War raging then in Europe, was most curious to know how we Europeans managed to eat such enormous quantities of human flesh," says Bronislaw Malinowski. "When I told him that Europeans do not eat their slain foes, he looked at me in shocked horror and asked what sort of barbarians we were to kill without any real object."

2381. Sir Douglas Haig after World War I told a group of clergymen in Scotland: "It is your business to put my business out of business."

2382. A British sergeant on the Somme has said that through those long months when the two battle lines kept up their continuous exchange of shells he could not get away from the feeling that Christ was out between the lines and that the shot passed through his body. Certainly

war between fellow Christians pierces and tears the Body of Christ, which is the church.—HENRY SLOANE COFFIN

2383. A Y.M.C.A. secretary held by the Japanese after the nonviolent Independent Movement in Korea in 1918 was asked: "Do you know who started this revolution?" He answered: "Yes. God."

WASHINGTON

2384. The inscription at Mount Vernon reads:

Washington, the brave, the wise, the good,
Supreme in war, in council, and in peace,
Valiant without ambition, discreet without fear,
Confident without presumption.
In disaster, calm; in success, moderate; in all, himself.
The hero, the patriot, the Christian.
The father of nations, the friend of mankind,
Who, when he had won all, renounced all,
Then sought in the bosom of his family and of nature, retirement,
And in the hope of religion, immortality.

2385. The Washington Monument, one of the tallest monuments in the world, was built of 179 stones from various states, nations, cities, and organizations. At the top of the shaft is a pyramid of pure aluminum. On this metal tip are inscribed the Latin words "Laus Deo," meaning "Praise to God."

WEAKNESS

2386. "What a noble animal," said the Man as he gazed at the Lion. "What strength! What magnificence! No wonder every other animal quails at the thought of him; no wonder every other animal admits him to be the King of

Beasts." "Confound that Flea!" said the Lion as he made one more attempt to rid himself of his tormentor.

2387. "Whatever weakens your reason, impairs the tenderness of your conscience, obscures your sense of God, or takes off the relish of spiritual things, that is sin to you," wrote Susannah Wesley.

2388. One of Wesley's biographers judges: "Probably no public speaker ever ascended a soapbox with greater hesitation: certainly no public speaker ever stood on one with greater power."

WISDOM

2389. A motto on the wall of a business establishment reads:

To know what to do is wisdom.
To know how to do it is skill.
To do the thing as it should be done is service.

2390.
Wisdom is not finally tested in the schools,
Wisdom cannot be pass'd from one having it to another not having it,
Wisdom is of the soul, is not susceptible of proof, is its own proof.
　　　　—WALT WHITMAN,
　　　　　　"Song of the Open Road"

WONDER

2391. "I would sooner live in a cottage and wonder at everything," said John Ruskin, "than live in Warwick Castle and wonder at nothing."

2392. Carlyle in Sartor Resartus wrote: "The man who cannot wonder, who does not habitually wonder (and worship), were he president of innumerable Royal Societies, and carried the whole Mécanique Céleste and Hegel's Philosophy, and the epitome of all laboratories and observations with their results in his single head, is but a pair of spectacles behind which there is no eye."

WORDS

2393. In The Terrible Meek, Charles Rann Kennedy has the Roman captain speak: "There is great power in words. All the things that ever get done in the world, good or bad, are done by words."

2394. G. K. Chesterton suggested: "The world is filled with the knowledge of the last word, but knows nothing of the first word."

2395. "Some men never speak a wise word, yet do wisely," said Sir Thomas Overbury. "Some on the other hand do never a wise deed and yet speak wisely."

2396.
On wings of deeds the soul must mount!
　When we are summoned from afar,
Ourselves, and not our words, will count—
　Not what we said, but what we are!
　　　　—WILLIAM WINTER,
　　　　　　"George Fawcett Rowe"

WORK

2397.
This for the day of life I ask:
Some all-absorbing useful task;
And when 'tis wholly, truly done,
A tranquil rest at set of sun.
　　　　—AUTHOR UNKNOWN

2398. The following is "The Worker's Pledge" written by Washington Gladden: "One thing I am resolved upon: I will not be a sponge or a parasite. I will give an honest equivalent for what I get. I want no man's money for which I have not rendered a full return. I want no wages that I have not earned. If I work for any man or any company or any institution, I will render a full, ample, generous service. If I work for the city or the state or the nation, I will give my best thought, my best effort, my most conscientious and efficient endeavor. No man, no body of men shall ever be made poor by their dealings with me. If I can give a little more than I get every time, in that shall be my happiness. The great commonwealth of human society shall not be the loser through me. I will take good care to put into the common fund more than I take out."

Enjoyment of Work

2399. Charles Eliot, onetime president of Harvard, once confessed, many years after he had assumed his position as head of the university, that his job no longer offered him either novelty or fresh interest. He went so far as to say that nine tenths of it had become sheer routine, as dull and monotonous to him as the work of carpenters and blacksmiths is to them.

2400. On the wall of his office Dr. Charles Mayo kept the following motto: "There is no fun like work." Of these words Mayo wrote: "I have always liked that motto, for I believe in it. To be without work is almost to be without life. For it is work which creates interest in life."

2401. "It is not doing the thing which we like to do," Goethe wrote, "but liking to do the thing which we have to do, that makes life blessed."

2402. Archibald Rutledge once watched one of his Negro workmen making a thing of clean shining beauty out of a rusty, filthy old tugboat engine and asked him how he succeeded in doing it.

The Negro replied: "Well, it's this way —I got a glory."

Purpose of Work

2403. A spectator watched three men at work. "What are you doing?" he asked the first man. "Working for ten shillings a day." He asked the second man the same question. "Cutting stone." But when he asked the third man, the answer was: "Building a cathedral."

2404. When friends told Louis Pasteur that he was overworking, the scientist replied: "It would seem to me that I was committing a theft if I were to let one day go by without doing some work."

2405. Henry Ford has told of the purpose behind the first automobile with these words: "When we were building our first car, was it money we were thinking about? We realized, of course, that the new car—if it would run at all—would be profitable to manufacture. But making a fortune for ourselves was not in the front of our thoughts. What we wanted to do was build a car which would cost so little that every family in the United States would be able to buy it. So we worked morning, noon, and night. We worked till our muscles ached, worked till our nerves were so ragged that we could not endure the word 'automobile.' One day when all of us were near the breaking point I laid down my tools and said, 'Well, boys, there's one consolation anyway. Nobody can take this thing away from us unless he's willing to work on it harder than we've worked. And so far I haven't seen anyone who's willing to do that!' "

Satisfaction in Work

2406. Dr. George Washington Carver, when asked how he got started in his scientific discoveries, said: "I took a peanut and put it in my open hand and said, 'Mr. Creator, what's in that peanut?' and the Creator answered and said, 'You have brains. Go and find out.'"—E. STANLEY JONES, *Christ of the American Road*

2407. In his later years Sir Christopher Wren, designer of many of the finest churches in London, built a house for himself on a hill near the city. From his new home he could look toward London and see the dome of his finished masterpiece, St. Paul's Cathedral. He said that the satisfaction found in looking back upon his lifework was a great joy.

2408. Michelangelo the great Italian sculptor and architect, once said, "It is only well with me when I have a chisel in my hand."

2409. "Yours must be a dog's life!" someone said to a traffic officer at a busy intersection. "It would be if I were a dog," the policeman answered. "But I'm not a dog; I'm a saver of lives. Already I've saved three today, right here at this corner. How many have you saved?" —ROY L. SMITH

2410.
No man is born into the world whose work
Is not born with him; there is always work,
And tools to work withal, for those who will;
And blessed are the horny hands of toil!
   —JAMES RUSSELL LOWELL,
   "A Glance Behind the Curtain"

2411. The story was told by Plato that the spirits of the other world came back to find bodies and places to work. One took the body of a poet and did his work. Finally Ulysses came and said: "All the fine bodies have been taken and all the grand work done. There is nothing for me." "Yes," said a voice, "the best has been left for you—the body of a common man, doing a common work for a common reward."

WORLD

2412. George Jackson in *First Things First* tells how one of his colleagues at a church meeting cried out: "Mr. Chairman, I move we move the world," to which Jackson replied: "The early Christians not only moved the world; they turned it upside down."

2413. Rufus M. Jones wrote: "It is not accident that wherever we point the telescope we see beauty, that wherever we look with the microscope there we find beauty. It beats in through every nook and cranny of the mighty world."

2414. William Makepeace Thackeray in *Vanity Fair* wrote: "The world is a looking glass and gives back to every man the reflection of his own face. Frown at it, and it will in turn look sourly upon you; laugh at it and with it, and it is a jolly kind companion."

2415. A boy was given a jigsaw puzzle by his father. The puzzle was a map of the world. In a very short time the boy had completed the puzzle and showed it to his father. When asked how he finished so difficult a task in such a brief time, the boy said: "On the back of the puzzle was the picture of a man. I figured that if I got the man right, I could get the world right."

2416. Someone, speaking of the author of "The Hound of Heaven," said: "It was the tragedy of Francis Thompson's life that he never felt at home in this world." To this a second person rejoined: "It is our tragedy that we do."

2417. When a friend questioned Henry Thoreau during his last illness concerning his faith in the hereafter, the New England poet-philosopher said: "One world at a time, brother, one world at a time!"

2418. "There are two worlds: the world that we can measure with line and rule, and the world that we feel with our hearts and imaginations," wrote Leigh Hunt.

Better World

2419. One of the characters in *Faraway* by J. B. Priestly says: "It's not a matter of Englishmen and Frenchmen. . . . It's a matter of men and women. . . . Every time you ignore national boundaries you bring the possibility of a sane, happy, peaceful world a bit nearer. . . . I'm an Englishman, and I love England. . . . I owe a lot to England. But I owe still more to the world. . . . You say . . . let's do something for England for once. But I say, for God's sake, let's do something for civilization for once."

2420. "Confucianists do not try to change the order of the world," said a Chinese student attending an American college. "They conform to it."

2421. S. Parkes Cadman used to tell a Persian legend which pictured four angels watching God create the world. "Why did he make it?" said one. "How did he make it?" asked another. "Give it to me!" demanded the third. The fourth angel said nothing but eagerly went forth to make another world. The first represented the philosophical attitude, the second the scientific, the third the selfish, and the last the essentially religious and creative attitude whereby the Christian goes forth to make a better world.

2422. "We believe in a Christlike world," someone has written. "We can conceive of nothing better. We can be satisfied with nothing less."

2423. Lord Eustace Percy said: "A regenerated society can only be composed of regenerated men. To expect a change in human nature may be an act of faith; but to expect a change in human society without it is an act of lunacy."

2424. "The world," writes the English author H. M. Tomlinson, "is what we think it is. If we can change our thoughts, we can change the world. And that is our hope."

One World

2425. Inscribed on a monument to Brazilian Marshal Manuel Luiz Osario, are these words: "The happiest day of my life will be that day when they bring me the news that the civilized peoples are celebrating the festival of their brotherhood by burning down their arsenals."

2426. Virginia Woolf in *Three Guineas* wrote: "As long as there is a dictator, we cannot dissociate ourselves from that figure. We are it. It suggests that we are not passive spectators doomed to unresisting obedience, but by our thoughts and actions can ourselves change that figure. A common interest unites us: it is one world, one life."

2427. G. A. Studdert-Kennedy, onetime chaplain to George V, said after World War I: "You can't buck the universe. The world was meant to be a family. If you treat it as a battleground, everybody loses."

2428. During World War I, Lloyd George said, "When this war is over, this is going to be everybody's world."

WORRY

2429. "To worry about what we can't help is useless," someone has said. "To worry about what we can help is stupid."

2430.
Worry is an old man with bended head,
Carrying a load of feathers
Which he thinks are lead.
—Author Unknown

2431. An old Chinese proverb reads: "The legs of the stork are long, and the legs of the duck are short. You cannot shorten the legs of the stork, nor can you lengthen the legs of the duck. Why worry?"

WORSHIP

2432. The inscription on the Plymouth Rock monument is a challenge to every generation of Americans: "This spot marks the final resting place of the Pilgrims of the Mayflower. In weariness and hunger and in cold, fighting the wilderness and burying their dead in common graves that the Indians should not know how many had perished, they here laid the foundations of a state in which all men for countless ages should have liberty to worship God in their own way. All you who pass by and see this stone remember, and dedicate yourselves anew to the resolution that you will not rest until this lofty ideal shall have been realized *throughout the earth.*"

2433.
For worship
   is a thirsty land crying out for rain,
It is a candle in the act of being kindled,
It is a drop in quest of the ocean, . . .

It is a voice in the night calling for help,
It is a soul standing in awe before the
   mystery of the universe, . . .
It is time flowing into eternity,
. . . a man climbing the altar stairs to
God.
—Dwight Bradley

2434. "To worship," the late Dr. William Temple wrote, "is to quicken the conscience by the holiness of God, to feed the mind with the truth of God, to purge the imagination by the beauty of God, to open the heart to the love of God, to devote the will to the purpose of God."—*The Hope of a New World*

2435. The story is told of "Golden Rule Nash," a tailor in Cincinnati, who tried to run his business on the principle of the golden rule of Jesus. "I feel more in the spirit of worship when I come into this shop," he used to tell friends, "than I ever did in a church."

2436. "It is only when men begin to worship that they begin to grow," said Calvin Coolidge.

2437. Lyman Beecher Stowe in *Saints, Sinners and Beechers* told that on one occasion Thomas K. Beecher substituted for his famous brother, Henry Ward Beecher, at Plymouth Church, Brooklyn. Many of the people who had come to hear Henry became restless when Thomas appeared in the pulpit. Some started for the door. Thomas raised his voice and said: "All those who came here this morning to worship Henry Ward Beecher may now withdraw from the church. All who came to worship God may remain."

2438. The Allen Memorial Church in Shanghai is considered the Mother

Church of Methodism in China. One day the ministers of the Japanese Mission asked the Chinese Christians to permit them to use this historic church as a place of worship for the many Japanese soldiers stationed in Shanghai after the capture of the city. At first the Chinese hesitated, but after praying over the question granted full permission, saying: "We would not want the world to hear that the doors of our church had been closed to any group that wanted to worship God."—GRACE NOLL CROWELL

False Worship

2439. When Calvin Coolidge was asked, "Cannot I worship God in the green fields?" he answered: "You can, but you don't."

2440. A patient in a hospital for the mentally sick thought of himself as a God-maker. When visitors came to his ward, he would take from his locker a block of wood. The block was of cube shape and showed that great care had been taken that the edges should be square and the surface smooth. After showing the block the patient would say: "This is my God. I made him. I worship him daily." A doctor tried desperately to interpret to the patient the true meaning of God in an effort to show that man does not make his God but that God makes man. When the significance of this teaching was at last realized, the mental sickness passed.

WRONG

2441. G. K. Chesterton tells the story of an architect who so disliked an especially ugly house in London that he bought the building, moved in, and never left the house again. Of course this didn't change the ugliness of the house which other people had to continue to see each day.

2442. A member of the congregation almost upset a service of worship by first removing a shoe and then removing a sock. Asked the reason for such strange behavior, the member said: "I just noticed that one of my socks was on wrong side out. When I find I am wrong, I always proceed at once to get right."

2443. American Colonial history records a certain town meeting in a Massachusetts Bay Colony village. The people were called together to consider a resolution drawn up by the pastor of the village church in condemnation of a community evil. In speaking of this undesirable situation the resolution read: "It is wrong." One of the citizens asked: "Why did you not make the statement stronger?" The minister replied: "At first I wrote, 'It is exceedingly wrong,' then I took out the word 'exceedingly' to make it stronger."—BRUCE R. BAXTER

2444. It is said that the last entry in the diary of Alexander Hamilton, written on the eve of that ill-fated duel with Aaron Burr, was this: "I know this is wrong, but I am afraid not to do it."

Y

YOUTH

2445. Alexander the Great ascended the throne at twenty and conquered the known world by thirty-three. Julius Caesar at a young age captured eight hundred cities, conquered three hundred nations, defeated three million men, became a great orator and one of the greatest statesman known. Washington was appointed adjutant general at nineteen, was sent at twenty-one as an ambassador to treat with the French, and won his first battle as a colonel at twenty-two. Lafayette was made general of the whole French army at the age of twenty. Charlemagne was master of France and of Germany at thirty. Galileo was but eighteen when he saw the principle of the pendulum in the swinging lamp in the cathedral at Pisa. Peel was in Parliament at twenty-one. Gladstone was in Parliament before he was twenty-two and at twenty-four was Lord of the Treasury. Luther was but twenty-nine when he nailed his famous theses to the door of the cathedral and defied the pope. Shakespeare wrote his masterpieces at thirty-six.—ANDERSON M. BATEN, *The Philosophy of Success*

2446. Wrote Samuel Ullman: "Youth is not a time of life—it is a state of mind. It is not a matter of red cheeks, red lips, and supple knees. It is a temper of the will, a quality of the imagination, a vigor of the emotions; it is a freshness of the deep springs of life. Youth means a temperamental predominance of courage over timidity, of the appetite for adventure over a life of ease. This often exists in a man of fifty more than in a boy of twenty. Nobody grows old by merely living a number of years; people grow old by deserting their ideals."

2447. Great expressions of the faith of youth are to be found in the hymnal. Watts and Wesley were young men when they wrote some of their finest hymns. Joseph Grigg at ten wrote "Jesus, and Shall It Ever Be"; Milton at fifteen wrote "Let Us with a Gladsome Mind"; Anna L. Coghill, eighteen, "Work, for the Night Is Coming"; Arthur C. Coxe, twenty-one, "O Where Are Kings and Empires Now?"; Palmer, twenty-two, "My Faith Looks Up to Thee"; Howard A. Walter, twenty-three, "I Would Be True"; Samuel F. Smith, twenty-four, "My Country, 'Tis of Thee"; Samuel John Stone, twenty-six, "The Church's One Foundation"; and Newman, thirty-two, "Lead, Kindly Light."

2448. A tablet in Woolsey Hall, Yale University, honors more than two hundred Yale men who lost their lives in World War I with these words:

O youth foregone, foregoing!
    O dreams unseen, unsought!
God give you joy of knowing
    What life your death has bought.

Index of the Christian Year

Index of Children's Stories

Index of Hymn Stories

Index of Names

Abbott, Lyman (1835-1922, Am. clergyman, author, and editor), 323, 1141, 1261

Adams, John (1735-1826, second president of the U.S.), 33

Adams, John Quincy (1767-1848, sixth president of the U.S.), 12, 146, 1735

Addams, Jane (1860-1935, Am. social worker and peace advocate), 421, 1295, 1493

Adler, Alfred (1870-1937, Viennese psychologist), 308

Agassiz, Louis (1807-73, naturalist), 1723

Alexander the Great (356-323 B.C., world conqueror), 1759, 2258

Alford, Henry (1810-71, Eng. clergyman and scholar), 720

Allen, Hervey 1889-1949, Am. author), 470

Andersen, Hans Christian (1805-75, Dan. author), 1760, 1850

Anderson, Marian (contemp. Am. concert contralto), 1845, 1966

Applegarth, Margaret (contemp. Am. author), 781

Aristotle (384-322 B.C., Gk. philosopher), 44, 2072

Armstrong, Samuel Chapman (1839-93, Am. educator), 760

Arnold, Matthew (1822-88, Eng. poet and critic), 346, 348, 451

Asbury, Francis (1745-1816, Am. clergyman), 736, 1896

Atkins, Gaius Glenn (contemp. Am. clergyman), 2178

Augustine (354-430, Christian philosopher), 659, 726, 1157, 1222, 1244, 1332, 1742, 1876, 2097, 2207

Aurelius, Marcus (188-217, Roman emperor), 628, 914, 2212

Austen, Jane (1775-1817, Eng. author), 1901

Axling, William (contemp. Am. missionary), 416

Babcock, Maltbie (1858-1901, Am. clergyman and author), 1900

Babson, Roger (contemp. Am. financial statistician), 1638, 2209

Bach, Johann Sebastian (1685-1750, Ger. organist and composer), 1109

Bacon, Francis (1561-1626, Eng. philosopher and author), 560, 2302

Baden-Powell, Sir Robert (1857-1941, Eng. general and founder of the Boy Scout movement), 722

Baillie, John (contemp. Eng. clergyman), 1174

Barrie, James M. (1860-1937, Scot. novelist and dramatist), 1851

Barth, Karl (contemp. Swiss theologian), 518

Beard, Charles A. (1874-1948, Am. historian), 1333, 1578

Beebe, William (contemp. Am. naturalist), 578

Beecher, Henry Ward (1813-87, Am. clergyman), 19, 151, 203, 534, 537, 932, 1010, 1141, 1492, 1854, 2118, 2185, 2437

Beecher, Lyman (1775-1863, Am. clergyman), 19, 1923

Beethoven, Ludwig van (1770-1827, Ger. composer), 1269, 1359

Bell, Alexander Graham (1847-1922, Am. inventor), 1472, 1781

Bell, Bernard Iddings (contemp. Am. clergyman and educator), 2131

Bennett, Arnold (1867-1931), Eng. novelist and dramatist), 2307

Berdyaev, Nikolai (1874-1948, Russian philosopher) 2208

Bernard of Clairvaux (1091-1153, Fr. ecclesiastic), 1908

Bernard of Menthon (923-1008, patron of Alpinists), 1314

Beveridge, Albert J. (1862-1927, Am. politician and historian), 741

Billings, John (pseud. of Henry Wheeler Shaw, 1818-85, Am. humorist), 1287

Blake, William (1757-1827, Eng. poet and artist), 60

Boardman, George Dana (1838-1903, Am. clergyman), 1690

Bonnell, John Sutherland (contemp. Am. clergyman), 1326

Boone, Daniel (1734-1820, Am. pioneer), 796

Booth, Edwin (1833-93, Am. actor), 790, 1182, 1281

Index of Topics

The numbers in italic refer to main entries.